SACRED MUSIC DRAMA
The Producer's Guide Second Edition
Second Edition

by
CARL GERBRANDT

Bloomington, IN   Milton Keynes, UK

AuthorHouse™ *AuthorHouse*™ *UK Ltd.*
1663 Liberty Drive, Suite 200 *500 Avebury Boulevard*
Bloomington, IN 47403 *Central Milton Keynes, MK9 2BE*
www.authorhouse.com *www.authorhouse.co.uk*
Phone: 1-800-839-8640 *Phone: 08001974150*

© 1993, 2006 Carl Gerbrandt. All rights reserved.

No part of this book may be reproduced, stored in a retrieval system, or transmitted by any means without the written permission of the author.

First published by AuthorHouse 12/20/2006

ISBN: 978-1-4259-6847-2 (sc)

Library of Congress Control Number: 2006910502

Printed in the United States of America
Bloomington, Indiana

This book is printed on acid-free paper.

SACRED MUSIC DRAMA
THE PRODUCER'S GUIDE

TABLE OF CONTENTS

PREFACE	13
PREFACE TO THE SECOND EDITION	14
ACKNOWLEDGMENTS	16
SETTING THE STAGE – AN INTRODUCTION TO SACRED MUSIC DRAMA	18
The Purpose for this Research	19
Some Historical Aspects of Sacred Music Drama	20
Pre-Christian Greek Drama	21
Liturgical Music Drama	21
The Mystery Plays	22
Handel	23
The Eighteenth and Nineteenth Centuries	24
The Twentieth Century	24
Beyond the Twentieth Century	27
DESCRIPTION OF ANNOTATIONS AND APPENDICES	28
ABBREVIATIONS USED IN THIS BOOK	31

THE MUSIC DRAMA REPERTOIRE

JOHN ADAMS	
El Niño	35
SAMUEL ADLER	
The Wrestler	36
NOA AIN	
The Outcast	37
EUGEN D'ALBERT	
Der Golem – The Golem	38
WILLIAM P. ALEXANDER	
Samson at Gaza	39
DOMINICK ARGENTO	
Jonah and the Whale	40
The Masque of Angels	41
PIETRO ARIA	
Jericho Road	42

MALCOLM ARNOLD
    Song of Simeon — 43

JOHANN SEBASTIAN BACH
    Johannes Passion – St. John Passion — 44
    Matthaeus Passion – St. Matthew Passion — 45

GRANVILLE BANTOCK
    The Pilgrim's Progress — 46

SEYMOUR BARAB
    Father of the Child — 47
    Only A Miracle — 48

FRANCIS BARNARD
    The Glory Coach — 49
    A Nativity In Threes — 50

CLAUDE L. BASS
    The Father's Love — 51

JACK BEESON
    Jonah — 52

JEAN BERGER
    Birds of A Feather — 54
    Cherry Tree Carol — 55
    Yiphtah and His Daughter — 56

LENNOX BERKELEY
    Ruth — 57

HECTOR BERLIOZ
    L'enfance du Christ – The Childhood of Christ — 58

LEONARD BERNSTEIN
    Mass — 59

THOMAS BEVERSDORF
    The Vision of Christ — 61

SUSAN HULSMAN BINGHAM
    The Awakening — 62
    The Birth of Our Lord — 63
    By the Pool of Siloam — 64
    A Conversation Between Mary and the Angel Gabriel — 65
    Magdalene — 65
    On the Road to Emmaus — 67
    Piece Together — 68
    The Raising of Lazarus — 69
    Ruth — 70
    The Sacrifice of Isaac — 71
    Simeon — 72
    Tales of A Magic Monastery — 73
    The Woman At Jacob's Well — 75

HARRISON BIRTWISTLE
    The Last Supper — 76

ARTHUR BLISS
    Tobias and the Angel — 77
BENJAMIN COLMAN BLODGETT
    A Representation of the Book of Job — 78
MURRAY BOREN
    Abraham and Isaac — 79
    The Christymas Playe — 80
    Emma — 81
RUTLAND BOUGHTON
    Bethlehem (Full-length version) — 83
    Bethlehem (Abridged version) — 84
ROYAL BRANTLEY
    Samuel — 84
LESLIE BRICUSSE
    Scrooge — 86
FRANK BRIDGE
    The Christmas Rose — 87
BENJAMIN BRITTEN
    The Burning Fiery Furnace — 88
    Curlew River — 89
    Noye's Fludde – Noah's Flood — 90
    The Prodigal Son — 92
    The Rape of Lucretia — 93
R. R. BROOME
    The Finding of the King — 94
RICHARD E. BROWN
    The Gift of the Magi — 95
DAVID WARREN BRUBECK
    Beloved Son — 96
    La Fiesta de la Posada — 97
    The Light in the Wilderness — 98
GEOFFREY BURGON
    The Fall of Lucifer — 99
PAUL BURKHARD
    Die Zeller Weinacht – A Swiss Nativity — 100
BOB BURROUGHS
    David — 101
GORDON BUSH
    The Visitation — 102
EUGENE BUTLER
    God's Word in Their Heart — 103
    Samuel — 103
MARY ELIZABETH CALDWELL
    A Gift of Song — 104
    In the Fullness of Time — 106
    The Night of the Star — 108

  Pepito's Golden Flower   109
MARIO CASTELNUOVO-TEDESCO
  Saul   111
  Song of Songs   112
  Tobias and the Angel   112
EMILIO DE' CAVALIERI
  La Rappresentazione di Anima e di Corpo –
  The Representation of the Soul and Body   113
GEORGE WHITEFIELD CHADWICK
  Judith   115
DAVID CONTE
  The Gift of the Magi   116
CARSON P. COOMAN
  Thieves   117
CARSON P. COOMAN and SANDRA GAY
  See the Promised Dawn Arise   118
ROBERT CUNDICK
  The Redeemer   119
LUIGI DALLAPICCOLA
  Job   120
MELVIN L. DANIELS
  Lazarus   121
PETER MAXWELL DAVIES
  The Martyrdom of St. Magnus   122
ANTHONY DAVIS
  X (The Life and Times of Malcolm X)   123
CLAUDE DEBUSSY
  L'enfant prodigue – The Prodigal Son   124
VICTOR DE LISA
  Moses, Prince of Egypt   125
LYUBOMIR DENEV
  Cain   126
PETER DICKINSON
  The Judas Tree   128
HUGO DISTLER
  Dance of Death   129
ROBERT DOWNARD
  Martin Avdeich: A Christmas Miracle   130
THÉODORE (FRANÇOIS CLÉMENT) DUBOIS
  Les sept paroles du Christ – The Seven Last Words of Christ   131
ZSÓLT DURKÓ
  Mózes – Moses   132
LINDA EKMON and ELIZABETH FYFFE
  The Nativity: A Mystery Play   134
PETER EKSTROM
  The Gift of the Magi   134

MYRON S. FINK
    Jeremiah   135
    Judith and Holofernes   136

JOHN FRANCESCHINA
    The Lord's A Wonder   137
    To the Ends of the Earth   138

DON FREUND
    Passion With Tropes   139

CHARLES HUTCHINSON GABRIEL
    Saul, King of Israel   140

PAOLA GALLICO
    The Apocalypse   141

JOHN GARDNER
    Bel and the Dragon   142

DON GILLIS
    The Gift of the Magi   143
    The Nazarene   144

ALEXANDER GOEHR
    Naboth's Vineyard   145

NOËL GOEMANNE
    The Walk   146

EDWARD M. GOLDMAN
    David   147

WILLIAM ARTHUR GOLDSWORTHY
    The Judgment of Sheba   148

EUGENE GOOSSENS
    Judith   150

FRANÇOIS-JOSEPH GOSSEC
    La Nativité – The Nativity   151

JACK GOTTLIEB
    Sharing the Prophets: A Musical Encounter For Singers   152

CECIL GRAY
    The Temptation of St. Anthony   153

PHILIP HAGEMANN
    Ruth   154

GEORGE FRIDERIC HANDEL
    Athalia   155
    Belshazzar   156
    Deborah   158
    Esther   159
    Jephtha   160
    Joseph   161
    Joshua   162
    Judas Maccabaeus   163
    Samson   165
    Saul   166

Solomon	167
LOU HARRISON	
Jephthah's Daughter	168
JONATHAN HARVEY	
Passion and Resurrection	170
PAUL HINDEMITH	
Das lange Weihnachtsmahl – The Long Christmas Dinner	171
JEROME HINES	
I Am the Way	172
LEE HOLDRIDGE	
Lazarus and His Beloved	173
GUSTAV HOLST	
Savitri	174
ARTHUR HONEGGER	
Jeanne d'Arc au bûcher – Joan of Arc at the Stake	175
Judith	177
ALAN HOVHANESS	
Pilate	178
EUSEBIA SIMPSON HUNKINS	
Wondrous Love	178
VINCENT D'INDY	
La légende de Saint Christophe – The Legend of Saint Christopher	179
MARTIN KALMANOFF	
Noah and the Stowaway	180
BRYAN KELLY	
Herod, Do Your Worst	181
EDGAR STILLMAN KELLY	
Pilgrim's Progress	183
The Shorter Pilgrim's Progress	184
GERSHON KINGSLEY	
God and Abraham	185
FREDERICK KOCH	
The Shepherds	185
LESLIE KONDOROSSY	
Ruth and Naomi	187
ROBERT EDWARD KREUTZ	
Francesco: A Musical Biography	188
EZRA LADERMAN	
And David Wept	190
Galileo Galilei	191
JOHN LA MONTAINE	
Erode the Greate	192
The Lessons of Advent	195
Novellis, Novellis	195
The Shephardes Playe	197

STANLEY LEBOWSKY
    The Children's Crusade   198
DAN LOCKLAIR
    Good Tidings from the Holy Beast   199
RUTH TAYLOR MAGNEY
    The Gift of the Magi   200
DENISE MAINVILLE
    The Christmas Troubadour   201
G. FRANCESCO MALIPIERO
    La cena – The Last Supper   202
FRANK MARTIN
    Le Mystère de la Nativité – The Mystery of the Nativity   203
BOHUSLAV MARTINU
    Griechische Passion – The Greek Passion   204
    What Men Live By   205
JULES MASSENET
    Hérodiade – Herodias   206
    Marie-Magdeleine – Mary Magdalene   207
WILLIAM MATHIAS
    Jonah   209
WILLIAM MAYER
    One Christmas Long Ago   210
JOHN McCABE
    The Lion, the Witch, and the Wardrobe   211
HOWARD D. McKINNY
    A Mystery for Christmas   213
KIRKE MECHEM
    The King's Contest   214
ÉTIENNE NICOLAS MÉHUL
    Joseph   215
FELIX MENDELSSOHN BARTHOLDY
    Elias – Elijah   216
    Saint Paul   218
GIAN-CARLO MENOTTI
    Amahl and the Night Visitors   219
    The Death of the Bishop of Brindisi   220
    The Egg   221
    Martin's Lie   222
JAN MEYEROWITZ
    Esther   224
P. NAPIER MILES
    Good Friday   225
DARIUS MILHAUD
    David   227
CLAUDIO MONTEVERDI
    Il Combattimento di Tancredi e Clorinda – The Combat of Tancredi and Clorinda 228

DOUGLAS MOORE
    The Greenfield Christmas Tree   229
FRANK LEDLIE MOORE
    The Perfect Choir   231
WOLFGANG AMADEUS MOZART
    Die Schuldigkeit des ersten Gebotes – The Obligation of the First Commandment   232
THEA MUSGRAVE
    A Christmas Carol   233
ALFRED NEUMANN
    An Opera for Christmas   235
    An Opera for Easter   236
    An Opera for Everyman   237
    The Rites (Rights) of Man   238
CARL NIELSEN
    Saul and David   239
CARL ORFF
    Comoedia de Christi resurrectione – A Comedy during Christ's Resurrection   240
HAROLD JOHN OWEN
    The Passion of Our Lord Jesus Christ According to Saint Mark   241
RICHARD OWEN
    A Fisherman Called Peter   242
ALICE PARKER
    The Martyrs' Mirror   243
    Singer's Glen   245
HORATIO W. PARKER
    The Legend of St. Christopher   246
THOMAS PASATIERI
    Calvary   248
PETER PATENTE
    Behold Your King   249
STEVEN PAULUS
    The Village Singer   249
KRZYSZTOF PENDERECKI
    Paradise Lost   250
    Passio et mors domini nostri Jesu Christi secundum Lucam –
    The Passion and Death of Our Lord Jesus Christ According to St. Luke –
    St. Luke Passion   252
EDMUND J. PENDLETON
    The Miracle of the Nativity   253
DAVID PENINGER
    The Door   254
HANS PFITZNER
    Palestrina   255
GABRIEL PIERNE
    The Children's Crusade   256

DANIEL PINKHAM
    Daniel in the Lion's Den   258
ILDEBRANDO PIZZETTI
    L'Assassinio nella cattedrale   259
FRANCIS POULENC
    Les Dialogues des Carmélites – The Dialogues of the Carmelites   260
RICHARD PROULX
    The Pilgrim   261
L. NATALIA RAIGORODSKY
    The Promise of Peace   263
LICINIO REFICE
    Cecilia   263
OTTORINO RESPIGHI
    Lauda per la Natività del Signore – Laud to the Nativity   264
    Maria Egiziaca   265
HERMANN REUTTER
    Saul   266
E. N. von REZNICEK
    Holofernes   267
PHIL RIZZO
    Christ, the Man from Galilee   268
RICHARD RODGERS
    Two by Two   269
GEORGE F. ROOT
    Belshazzar's Feast or the Fall of Babylon   271
ANTON RUBINSTEIN
    Der Thurm zu Babel – The Tower of Babel   272
CAMILLE SAINT-SAËNS
    Samson et Dalila – Samson and Delilah   273
KAREL SALOMON
    David and Goliath   274
ERIC SALZMAN and MICHAEL SAHL
    Noah   275
GREGORY SANDOW
    A Christmas Carol   276
SIMON A. SARGON
    Saul, King of Israel   278
LELAND B. SATEREN
    Day of Pentecost   280
    Here Comes Our King   281
    Meditations on the Seven Last Words   281
    Our Faith   282
ALESSANDRO SCARLATTI
    Il primo omicidio – The First Murder   283
ARNOLD SCHOENBERG
    Moses und Aron – Moses and Aaron   284

HEINRICH SCHÜTZ
    Historia der . . . Auferstehungs . . . Jesu Christi – The Easter Story   285
    Historia der . . . Geburt . . . Jesu Christi – The Christmas Story   286

MARK SCHWEIZER
    Saturday, 29 A.D.   287

CHARLES KENNEDY SCOTT
    Everyman   288

RICHARD JAMES SHEPHARD
    Caedmon   290
    Good King Wenceslas   291
    St. Nicholas   292
    The Shepherd's Play   293

FREDERICK SILVER
    Exodus and Easter   294
    Hannah   295

FAYE-ELLEN SILVERMAN
    The Miracle of Nemirov   297

STANLEY SILVERMAN
    Up From Paradise   297

LARRY SITSKY
    The Golem   299

THOMAS M. SLEEPER
    Aceldama   300

DOUGLAS SMITH
    Judith   302

JOSEP SOLER
    La tentation de Saint Antoine – The Temptation of Saint Antoine   303

DAVID SOSIN
    Esther   304

RICHARD STRAUSS
    Salome   305

IGOR STRAVINSKY
    The Flood   306

PAUL O. STUART
    The Little Thieves of Bethlehem   307

CONRAD SUSA
    The Wise Women   308

DONALD SWANN
    Baboushka   310
    Bontzye Schweig   311
    Candle Tree   312
    Perelandra   313
    The Visitors   315

ALEXANDER TCHEREPNIN
    Le jeu de la Nativité – Nativity Play   316

RANDALL THOMPSON
    Nativity According to St. Luke   317
KARI TIKKA
    Luther   319
STEPHEN TOSH
    A Christmas Carol   320
BRUCE TRINKLEY
    Eve's Odds   321
ISAAC VAN GROVE
    The Other Wise Man   323
    Ruth   324
RALPH VAUGHAN WILLIAMS
    The First Nowell   325
    The Pilgrim's Progress   326
    The Shepherds of the Delectable Mountains   328
GIUSEPPE VERDI
    Nabucco   328
ANTONIO VIVALDI
    Juditha triumphans – The Triumph of Judith   330
JOHN WEBBER
    The Nativity   331
DAN WELCHER
    Della's Gift   332
RONALD K. WELLS
    Who is My Neighbor?   333
WILMER HAYDEN WELSH
    Faith and the Sewing Circle   334
    Judas Iscariot   335
    The Passion According to Pilate   336
    Please Get Out of the Way While We Rehearse   338
MALCOLM WILLIAMSON
    Dunstan and the Devil   339
    The Red Sea   340
ALEC WYTON
    The Journey With Jonah   341
PHILIP M. YOUNG
    Samuel: The Boy Who Talked With God   343
EUGENE ZÁDOR
    Yehu   344
CARL ZYTOWSKI
    The Play of Balaam and His Ass   345
    The Play of the Three Maries at the Tomb   346
    The Play of the Three Shepherds   347
    Thomas of Canterbury   348
ANONYMOUS EDITIONS, TRANSCRIPTIONS, ARRANGEMENTS   350
    The Maastricht Easter Play   350

Officium Pastorum – The Shepherds at the Manger ... 351
Peregrinus – The Stranger ... 351
Planctus Mariae – The Lament of Mary ... 352
The Play of Daniel ... 353
The Play of Herod ... 354
The Play of Saint Nicholas ... 355
Rachel ... 357
The Shepherds ... 357
Sponsus – The Bridegroom ... 358
The Star ... 359
Visitatio Sepulchri – The Visit to the Tomb ... 360

APPENDICES

APPENDIX A: SUPPLEMENTAL LIST ... 363
APPENDIX B: PUBLISHERS AND DISTRIBUTORS ... 367
APPENDIX C: COMPOSERS, TRANSLATORS, EDITORS, RESOURCES ... 379
APPENDIX D: REFERENCES ... 387
APPENDIX E: WORKS FOR ALL-MALE OR ALL-FEMALE VOICES ... 388
APPENDIX F: WORKS ESPECIALLY SUITABLE FOR YOUNG AUDIENCES ... 389
APPENDIX G: LISTING BY TEXTUAL SOURCE ... 391
APPENDIX H: LISTING BY SUBJECT ... 399
APPENDIX I: LISTING BY TYPE OR STYLE OF WORK ... 403
APPENDIX J: WORKS INCLUDING CHILDREN'S VOICES ... 411

TITLE INDEX ... 413

PREFACE

Nine years ago I found myself faced with the responsibility of producing a sacred opera. Until that time, it had never seriously entered my mind that Biblical truths could be dramatized in an operatic setting. My career had been filled with my own performing, voice teaching and traditional opera directing, and it had not occurred to me to combine the power of the stage with the power found in Biblical or "sacred" ideology.

I had been the director of the Opera Theatre program at Peabody Conservatory of Music of Johns Hopkins University and a member of their music staff for twelve years. Then in 1979, I accepted the challenge of building a music drama program for the Southern Baptist Theological Seminary School of Church Music in Louisville, KY. I soon realized the extensive deficiency of a comprehensive knowledge and understanding of sacred opera and sacred music drama repertoire. I, like a majority of opera directors when faced with the question, "What operas do you know that have the potential for being presented in a house of worship," replied with the all too-familiar, "Well, there is *Amahl and the Night Visitors*, the Britten church trilogy, the medieval *Play of Daniel* and *Play of Herod*, and......"; that's where the answer would end.

Thus began my search! When asked by the National Association of Teachers of Singing to present a sacred music drama for their National Convention in 1981, my search intensified dramatically! I gave them La Montaine's *Novellis, Novellis*, staged in Louisville's Christ Church Cathedral. This event prompted a plethora of questions from the Association's membership and convinced me of the need for further investigation and research into sacred opera production and repertoire.

In 1983, my Seminary Opera Workshop toured with Mary Elizabeth Caldwell's *A Gift of Song*, culminating with a performance for a national Church Music Convention in Pittsburgh. Following these productions, I received letters, titles and scores from people across the country who were learning of my interest in sacred music drama. Thus began a "Director's Guide" that has evolved from information provided by many colleagues, composers and publishers, culminating with an extended period of intensive personal research in England, a country rich in the medieval tradition of sacred music drama. In 1990, I was fortunate to be granted a Visiting Scholar position at Wolfson College of Cambridge University in order to complete my research and find answers to questions of style, performance practices and historical traditions in sacred music drama. The highly stimulating Cambridge setting also provided the motivation to complete this "Director's Guide."

PREFACE TO THE SECOND EDITION

Since the 1993 publishing of my original manuscript, it never occurred to me that there would be sufficient demand for a second edition. From the beginning of my interest in this subject, researching and studying sacred music dramas have been a labor of love and artistic curiosity. Stimulation has come from many sources. Most unforgettable and motivating was my time spent in Cambridge Unversity, England in 2004, where for the second time I was privileged to be in residence, this time as a "Visiting Fellow". However, it has been the support and encouragement of my wife, Marilyn, and our children, along with many individuals who have brought this Second Edition to reality.

The purpose then of this Second Edition is to supply the on-going demand for this book, update the information, and provide detailed data on sacred operas which have been composed in the last 14 years. Naturally, certain changes and corrections have been made to improve the content of this book and the new information available in this field.

Twenty-one new operas (see Table of Contents and Appendix A) have been added to this book.

John Adams – *El Niño*
Harrison Birtwistle – *The Last Supper*
Marc-Antoine Charpentier – *David et Jonathas*
David Conte – *The Gift of the Magi*
Carson P. Cooman – *Thieves*
Carson P. Cooman and Sandra Gay – *See the Promised Dawn Arise*
Lyubomir Denev – *Cain*
Tsippi Fleischer – *Cain and Abel*
Philip Hagemann – *Ruth*
Robert Edward Kreutz – *Francesco: A Musical Biography*
Matthew Kenneth Peterson – *The Binding of Isaac*
Mark Schweizer – *Saturday, 29 A.D.*
Richard James Shephard – *Caedmon, Good King Wenceslas, St. Nicholas, The Shepherd's Play*
Thomas M. Sleeper - *Aceldama*
Paul O. Stuart – *The Little Thieves of Bethlehem*
Conrad Susa – *The Wise Women*
Kari Tikka – *Luther*
Bruce Trinkley – *Eve's Odds*

In studying the operas which have been composed and produced within the past fourteen years, I have found a curious pattern in the plot content and the manner in which these works have been directed toward the audience. If indeed history tells us that works of art are a reflection of who we are and of our times, then how can we ignore the fact that of these new operas, three have been written on the violent story of Cain and Abel – brother killing brother! Does this speak to the violence of recent world history and events? It is also intriguing that a number of these works are presented with direct and searching questions. No longer are these works simply telling a story and providing an answer, but are leaving very personal ethical and moral questions to be answered by the listener.

One of the great joys in the pursuit of this information is the personal contact with some of the world's great composers. My deepest appreciation is extended to them, especially Conrad Susa, and their publishers for allowing me access to their scores and in some cases sharing intriguing personal perspectives of their compositions.

Since the writing of my original manuscript, I have had the privilege of advising many doctoral students in the preparation of their dissertations, a process that is most often tedious and consuming! Two of these students, Juliana Bishop and Lisa Grevlos, have ventured into the arena of sacred music drama research and production, studying the works of American, Robert Edward Kreutz and Britain's Richard James Shephard respectively. I am deeply grateful to both these scholars for contributing their insights to this Second Edition.

I have left the Acknowledgement section of this book intact because of my on-going gratitude to all those people who so conscientiously and lovingly guided me through this process. Thank you all once again.

ACKNOWLEDGMENTS

Over the course of my work on this project, I have built up a rather extensive list of debtors, many of whom I shall never be able to repay. I am aware of the risk involved in mentioning names for fear of committing "sins of omission;" however, I am genuinely grateful to the many who have stood beside me throughout the writing of this work and must specifically mention the names of these wonderful people.

The work on this project culminated in England where David G. T. Williams, President of Wolfson College and Vice Chancellor of Cambridge University, made possible my research through a Visiting Scholar position at Wolfson College, an experience I shall never forget and for which I am deeply grateful.

Both Dr. Howard Skinner, Dean of the College of Performing and Visual Arts and Dr. Shirley Howell, Director of the School of Music of the University of Northern Colorado enthusiastically supported me in my request for a sabbatical leave and funding to complete this project. Valuable encouragement was given me by the Graduate School and Faculty Research and Publication Board of UNC who believed in my project and enthusiastically supported me.

I am indebted in a special way to those librarians and organizations who have "plumbed the depths" in answering my many questions. Norman Savig and Sharon Salzman of UNC's Music Library reached far beyond the call of duty in locating and acquiring scores for my perusal. The personnel of Pendlebury Library and the Cambridge University Library in Cambridge, England spent valuable hours in assisting me with locating important documents and scores, while Deborah Meth at ASCAP so capably pried information from files and composers alike. Maria Rich and her able staff at Central Opera Service, New York City, provided materials and information with kindness and promptness; Thurston Dox, author of *American Oratorios and Cantatas: A Catalog of Works Written in the United States from Colonial Times to 1985*, willingly supplied valuable information from his wealth of knowledge on the subject.

Music publishers, without exception, were courteous, lending scores without cost and answering a myriad of questions. While I would like to mention them all and I am grateful to every one of them, particular thanks must go to Ursula Eastman of G. Schirmer, Stephen Gerber of E.C. Schirmer, Marie Iannacone of Theodore Presser, Simon Wright and Antonia Walker of Oxford University Press in Oxford, England, Mark Wilson and Sue Klein of Boosey and Hawkes, Arthur Cohn of Carl Fischer, and Geoffrey Barlow of Sussex, England.

Then there are those greatest of all heroes, the composers who gave of their compositions and responded with enthusiasm and promptness to my numerous inquiries. Again, I should like to mention every one but several stand out as having been particularly helpful and supportive of this project: Susan Bingham, Alec Wyton, Donald Swann of England, Royal Brantley, Alfred Neumann, Wilmer Hayden Welsh, Seymour Barab, Francis Barnard, Jean Berger, Mary

Elizabeth Caldwell, John La Montaine, Jerome Hines and Derek de Cambra, Carl Zytowski, Alice Parker, Stanley Silverman, Stephen Tosh, Gregory Sandow, Richard Proulx, Leland B. Sateren and Simon A. Sargon.

My warm gratitude goes to the expert opinions of individuals who assisted in reading and re-reading the manuscript, tirelessly looking for flaws and errors; and to those dedicated enthusiasts who provided valuable editorial suggestions to make this the best possible informational source on sacred music drama.

I would have succumbed to defeat had it not been for my loving wife, Marilyn, daughter Lynée, and son Gregory, who provided encouragement and an atmosphere conducive to the countless hours of writing and analyzing.

And finally, my eternal gratitude is extended to Dr. Ray Robinson, whose encouragement, expertise, and confidence provided the impetus for this project. Without him, this book would never have become reality.

SETTING THE STAGE

AN INTRODUCTION TO SACRED MUSIC DRAMA

Throughout the preparation of this book, I have attempted to brace myself for the barrage of responses reminding me of the omission of their favorite work. Indeed, the selection process has been one of the most soul-rending tasks of my work. As can be well imagined, a very thin and fragile maché, if indeed there is any at all, separates compositions from being either stageworthy or not stageworthy. This is particularly true with respect to oratorios, cantatas and Passions, i.e., those works normally relegated to concert presentation but containing designated characters and dramatic potential.

Others, finding their "pet" concert works included in this book, will argue strongly against even the slightest hint of stage treatment. These matters are indeed very personal and I leave to your individual judgment the matter of stage treatment versus concert presentation.

In selecting this repertoire, I have looked carefully at the composer's intent which in the case of designated operas and music dramas is generally self-explanatory.

With regard to predominantly choral works where composers have been vague or non-committal, I have used this criteria: if a work has designated characters AND/OR any stage directions indicated by the composer, or if the work over the course of trial and error has received successfully staged performances, I have included that work. For example, the Bach Passions, Dubois' *Seven Last Words of Christ* and Mendelssohn's *Elijah* were all intended as concert works, yet in all cases, highly successful staged productions have proven their dramatic potential.

In one case, a work designated as an oratorio by the composer contained but one stage direction in the score: "Lift curtain here." This provided the impetus for further study of the score. I found it "crying out" for stage treatment.

With regard to more dated and obscure works, particularly of the seventeenth and eighteenth centuries, I have included only a sampling of the most accessible scores. This sampling will hopefully simulate further research into the sacred dramatic works of those centuries. Since this book is designed to be practical, I felt that scores and parts should be accessed with relative ease. Certainly scores and parts from those periods can cause no end of searchings.

I have also chosen to include some works which may be hotly debated as to their sacred or secular nature. In most cases, these works have some association with sacred ideas and in my weaker moments of entertainment-proneness, have included what I felt would be appropriate for an evening of light entertainment. *The Perfect Choir* by Frank Moore or Silverman's *Up From Paradise* are two such works. Other compositions conducive to light-hearted humor and entertainment but religious or sacred in content have been so identified and are listed in Appendix I.

The Purpose for this Research

This book is intended to be a practical guide for opera directors and producers, performers, students, music scholars and writers, church musicians and curious enthusiasts of opera and sacred music drama.

Sufficient factual information has been sought and provided in order to assist the opera director in determining the appropriateness of a given work to his/her situation, be it a church, synagogue, college or professional organization.

The repertoire selected extends from the very simplistic to the most difficult both in musical requirements and production demands. While providing as thorough a factual basis as possible, I have added concise production suggestions as guidelines, which at times have come from composers but most often from my own studied observations of the scores. It is not my intent to infringe on the artistic prerogative of the director, but in making these suggestions, I hope to provide a more complete picture of the work being considered and thus to assist the director in making preliminary repertoire decisions.

Opera producers will find at a glance information on orchestration, chorus requirements, number of scenes, acts, settings, solo cast with voice classifications, dance requirements, and duration of performance. Additionally, he/she can learn where to acquire the score and materials.

Performers will be aided in finding the appropriateness of a specific role to their voice. Normally, ranges and tessituras are only indicated if they exceed the average singer's capabilities. Likewise, any unusual or problematic vocal or dramatic demands are noted.

Students should find adequate information on each work to familiarize themselves with its general concept, its plot, musical style and concise historical data.

The scholar and writer can learn of the librettist and source of the libretto, as well as a brief musical description of the work. I have attempted to show by the inclusion of works from all periods of music history that, while sacred music drama flourished at certain times, each era produced at least some works of this nature. The ebb and flow of interest in and composing of sacred music drama demands further research. Selected reference materials on sacred music drama have been listed in Appendix D. While many more works could be added, doing so would surpass the intent and confines of this work. Thus, I have selected those which seem to me to be the most helpful to the type of reader this book may attract, particularly the performer and director.

The numerous cross-reference Appendices will be of particular assistance to church musicians and ministerial personnel in coordinating worship service content. Biblical sources are arranged by book in Appendix G and by specific chapters and verses in the annotations. Other sources are likewise specified. Additionally, a Subject Appendix (H) should greatly assist the minister and musician in the planning of worship services and seasonal repertoire.

Interest in opera is at an all-time high. New professional companies are being chartered, and older companies are revitalizing. The church likewise is venturing new risks, finding the dramatization of sacred music effective and refreshing in the worship experience.

It is hoped that this book will fill a long standing void by acquainting directors, students, performers and interested laypeople with the numerous sacred music dramas which have been composed and are available; that it will stimulate a renewed interest in the presentation of this repertoire; and that it will bring about an awareness of the powerful impact of dramatizing Biblical truths.

Some Historical Aspects of Sacred Music Drama

While the stated purpose of this book does not include musicological renderings, a brief review of some historical perspective will perhaps further illuminate the reasons and purposes for the nature of music drama in the church. Certainly the tradition and history of the medieval music drama has been well documented. I refer you to the research and scholarly writing of men like William L. Smoldon, Noah Greenberg and Fletcher Collins, to cite but three.

Sacred music drama is but one small sibling in the larger family of music drama; and yet, it may very well be, rather than the sibling, the parent of all music drama. Music drama from its earliest known origins has been associated with religious belief. Music, ritual, dance or movement, spectacle, narrative and drama are all ingredients of worship. Combine these elements with the human need for make-believe and role-playing, and we find a form of communication which expresses facets of the meaning of life.

Throughout history, music drama has provided an important vehicle by which human beings have been afforded the opportunity of entering the world of make-believe; and in so doing he has gained the experience of the thing or personage being imitated. It is precisely in this experience that we gain a deeper understanding of the mysteries that surround us. When we assume the character of and imitate another's actions and personality, we begin to establish a relationship that reaches beyond our usual understanding.

A particularly vivid example of this growth process is found in John La Montaine's pageant opera *Novellis, Novellis*, based on two medieval Corpus Christi plays and written for church performance. A highly emotional scene evolves when Joseph learns that Mary is pregnant. The Biblical narrative leaves us with the bare facts, but without the probable emotional overtones. Pause for a moment and place yourself in Joseph's predicament with the hurt and bitter anger he must have felt. Both music and text bring us new insights into this particular Biblical episode and the psyche of Joseph, a real human being, with whom we can only relate if allowed to share some of his "gut" feelings in his situation. Both the music and text give us ample opportunity to associate with the reality of Joseph's experience and bring to a fact-oriented Biblical setting an emotional dimension which we human beings can understand.

Pre-Christian Greek Drama

It is commonly assumed that the origin of Western drama lies within the realm of Pre-Christian Greece. Certainly its direct influence upon the beginnings of opera around 1600 is well known.

Greek tragedy was not just spoken drama; it was music drama with singing and dancing. Furthermore, it was not only secular in nature, but sprang directly from religious ritualism. Ritual, of course, is not ritual unless it contains some manner of order and dramatized symbolic purpose. Thus, one ingredient, symbolic movement, is already present in ritualism, and it seems that such movement could hardly occur without the simultaneous involvement of rhythmic or melodic elements.

I am indebted to the stimulating and insightful writings of John D. Drummond in his book *Opera in Perspective* (see Appendix D). In the early chapters, Mr. Drummond elaborates extensively on man's need for exploring the mysteries of life and the connection between man's music drama and his religious beliefs. Mr. Drummond states: "Man is still concerned with exploring the mysteries of life through images which transform reality. His religious beliefs may alter, and the details of his music-drama change, but he perpetually remains the curious and mystified animal, seeking to find some connection between himself, the things he knows and the things he can imagine."

Myth was the basic ingredient of Greek tragedy. In the world of myth, we move beyond reality and are switched into an imaginary or make-believe world. Through this state of fantasy, the Greeks brought about a relationship and an avenue of communication between man and the gods. Thus, it follows that through the music drama of the Greeks, we find man attempting to come to an understanding of the mysteries that surrounded his existence and his relationship between himself and a higher being. Certainly the connection between man's music drama and his religious beliefs is undeniable.

Man's numerous myths, religions, cults and superstitions are his attempts to earn his right to life, to justify his existence before a higher being and to somehow bring about truth to his life. Once a religion or cult is established, it may provide a temporary answer, right or wrong, based on belief and faith in something which has no logical explanation nor can it be proved. Likewise, Christianity is void without faith and belief in Christ. It is, in a sense, a mystery in which we constantly strive to find deeper meaning. I am reminded that the method of teaching used so often and effectively by Jesus was the parable, a story of fantasy often drawing upon the familiar yet mysterious for the purpose of teaching a truth.

Liturgical Music Drama

The historical evolution of the church's liturgy and development of the Mass is in itself an example of ceremonial music drama. The Mass contains nearly all the ingredients of a music drama with members of the clergy serving as the solo performers and the congregation becoming the responsatory chorus. The varying rituals, the choreographed physical movement, the chanting (music) and the text are all in place to create a drama.

From about the tenth to the late thirteenth century, a form of liturgical music drama occupied an important place in the church's worship activities. Various personages, at first only members of the clergy, were selected to portray the characters represented in the scripture reading of the service. Thus, a very simple scene was visually dramatized in the midst of the liturgy. The most commonly enacted scenes were taken from the Gospels and centered on seasonal events such as the Marys visiting the tomb of Christ and the activities and characters surrounding the birth of Jesus.

The Mystery Plays

By the fourteenth century, cycles of such scenes known as "Mystery Plays" were being performed which covered the entire range of Biblical history from the Creation to the Last Judgment. With few exceptions, these plays grew into an elaborate entertainment with lavish scenery, costumes and large casts.

The fourteenth and fifteenth centuries saw the flourishing of the mystery and miracle plays, direct descendents of the earlier liturgical music dramas. At first, these plays were presented entirely in Latin and within the walls of the church. They became so popular that it was thought necessary to intersperse a vernacular commentary and translation. Within a century, many dramas had been entirely translated into the vernacular. Secular music forms appeared (sound familiar?), performances began to take place outside the confines of the church, and to the horror of some, non-clerical performers assumed important roles. Soon these Biblically based plays, while purporting to retain doctrinal purpose, made their appeal largely as popular entertainment.

In England, these plays, and particularly the miracle plays, were acted with little or no music, and without costumes and often without any scenery. They were instead played with ordinary everyday attire and in natural surroundings. Mary and Joseph wore the ordinary dress of English peasants while the Wise Men appeared in courtiers' attire, no doubt borrowed from their lord's armoury. It was as though the events represented were contemporary; even appropriate jokes and improvised horseplay did not seem incongruous.

In each era, these religious or sacred music dramas were as intensely real and actual to the players and audience as any other era. They were not something removed, distant or legendary. They were events of living reality and thus part of the lives and experiences of the people. Just so, Mary was a real person with real events in her life and real emotional responses.

What is more natural therefore, than for the Biblical events to be acted and played out in an attempt to bring them closer to the reality of each contemporary age. What is more fitting than for these events to be represented as actual living realities?

It was only when the peoples' religions, beliefs, and faith (occurring at most only on Sundays) became divorced from life that the miracle plays ceased. The chief enemy of the plays had become, ironically, the church. By around 1525, dramatic representation of Biblical personages and events was anathema to all but the most liberal factions of both Catholicism and the newly born Protestantism. By 1580, the "Mystery Plays" had alas died out, partly as a result of religious suppression and partly because of a dying faith.

Following the demise of the mystery and miracle plays, very little remained in the way of musico-dramatic treatment of religious subjects. A few music dramas/operas appeared in Italy and Germany in the late sixteenth and early seventeenth centuries. With few exceptions, a drought was in progress which lasted over three centuries. A few glimmers however bear mentioning.

The solo oratorios of Scarlatti, the Passions of Bach and the dramatic oratorios of Handel and his contemporaries mark the next occurrence of dramatizing Biblical events through music.

Handel

Scarlatti treated the solo cantata as a dramatic work, focusing on a single character who may not have played out his actions at all but rather allowed the audience to view his state of mind. In essence, the solo cantata became a chamber opera, frequently acted and sung by a single singer or actor in the home of a politician or artisan. Scarlatti, in many respects, became a model for Handel, the eighteenth century Italian opera composer. This influence naturally followed Handel into his other dramatic endeavors and especially his English oratorios. One need only look at music he composed for special events such as *Ode for Queen Anne's Birthday*, and celebration works such as the *Utrecht Te Deum* or the introduction to *Zadok the Priest*, to sense the dramatic intent and theatrical nature of Handel. In his own right, Handel's sense of theatre was as strong as any of his contemporaries and perhaps even of those noteworthy opera composers of the 19th century.

Handel is generally thought of as a synthesizer of musical forms in the Baroque, much as we think of Bach. However, Handel's one truly original contribution to musical art form was that of the dramatic oratorio. The oratorio of Handel was not a consciously contrived form, but rather grew out of the ever-popular and dominant Baroque opera. Dramatically for Handel, setting a Biblical or religious plot to music was no different than composing an opera on a secular theme. In all his sacred oratorios, Handel was not writing for the church, even in *Messiah*, but for entertainment. His oratorios without exception received their premieres in a theatrical or concert location and not in a house of worship.

The theatrical or dramatic intent of Handel's oratorios goes far beyond speculation. Most of the works declare in the titles their intent: "oratorio or sacred drama," "musical drama," "sacred drama," etc. *Samson* was specifically designated as "alter'd and adapted to the stage." In nearly all of his oratorios, Handel and his librettists went to considerable length to place, at times elaborate stage directions in the autographs. Handel's artistic and theatrical inclinations are clearly observed both in his music and his instructions. Librettos are set in the form of stageworthy dramas and frequently include dramatic events which become mundane without visual enforcement. In the case of *Belshazzar*, the opening chorus is dramatically unclear and nearly incomprehensible without action – yet with dramatization, it becomes a *tour de force*.

Various writings during Handel's time make it clear that many of his sacred oratorios were not only first performed in staged versions, but that subsequent concert performances were met with public distaste due to a lack of dramatic treatment.

The chorus in Handel's oratorios is a continuing area of concern for both stage directors and chorus masters. His oratorios are characterized by a vastness of choral music which in itself presents memorization problems if the chorus is to be included in the action. Chorus characterization presents additional production problems for the director. This is exemplified in *Belshazzar*, in which the chorus assumes the responsibility of characterizing three different groups of people: Jews, Persians, and Babylonians, all of which are contrasted both musically and dramatically by Handel. In certain instances, a director would be well advised to place his chorus members in an off-stage area and use them as observing commentators, i.e., a Greek Chorus. If action is desired, the use of a dance troupe or pantomime group is not only advisable but can be enormously effective and highly practical. I refer you to my commentary under the annotation of Mendelssohn's *Elijah*.

It should not be considered a breach of musical integrity to make cuts or rearrange the order of certain numbers. Most of the larger oratorios discussed in this book will benefit dramatically from cuts particularly for today's audiences. The use of dancers and mime artists will likewise generally improve the dramatic impact of a production.

Five sacred oratorios of Handel have been omitted from discussion in this book: *Alexander Balus, Israel in Egypt, Messiah, Susanna,* and *Theodora*. While each have dramatic moments conducive to stage treatment, they represent the dramatically weakest of Handel's sacred oratorios. Solutions to the numerous and difficult production problems in these works cannot be measured against the advantages of staging and it is doubtful that stage action would add to the effectiveness of these works. Musically, they are certainly capable of standing on their own. Of these five works, *Susanna* is perhaps the most adaptable to the stage. However, while the plot contains religious elements, the overall nature of the libretto is more secular than sacred in spite of the fact that the libretto is loosely based on events from the Apocrypha.

The Eighteenth and Nineteenth Centuries

The eighteenth and nineteenth centuries saw little interest in incorporating religious ideas into dramatic music. Several composers did include Biblically-based moralities and characters in their librettos, but these were treated in much the same manner as any secular subject, e.g., Strauss' *Salome*, Rossini's *Moses*, Wagner's *Parsifal*, Puccini's *Suor Angelica*, and Saint-Saëns' *Samson et Dalila*. Isolated scenes of a religious nature were occasionally inserted into a secular framework, e.g., the "Ave Maria" in Verdi's *Othello*, the church scene in Gounod's *Faust*, and the Easter morning church setting in Mascagni's *Cavalleria Rusticana*.

The Twentieth Century

This practice of inserting short religious scenes into secular operas has continued into the twentieth century with religious ideas playing an increasingly important role, e.g., the vivid and realistic revival scene in Carlisle Floyd's *Susannah*, the religious fervor exhibited in

Robert Ward's *The Crucible*, pitting the power of God against the witches of Salem, and the beautiful prayer of Mary in Douglas Moore's *The Devil and Daniel Webster*.

If indeed the demise of the miracle and mystery plays in the sixteenth century was, at least in part, due to a diminishing faith, then the resurgence of interest in sacred music drama in the twentieth century certainly stirs the curiosity. Western Europe and England in particular have been a welcome harbor for this avenue of expression. That the American composers, churches, and church related colleges should now be turning their attention to sacred dramatic works demand inspection and the ultimate questions of "why" and "what is the motivating force?" Perhaps the answers can only be found in succeeding generations whose hindsight will be far less biased, hopefully better enlightened and capable of evaluating the landscape from a broader perspective.

The industrialization and humanistic movement of the nineteenth century, among other phenomena, brought to the highly pious and conservative American church a gradual liberalization of thought. The materialism and scientific explosion of the twentieth century continued this movement of secularization along with a departure from the church and its religious mores.

America's church, so long ruled by the conservative tradition of its early Puritan founders may have finally asked itself what new avenues can we probe in order to breathe new life into the church and stimulate the highly fragile and frayed spiritual nerve endings of the church.

As the rebirth of Western drama during the middle ages occurred in the church, so, according to William L. Smoldon, the modern-day recovery of music drama is also finding the church to be an appropriate incubator. Curiously, many modern composers are turning to the medieval sources and finding meaningful material as a basis for original music dramas. Benjamin Britten, John La Montaine, Geoffrey Burgon, Richard Proulx, and Carl Zytowski, to name but a few, have been inspired by the straight-forward presentation of Biblical narratives and truths found in the medieval plays. Others, such as Gian-Carlo Menotti, Wilmer Hayden Welsh and Mary Elizabeth Caldwell are appropriating contemporary texts, plots and musical idioms, and adapting them to medieval concepts of presentation.

In the *Adoration of the Shepherds*, taken from the "Chester Cycles," one becomes acquainted with the shepherds as individuals. The play depicts a marked departure toward real characters, i.e., references to the mundane everyday life of the shepherds, the problems of sheepherding, the herbs and salves used to heal the wounds of sheep, and the loneliness of the shepherd's life. The shepherds were ordinary human beings faced with a mystery: angels confronting and singing to them. How unbelievable! And yet through music dramatization, our minds are stirred as we observe the shepherds' attempt to come to terms with this anomaly. The shepherds deal with the angel's song by singing their own rather than rationally attempting to solve this problem and scientifically explaining it away. They simply believed and rejoiced in their beliefs.

History has undoubtedly had its siphonic effect on works from the past but never since the medieval era has sacred music drama seen such activity and interest. I would draw attention to examples such as the Chancel Opera Company of Connecticut, an organization led by composer Susan Hulsman Bingham, devoted exclusively to the performance of sacred music dramas in the church. Other organizations such as the American Guild of Organists and National Association of Teachers of Singing are commissioning and promoting sacred music dramas. Sidney Opera House of Australia has recently commissioned the yet to be performed opera, *The Golem*, based on Jewish legend and religious ideology. The British Broadcasting Corporation has been active in broadcasting and promoting sacred opera. John La Montaine's three sacred operas, "Christmas Trilogy," were commissioned and premiered by the Washington Cathedral and televised by NBC-TV. The list could go on and on. The exposure of sacred music drama through other broadly based organizations is documented in this book.

Another relative of sacred music drama has in the past few decades grown out of the gospel music movement: the youth-oriented gospel or pop-musical. The plots are generally contemporary, the music of a popular, rock, or folk nature with relatively simplistic musical demands and often simple folk-oriented plots. Buryl Red's *Celebrate Life* is an early example of this type of dramatized sacred music. The plethora of works now available in this genre would fill an additional volume. Thus I have chosen not to include in this study works which might fall exclusively into this style of musical composition.

The proliferation of children's operas and musicals is also a phenomenon of the mid-twentieth century. While I have included some works particularly suitable for young audiences, only those which include adult (college age and up) singers will be found here. Works for children and sung by children have been excluded as the enormous number of these compositions also would require an additional volume. Central Opera Service, now Opera America, (see COS in Appendix B) has graciously compiled an extensive list of such works.

In all eras, and ours is no exception, artists, playwrights and composers have responded out of their experience, the sum of which includes the observation of life around them as it relates to historical knowledge and personal perspective. While we have already touched on some philosophical reasoning behind the influx of sacred music drama works in the mid-twentieth century, several factors not yet mentioned also play upon this resurgence.

Notable activity in literary and musicological research has resulted in performable editions of medieval dramas. Beginning in the late 1940s, scholars such as William L. Smoldon along with performers like Noah Greenberg began to produce performing editions of complete liturgical dramas. In turn, composers such as Benjamin Britten, John La Montaine, and Francis Barnard have been strongly influenced by these efforts in composing their own works.

A second reason behind this renewed interest has been the movement by a substantial part of the church toward spiritual revitalization and a renewal of its forms or expressions of worship. Certainly Vatican II was influential among Roman Catholics in re-thinking worship, Biblical application and personal participation in worship. Evangelical churches experimented with new practices which could be used along with or in place of the traditional service to communicate the Biblical message. More dramatic forms of worship as observed in the growing role of charismatic groups, holiness rallies, and in general, a more open expressiveness of personal beliefs, have stimulated increased visual expressions.

Third, the media is perhaps the single most influential stimulus in the revolutionary changes of the past fifty years. For better or for worse, television has become the primary medium for entertainment, current events, and teaching-learning situations. Our contemporary perception and learning patterns have been undeniably affected by the visuals we witness, so much so, that we have become a people with very strong eyes and somewhat dull ears.

The revival of religious music drama may then be seen as a natural result of the converging currents I have mentioned: historical research, religious or spiritual evaluation and renewal, and revolutionary changes in communication between people.

Measuring by the yardstick, the poignancy of sacred music drama upon its viewers would be impossible. The indelible imprint of sacred music drama throughout history is undeniable.

It is my intent and hope that this book will familiarize many people with repertoire which has heretofore been in the domain of only a few, and to engender a growing interest in and performance of sacred music drama, be it in churches, synagogues or opera theatres. My enthusiasm will not wane – I trust yours will be stimulated through the efforts of these pages.

Soli Deo Gloria
Cambridge, England – 1993

Beyond the Twentieth Century

I believe today's composers and lyricists are unashamedly documenting in their works vivid and striking pictures of our times. As I have studied the sacred opera repertoire composed since 1993, I have observed composers speaking to the violence in our world, attempting to make more direct and meaningful contact with the listeners and audiences, and delving more deeply into people's imagination with probing questions that desperately seek answers. Three of the twenty-one new operas in this Second Edition deal with the Biblical story of Cain and Abel and the violence of fratricide – brother killing brother. Four of the works include the use of familiar tunes and invite the audience to participate in the music and drama. Several operas provide no answers to the issues raised, leaving the dilemma in the hands of the audience. These works are not simply telling a story and providing an answer, but are leaving personal ethical and moral questions to be answered by the listener.

Though I am reflecting on only 14 years of history, I believe composers are cognizant of our times and speaking to the critical issues at hand. If we indeed believe that works of art are a reflection of who we are and of our times, then we cannot ignore the messages being sent to us by our composers of sacred operas. Will these trends continue? Only time and great works of art will tell us.

Greeley, Colorado – 2006

DESCRIPTION OF ANNOTATIONS AND APPENDICES

Numerous abbreviations are used in the annotations and explanations of works in this book. Understanding and readability will be assisted by first thoroughly familiarizing yourself with the following explanations.

The works in this book have been alphabetically arranged by composer. Titles are listed both in their original language and English translation. The Title Index lists both as well. However, in all of the Appendices, titles are listed by their most familiar title, usually in English.

Paragraph 1: The opening paragraph identifies the composer's name and dates, the type of work, its original language, librettist and source of libretto. All abbreviations are given either on page 31 or Appendix B.

Paragraph 2: The date and location of the first performance is indicated here, and where available, the commissioning agency.

Paragraph 3: With great difficulty I have attempted to indicate in a broad and general sense what musical characteristics are inherent in the score. Specifically, I have noted whether its harmonic structure is tonal, modal, or serial; whether its lines are melodic or disjunct; if its form is built on set numbers with arias, recitatives, and ensembles; if it contains spoken dialogue; and whether it is continuous in action or through-composed.

Paragraph 4: In this paragraph I have noted the number of acts and scenes and a description of each. Duration in all cases can only be approximate, fluctuating according to individual tastes and cuts. Where specific timings of works were not available, I have approximated the timing or in the case of works in excess of two hours duration, simply indicated "full length."

Roles: For each work, the individual characters are listed by name and voicing. I have noted the extremities of range when that range may be below or above the average singer's capabilities. I have also made note of any tessitura problems or other unusual vocal demands. The range or pitch identification system which I have employed begins with low C below the staff as C1. Each consecutively higher C then is listed as C2, C3, C4, and C5. The following illustration should clarify the system used.

Chorus: This section identifies the choral needs of the dramatic presentation, which the chorus represents as characters, and whether or not they are involved in the action. Unusual vocal or dramatic demands are indicated.

Dance: The type and extent of dance, mime, or choreography is identified.

Orchestration: The instrumentation requirements are given here together with any alternatives. Instruments which double are noted in parentheses, e.g., ob (Eng hrn), meaning the oboe may also play the English horn part. Abbreviations are listed on page 31.

Synopsis: As often as is warranted, a background to the plot precedes the story itself. A synopsis can frequently be supplemented by referring to the Scripture or libretto reference in paragraph 1.

Materials: Locating and securing all the necessary materials is not always as simple as one might wish. The frequency with which publishers are being bought and sold in recent years further complicates the problem. I have tried as best as possible to identify the source (the various Appendices will list names and address of publishers, composers and other sources). Also listed here are available English translations.

Notes: I have taken the liberty in this one paragraph of deviating from factual non-critical annotating. Occasionally, noteworthy production problems, critics' reviews and composers' comments will appear here. Additionally and because this has been a matter of greatest interest on the part of my students and inquiring directors, I have indicated my personal opinion as to the appropriate performance location, i.e., a theatre, auditorium, or house of worship. In some instances composers have voiced their preference. It is my hope that these notes will be helpful rather than dictatorial.

Appendix A: I have included a short list of works with limited or partially religious themes. These works are largely full-length operas. Included here also is a comprehensive listing of musical settings to Dickens' "A Christmas Carol." Of these, four have been selected for detailed annotation in the main portion of this book due to their diversity, dramatic potential and availability.

Appendix B and C: Here can be found a limited list of publishers and composers with contact information.

Appendix D: The list of references has been kept brief and selective, citing those sources which will be immediately and directly helpful to primarily the director, producer, and performer. Appendix C also includes several resources.

Appendix E and F: Works particularly suitable for young audiences or works which have been written for all-male and all-female casts are listed here.

Appendix G: This Appendix of textual sources lists works by Old Testament, New Testament, Apocrypha, legend/folk, or medieval plays/dramas/hymns. The first three categories are further sub-divided by specific books.

Appendix H: The subject Appendix indicates whether a work is appropriate for Advent/Christmas, Passion/Easter, Missions, or Pentecost, and whether it deals with Parables or Miracles.

Appendix I: I have categorized the works according to their musical style and dramatic type. Occasionally the same work may be found under more than one heading such as *Planctus Mariae*, edited by Smoldon, a medieval play and also appropriate for inclusion in a worship service. Also included here is a list of works which will interest the choral director. These works are predominantly choral in content or specifically designated as choric dramas.

Humorous and light-hearted entertainment works will be found in a separate category. It is not uncommon for directors and church musicians to seek out an evening away from the chancel where singers can, still within "sacred music" bounds, become a bit more informal.

A separate listing of compositions intended for or adaptable to multi-media presentation, meaning various combinations of singing, acting, dancing and visual aids are also in Appendix I. Certain works are included which are designated as or in the style of Musical Theatre. These works cater in part or in whole to a more "pop" musical style, though with quite different textures than the youth "pop" or "gospel" musical which I have chosen not to include in this book.

Appendix J: The use of children's voices is a matter of considerable concern for most conductors and directors. Likewise, children's chorus directors are constantly on the lookout for repertoire which will challenge their groups. Thus, I have included a list indicating which of the works in this book require some combination of children's voices.

ABBREVIATIONS USED IN THIS BOOK

alt	alto	lg	large
b	born	med	medium
bar	baritone	m-sop	mezzo-soprano
bs	bass	ob	oboe
bs-bar	bass-baritone	opt	optional
bsn	bassoon	org	organ
©	copyright	P	Parts (instrumental)
ca	circa	perc	percussion
cb	contrabass (string bass)	pia	piano
cel	celeste	picc	piccolo
ch	chorus	rec	recorder
cl	clarinet	SATB	Soprano, Alto, Tenor, Bass (Chorus)
col	coloratura	sax	saxophone
cont	contralto	sc	scene
corn	cornet	sd	side drum
ct	counter (tenor)	sm	small
cym	cymbal	sn	snare drum
Dan	Danish	sop	soprano
dr	drum	sp	spoken
dram	dramatic	str	string(s)
elec	electric	sus	suspended
Eng	English	synth	synthesizer
Eng hrn	English horn	tamb	tambourine
euph	Euphonium	tba	tuba
fl	flute	ten	tenor
Fr	French	tess	tessitura
FS	Full score (conductor's score)	timp	timpani
Ger	German	trb	trombone
glock	glockenspiel	tri	triangle
gui	guitar	trp	trumpet
Heb	Hebrew	vc	violincello (cello)
hp	harp	vib	vibraphone
hpsch	harpsichord	vla	viola
hrn	horn	vln	violin
It	Italian	VS	vocal score
LC	Library of Congress	xyl	xylophone

The Music Drama Repertoire

JOHN ADAMS

El Niño

Music by **John Adams** (b. 1947). Dramatic Oratorio with libretto by John Adams and Peter Sellars taken from the Bible, Haggai, *Wakefield Mystery Plays, Documents for the Study of the Gospels*, and select texts adapted from Latin American poets – many of them female – such as Sor Juana Inés de la Cruz, Rosario Castellanos, Rubén Darío, Vicente Huidobro, Hildegard von Bingen, and Gabriela Mistral. English, Latin, and Spanish texts.

Commissioned by Châtelet, San Francisco Symphony, Barbican Centre, London and the BBC, and Lincoln Center for the Performing Arts. World premiere December 25, 2000 in the Thèâtre du Châtelet in Paris, with the Deutsches Symphonie Berlin and the London Voices. It was performed under the title *La Nativité* at its premiere in Paris. American premiere by San Francisco Symphony.

Rhythmic and tonal complexities. Highly melodic. Atonality dominates. Set numbers; arias, ensembles.

Time and place for the action is not specified, though the story line of the Nativity dictates Biblical times. Duration: 105 minutes

Major Roles: SOP (top C5); M-SOP (top A4); BAR (G#1-F3) – some melisma; ensemble of 3 COUNTER-TENORS. The soloists are not bound to specific characters. Each of the three soloists embodies various figures or takes on a narrative role. All roles difficult.

Chorus: SSSAATTTBB – considerable choral music, extremely difficult at times.

Dancers: Optional but desirable

Orchestration: 2 fl (2 picc), 2 ob (2 Eng hrn), 2 cl (bs cl), 2 bsn (ctr bsn), 3 hrn, 3 trb, 3 perc (numerous percussion instruments), hp, pia (cel), synth, 2 steel string gui, str (minimum 14.0.6.6.4) (for complete technical requirements go to: http://www.earbox.com/tech-guide/eq/ja-elnino-eq.htm

Synopsis: *El Niño* tells the story of Jesus, Mary, and Joseph through a sequence of separate numbers, shifting between narration and reflection, but always through the image of modern-day Marys. According to librettist Peter Sellars, it depicts the birth of Christ simultaneously from several different – largely female – points of view.

El Niño tells the story of the Nativity, along with reflections on the wonders and tribulations of motherhood itself. Mary's virtue is praised; she is visited by the Holy Spirit, who tells her of the miracle to come. Joseph is angered to discover that Mary is pregnant. He is reassured by an angel of the Lord. The birth of Jesus is heralded by a star in the east. Three wise men arrive in Jerusalem in search of the child; Herod, hearing that a new King of the Jews has been born, sends the wise men to find him. They present Jesus with precious gifts. An angel of the Lord tells Joseph and Mary to flee to Egypt, for Herod wants to destroy the child. Herod, who has been mocked by the three wise men, orders that all of the children in Bethlehem shall be killed. Jesus performs miracles to rescue and protect his mother as they travel with Joseph through the desert to safety.

Materials: BH – corrected edition published August 2002.

Notes: This work is most suitable to a theatre stage. Large forces are needed for the chorus and orchestra, while professional/advanced level soloists are required. CD and DVD recordings of the world premiere production are available.

SAMUEL ADLER

The Wrestler

Music by **Samuel Adler** (b. 1928). A Sacred Music Drama with libretto in English by Judah Stampfer, based on the Biblical story of Jacob and Esau as found in Genesis 25-35.

Commissioned by the American Guild of Organists and first performed at its biennial meeting in Dallas, Texas, June 22, 1972.

Tonally conceived with frequent use of dissonance. Lyricism dominates the vocal lines with occasional awkward intervalic skips.

One act. Set in Biblical times. Duration: 40 minutes.

Major Roles: JACOB (bar); THE ANGEL, sung by the voice of Jacob; ESAU (bs-bar); RACHEL (sop); LEAH (m-sop).

Minor Roles: OBADIAH (bs-bar), Jacob's Servant; 2 MESSENGERS (tenors); 3 SHEPHERDS (tenors).

Chorus: Children's Chorus divided into seven groupings;
Women's Chorus (should have at least 16 voices);
Men's Chorus (TTBB).

Orchestration: 1 picc (doubling fl 2 and alto fl), fl, ob, cl, bsn, 2 tpt, 2 trb, hrn, 2 perc, pia (cel), org, 4 vla, 2 vc, cb.

Synopsis: A series of flashbacks is outlined through the narrative of Jacob: his buying of Esau's birthright, his deception of Isaac and flight from Esau's vengeance, and his successive marriages to Leah and Rachel. On the eve of his encounter with Esau, he meets and wrestles with an angel. Blessed by the angel, his life is changed. Eventually he meets and is reconciled with Esau.

Materials: OUP.

Notes: Most suitable for performance in a house of worship, but may also be presented in a theatre. Dramatically effective work.

NOA AIN

The Outcast

Music by **Noa Ain** (b. 1942). A Biblical Opera with libretto in English by the composer, freely based on the Book of Ruth.

Premiered June 17, 1990, Aaron Davis Hall, New York City.

Classical, jazz, folk and gospel influences present. Frequent meter changes. Tonal. Some rhythmic declamatory speech; spoken lines. Occasional improvisation and non-traditional vocal effects.

Two acts. Setting: Bethlehem during the time of Ruth. Duration: 100 minutes.

Roles: All roles require a mixture of jazz and classical styles with the latter dominating. RUTH (dram sop – A2-A4); NAOMI (m-sop – low El); GIDEON (ten – Ab1-Ab3); BOAZ (bar – top G3, falsetto C4); AR (bs), High Priest of Moab; THE BLUE WOMAN (jazz voice with low tess).

Chorus: SATB – Moabites and Jews.

Orchestration: Fl/alt fl, ob/Eng hrn, cl/bs cl/sax, bsn, vln, 4 vc, cb, pia, synthesizer, perc. The premiere was performed with rec, vc, pia, synthesizer, and dr.

Synopsis: Naomi and her son, Gideon, escaping from a famine in the Jewish city of Bethlehem, arrive in the country of Moab. Despite the wishes of the guards and some of the young men that these strangers be sacrificed to their goddess Ar, the High Priestess of Moab allows the Jews to live among them in peace. Soon after their arrival, Ruta, daughter of Ar, and Gideon are passionately attracted to each other, and in a mad pagan ceremony are wed. Naomi is despondent, but slowly, wooed by the goodness of Ruta, she begins to love Ruta. One night when Ruta and Gideon are walking in the mountains, three guards wearing masks of the goddess Inanna attack them. Ruta escapes; Gideon kills two of the guards, but the third murders him. The scene transforms into a funeral. The bodies of the murderers and Gideon are burnt in front of the goddess. The murderer, Beor, arrives still wearing the mask with blood on it. As he takes off his mask, Ruta declares passionately that he has "broken the heart of her dream" and tells Ar she must leave. Naomi rips Ruta's skirt in the Jewish manner of mourning, and together they leave for Bethlehem.

In Bethlehem, Naomi is punished by the Jews for her ten years among idolaters; she is made an outcast for one year while Ruta is allowed to gather wheat in the fields of Boaz, a former cousin of Naomi's husband. Boaz begins to love her and she him. Boaz tells Ruta he wishes to marry her, but Ruta says she still hears the voice of Gideon in her heart and she wishes to speak with him. Seeing that this is his only chance to win her, Boaz tells her of a woman who calls spirits. Ruta goes at night into the mountains where the Blue Woman appears to her in a crystal cave. The voice of Gideon tells her to let go of her love for Gideon, that she must marry another Jew, but first she must marry his people and they must marry her. Ruta returns to Bethlehem where she is ridiculed for speaking to spirits. She falls to her knees and asks the Jewish God to "give her a sign." A chorus of angels answers her, telling her she is not only already one of His people, but an example of loyalty and goodness for the rest of the Jews. The clouds part, and the angels descend slowly to the stage and then disappear. The Jews, moved by the magic of the event and God's acceptance of Ruta, one by one go to her, and in a wedding where the stage is slowly covered by an unfurling Chups, they marry her to themselves.

Materials: Unpublished. From the composer.

Notes: Best performed in a theatre.

EUGEN D'ALBERT

Der Golem – The Golem

Music by **Eugen d'Albert** (1864-1932). A *Musikdrama* with libretto in German by F. Lion, based on Jewish legend.

Premiered November 14, 1926, Frankfurt.

Extensive chromaticism, tonal. Declamatory accompanied recitative. Predominantly soloistic with little ensemble.

Three acts. Setting: Prague around 1600. Duration: approximately 120 minutes.

Roles: DER GOLEM (bar); RABBI LOEW (bs); HIS SON (ten); LEA (sop); KAISER RUDOLF DER ZWEITER (bar).

Chorus: SATBB – Jews, villagers.

Orchestration: 3 fl (picc), 2 ob, 2 Eng hrn, 2 cl, bs cl, 3 bsn, 4 hrn, 4 trp, 3 trb, tba, 3 perc, 2 hp, strings. Off-stage: 2 corn, 2 trb, bs dr, Becken, Baskische trommel.

Synopsis: The subject of this plot is a legendary occurrence in fifteenth century Prague, wherein the Rabbi of the Jewish ghetto, fearful of persecution, makes a Golem: an artificial being molded from the clay of the banks of the river Moldau. The appearance of the fearful Golem strikes terror in the hearts of both Christians and the Jews, precipitating a series of events, many historically verifiable, which culminates in the destruction of the Golem by the same magical means by which it was created. Many ideas are dealt with in this plot: the matter of magic, both black and white, religious persecution and intolerance, and historical drama. A love story is woven through the fabric of all these events and ideas as the Golem, gradually acquiring human characteristics, falls in love with the Rabbi's daughter, Rachel.

Materials: Universal Edition (© 1926) (Ger).

Notes: Best suited for theatre performance. This work and Sitsky's of the same title make an interesting comparison. The works are remarkably different in every aspect with the exception of orchestra size. This plot in this work is considerably simplified.

WILLIAM P. ALEXANDER

Samson at Gaza

Music by **William P. Alexander** (b. 1927). Sacred Chamber Opera with libretto in English by Ralph Church, based on the Old Testament story of Samson and Delilah as recorded in Judges 16.

Commissioned and premiered by Edinboro State College, PA, 1980.

Modal; conventional harmonies with considerable chromaticism.

One act. Setting: Gaza in Old Testament times. Duration: 20 minutes.

Roles: SAMSON (bar); DELILAH (sop).

Orchestration: Piano four hands. To be orchestrated for five winds.

Synopsis: This work covers the period toward the end of Samson's incarceration until his death in the collapse of the temple. The work is primarily a dialogue between Samson and Delilah.

Materials: Unpublished. AMC.

Notes: Suitable for performance in either a theatre or house of worship.

DOMINICK ARGENTO

Jonah and the Whale

Music by **Dominick Argento** (b. 1927). A Dramatic Oratorio with libretto in English, adapted from anonymous medieval English, the Biblical Books of Jonah and Psalm CXXX, sea shanties, and work songs. Suitable for both adults and children.

Premiered at Plymouth Congregational Church, Minneapolis, MN, March 19, 1974.

Tonally conceived but considerable use of dissonance and non-traditional harmonies.

Two parts. Setting: Biblical times in various places of the Jonah story (see synopsis). Duration: 60 minutes.

Major Roles: JONAH (ten); VOICE OF GOD (bs); NARRATOR (should be amplified).

Chorus: SATB

Orchestration: 2 trb, bs trb, 2 perc, timp, hp, pia, org.

Synopsis: God gives Jonah his mission to go to Nineveh, but Jonah refuses and flees by ship. During a storm at sea, Jonah is thrown overboard and is swallowed alive by a whale. When Jonah finally repents, God causes the whale to spit Jonah out. In Part II, Jonah goes to Nineveh and warns the people of God's anger. The people of Nineveh repent and God forgives them. Jonah becomes angry with God thinking that God has not kept His part of the bargain to destroy wicked Nineveh. God gives Jonah the sign of the Woodbine, a sign of God's eternal faithfulness, but Jonah's contrite spirit is not easily soothed.

Materials: BH. Recorded by CRI.

Notes: Sets can be sparse and simple. Particularly adaptable to a house of worship sanctuary or may be staged in a theatre. Staging and production problems include a storm, a whale, and the growth process of a Woodbine plant. Some productions have used dance or mime to represent these situations. Particularly well suited for young audiences.

The Masque of Angels

Music by **Dominick Argento** (b. 1927). A Sacred Music Drama of chamber opera proportions with libretto in English by John Olon Scrymgeour.

Commissioned by the Community Center Arts Council of Walker Art Center, Minneapolis, MN. Premiered in Minneapolis, January 9, 1964.

Tonally conceived, highly melodic, harmonically conventional, frequently comic. Harmonic structures and usage delineate between "sacred" and "secular." Folklore with strong moralistic and religious tendencies.

One act. Setting: The present time in a church. Duration: 75 minutes.

Major Roles: JOHN (ten – C#2-B3), a young man; ANN (sop – top B4), a young woman; METATRON (bar – G1-F3), Captain of the angels; SANDOLFON (ten – C#2-Bb3), his aide-de-camp; SADRIEL (ten), company clerk; JEREMIEL (ten – Bb1-Ab3), a Principality; RAGUEL (bar – F#1-Eb3), a Principality; THE SPINSTER (m-sop – A#2-Eb4); THE PROFESSOR (bs – F#1 (F#2 opt.)-E3).

Chorus: SSAATTBB. Very important, with much use of melisma. Semi-chorus of Powers (ABADDON, solo). Semi-chorus of Cherubim (CHERUBIEL, bs solo). Semi-chorus of Seraphim.

Dance: Ballet. Four Virtues who dance; four who dance the comic "Tie That Binds"; eleven Virtues who play on instruments.

Orchestration: 2 ob, bsn, 2 trp, trb, perc, hp, 2 vla, 2 vc.

Synopsis: On a routine inspection, a group of angels find themselves in a church making plans to stimulate the courtship of a young couple, Ann and John. Metatron, Captain of the angels, instructs his angelic troupe but is perplexed with the small number of available dancers. He is told that the usual *corps de ballet* for such occasions suffered an accident when too many tried to dance on the head of a pin. An embittered Spinster and frustrated old Professor, who are uncertain about their own love, offer advice to the young couple. Eventually, the angelic host accomplishes its mission even without the aid of the "Tie That Binds" dance, which is clumsily performed by the depleted ballet. The angels move on to their next task which is to stimulate success in the marriages of all heads of state, hoping thereby to benefit the entire world.

Material: BH.

Notes: This work may be staged in a theatre but is particularly well suited to a church presentation.

PIETRO ARIA

Jericho Road

Music by **Pietro Aria** (20th century American). A Biblical Opera/Play with libretto in English by Isabel Harriss Barr, based on a miracle play and the Biblical account in Mark 10. Suitable especially for children as well as adults.

Composed 1965; premiered by the Philadelphia Grand Opera on March 12, 1969.

Traditional harmonic structures, tonal with some chromaticism. Melodic, through-composed.

Two acts. Setting: Act I: The home of Timeus; Act II: A square on Jericho Road, just before Passover, 33 A.D. Duration: 60 minutes.

Major Roles: BARTIMEUS (ten – top A3), a blind beggar; TIMEUS (bar), his father; RUTH (cont), his sister; MARIAM (sop), a young girl.

Minor Roles: SETH (treble – top G4), a young boy; DISSENTER (bs); A VOICE (small boy); 2 LEPERS (tenors); OLD WOMAN (m-sop); MALE VOICE; SHELEM (bar); PHARISEE (ten); SCRIBE (ten); VENDOR (ten or sop); EMISSARY (bs); FORTUNE TELLER (alt - must dance); PROSTITUTE (alt); SAMARITAN (bar – top A3); OLD BEGGAR WOMAN (alt); POTTER (m-sop or bar).

Chorus: Two choirs: SATB and SA – Crowd, Potters, Soldiers, Guards, Emissaries.

Dance: Fortune Teller must dance. Folk dancing by the crowd, frantic at times.

Orchestration: Chamber orchestra.

Synopsis: Timeus is worried and fearful for the future of his people, the Israelites. His children try to console him. Mariam comes to take the blind Bartimeus to town as is her custom. She confides in Ruth, his sister, that she is at the age in her life she no longer wants to be bothered by continually escorting Bartimeus from place to place. Meanwhile in the village, crowds have already gathered to catch a glimpse of the stranger who is coming to town. Some call Him an imposter, others claim He heals the sick. Mariam urges Bartimeus to approach the stranger with his blind condition; he finally consents. Suddenly a cry of "He can see" erupts from the crowd. The stranger has healed Bartimeus, giving him his sight. Dancing and rejoicing by the crowds bring the work to its conclusion.

Material: Unpublished. AMC.

Notes: May be performed in a church or auditorium. This work is particularly well suited for children but must be performed by adults. J. Parker of the *Philadelphia Gazette* says: "Traditional values of communication in a rich instrumental score... the emotional impact of its drama [is a] cry for peace."

MALCOLM ARNOLD

Song of Simeon

Music by **Malcolm Arnold** (b. 1921). A Nativity Masque with words in English by Christopher Hassall, based on the Biblical story of Simeon as recorded in Luke 2:25-35.

Premiered in Theatre Royal, London, January 5, 1960, conducted by the composer.

An emulation of the Renaissance masque form and style in which the principal characters are portrayed in mime while sung by off-stage soloists or ensembles. Spoken dialogue, some rhythmic speech. Twentieth century influences mixed with modality and plainchant. Continuous action.

One act. Setting: Sc. 1: The place of the Annunciation; sc. 2: The Inn at Bethlehem which overlooks the stable; sc. 3: Outside the Temple at Jerusalem. Duration: 30 minutes.

Major Roles: MARY (sop); JOSEPH (bs); THE INNKEEPER (bs); HIS WIFE (cont); SIMEON (ten).

Minor Roles: A WOMAN FROM GALILEE (sop); ARAK (sp), her son; SUSANA (sp/dancer), her daughter; FOUR SHEPHERDS (basses).

Chorus: SSATTB – guests at the Inn and narrate the Angel Gabriel's part.

Dance: Susana must dance.

Orchestration: 3 trp, 3 trb, tba, timp, perc, cel, hp, and strings. Opt: 3 rec, timp, perc, pia duet, str

Synopsis: The story of the Annunciation and birth of Christ is told with simplicity and clarity. It is revealed by the Holy Spirit to the aging man Simeon, that he should not die without seeing the promised Messiah. Simeon indeed meets the Christ, Mary and Joseph, and holding the child in his arms, blesses God, declaring that this child will be the salvation of all people.

Material: OUP.

Notes: Best suited to performance in a church/cathedral. VS contains numerous staging suggestions. *Making Music* states: "The music, as one might expect, is powerful and dynamic, free from the sentimental approach so often associated with Nativity plays, yet has a direct appeal to the listener."

JOHANN SEBASTIAN BACH

Johannes Passion – St. John Passion

Music by **Johann Sebastian Bach** (1685-1750). A passion with text in German based on the Passion of Christ according to the New Testament Book of John. The majority of the text comes from the Gospel of John, chapters 18 and 19. Two passages from Matthew are added, one from chapter 26, dealing with Peter's denial of Jesus and another from chapter 27, describing the earthquake at the time of Jesus' death. Eight parts of the text were borrowed and adapted from *Der gemarterte und sterbende Jesus* by Barthold Heinrich Brockes. The poetry for the tenor aria in Part I was written by Christian Weise. Three other sections are scripturally based or original and are assumed to be the work of Bach.

Probably written in 1722-23, with the first performance in Leipzig, April 7, 1724.

Two parts. Duration: approximately 2 hours.

Major Roles: EVANGELIST (ten – high tess and vocally demanding); JESUS (bar), must possess warmth and lyric qualities.

Minor roles: SOPRANO, ALTO, TENOR, AND BASS SOLOISTS, all sing very difficult arias. PETER (bar), only recitative; JUDAS (bs), only recitative; PILATE (bs), only recitative; HIGH PRIEST (bar), only recitative; SOLDIER (bar), only recitative. Depending upon the dramatic interpretation, it is possible to double some of these soloists.

Chorus: SATB. Very important. Townspeople, on-lookers, soldiers, and commentators on the action.

Orchestration: 2 fl, 2 ob, 2 ob d'amore, 2 ob da caccia, lute/org/hpsch, strings, continuo

Synopsis: The story of the arrest, trial, and crucifixion of Jesus as told by the apostle John. The Evangelist narrates the action while the drama progresses through the action of the individual characters and dramatic choruses. The chorales represent moments of individual reflection.

Material: BAR (Ger); GS (Mendel edition); CFP (Ger); NOV (Eng by T.A. Lacey).

Notes: While this work was intended for concert presentation, the dramatic flow is quite adaptable for the stage, and can be visually effective. The chorus may be involved in the action but is best used as a Greek chorus. Dramatic involvement of the chorus could be enacted by a dance or pantomime troupe. Twelve chorales are used at strategic points throughout the work. It was intended by Bach that these chorales be sung by the congregation. May be staged in a theatre, but is most suitably adapted in a sanctuary with a large stage and chancel area.

Matthaeus Passion – St. Matthew Passion

Music by **Johann Sebastian Bach** (1685-1750). A Passion with text in German, based on the arrest, trial, and crucifixion of Jesus as told by the apostle Matthew in the New Testament Book of Matthew 26-28.

First performance April 11, 1727 or April 17, 1729.

A musical score of considerable difficulty for to integrate. Requires excellent musicians. Double chorus and double orchestra.

Two parts. Duration: 3 hours, 15 minutes.

Major Roles: EVANGELIST (ten – high tess), very difficult; JESUS (bar), requires great warmth and lyricism.

Minor Roles: SOPRANO, ALTO, TENOR, AND BASS SOLOISTS who sing very demanding arias. JUDAS (bs), recitative only; PETER (bar), recitative only; HIGH PRIEST (bar), recitative only; PILATE (bar), recitative only; MARY (sop), recitative only. It is possible for some of these roles to be doubled.

Chorus: SATB double chorus. Townspeople, observers, crowds, and commentators on the action. Very important and difficult.

Orchestration: Double orchestra. I: 2 rec. 2 fl, 2 ob, 2 ob d'amore, 2 ob da caccia, strings, continuo. II: 2 fl, 2 ob, 2 ob d'amore, str, continuo.

Synopsis: The story of the arrest, trial, and crucifixion of Jesus as told by the apostle Matthew. The Evangelist narrates the action while the drama evolves through the individual characters and chorus. Frequent moments of individual reflection are provided through the chorales.

Materials: BAR (Ger); GS (Eng by Robert Shaw); NOV; CFP (Ger).

Notes: While this work was intended for concert presentation, the dramatic flow of the text can be effectively adapted to the stage. The chorus may be involved in the stage action, or better, take on the form of a Greek chorus, in which case a dance or pantomime troupe may enact the drama as sung by the chorus. The chorales were intended by Bach to be sung by the congregation.

GRANVILLE BANTOCK

The Pilgrim's Progress

Music by **Granville Bantock** (1868-1946). A Dramatic Oratorio with libretto in English adapted from John Bunyan's *Pilgrim's Progress* by Bowker Andrews, with some text by Andrews and Milton's *Paradise Lost*.

Premiered at the Queen's Hall in London, November 23, 1928, under the direction of the composer. The work was requested by the BBC in commemoration of the John Bunyan Tercentenary.

Conventional harmonic structures with Romantic chromaticism. Numerous accompanied recitatives, set numbers, some arias and ensembles. Many orchestral interludes. The work is musically not difficult.

Two acts, twelve scenes. Minimal scenery required as little time is allowed for scene shifts. Duration: full length.

Major Roles: BUNYAN (bs – low D1 (opt), low tess); CHRISTIAN (ten – top Bb3); APOLLYON (bar – top F#3), requires a wide range with strong top.

Minor Roles: THE THREE SHINING ONES (sop, m-sop, cont).

Chorus: SSAATTBB – Angels, Pilgrims, Wayfarers, Devils, and Lost Souls.

Orchestration: Full orchestra.

Synopsis: The story is kept intact in its condensation. Bunyan, currently in prison, narrates the story of Pilgrim as he journeys. He seeks to be freed from his heavy burden which he carries on his back. He eventually comes to the foot of the cross where in humility he kneels and finds that his burden rolls off his back. He meets The Three Shining Ones who guide him on his way. Christian (Pilgrim's new name) is heard singing as he enters the Valley of the Shadow of Death. Here he meets Apollyon, the devil, with whom he does battle and is victorious. Able to continue his journey, he goes to the city of Vanity Fair where he and his friend Faithful are cast into prison. Faithful is put to death for his beliefs but Christian escapes and finally after successfully crossing the river of death, his journey ends in triumph at the gates of the Celestial City.

Material: SWAN (© 1928).

Notes: This work was intended as a concert piece, but because of the dramatic exchanges between the solos and the choruses, there is considerable potential for stage treatment. Numerous orchestral interludes allow for pantomime, dance, and actors to carry out the drama. Best performed in a theatre, though a large chancel area would suffice.

SEYMOUR BARAB

Father of the Child

Music by **Seymour Barab** (b. 1921). A Christmas Opera with libretto in English by the composer, suggested by William Gibson's play, *The Butterfingers Angel, Mary and Joseph, Herod the Nut and the Slaughter of 12 Hit Carols in a Pear Tree.*

Composed in 1985; premiered October 6, 1985 by Queensborough Community College, Bayside, NY.

Humorous throughout. While the setting is period, the language is contemporary. Tonally conceived with frequent dissonances. Melodically rewarding and linear but requiring good musicianship in the solo roles. Through-composed, spoken dialogue, considerable recitative, a few arias and frequent ensemble sections.

One act. Setting: From the conception to the birth of Jesus. Sc. 1: Nazareth, in an abstract structure representing Joseph's house; Sc. 2: In Bethlehem, the stable. Scene change occurs within the action. Duration: 75 minutes.

Major Roles: JOSEPH (bar), good actor required; MARY (sop); SATAN (bs – occasional low tess), must impersonate at least six different characters requiring excellent acting; GABRIEL (ten – top A3), youthful looking. All roles are mid-range and easily manageable.

Minor Roles: DONKEY (sop); CHERRY TREE (m-sop). The three Kings who comment on the action throughout the opera, frequently singing snatch phrases of Christmas Carols: GASPAR (ten), MELCHIOR (bar), BALTHAZAR (bs),

Orchestration: Piano. Orchestration is planned.

Synopsis: The Angel Gabriel descends to earth in human form to protect Mary from Satan, who throughout the opera appears in various forms, threatening to prevent the birth of God's Son. Joseph, doubting the Holy Conception and Gabriel's divinity, suspects him of being the father of Mary's child. Joseph demands a miracle of Gabriel before he will believe. Satan intervenes to sabotage the miracle but Gabriel sacrifices himself so the birth can occur.

Material: GS.

Notes: Sets should be simple, using set pieces. May be staged in a theatre, but particularly adaptable to a cathedral/church. Special costumes needs for Donkey and Cherry Tree.

Only A Miracle

Music by **Seymour Barab** (b. 1921). A Christmas Opera with libretto in English by the composer. A festival account of events immediately following Christ's birth.

Premiered by the Illinois University Opera Theatre, Urbana, December 1, 1983.

Tonal but dissonant at times with considerable chromaticism. Rythmic complexities within recitative sections which flow quite naturally with the contour of the English. Melodic within safe vocal ranges. Serious drama with occasional humor. Considerable recitative with arias and some set numbers.

One act. Setting: Outside the Inn at Bethlehem some days after the Holy Birth. Duration: ca. 50 minutes.

Major Roles: SYLPHINIA (sop – top G4), a slave girl of the Landlord; SOLDIER (ten); LANDLORD (bar – E1-F3, high tess at times).

Minor Roles: MESSENGER (bs); KING HEROD (bs). These two roles may be sung by the same person.

Orchestration: fl, ob, 2 cl, bsn, 2 hrn, tpt, trb, timp, perc, str

Synopsis: A Messenger is looking for Joseph. He goes by an Inn where a kind-hearted servant girl, Sylphinia, and a brutal Landlord are discussing the absence of his food.

The Landlord recalls turning away a couple, Mary and Joseph, who were about to give birth to a child. Sylphinia secretly recalls that she took them to the stable behind the Inn. A Soldier and King Herod enter. Herod is furious that the Wisemen left without telling him the location of the Christ child. Herod makes plans to offer a reward in exchange for the child. The Soldier is appointed to carry out this mission. The Soldier meets Sylphinia who tells him of the miracles that she has seen in connection with the birth of the child. He pleads with Sylphinia to reveal the child's location but to no avail. The Landlord then demands to know where the child is. He starts to beat Sylphinia, the Soldier attempting to protect her, but the Landlord prevails. He ties up the Soldier and threatens him with death if he does not reveal the location of the reward. The Landlord is about to kill the Soldier when the Messenger reappears saying that it is too late: the child is safe having escaped to Egypt. The Messenger then reveals that he is an angel. He frees the Soldier and Sylphinia, and causes the Landlord to speak like a donkey. The opera ends with a rousing ensemble given as a gift to the audience in celebration of Christmas.

Materials: GS. Tape available.

Notes: Adaptable for either church or theatre performance.

FRANCIS BARNARD

The Glory Coach

Music by **Francis Barnard** (? - 1985). A Sacred Folk Opera with libretto in English by the composer, patterned after two of the plays from the Wakefield Mystery Play Cycle, *The Creation*, and *The Deliverance of Souls*. Thematic material used in the course of the score is taken from numerous American hymn and folk tunes.

Premiered at the First Presbyterian Church, 12 West 12th St., New York City 10011, on March 28, 1982, Herbert Grossman, conducting.

Tonally conceived with considerable chromaticism. Some solo parts and choral numbers are difficult but melodic. Set numbers, spoken dialogue; rhythmic complexities.

Three acts. Setting: Act I: The creation of earth. Act II: During the time of Christ. Act III: The final judgment and aftermath. Duration: ca. 90 minutes.

Major Roles: GOD (a Trivinity sung by a soprano in Act I, tenor in Act II, and bass in Act III), voices need authority – all sing in mid-range; JESUS (bar – A1-Gb3); LUCIFER/SATAN (ten – F2-C4), requires top musical and vocal skills along with an acting talent that projects irony; ADAM (bar – top G3 with high tess; GABRIEL (bar – top Gb3).

Minor Roles: EVE (sop); BEELZEBUB (bs – low F1; RIBALD (ten – top G3; SUN (m-sop); MOON (treble voice); DOG (ten); CAT (m-sop); 1st ANGEL (ten); 2nd ANGEL (bar).

Spoken Roles: FLORA, FAUNA, WHALE, DODO BIRD, LOON BIRD, MICHAEL.

Chorus: SSAATBB. Representing 7 Planets, Trees, Extinct Species, Seraphim, Birds, Angels. Choral parts at times difficult. Very important to the drama and often acts as a Greek chorus. Children's choir unison.

Dance: Stylized not mandatory but can be incorporated effectively.

Orchestration: fl, ob, cl, bs cl, 2 trp, strings without cb. Organ accompanies the large choruses. The "Coach" chorus requires soprano and alto recorders.

Synopsis: This opera takes a look at the history of time with three stops: the creation, the life of Jesus, and the final judgment. The opera begins with the creation and subsequent fall of man. Act II takes us to the sending of God's Son to earth, with the trial of Jesus, His triumph over death and hell, and the freeing of the hell-bound. The third act sums up the gospel message and takes us to the final judgment.

Materials: FPC or CG.

Notes: Designed to be performed with minimal sets in a church sanctuary with ample space. Requires well-trained singers in all parts.

A Nativity In Threes

Music by **Francis Barnard** (? - 1985). A Christmas Opera with libretto in English by the composer, patterned after the medieval mystery plays.

Composed for the After Dinner Opera Company as an occasional piece to serve as the entertainment for a Christmas party honoring the late John Steinbeck. It was previewed in Vienna at the home of the American cultural attaché for Austria for friends of the embassy. Composed ca. 1975.

Traditional harmony with some dissonance and chromaticism. Some mixed meters and complex rhythms. Vocally lyric. Light comedy until the final number, "Lament," which must be sung with all solemnity. Set numbers.

One act. Setting: The manger scene during the birth of Christ. Duration: ca. 45 minutes.

Major Roles: The opera is performed by three singers, SOPRANO, ALTO, and BASS, who sing all the parts, assuming the roles of three Angels, Mary, Joseph, the Donkey, the Innkeeper, three Kings and three Shepherds. Additionally, three property people who participate in the action and help the singers with their costume changes in view of the audience. If one of these people were a mezzo-soprano, she could sing the alto part in the chorale at the beginning and the end, although the part can be left out without serious impairment. Ranges for the three soloists are easily accessible.

Chorus: SATB optional. Although originally conceived as a miniature, this work could be enlarged by the addition of a chorus of angels who would sing the chorale at the beginning and the end, the processional, "We Offer Our Nativity", the choral bits in the "March", the "Gloria", and the choral section in the "Lament".

Orchestration: Piano or organ and handbell in D.

Synopsis: The opera opens with a chorale asking the question, "Where is He?" The processional follows in which all six performers start down the aisle playing children's games. The three singers dress like angels and the Nativity story begins. The story line takes us on the journey to Bethlehem, the search for an inn, the presentation of gifts by the Magi, and the three shepherds' encounter with the angelic host. The final scene shifts to the mourning of the death of Jesus, concluding with the opening chorale, "Where is He?"

Materials: FPC or CG.

Notes: A delightful and easily produced opera. Costumes for all characters must be kept simple in order to accommodate quick changes. With a triptych placed in the chancel consisting of three translucent panels upon which are painted three medieval angels, the sanctuary of a church is an ideal performing environment.

CLAUDE L. BASS

The Father's Love

Music by **Claude L. Bass** (b. 1935). A Dramatic Cantata with libretto in English by the composer based on the Biblical parable found in Luke 15.

Composed in 1970.

Twelve set numbers with spoken dialogue and continuous action. The Greek chorus is significant. Tonal and harmonically conventional; melodic.

One act. Setting: Biblical times, mostly outdoors. Duration: 40 minutes.

Major Roles: THE PRODIGAL (ten), the younger of two brothers; two men are needed, one sings and narrates, the other pantomimes during the "flashback" sequence. If possible they should be of the same build and coloring, and should be costumed identically, except that the singer's costume should be torn and dirty. THE FATHER (bs-bar), appearing to age as time passes.

Minor Roles: THE MOTHER (non-singing role); THE BROTHER (non-singing role); SERVANTS AND WORKERS (these may sing on stage if desired, but it is not necessary); COMPANIONS (revelers in the far country – pantomime only).

Chorus: SATB – comment on the action and act as a Greek chorus.

Dance: The "Celebration" scene may be choreographed as stylistically or simply as desired. Folk dancing is appropriate.

Orchestration: Scored for piano, however, it may be adapted for organ or piano-organ combination. A tambourine may be used *ad libitum* in the "Celebration" scene.

Synopsis: The Prodigal Son reflects back to the time when he had food, home, and family, and is questioning his decision to leave. In a flashback scene, his mind and the action go back to the time when he worked at home in the fields. He recalls his father's admonitions for day dreaming and his decision to ask for his inheritance and leave home. He remembers the loneliness, hunger, poverty, and realizes he is no better off than his father's slaves. Waking from his day dreaming, he faces the reality of his condition and resolves to go back to his father. A celebration follows the Prodigal's return, evoking jealousy in the heart of his older brother. The Father attempts to reason with him. The celebrating continues and climaxes with a final choral alleluia.

Material: BP or composer.

Notes: This work may be produced as simply or as elaborately as desired. It is designed to be performed in the church with action taking place throughout the sanctuary. The chorus should not be in the loft, but should be seated in the pews to the left or right front of the church. The vocal score contains basic stage directions.

JACK BEESON

Jonah

Music by **Jack Beeson** (b. 1921). A Biblical Opera with libretto in English by the composer based on the play *Jonah* by Paul Goodman.

Completed in 1950.

Chromatic, tonal, with vocal parts largely declamatory. Ariosos with some solos and ensembles. Comic, dramatic.

Two or three acts. Act I, sc. 1: Jonah's home; sc. 2: Deck of a ship. Act II, sc. 1: Inside the fish; sc. 2: A public square in Nineveh; sc. 3: A throne room. Act III, sc. 1 or II, sc. 4: Outside Nineveh; sc. 2 or 5: The same. Duration: 120 minutes.

Roles: JONAH (buffo bs), vocally and dramatically demanding; HEPHZIBAH (m-sop), his wife; AN ANGEL and CAPTAIN OF THE GLORY OF TAMMUZ (bar); 1st IDOLATRESS and 1st LADY (col sop); 2nd IDOLATRESS and 2nd LADY (sop); 3rd IDOLATRESS and 3rd LADY (m-sop); 1st SAILOR and A DUKE (ten); 2nd SAILOR and AN URBAN GUIDE (bar); 3rd SAILOR and A PEASANT (bs); A MEDITATIVE MAN and AN ASTROLOGER (bs); THE KING (ten).

Chorus: SATB – Ninevites. Six bit-parts from the chorus.

Dance: Four or five dancers.

Orchestration: 2 fl (picc), ob, 2 cl (bs cl), 2 bsn, 2 hrn, 2 trp, trb, pia, hp, 2 perc, str

Synopsis: Jonah is awakened by the thunderous knocks of the Angel who has come to send him on another unwelcome mission. After a fight, he is commanded to go to Nineveh and to cry out the destruction of the city in forty days. The Angel leaves and Jonah decides to flee from his duty. Jonah is at sea, deliberately going the opposite direction from Nineveh. A fierce storm threatens the ship's safety. It is determined that Jonah is the culprit and he is thrown overboard, whereupon the nose of a great fish appears. The storm ends suddenly and objects thrown overboard come flying back on board. Inside the great fish, Jonah sleeps. When he awakens, he realizes that the whale has been provided in order that he may carry out his duty; he resigns himself to the will of the Lord. The Angel enters with a lamp and announces that they have arrived. They shout their farewells to their host and leave. In Nineveh, Jonah is dressed as a dignitary and makes his prophecy. The people find him charming and are soon dancing to a popular tune improvised on the prophet's words. The King and courtiers are delighted with Jonah's prophecy and decide to wear sackcloth and cover themselves with ashes in preparation for their destruction.

Outside the city, Jonah sets up a booth from which he will watch the destruction of the city. The Astrologer sees a vision of the destroyed city. The Duke and Urban Guide lay bets on the outcome and leave as the Imperial Odds are announced. At the same moment the final day is torn off the calendar. Shouts and laughter are heard, disclosing a blinding hot morning. Crowds troop out in holiday mood to thank Jonah for forty days of diversion. Enraged at having been tricked by the Lord and taunted by the Ninevites, he upbraids the Angel. Overcome by anger, he faints and the Angel draws from the earth a melon-tree to protect him from the sun. When he awakens he discovers that one of the melons is provided with a spigot and a never-ending supply of wine. Soon a party is in progress, interrupted by the Angel, who explodes the melon.

Jonah again turns on the Angel. Jonah pities the melon for which he did not labor; the Lord, who has labored long, pities and spares Nineveh "wherein are seven million, innocent at heart, who mean no harm."

Materials: From the composer.

Notes: Best performed in a theatre.

JEAN BERGER

Birds of A Feather

Music by **Jean Berger** (1909-2002). A Dramatic Choral work (an entertainment) with libretto in English by the composer, based on the poem *Similar Cases* by Charlotte Perkins S. Gilman.

Tonal with some harmonic surprises, but very melodic and singable. Highly rhythmic with some complexities. Many imitative devices in the choral sections. Through-composed. A few unaccompanied sections.

Premiered at Southern Illinois University, Carbondale, October 24, 1974.

One act. Setting: An open stage area. Duration: 32 minutes.

Roles: THE TRIO (sop, ten, bar) – this group stands outside the action, commenting on it. They may be presented as specified characters if desired. Good acting required. EOHIPPUS (sop), should appear very young and in the guise of a 6-year old girl; COMPANIONS, her Companions should be of similar age (all females). ANTHROPOIDAL APE (ten), virile, athletic looking; COMPANIONS (all male), should have similar appearance – no ape costume NEOLITHIC MAN (sp), should have the appearance of the proverbial demagogue, filled with empty promises.

Chorus: SSAATTBB. The chorus fills a double role: one, to stand outside the action and comment on it; second, to participate in the action including the part of the Companions. Three soloists are from the chorus: 1 alto, 2 sopranos. Actions of the chorus should be highly stylized or choreographed.

Dance: A group of dancers is optional but recommended. Action is stylized and choreographed as expressive clowning, miming, and caricaturing.

Orchestration: 2 fl, 2 trp, melodica (2 cl opt), 1 pia, 1 elec pia, cb, perc, timp.

Synopsis: Whether this work is a farce, satire, an heir to the madrigal comedy or something else must be decided by the director of the production. Eohippus, Anthropoidal and Neolithic each want to become something other than what they are. In each case it is decided that they cannot change their nature. The final conclusion expresses hope for the "nature of humankind." The chief purpose of this work is to show this hope and not to convey a plot. The participants are involved in rendering a concept rather than a story, and thus the staging or the choreography should not aim at any realism or naturalism. Stylization is the password, and motion per se, be it comic, pathetic, ecstatic or other, should be the goal.

Materials: JS. Sole agent is JB.

Cherry Tree Carol

Music by **Jean Berger** (1909-2002). After a Medieval Christmas Liturgical Drama based on the medieval play of the same name.

Through-composed with considerable mixed meter though the rhythmic complexities are for the most part confined to the instrumental sections. Melodically and vocally conceived with accessible ranges; the work is primarily choral with soloists playing minor roles.

One act with a number of different scenes possible, though all scenes should follow each other with only momentary interruptions. Duration: 19 minutes.

Roles: All roles are very brief and not vocally difficult. MARY (sop); JOSEPH (ten); CHILD (boy sop); SOLO QUARTET (S,A,T,B).

Chorus: SSAATTBB. Best used as a Greek chorus, though they should be involved in the processional and recessional and could be included in some of the action.

Dance: Dancers are optional but desirable. Frequent instrumental interludes suggest activity and drama. Dancers may also be included with choral passages using choreography which is fanciful, playful, imaginative, and even irreverent at times.

Orchestration: pia (elec, if available), bs, fl, mandolin (opt), ob/Melodica (opt), perc (bs drum, cym, finger cym, glock, sd dr, sus cym, tamb, tri). It is suggested that if the treble instruments indicated are not available, other compatible instruments may be used. If an electric piano is not available, a conventional piano may be used. For church performance, an organ may be used instead of piano. Contrasting organ combinations could substitute for the treble instruments. Of all the treble instruments, the flute is the most important.

Synopsis: Joseph and Mary are walking through an orchard. Mary asks Joseph to pluck her a cherry for she is with child. Enraged, Joseph refuses. The Babe within Mary's womb asks the cherry tree to bow down its limbs, and in obedience, does so. Joseph, understanding what has occurred, confesses his error. Mary asks her Son what the world will be like in the future. The Child tells her of His coming death and resurrection. A recessional concludes the work.

Materials: AUG (© 1975).

Notes: Best performed in a church/cathedral. Sets not necessary though a stylized cherry tree and a few props may be desirable. Some stage directions are included in the VS. Some costuming of the chorus may be desirable. A functional and appealing work for a choral organization. Could fit into a Sunday worship service.

Yiphtah and His Daughter

Music by **Jean Berger** (1909-2002). A Sacred Opera with libretto in English by the composer, loosely based on the Old Testament story as found in Judges 11-12.

Harmonically conventional but infused with chromaticism and occasional straying tonalities. Vocally conceived. Highly colorful orchestration. Set numbers.

One act. Setting is not specified but would seem to be outdoors. Duration: 22 minutes.

Major Roles: YIPHTAH (bar – top sustained F3), a warrior; YIPHTAH'S DAUGHTER (sop).

Minor Roles: SOPRANO SOLO; TOWN CRIER (sp or chanted), a declamatory voice; DRUMMER BOY (acting and drumming).

Chorus: Double chorus of SSA and SATBB – acting as townspeople as well as commenting on the action. The score is predominantly choral.

Dance: A single dancer who impersonates Yiphtah's Daughter.

Orchestration: fl, trp, elec pia (a second acoustic pia may be used), acoustic pia, cel, cb, perc.

Synopsis: The warrior, Yiphtah, exiled by his brothers, is summoned by the Israelites to lead an armed force against the Ammonites. He vows that, should the Israelites win the battle, he will sacrifice to the Lord the first member of the returning victory party. Israel is victorious. Yiphtah returns home to be greeted first by his own daughter. The deep despair experienced by both father and daughter is the primary focus of the opera.

Materials: CF.

Notes: A house of worship would be an appropriate setting for this opera. The FS contains basic lighting and stage directions.

LENNOX BERKELEY

Ruth

Music by **Lennox Berkeley** (1903-1989). A Sacred Opera with libretto in English by Eric Crozier, based on the Old Testament story as found in the Book of Ruth.

Premiered at the Scala Theatre, London, England, October 2, 1956, by the English Opera Group.

Tonal, conventional harmonies, but highly chromatic. Some set numbers, using both secco and accompagnato recitatives. Few arias. Orchestral prelude to Scene 3.

One act, three scenes. Setting: Biblical times. Sc. 1: In the hills near Bethlehem; Sc. 2: The field of Boaz; Sc. 3: A threshing floor at night. Duration: ca. 80 minutes.

Roles: RUTH (m-sop – B2-G#4); BOAZ (ten – top Bb3), some unaccompanied sections; NAOMI (sop - top B4); ORPAH (sop – top B4, high tess); HEAD REAPER (bar – top F#3).

Dance: Celebration dance in Sc. 3.

Chorus: SATB – Friends of Ruth and Boaz, Townspeople. Considerable choral involvement throughout.

Orchestration: 2 fl (picc), hrn, pia, perc, str

Synopsis: Naomi has returned to Judah with her daughters-in-law Orpah and Ruth. She persuades Orpah to go back to Moab, but Ruth insists on staying with her. Reapers on the way to the harvest field are joined by some women asking permission to glean. Ruth's arrival a little later provokes an outburst of hostility. She is saved from violence by the arrival of Boaz, a distant kinsman of Naomi's, who rebukes the laborers. He then questions Ruth and sends her to Naomi with a gift of corn. The "harvest-home" is to be celebrated. Naomi brings Ruth to the threshing floor and persuades her to offer herself in marriage to Boaz. The effigy of the Corn King is brought in amid harvest songs and dances. The festivities conclude with a prayer of thanksgiving by Boaz before they retire to sleep. Ruth makes her presence known to Boaz and asks him to take her as his wife. Boaz, deeply moved by the selflessness of the young woman, consents and calls together his people to witness the marriage.

Material: CHES.

Notes: May be staged with minimal scenery in either a theatre or house of worship.

HECTOR BERLIOZ

L'enfance du Christ – The Childhood of Christ

Music by **Hector Berlioz** (1803-1869). A Sacred Music Drama (trilogy) with libretto in French by the composer based on New Testament accounts.

Premiered in its entirety in Paris, December 10, 1854.

Typically lush romantic chromatic harmony. Long melodic lines. Some unaccompanied sections. Set numbers: arias, duets, and large ensembles. Considerable number of orchestral sections.

Three parts. Part I: King Herod's Dream; Sc. 1: A street in Jerusalem; Sc. 2-4: The palace of Herod; Sc. 5-6: The stable at Bethlehem. Part II: The Flight into Egypt and the stable at Bethlehem. Part III: The Arrival at Sais, then within the city of Sais. Duration: ca. 90 minutes.

Major Roles: NARRATOR (ten); HEROD (bs), vocally and dramatically demanding at times; MARY (m-sop); JOSEPH (bar).

Minor Roles: POLYDORUS (bs); CENTURION (ten); 2 CENTURIONS (non-singing); FATHER OF THE FAMILY (bs – low Fl).

Chorus: SSAATTBB – Magicians, Angels, Shepherds, Romans, Egyptians, Ishmaelites, Servants.

Dance: Several orchestral sections may be choreographed.

Orchestration: 2 fl (picc), ob, Eng hrn, 2 cl, 2 bsn, 2 hrn, 2 trp, 2 corn, 3 trb, timp, hp, org, str

Synopsis: PART I – HEROD'S DREAM. A Roman detachment patrols the empty streets of Jerusalem. Their watch is briefly interrupted as two soldiers discuss the

strange terrors of King Herod. Alone and unable to sleep, Herod reflects on the loneliness of his life and goes over in his mind the dream that haunts him: a child who will overthrow his power. He consults his soothsayers and learns that his throne will be preserved only if all the children lately born in his kingdom are put to death. He gives orders for the massacre of the innocents. The scene moves to the stable in Bethlehem where Mary and Joseph worship the Child. In a vision they are warned by angels of the danger to Jesus and are told to leave for Egypt at once.
PART II – THE FLIGHT INTO EGYPT. The shepherds gather at the stable and say goodbye to the Holy Family. The Narrator describes Mary, Joseph, the baby and the donkey resting at an oasis, watched over by angels. PART III – THE ARRIVAL AT SAIS. The Narrator tells how the travelers, after great hardships, reach the city of Sais. They knock at many doors but are driven away. At last, fainting from hunger, they are hospitably received by the family of an Ishmaelite. The Father of the family invites them to stay and live with him and his household. The pilgrims gratefully rest, entertained with music by the children and then retire to bed. In an epilogue, the Narrator tells of their long sojourn in Egypt, their eventual return to Palestine, the child's fulfillment of His redeeming mission, and the final sacrifice. Chorus and Narrator pray that men's pride may be abased before such a mystery, and their heart filled with Christ's love.

Material: GS edition has an acceptable Eng translation but without the Fr. Eng translation also by Jacques Barzin available.

Notes: Frequent orchestral interludes present staging challenges. Most often performed as a concert piece but adaptable to the stage in either a theatre or large chancel area.

LEONARD BERNSTEIN

Mass

Music by **Leonard Bernstein** (1918-1990). A Theatre Piece for singers, players and dancers with libretto in English and Latin, taken from the Liturgy of the Roman Mass with additions by Stephen Schwartz and the composer.

Premiered at the Kennedy Center for the Performing Arts, Washington, D. C., September 8, 1971.

Uses nearly every musical style within reach: folk, rock, jazz, chorale, chant, gospel, pop, show tunes, marching bands, traditional classical. At times melodically disjunct, bordering on atonal. Set numbers, following the order of the Roman Mass.

Continuous drama with seventeen thematic sections. Time is contemporary. Setting is non-designated. Duration: ca. 2 hours.

Major Roles: CELEBRANT (ten), a gifted musician capable of singing in many styles ranging from classical to pop and jazz; must have a wide range, and should be able to play acoustical guitar.

Minor Roles: Numerous small solo parts exist throughout the work and include: boy sop; six solo voices (2 sop, alt, ten, bar, bs); Acolytes; three rock singers (sop, 2 ten); blues singers (sop, alt, ten); sop solo; preacher; m-sop solo.

Dance: Dancers capable of a variety of dance styles, particularly popular.

Chorus: SATB – A large chorus inclusive of a Street Chorus; SATB – Ecclesiastical Choir; rock singers; blues singers; boys choir.

Orchestration: 2 fl (picc), 2 ob, 3 cl, alt sax, 2 bsn, 4 hrn, 4 trp, 5 trb, tba, 3 perc, keyboard, hp, gui, bs gui, vln, cb. Reduction possible. Specialty groups taken from the above orchestration include a marching street band, rock band, and blues combo.

Synopsis: The Celebrant, representing Church, Everyman and Christ, strums his guitar singing a hymn to God. Soon the people joyously march to MASS singing the traditional Greek and Latin words to music they understand. The boys place vestments on the folk singer as he assumes the role of the Celebrant. As the boys and Celebrant sing of their faith in God, they are interrupted by a rock band complaining about the difficulty of confession. The blues singers state that it's so easy if you don't care. An ecclesiastical choir pleads with the Virgin Mary to pray for them amid the interruptions of the rock and blues musicians. Although the people are discontent, the Celebrant struggles to continue the Mass. When the crowd continues to mock him, however, he calls to heaven, "Lord, I am not worthy." Like Moses on Mount Sinai, the Celebrant hurls the sacred vessel to the ground. He defrocks himself and rapidly loses his sense of reason. The crowd is frozen to silence by his sacrifice until a child sings a praise to God. Little by little the people pass the kiss of peace as the choirboys descend into the audience to touch the audience, saying "Pass it on."

Material: GS.

Notes: Musically, large and well-trained forces are required. May be staged in a theatre or house of worship with a large stage area. Sets may be minimal or as elaborate as desired. Platforms or a multi-level stage works well.

THOMAS BEVERSDORF

The Vision of Christ

Music by **Thomas Beversdorf** (1924-1981). On the order of a Mystery Play with libretto in English by John Wheatcroft, based on *The Vision of William Concerning Piers the Plowman* by William Langland (1332?-?).

Composed 1970-71. Premiered May 1, 1971, Bucknell University, Lewisburg, PA.

Both vocally and instrumentally, a mixture of musical styles from that of the Middle Ages and modern eras. Modality, chant-like solo passages, ensembles, and solos. Conventional harmonies throughout. Instrumental interludes between episodes.

Three parts plus a Prologue. Part I: The Annunciation through the birth of Christ; Part II: Christ's earthly life through his death; Part III: Christ's burial through his resurrection. Duration: 40 minutes.

Roles: POET (male voice); MARY, PEACE (sop); IMAGINATIVE, HOLY SPIRIT, FAITH (ct ten or alt); WILL, LONGINUS, GOOD SAMARITAN (ten); CHRIST (bar); JUDAS, SATAN (bs); BEELZEBUB (bs).

Chorus: SATB. Small mixed Chorus who comment on the action and often narrate the story.

Dance: Four young female dancers (Mercy, Peace, Righteousness, Truth).

Orchestration: 3 rec (sop, sop-alt, alt-ten), picc (wooden), fl (wooden), alt fl, 2 ob (Eng hrn), 2 cl, 2 bsn (contra bsn), 2 hrn, 2 trp, trb, bs trb, hp, hpsch, portative org (autoharp), 3 vla, cb, 5 perc players.

Synopsis: Langland's *The Vision of William Concerning Piers the Plowman*. After a processional by the entire cast, the Poet is found wandering throughout the wide world in search of Christ. Poet meets Imaginative and Will who help him on his way. Mary is told of her part in the salvation of the world. The Nativity scene concludes Part I. Christ's miracles, His confrontation with Satan, the Last Supper, Judas's betrayal, Christ's trial and His crucifixion all are played out in Part II. The action surrounding the death of Christ continues into Part III. Satan is defeated. The friends of Jesus mourn His death. In the last scene, Poet paints a picture of rejoicing over the resurrection of Jesus. A recessional of the entire cast concludes the work.

Materials: Unpublished. IUML.

Notes: Equally suitable for presentation in church or theatre.

SUSAN HULSMAN BINGHAM

The Awakening

Music by **Susan Hulsman Bingham** (b. 1944). A Chancel Opera with libretto in English by Neil Olsen based on Scripture from John 2:1-11, Luke 10:38-42, Matthew 27, Mark 15:46-47, Luke 23:53-56, and John 19:40-42.

Premiered in 1980, Trinity Church on the Green, New Haven, CT.

Tonal with traditional harmonic treatment. Highly melodic with many recitative passages, arias, ensembles. Mostly chordal and arpeggiated accompaniment. Contemporary language usage.

One act, five scenes. Short interludes between scenes. Sc. 1: The present; sc. 2: The wedding at Cana during Jesus' early ministry; sc. 3: The house of Mary and Martha; sc. 4: At the tomb of Jesus just after the crucifixion; sc. 5: The present. Duration: 25 minutes.

Roles: All roles easily accessible. MARY (sop – top G#4), must act four different Mary characters: modern, Mary the Mother of Jesus, Martha's sister, and one of the two Marys at the tomb; MARTHA (m-sop), must act four different Martha characters: modern, Martha as a kitchen servant, Mary's sister, and one of the two Marys at the tomb; JESUS (bar – top F3).

Orchestration: Piano.

Synopsis: Martha and her friend Mary discuss their economic situation. Mary envies Martha, who seems to have all the comforts of modern life while Martha sees Mary as serene and secure. Martha confesses that she is deeply troubled and suffers from a "sense of lack." She asks Mary for help. The scene changes to the wedding in Cana. The kitchen servant (Martha) in her carelessness has allowed the wine to run out. Jesus comes to the wedding and is coerced by His mother to assist. He miraculously turns the water into wine. Martha withdraws in awe and fear from the man who has such power and control over the elements. Again the scene changes to the home of Mary and Martha. Martha is bustling around the house in preparation for Jesus' visit. Mary, meanwhile, is blessed for sitting at the feet of Jesus and listening to His teaching. Martha is rebuked ("awakened") by Jesus and sees her mistaken view of the world. The scene changes to the tomb of Jesus. The two Marys bitterly mourn the death and their own personal loss of Jesus. In the final scene, sometime later, we again visit the modern friends, Mary and Martha. Martha is still troubled. She has seen the transforming and enlightening power of Jesus but still questions her sense of loss. Jesus, across death and centuries, and despite doubt, touches her with the touch of the healer.

Materials: Unpublished. From the composer.

Notes: Minimal sets and properties needed. May be performed in either a theatre or cathedral/church.

The Birth of Our Lord

Music by **Susan Hulsman Bingham** (b. 1944). A Christmas Chancel Opera with libretto in English by the composer adapted from the nativity story in the New Testament Gospels and the Book of Psalms.

Composed in 1990. Not yet premiered.

Traditional harmonies. Highly melodic with chant-like passages during Scriptural quotations. One aria, ensembles. Mostly contemporary language usage; simple chordal and arpeggiation accompaniment.

One act. Setting: During the time of the birth of Jesus; in a stable. Duration: 17 minutes.

Roles: MARY (sop – top G#4); JOSEPH (bar – F#1-G3), requires strong low range; RACHEL (sop), a midwife; SUSANNAH (sop), her assistant; INNKEEPER (mime).

Chorus: All roles should sing chorus parts at different points in the opera. A separate chorus may also be used (unison and 3-part). Chorus is mostly narrative.

Orchestration: Piano.

Synopsis: Joseph is desperately attempting to locate an inn in which Mary could give birth to her son; she is obviously already experiencing labor pains. Two women rush to help as Mary and Joseph, in desperation, find shelter from the cold night air in a stable. Joseph is invited to wait outside while the women attend to Mary, whose pains are depicted by half-sung cries. The Child is born. The women forget their frenzy as they worship and adore the newborn Child. Joseph is invited in to greet the Babe. Overwhelmed, he leaves the stable, puzzled over the events leading to the birth. As he finishes his song, he sees, in the distance, shepherds approaching with the help of a guiding star.

Materials: Unpublished. From the composer.

Notes: Intended to be performed as a part of a worship service in a cathedral/church. Set requirements include a manger scene with several animals and hay.

By the Pool of Siloam

Music by **Susan Hulsman Bingham** (b. 1944). A Chancel Opera with libretto in English by the composer based on John 9:1-38 from the New Testament.

Composed in 1983 with revisions in 1990. Not yet premiered.

Tonal; traditional harmonies. Recitative passages with chant-like vocal lines. A few spoken lines. Continuous texture. Non-scripture passages use contemporary language. Mostly arpeggiated accompaniment with frequent key changes.

One act. Setting: Near the Pool of Siloam during the time of Jesus' ministry. Duration: 25 minutes.

Roles: JESUS (bar – top F#3); DISCIPLE #1 (ten or high bar); DISCIPLE #2 (ten or high bar); MAN BORN BLIND (ten or high bar); YOUNG BLIND GIRL (sop); PHARISEE #1 (ten or high bar); PHARISEE #2 (ten or high bar); FATHER OF BLIND MAN (bar); MOTHER OF BLIND MAN (sop or m-sop).

Chorus: TBB – Additional disciples and two groups of Pharisees; Mixed voices – Villagers, which may be sung in three parts or in unison depending on the capabilities of the singers.

Orchestration: Piano.

Synopsis: A blind man is seated by a pool. Several of Jesus' disciples ask Jesus if the man's blindness was caused by his own sin or the sin of his parents. Jesus answers that it is for the glory of God that he was born blind. Jesus then makes a paste out of His own spit and some dirt. Spreading it over the eyes of the blind man, Jesus instructs him to wash in the pool. When he does, the man is able to see. A young girl, also blind, tries to obtain healing in the same manner and, though she remains blind, her spirit is healed. The on-looking crowd of Pharisees, villagers and disciples express their varying opinions of the event. The now-healed man kneels before Jesus praising God while a large chorus of converted Pharisees and villagers join him.

Materials: Unpublished. From the composer.

Notes: Best performed in a house of worship. May be incorporated into a service of worship.

A Conversation Between Mary and the Angel Gabriel

Music by **Susan Hulsman Bingham** (b. 1944). A Christmas Chancel Opera with libretto in English by the composer, loosely based on the Annunciation as found in Luke 1:26-38. After the manner of a medieval play.

First performed December, 1978, Trinity Church on the Green, New Haven, CT.

Tonal; vocally conceived. Contemporary language usage. Sparse accompaniment with simple traditional harmonic treatment. Light but not comic. Continuous texture.

One act. Setting: Mary's home. Duration: 10 minutes.

Roles: Both roles accessible and mid-range. MARY (sop); GABRIEL (treble, sop, or ten), may be an adult or child.

Chorus: SAT – chorus of Angels not involved directly in the action.

Dance: Optional stylized dance for Gabriel.

Orchestration: pia or org, fl, tamb.

Synopsis: Alone and feeling a bit uneasy, Mary is approached by Gabriel bringing a message from God. Mary listens excitedly as Gabriel explains how God has chosen her to bear His Child. She gently protests, saying she is not yet married and too young; furthermore, Joseph would be very angry and think she is making up a tale. Gabriel says he will give her time to think over her decision. Mary finally agrees and with some fear calls upon Joseph to help her and to understand her. Her fear turns to joy as she realizes that she is indeed "the handmaid of God. Let it be according to your word." Gabriel and the angel chorus respond with joyful "Tra-la-las."

Materials: Unpublished. From the composer.

Notes: A simple but effective dramatization ideally suited for performance in either a service of worship or concert. Best suited for presentation in a cathedral/church.

Magdalene

Music by **Susan Hulsman Bingham** (b. 1944). A Chancel Opera with libretto in English by the composer, based on texts from the Bible, the Gnostic Gospels, *Pistis Sophia* and Wedeck's *A Treasury of Witchcraft*.

Composed in 1987. Not yet premiered.

Traditional harmony; some contemporary "pop" sounds and rhythms. Frequent key changes. Vocally conceived. Some spoken lines. Non-scripture passages use contemporary language. Arias, ensembles, recitative passages often with chant-like treatment. Continuous texture except between scenes.

One act, six scenes. Setting: In and around Jerusalem during Jesus' ministry. Scene 1: Unclean spirits cast out; sc. 2: Jesus and Mary walk together; sc. 3: In the house of Simon the leper; sc. 4: A meeting room; sc. 5: The crucifixion of Jesus on Golgotha; sc. 6: At the tomb of Jesus after the resurrection. Duration: 30 minutes.

Major Roles: MARY MAGDALENE (sop – top Bb4); JESUS (bar – A1-F3).

Minor Roles: JOANNA (sop); MARY THE MOTHER OF JAMES (m-sop); MARY OF BETHANY (sop); 2 ANGELS (sop, sop); ANDREW (ten); PETER (bar); MATTHEW (bar). Some discrepancy exists between the printed libretto and the score in regard to cast assignments: i.e., Susannah, Mary the Mother of James, and Joanna appear in the libretto, but not in the score.

Speaking Roles: THREE MEN (lines may be spoken either as a group or individually); SIMON; JUDAS ISCARIOT; CRIMINAL #1; CRIMINAL #2; CENTURION.

Chorus: SA – Seven Unclean Spirits (hooded and not recognizable, they appear only in Scene 1 and therefore may play other parts later in the opera); SSA – Women mourners at the cross. Supers: Soldiers, villagers.

Orchestration: pia or org.

Synopsis: The plot traces the relationship and encounters between Mary Magdalene and Jesus. Mary Magdalene is healed and purged of her seven unclean spirits by Jesus. She falls before Him in thanksgiving. A short time later, she complains to Jesus that His male disciples do not approve of her and that she is uncomfortable in their presence because of Him. Jesus reassures her of her importance. In the home of Simon the leper, Mary anoints Jesus' head and feet with oil and perfume while other guests mumble about the high cost of such extravagance. Jesus gives them a morality lesson and tells Mary that "your faith has made you whole, your sins are forgiven." Later, Mary and a few other disciples argue about who is closer to Jesus. She tells them how such jealousy is not necessary. Scene 5 takes us to the crucifixion with commentary from the criminals, Centurion, soldiers, villagers, and the words of Jesus from the cross. After Jesus dies, Mary assures her stricken friends that His promises are true. At Jesus' tomb, Jesus appears to the surprised Mary. The women rush into the village to tell the other disciples, who challenge Mary's honesty. She is hurt but then reassures them that "This is no vision. He is with us here and now, continuing."

Materials: Unpublished. From the composer.

Notes: Intended to be a part of a worship service. May be performed in either a house of worship or theatre. Production problem: Jesus hanging on the cross. Sets may be elaborate or simple, using the decor of a cathedral as the setting.

On the Road to Emmaus

Music by **Susan Hulsman Bingham** (b. 1944). A Chancel Opera (Liturgical operetta) with libretto in English by the composer, based on Luke 24 of the New Testament. After the manner of a mystery play.

Premiered April 13, 1980, at Trinity Church on the Green, New Haven, CT.

Tonal, highly melodic with traditional harmonic texture. One aria for Jesus; numerous recitative passages with modal chant-like melodic lines. Non-scriptural passages in contemporary language. Mostly simple chordal accompaniment.

One act. Setting: One week after the crucifixion of Jesus on the road to Emmaus and then in the home of Cleopas. Duration: 20 minutes.

Roles: JESUS (bar – G1-F3); CLEOPAS (ten – top G#3); SIMON or JUDITH (ten or sop). "One of the disciple's parts may be sung by a soprano, as the unnamed disciple may have been a woman. It is recommended that the part of Cleopas, which is higher than the part of Simon, be given to the soprano in this case." SHB

Chorus: TTT (an offstage chorus).

Orchestration: fl, hp (opt), pia or org.

Synopsis: Only one of the two disciples in Luke 24 is named and their relationship to one another is unclear. The two disciples are walking toward the town of Emmaus discussing the events leading up to the crucifixion and the fact that Jesus might have risen from the dead. They are joined by a stranger who appears not to have heard about these events. Eagerly, the two disciples retell the story. It becomes clear that the two have some doubts as to the truth of some of the facts. The stranger reminds them that Scripture is full of references and prophesies concerning these events. As the stranger quotes Moses, Zechariah, Micah and others, Cleopas and Simon playfully interrupt him, eager to exhibit their knowledge. As the three approach town, Cleopas invites the stranger to join them for their evening meal. Before they eat, the stranger offers thanks for the food. When they open their eyes, the stranger is gone. The two astounded disciples gather their belongings and begin their return to Jerusalem to tell the others what they witnessed.

Materials: Unpublished. From the composer.

Notes: A simple but highly effective dramatization. To be performed in a cathedral/church as part of a worship service. Simple props required.

Piece Together

Music by **Susan Hulsman Bingham** (b. 1944). A Chancel Opera with libretto in English by the composer, loosely based on Matthew 9:18-26, Mark 5:21-43, and Luke 8:40-56. For all-female cast.

Premiered March 12, 1987, at Trinity Church on the Green, New Haven, CT.

Considerable recitative and plainchant; modal, tonal, traditional harmonic textures; several arias. Mostly contemporary language.

One act. Setting: At a well outside Jerusalem, sixteen years after the crucifixion of Jesus. Duration: 25 minutes.

Major Roles: JUDITH (sop – C3-Ab4), the now-cured woman; KAROL (sop – top A#), the raised daughter of Jairus; CAROL (m-sop – A2-F4, low tess), who remembers what Jairus said.

Minor Roles: KATHERINE (sop), a friend; CANDYCE (sop), a friend; MICKI (sop), a friend; SANDY (sop), a friend; JOAN (sop), a friend; JULIET (silent), Karol at age 12 (this role may be mimed by any young member of the cast if a dancer is not available).

Dance: Optional solo dance for Juliet, who pantomimes the events when Karol, whom she is impersonating, was miraculously raised from death.

Orchestration: piano or organ.

Synopsis: It is sixteen years after the death and resurrection of Jesus. A group of women gather at a water well on the edge of their village. A stranger, Karol, whom they do not know shyly approaches to fetch water. It is soon discovered that she is the daughter of Jairus who at age twelve was raised from death by Jesus. On that very day, another woman was cured of a blood disease when she touched the garment of Jesus. As discussion continues, it is learned that Judith is that woman. Judith and Karol meet and their friends help them piece together the events of their healing. Having reflected on the goodness of the Lord, they leave each other refreshed in spirit and renewed in their bond of friendship.

Materials: Unpublished. From the composer.

Notes: To be performed as part of a worship service in a cathedral/church setting. A moving and touching dramatization. *"Piece Together* was originally written for men and women. Then the problem of finding enough men who were free and eager to sing presented itself. My husband suggested that I rewrite the opera from the perspective of the women who had been healed or who had witnessed the healings. This suggestion set me free in a number of ways: I could call on my friends who regularly express a desire to sing in these little operas; I could write the parts for them personally, taking into account their unique vocal needs and abilities; and I could enjoy the pleasure of working with them again." SHB

The Raising of Lazarus

Music by **Susan Hulsman Bingham** (b. 1944). A Chancel Opera with libretto in English by the composer, based on John 11:1-53 of the New Testament.

Composed and premiered in 1979, Trinity Church on the Green, New Haven, CT; revised in 1981.

Traditional harmony with some chromaticism and twentieth century influences. Mostly modern language. Declamatory recitatives, some arias, mostly soloistic.

One act, four scenes. Setting: On a quiet hill in Judea during Jesus' ministry. Sc. 1: On a hillside; sc. 2: Mary and Martha's house; sc. 3: Same a sc. 1; sc. 4: Same as sc. 2. Duration: 28 minutes.

Major Roles: JESUS (bar), requires strong actor; JAMES (listed as ten, but bar may be more suited to the low tess – B1-F#3).

Minor Roles: MESSENGER (treble – top F#4); JOHN (bs-bar); THOMAS (ten); ANDREW (bar – top F#3); PETER (bar); MARTHA (sop); MARY (m-sop); DOUBTER (cont or bar); TWO MEN (bar, bs); CAIAPHAS (bs); LAZARUS (silent).

Chorus: SATB – mourners.

Orchestration: – pia, fl or rec (opt).

Synopsis: On a quiet hillside, the disciples of Jesus converse among themselves. A Messenger enters announcing that Lazarus, a beloved friend, is gravely ill. The disciples try to prevent Jesus from going to him because of the danger to Jesus' life from those who would kill him. A short scene depicts the mourning in Mary and Martha's house. In spite of their protests, Jesus begins walking along the road toward Bethany. The disciples fearfully follow behind. The Messenger announces the arrival of Jesus. The disciples, as a release to their anxieties, sing a raucous song about whether Jesus can manage to perform such an enormous miracle as raising a man from the dead.

Under their frivolity, they still have doubts as to His power. Their song is interrupted by Martha, who throws herself at Jesus' feet begging for help. Jesus reassures her that He is the resurrection and the life. Mary enters and boldly admonishes Jesus for not coming prior to Lazarus' death. Jesus groans and asks where Lazarus has been laid. Upon seeing the tomb, Jesus weeps. He then asks them to remove the stone. They protest, saying that Lazarus has been dead four days and already stinks. However, the stone is removed. Jesus, undaunted, prays to God and in a loud voice cries, "Lazarus! Come out!" Lazarus appears! The awed and terrified mourners reach out to him fearfully. As Jesus prays, the mourners sing through their disbelief and into joy as they realize that, by removing the stone from their hearts and by walking out into the sun, they too can emerge from darkness and death into the light.

Materials: Unpublished. From the composer.

Notes: Intended for performance in a cathedral/church as part of a worship service. A graphic dramatization of changed lives. Minimal sets required; Lazarus' tomb necessary.

Ruth

Music by **Susan Hulsman Bingham** (b. 1944). A Chancel Opera (Liturgical drama) with libretto in English by the composer, based on events in the life of Ruth as recorded in the Old Testament Book of Ruth. After the manner of a mystery play.

Composed and premiered in 1983, Trinity Church on the Green, New Haven, CT.

Traditional harmonic treatment; considerable plainchant and modality. Arias and much recitative with mostly simple chordal accompaniment. Mostly King James English.

One act, seven scenes. Setting: During the time of Ruth in Moab and Judah. Sc. 1: In Moab; sc. 2: Naomi's home village in Judah; sc. 3: Inside Naomi house near Boaz's fields; sc. 4: In Boaz's fields; sc. 5: Same as sc. 3; sc. 6: On the threshing floor where Boaz is sleeping; sc. 7: Same as sc. 3. Duration: 28 minutes.

Roles: All roles easily accessible with low tessituras. NAOMI (sop); RUTH (listed as sop, but low tess may be better suited to an alt); BOAZ (bar); ORPAH (sop).

Chorus: SATB – harvesters and townspeople.

Orchestration: piano or organ.

Synopsis: Naomi laments the loss of her husband and sons. She makes plans to return to her birthplace in Judah, leaving her two daughters-in-law, Ruth and Orpha, behind in Moab. Ruth, however, insists on coming with her, leaving all she possessed. Ruth and Naomi arrive in Naomi's home village where townspeople hardly recognize her, so great has been her trouble and sorrow. The two find a home and set up housekeeping. They are desperately poor, so Ruth finds employment in the grain fields of Boaz, a kinsman of Naomi. Boaz takes notice of her, welcomes her, feeds her and tells her she should feel free to glean in his fields. Ruth returns home with her apron filled with grain, given to her by Boaz. Naomi, realizing that Boaz being a kinsman, might be willing to marry Ruth. She suggests to Ruth that she go to the threshing floor late at night and place herself at the feet of Boaz as he sleeps. (This odd and bold plan was in keeping with a custom of the time.) With modesty and shyness, Ruth carries out her mother-in-law's suggestion. Boaz is touched and amazed. Soberly, in the dark, the two shape their plans. Later, Boaz announces that he has bought land from Naomi's family, and that he has taken Ruth for his wife. Ruth bears a son named Obed, who later fathers Jesse, who fathers King David. The townspeople sing of the birth of Obed and prophesy that this holy line will lead to the birth of the Messiah, Jesus.

Materials: Unpublished. From the composer.

Notes: Intended for performance in a cathedral/church as part of a worship service. Sets and properties should be kept simple.

The Sacrifice of Isaac

Music by **Susan Hulsman Bingham** (b. 1944). A Chancel Opera with libretto in English by the composer, based on episodes in the life of Abraham, Sarah and Isaac as recorded in the Book of Genesis 18:1-15, 21:6-7 and 22:1-18. Additional texts are taken from Psalms 6, 33, 51, 127, and Habakkuk 3:17-19.

Premiered October 25, 1981 at Trinity Church on the Green, New Haven, CT.

Tonal with occasional modality. Traditional harmony with some rhythmic complexities and chromaticism. Frequent plainchant in vocal lines. Uses mostly contemporary language. Light and comic at times.

One act, five scenes. Setting: In and around Abraham and Sarah's tent in the desert of Israel and on Mt. Moriah. Sc. 1: Early one morning in Abraham's tent; sc. 2: Later, in the tent; sc. 3: The same, one year later; sc. 4: The same, twelve years later; sc. 5: The same, late that night; then on Mt. Moriah the next morning. Duration: 25 minutes.

Roles: ABRAHAM (bar – G1-F3); SARAH (m-sop – B2-G4); ISAAC (boy sop – top E4); GOD, in the form of Three Angels (TTB or SSA).

Orchestration: pia or org.

Synopsis: Abraham is surprised to find Sarah up so early. She is weeping and praying to God for a son. Abraham flippantly excuses the situation by quoting some Scripture, which provokes Sarah to anger; she leaves the room. Alone, Abraham is visited by God in the form of Three Angels. He offers them a meal and then hears their promise of a son to be born to Sarah. Sarah, overhearing the conversation in the next room, cannot contain her laughter. The Angels leave and Sarah, believing herself to be alone, recounts her anger at not having been able to bear children. She remorsefully admits that devotion to Him is what she has really lacked. One year passes. Sarah enters with baby Isaac in her arms. She and Abraham sing a joyful duet of praise.

Twelve years later. God appears to Abraham and asks him to sacrifice his son to Him. Abraham first tries not to hear what God is saying, then bursts into loud pleas for mercy. Sarah, overhearing him, is at first stricken, then enraged. After a crazed night, Sarah finally falls asleep. Abraham steals to Isaac's bed, wakens him to prepare for a journey. Sarah hears them and a terrible struggle ensues. Abraham pushes her away from Isaac and the two make their escape. On the road to Mt. Moriah, Isaac inquires about the lamb to be sacrificed. At the altar on Mt. Moriah, Abraham begs God for mercy and contests that what God really wants is a "broken and contrite heart." Abraham clutches Isaac to his breast as he raises his knife. At the last moment, loud cries from the Angels of God stop Abraham. The excited Isaac, seeing a ram in the distance, tells his "silly father" that a mistake was almost made. As the two prepare to catch the ram, the Angels appear, praise Abraham's faithfulness and tell him that his seed shall prosper and multiply; in his seed shall all nations be blessed.

Materials: Unpublished. From the composer.

Notes: Intended to be presented in a cathedral/church as part of a worship service. Production problem: the time allowed for setting up the altar.

Simeon

Music by **Susan Hulsman Bingham** (b. 1944). A Chancel Opera with libretto in English by the composer based on Luke 2:25-35 of the New Testament.

Premiered October 26, 1980, Trinity Church on the Green, New Haven, CT.

Mostly traditional harmony with some twentieth century dissonances and chromaticism in the accompaniment and choral sections. Frequent key changes. Vocally conceived, numerous recitative passages; arias and choral ensembles. Some *a cappella* passages.

One act, two scenes without break. Setting: In the Temple of Jerusalem at the time of Mary's purification. Sc. 1: In the temple; sc. 2: Outside the temple. Duration: 25 minutes.

Roles: SIMEON (bar – B1-F#3, several sustained F#3); ANNA (m-sop), a Prophetess; MARY (sop), the mother of Jesus; JOSEPH (ten), husband to Mary.

Chorus: SATB (act as a Greek chorus) – Narrators, the Holy Spirit, the Voice of the infant Jesus.

Orchestration: piano and organ.

Synopsis: Little is known about Simeon, except that he begged God for the privilege of seeing the Messiah before he died. Simeon is alone in the temple praying. His loud pleas and yearnings alarm Anna, who is also in the temple. As the Holy Spirit speaks to Simeon, both exult the name of God. Mary and Joseph approach the Temple with their newborn Son, Jesus. They have come for the rights of purification. Mary is concerned about having Jesus outdoors for so long a period of time. Joseph consoles her and reassures her of his protection. They see an old man (Simeon) excitedly watching them approach, though they do not know who he is. Simeon meets them on the front steps of the Temple, greeting them and adoring the Child. In his excitement and inspired by the Holy Spirit, Simeon takes the Child in his arms, prophesying of the Child's death and His salvation to many. Having seen the Child, he now departs in peace tenderly leaving the young family as they enter the Temple.

Materials: Unpublished. From the composer.

Notes: Intended for presentation in a cathedral/church setting as part of a worship service.

Tales of A Magic Monastery

Music by **Susan Hulsman Bingham** (b. 1944). A Morality Musical Play with words taken from the writings of Theophane the Monk.

Composed and premiered December, 1985, Spuyten Duyvil Church, Edgehill, The Bronx, New York.

Disjunct harmonies; fragmentary texture with motivic tendencies. Melodic with numerous chant-like passages; entirely soloistic. Musical style reflects the idiosyncratic libretto of the author.

A series of eight musically detached and unrelated scenes which may be performed as a whole or individually. Duration: 24 minutes.

Roles: YOUNG MONK (ten – B1-F#3), requires strong actor; OLD MONK (ten – B1-F#3, darker timbre). These roles may be played by females (Nuns) if desired.

Chorus: Two groups of Monks (Nuns), ten and bar (sop and alt).

Orchestration: Yamaha DX-7 synthesizer or piano.

Synopsis: Scene 1: The Young Monk asks, "Father, could you tell us something about yourself?" The Old Monk replies, "My name used to be Me. But now it's you."

Scene 2: The Young Monk is looking for the Pearl of Great Price. The Old Monk gives it to him with the question, "Is it better to have it, or to give it away?" The Young Monk questions himself, "How long will that question rob me of my joy?"

Scene 3: The Young Monk tells the Old Monk that he would like to become a real monk. The Young Monk is taught a lesson: to become a real monk means to see the beauty in others and to be silent.

Scene 4: A Monk was present at the Transfiguration on Mt. Tabor. He was more taken by the music he heard than the bright light. He asked the Father to call him into the cloud, now. The Father took his head to His heart, and he heard that music. The cloud settled around them.

Scene 5: The Young Monk asked, "What is the audacity of humility?" The Old Monk replied, "To be the first to say 'I love you.'"

Scene 6: The Young Monk went to the monastery to give himself completely to God. An Old Monk asked him, "What is it you want?" "To give myself to God," replied the Young Monk who expected a gentle, fatherly reply. Instead, the Old Monk shouted "NOW!" again and again. Then reached for a club and came after the Young Monk. That was years ago, and still the Young Monk sees the club and hears that "NOW!"

Scene 7: A monk had been in a monastery a few years and things were not going well. He persuaded someone to inquire around and find out what the other monks thought of him. The report was: "They call you nobody." The monk thought he was somebody while others called him "nobody." The debate continued for months – all in his head. One night someone came to visit him and invited him to the magic monastery. The monk accepted and as he approached the great door, the bells began to ring; the Abbot came to greet him. He was placed in the center of a great hall surrounded by hundreds of monks. A candle was placed in front of him, and throughout the night he heard them chanting: "Somebody, somebody, somebody at last. Welcome." The monk was told: "You can sing!" So he sang, he sang songs of his life. It was beautiful. He was somebody.

Scene 8: A monk with no legs sat by the wall calling out to passersby, "What will you give me?" Another Monk felt compelled to stop and apologize: "I am a monk myself, so I have nothing to give you." "Give me your unhappiness," he demanded. I did.

Materials: Unpublished. From the composer.

Notes: Equally suitable for performance in a house of worship or theatre. Minimal staging required. Sets may be as simple as two chairs.

The Woman At Jacob's Well

Music by **Susan Hulsman Bingham** (b. 1944). A Chancel Opera with libretto in English by the composer, based on John 4 of the New Testament.

Composed and premiered in 1979, Trinity Church on the Green, New Haven, CT.

Modality with Eastern influences. Simple traditional harmonic texture with sparse accompaniment. Plainchant recitatives; several arias. Highly melodic. Several unaccompanied sections. Uses contemporary language throughout.

One act. Setting: At Jacob well during Jesus' ministry, on the road from town and in the village. Space must be allowed for three different playing areas separate from each other. Duration: 25 minutes.

Roles: JESUS (bar); JAMES (ten); JOHN (bar); PETER (ten – low tess, could easily be sung by bar); SAMARITAN WOMAN (sop); FOUR GOSSIPS (sop, sop, alt, alt).

Chorus: SAB – townspeople (unison and 3-part). Four short solo parts may be taken from the chorus.

Orchestration: pia, 2 ten rec (opt), gui or string (opt).

Synopsis: As Jesus and several of his disciples are passing through Samaria, they come to Jacob's well. As they have no vessel for drawing water and no food to satisfy their hunger, the disciples go on to the village to buy food, leaving Jesus to rest at the well. A Samaritan Woman from the village comes to draw water for herself. She is distraught and surprised when Jesus, a Jew, asks her, a Samaritan, for some water. She distrusts Him at first, growing more suspicious as He tells her of her past life with five husbands and now living with a man who is not her husband. His non judging understanding and kindness lead her to believe that He is indeed whom He says He is: the Messiah. Meanwhile, the disciples are returning from the village discussing their doubts and misgivings about the life they now lead. Should they confide their troubles in the Master? As they approach the well, the Woman runs toward the town, shouting that she has found the Messiah. Townspeople question and ridicule her – however, she persists and her behavior convinces them that if her life can change, they too must meet this man who offers water that quenches thirst permanently and changes lives. They meet Him and rejoice in their new-found faith. They conclude that this indeed is the Messiah.

Materials: Unpublished. From the composer.

Notes: Intended for presentation in a cathedral/church as part of a worship service. The entire sanctuary should be used for the action.

HARRISON BIRTWISTLE

The Last Supper

Music by **Harrison Birtwistle** (b. 1934). A Dramatic Tableaux for soloists, small female chorus and chamber orchestra. Words by Robin Blaser have been taken from biblical and medieval sources, and quotations from numerous literary sources. Texts are in Latin and English.

Commissioned by Glyndebourne and Deutsche Staatsoper Berlin. World premiere April 18, 2000, at the Deutsche Staatsoper Berlin.

Changing meters, highly dissonant, frequent disjunct melodic writing, rhythmic complexities in all parts. Some rhythmic speech and *Sprechstimme.*

The opera is set in our own time, comprised of four tableaux which are continuous musically and dramatically, and may be played in the same area. The work is best performed without a break. Duration: 110 minutes.

Major Roles: CHRIST (bar – top G3); JUDAS (ten – top Bb3); GHOST (sop – G2-B4)

Minor Roles: LITTLE JAMES (ct); JAMES (ct); THOMAS (ten – top C4); ANDREW (ten); SIMON (ten); BARTHOLOMEW (ten); PHILIP (bar – top G3); JOHN (bar); Matthew (bs-bar); THADDEUS (bs); PETER (bs)

Orchestration: 2 fl (2 picc), 2 ob (2 Eng hrn), 2 cl (Eb cl), bs cl (double bs cl), 2 bsn (2 ctr bsn), 2 hrn, 2 trp, 2 trb (2 bs trp, bs trb), timp, 2 perc (numerous small instruments), synth, accordion, str: 6 vla, 4 vc, 3 cb

Chorus: CHORUS MYSTICUS (amplified) – 3 sop/3 ms-sop/3 alto
CHORUS RESONUS (pre-recorded) – 3 sop/3 ms-sop/3 alto
CHORUS IN VISIONS I-III (pre-recorded) – 3 sop/3 ms-sop/3 alto/3 ten/3 bar/3 bs

Synopsis: Ghost, a representative of ourselves, invites Christ and his disciples to join us once again for supper but in our own age. Eleven disciples enter, starting with Peter. They do not know why they have been called to be reunited, or whether Judas or Christ will reappear. They reassemble the table from fragments, dance in celebration, and sing the *Lord's Prayer.* Judas appears bearing a red cloth for the table. He attempts to explain his actions, but arguments and recriminations fly, leading to the question, "Who is the betrayer and what has been betrayed?"
VISION I – THE CRUCIFIXION. Christ suddenly appears among them. He tells the disciples that he has returned to wash the dust of twenty centuries off their feet. Starting with Peter, Christ washes each of the disciples' feet ending with Judas. He

then leads the twelve to the table saying: "Come take your places." Turning to Ghost (us), He says, "Ghost, dear heart, I've discovered your name. Come, join us here at the table."

VISION II – THE STATIONS OF THE CROSS begins with a pre-recorded chorus singing the *Pange Lingua* (Sing, my tongue). Christ reaffirms a faith of love after two millennia of vileness. The twelve disciples and Christ walk into the garden amidst the olive trees.

VISION III – THE BETRAYAL, in the garden, is a brief statement delivered by Ghost to the audience: "Here we are – you and I – sharing our lives. Death is not our own, and love, sweet love, where we find ourselves beyond ourselves, is not our own." Christ's voice is suddenly heard out of the dark of the stage, "Whom do you seek?" A cock crows.

Materials: BH. Libretto available for purchase.

Notes: Equally adaptable to both house of worship and theatre settings. Can be done without full set. Orchestration is large and colorful. High quality sound system is important. This is a difficult work with a powerful message and gripping questions for the audience.

ARTHUR BLISS

Tobias and the Angel

Music by **Arthur Bliss** (1891-1975). A Sacred Opera with libretto in English by Christopher Hassall based on the Apocryphal Book of Tobit.

Commissioned by BBC Television; first produced May 19, 1960.

Traditional harmonic textures, some chromaticism but melodic. At times highly declamatory. Accompanied recitatives. Continuous texture.

Two acts, seven scenes. Setting: Eighth century B.C., Israel in exile among the Assyrians. Act I, sc. 1: Nineveh, a market square; sc. 2: A back street; sc. 3: The river bank; sc. 4: The embattled city of Ecbatane, Raguel's garden. Act II, sc. 1: Sara's bedchamber and terrace; sc. 2: The same; sc. 3: Nineveh. Duration: 85 minutes.

Roles: BOZRU (bs – G#1-F3), a trader in humanity; RHEZIA (m-sop – top Ab4), an Ionian slave; TOBIAS (ten), son of Tobit and Anna; AZARIAS (bar – G#1-F#3), the hired man; TOBIT (bs), blind father of Tobias; ANNA (cont – low G#2), his wife; RAGUEL (bs), a merchant of Ecbatane; SARA (sop – top Bb4), his daughter; ASMODAY (sp), an evil spirit; A BEGGAR (mime).

Chorus: SATB – people of Nineveh (several small solo parts from the chorus); SSA – three young women for Sara's wedding.

Orchestration: 2 fl, 2 ob, 2 cl, 2 bsn, 4 hrn, 2 trp, 2 trb, tba, timp, 2 perc, hp, str

Synopsis: Bozru is selling slaves to the public in the market square. Tobias is in need of a hired man to assist him in making a trip to collect a debt owed to his father, Tobit. Tobit and Anna are desperately poor and without possessions. Tobias hires Asarias who says he is willing to work for nearly nothing. Tobias grows rather skeptical and fearful of Azarias' strange mannerisms as the journey nears its end. The two finally arrive at their destination and find the debtor, Raguel, who welcomes them into his home. His daughter, Sara, and Tobias instantly fall in love. However, it seems Sara is possessed by an evil spirit and has killed her first seven husbands on their wedding nights. Fearful but unable to live without Sara, the wedding plans proceed. Azarias offers his assistance and tells Tobias what to do should the evil spirit (Asmoday) suddenly indwell Sara. The wedding is held and Sara with Tobias enter the bedchamber. Asmoday's voice is heard and Azarias appears, not as a servant but as Raphael, God's archangel, and does battle with Asmoday. Sara and Tobias awaken the next morning realizing that the evil spirit has been defeated. Together, they return home with the debt payment and arrive just in time to buy Tobit and Anna out of slavery. Even Tobit's eyesight is miraculously restored. All realize that the God of Israel and his angel have protected them and rescued them from death.

Materials: NOV (© 1961).

Notes: Best performed in a theatre; quick scene changes can be problematic.

BENJAMIN COLMAN BLODGETT

A Representation of the Book of Job

Music by **Benjamin Colman Blodgett** (1838-1925). A Symphony (dramatic oratorio) in English based on the Book of Job from the Old Testament. For all-female cast.

Premiered June 13 and 14, 1890, at Smith College, Northampton, Massachusetts; the premiere was a fully staged and costumed production.

Romantic harmony, Wagnerian in style and color, particularly with regard to the orchestration. The work contains very little conventional choral music, but is primarily written in recitative style. The work is based on themes representing the various characters and sentiments for which the characters stand. The theme of Eliphaz expresses entreaty, Bildad that of indignation, and Zophar of sarcasm. Job is represented by five themes expressing despair, trust, integrity, justification, and at the end, triumph. The final theme of the postlude represents divine verdict.

Three cycles, orchestral Prelude and Postlude. Setting: Patriarchal times in the Arabian land of Uz. Duration: full length.

Roles: JOB; ELIPHAS; BILDAD; ZOPHAR. The premiere performance used four groups each of eight ladies.

Chorus: SSAA

Dance: No formal dance, though each of the four characters could be represented through pantomime.

Orchestration: fl, 2 ob, 2 bsn, hrn, trp, 3 trb, timp, org, vln I (2), vln II (2), vla, vc, cb

Synopsis: The prose prologue preceding the poem tells us that Job was an upright and God-fearing man, and that he had sons and daughters and great possessions. God permitted him to be tried by adversity. In a single day all his wealth was destroyed and his children perished. Later, he was smitten with leprosy, yet his faith in God remained unshaken. The plot begins with his three friends, Eliphas, Bildad and Zophar, who upon hearing of his trials come to mourn with him. Job is at first completely crushed by his afflictions and only occasionally distressed by his friends' lack of sympathy. His faith and confidence in God actually grow, and he pays less and less heed to the denunciations of his friends. According to them, his trials are great because his sins have been great. Finally, Job ignores his friends completely and fixes all his thoughts on God. The answer from God comes in the orchestral postlude. Men can only trust in God. Job is justified and his adversaries humbled.

Materials: Unpublished. SM.

Notes: Best performed in a theatre or auditorium with a large stage.

MURRAY BOREN

Abraham and Isaac

Music by **Murray Boren** (b. 1950 – American). A Music Drama for 17 singers and 21 instrumentalists. Libretto in English by Orson Scott Card based on the Biblical account in Genesis 22.

Non-conventional harmonies; melodic with twentieth century dissonances. Atonality pervades; rhythmic complexities. Use of *sprechstimme* in places. Some unaccompanied sections.

One act, fifteen scenes. Continuous texture. Action moves from the home of Abraham to Mt. Moriah. Duration: approximately 50 minutes.

Roles: ABRAHAM (bar – top G#3), vocally and dramatically demanding; SARAH (sop); ISAAC (ten); PRIEST (bar); VOICE OF GOD (*sprechstimme*).

Chorus: Thirteen voices all sing individual parts. SSAABBB (Orchestral voices); three sopranos representing Sarah; three baritones representing Abraham. Throughout the work, these voices at times respond to, at other times become the characters of Abraham and Isaac.

Orchestration: fl, ob, cl, bsn, 2 hrn, trp, trb, tba, timp, 2 perc, 2 pia, 2 vln, 2 vla, 2 vc, cb.

Synopsis: Abraham is awakened from a troublesome dream which he tries to forget in spite of Sarah's insistence that he tell her. God then speaks directly to Abraham, confirming what he thought he saw in his dream. He must take his only beloved son Isaac to Mt. Moriah, and there offer him on an altar, giving him back to God. Abraham painfully agrees to obey. The next day, he takes Isaac to Mt. Moriah to offer a sacrifice. When they arrive, he ties Isaac's hands, places him upon the altar, and is about to slay him when a voice stops him. Abraham and Isaac both rejoice and give thanks.

Materials: Unpublished. From the composer or BYU.

Notes: May be performed in either a theatre or more suitably, in a house of worship.

The Christymas Playe

Music by **Murray Boren** (b. 1950 – American). A Yuletide Opera with libretto in English by the composer based on the anonymous medieval *Travellers' Play*.

Premiered December 11, 1982, at Brigham Young University.

Avant-garde musical idioms, no meter or key signatures; aleatoric and often improvised. The vocal lines are linear and chant-like with complete rhythmic freedom. According to the composer, "each performer is expected to find rhythms which most comfortably enhance characterization for the performer." Continuous texture.

One act, six scenes. Sc. 1: The Annunciation; sc. 2: In Elizabeth's home; sc. 3: On the hills outside Bethlehem; sc. 4: The countryside; sc. 5: Herod's palace; sc. 6: The Stable. Duration: approximately 60 minutes.

Major Roles: No range problems with any role. MARY (sop – top A#4); GABRIEL (ten); JOSEPH (bar).

Minor Roles: ELIZABETH (m-sop); 1st SHEPHERD (bar); 2nd SHEPHERD (ten); 3rd SHEPHERD (bar); 1st KING (bs); 2nd KING (ten or high bar); 3rd KING (high bar – top F#3); MESSENGER (m-sop); HEROD (bs-bar).

Orchestration: 2 fl, hp, 2 pia, 3 perc, 4 vln, 2 vla, 2 vc, 2 cb. Composer's note: "piano reduction is not intended for performance – It does not, cannot, imitate the orchestra closely enough.'

Synopsis: Alone, Mary is approached by Gabriel and told she will have a child. Her disbelief is softened when Gabriel tells her that her cousin, Elizabeth, too is pregnant. No sooner has Gabriel left than Joseph addresses Mary, bewildered and demanding to know the father of the child she carries. Unshaken, Mary tells him it is his and God's. Only after Gabriel appears to Joseph and convinces him of the truth does he turn to Mary in repentance. Excited, the two hurry to visit Elizabeth. Meanwhile on the hills outside Bethlehem, the three Shepherds attempt to keep warm. Their "chit-chat" is interrupted by Gabriel who instructs them to go immediately to Bethlehem, for God's Son lies in a manger. In Scene 4, the three Kings meet, discuss their common interests and discover they all have the same destination; together they follow the guiding star. In Herod's palace, a Messenger tells Herod that according to three Kings he recently met, a new King has just been born. Angered, Herod sends for them and commands them to inform him of the Child's location. The final scene takes us to the stable, where Mary, Joseph and the new born Child rest. They are joined by the Shepherds, Kings, Elizabeth, and Gabriel in a glorious hymn of praise.

Materials: Unpublished. From the composer or BYU.

Notes: Minimal set and props required. Best performed in a church/cathedral.

Emma

Music by **Murray Boren** (b. 1950 – American). A Folk Opera with libretto in English by Eric Samuelson, based on historical facts surrounding Emma, the wife of Mormon leader Joseph Smith. An all-female cast.

Premiered by Brigham Young University Music Department, Utah, January 26, 1984.

Highly dissonant textures, avant garde, little use of meter. Much of the vocal treatment is in recitative style with emphasis on words rather than melodic considerations. Highly colorful orchestration. Difficult solo roles.

Three acts, nine scenes but continuous in action. Set in Nauvoo, Illinois, immediately after the martyrdom of Joseph Smith, founder of The Church of Jesus Christ of Latter-day Saints. Duration: 75 minutes.

Major Roles: EMMA SMITH (col sop); ELIZA R. SNOW (dram sop); ELIZABETH MARSH (m-sop).

Minor Roles: ANNE (m-sop); MARY (sop); ZINA (sop); FLORA (cont); SARAH (sop); HELEN (sop); VILATE (m-sop).

Orchestration: fl, ob, cl, 4 hrn, tba, 4 vln, 2 vla, 2 vc, 2 cb, hp, 2 pia, 5 perc.

Background and Synopsis: "In 1844, Joseph Smith was killed by a mob, and his followers were driven out of Illinois. The main body of Mormons rallied and migrated to the Utah territory, but many became disaffected and remained behind. Among these were most of the prophet's family and his wife Emma. In one long scene for ten women, Emma confronts decision (symbolically represented by a mountain) in all its wrenching agony; finally she sinks back into the relative security of the status quo, while others (including Eliza R. Snow, another of Smith's plural wives) decide to struggle on, despite bereavement and oppression." (Dorothy Stowe, Opera News, 3/31/84). The women of Nauvoo gather to mourn the death of the Prophet and solicit guidance from his wife, Emma. Her refusal to accept this mantle of leadership heightens their sense of loss. In scene 2, the sisters of the church in a meeting of its women's auxiliary, the Relief Society, clamor for direction. Eliza's enthusiastic call westward is tempered by Emma's vision of the difficulty of such a journey. As Eliza helps Emma pack for the exodus, scene 3 finds them reminiscing about their lives around Joseph. Unexpectedly, Elizabeth Marsh wanders in looking for the women. Emma directs her to them.

In Act II as Emma packs, objects remind her of her early love affair with Joseph, their mature years together, and the final horrors of mobs and the deaths of children. On the mountain side, Eliza is presiding at a funeral service. The women recount the losses they've suffered and confront Eliza with the hardships of their journey as she tries to console them. Elizabeth Marsh pleads with the Relief Society to include her once again. Her inability to admit her errors has driven her to the brink of madness. Act III opens with Elizabeth trying to convince Emma not to follow the sisters west by offering Emma contrived memories of Joseph to justify remaining in Nauvoo. It is a technique with which Elizabeth is very familiar. Emma "hears" voices from the mountain and follows them, searching for someone to make choices for her. Alone, Emma ponders her life and current situation and decides to stay in Nauvoo.

Materials: Unpublished. From the composer or BYU.

Notes: There is very little plot. The work consists mainly of Emma's state of mind, seeing her frustrations and what she is trying to hold on to. The work has no melodic feeling, but rather a series of emotional states. The work may be played on a single set which should be kept very simple. Best performed in a theatre.

RUTLAND BOUGHTON

Bethlehem (Full-length version)

Music by **Rutland Boughton** (1878-1960). A Folk Opera with libretto in English adapted by the composer from the *Coventry Nativity Play*.

Premiered 1915, at the Christmas Festival of the Glastonbury Festival School, England.

Conventional harmonies, largely homophonic. Melodic, accessible ranges. Not difficult.

Two acts. Prelude (choral). Act I, sc. 1: Home of Mary and Joseph; sc. 2: A moor at night; sc. 3: The stable. Act II, sc. 1: Outdoor plaza in Jerusalem; sc. 2: The stable. Duration: 2 hours, 15 minutes.

Roles: MARY (sop – C3-A4); GABRIEL (sop or boy/girl sop); JOSEPH (male alt – G2-D4). The three shepherds: JEM (sop), SYM (sop), DAVE (alt). 1st ANGEL (sop); 2nd ANGEL (alt). The three wisemen: ZARATHUSTRA (m-sop), NUBAR (sop – E3-A4), MERLIN (alt). 1st WOMAN (sop); 2nd WOMAN (alt); BELIEVER (sop); UNBELIEVER (m-sop); CALCHAS (bar), the Herald; HERODIAS (alt – low F2, low tess); HEROD (ten or male alt – top A#3). Roles are interchangeable with male or female voices or young trebles.

Chorus: SATB. The Prelude and Interludes for chorus should be sung by a choir stationed outside the action but arranged so that the Angels Chorus may take part in the action when called for.

Dance: A lengthy dance number before Herod, Herodias and the royal court.

Orchestration: fl, ob, 2 cl, bsn, 2 hrn, 2 trp, 2 trb, timp, hp, bells, strings. An arrangement for strings and piano available.

Synopsis: Gabriel appears to Mary telling her that the "second person of God on high" will be born to her alone. Although suspicion is aroused in Joseph's mind, he is soon reconciled to Mary and they begin their journey to Bethlehem. Meanwhile, on a moor near Bethlehem, the three shepherds are attracted by the brightness of a star and the singing of angelic voices. They understand the angels' message and hasten to worship the Child in Bethlehem. Guided by two angels, they present their gifts: Jem his pipe, Dave his hat, and Sym his mittens. In Jerusalem, the three wise men meet en route to find the Christ Child. Before they can depart, a crowd gathers before Herod's palace. The Palace doors suddenly swing open revealing Herod in pagan splendor. The three wisemen greatly disturb Herod with their story of the birth of a divine child who shall be "greater than all the kings of earth."

In the final scene, the three wise men present their gifts to the Child. Gabriel appears, warning them of the evil intentions of Herod, and under divine guidance, Mary and Joseph depart, taking the Child with them into Egypt.

Materials: CUR (GS) (© 1920). VS has some staging notes.

Notes: This work has been enhanced by the insertion of Early English carols. Some of these are used as choral interludes connecting scenes and may be sung by the audience. A flexible work, possible of being performed by mixed, women's or youth voices alone. Adaptable to either church or theatre performance. A "producer's copy" with lighting plots, stage directions and production suggestions is available from the publisher. See *Bethlehem*, the abridged version also.

Bethlehem (Abridged version)

Music by **Rutland Boughton** (1878-1960). A Dramatic Cantata with libretto in English, adapted by the composer from the *Coventry Nativity Play*, and further adapted for this abridged version by Trevor Widdicombe.

A reduction of Boughton's full-length version of the same title. Act II, sc. 1 is entirely omitted as are the roles of Herod, Herodias, Calchas, Unbeliever, 1st and 2nd Women. The Dance is likewise deleted. Duration: 50 minutes.

Materials: CUR (© 1966).

ROYAL BRANTLEY

Samuel

Music by Royal Brantley (20th century American). A Sacred Opera with libretto in English by the composer, developed from the Biblical account in I Samuel 15 and 16.

Premiered at West Texas State University, Canyon, November 16, 1978.

Traditional harmonies with twentieth century influences. Quite chromatic. Spoken dialogue with underscoring. Arias, few ensembles, mostly soloistic. Excellent for elementary and high school audiences.

Two acts. Setting: Biblical Palestine in the time of David's youth, around 1,000 B.C. Act I, Introduction: In the dark with Yaweh; sc. 1: The yard of Samuel's home; sc. 2: A hill-top nearby; sc. 3: Jesse's home in Bethlehem; Act II, sc. 1: A wilderness trail;

sc. 2: The yard of Jesse's home; sc. 3: A spot on the trail; sc. 4: David's sheep camp; sc. 5: The same as II, 3; sc. 6: The yard of Jesse's home. Duration: ca 95 minutes.

Major roles: SAMUEL (bs-bar), the Prophet in his old age; DAVID (ten), about 17; THE MOTHER of David (sop); JESSE (bar – top G3), father of David.

Minor roles: SAUL (sp), King of Israel and Judah; HANNAH (cont), Samuel's old housekeeper; JOAB (alt or ten), David's nephew, about 13 years old; TWO GUARDS (mute), of King Saul; AGAG (sp), captive King of Amalek; SARAH (sp), Hannah's young niece; PUPILS of Samuel (4 ten, 2 bar, 2 bs; ZERUAH (m-sop), Joab's mother, David's sister; ELIAB (bs), Jesse's oldest son; Elders of Bethlehem: EPHRAIM (ten), CALEB (bar), PHINEAS (bs), JOSHUA (ten), JOEL (bs); JUBAL (ten), Joel's grandson, in his teens; ELIHU (ten), Jesse's seventh son; ABINADAB (ten), Jesse's second son; SHAMMAH (bs), Jesse's third son; BENJAMIN (bar); NATHANIEL (bs), Jesse's fourth son; RADDAI (bar), Jesse's fifth son; OZEM (bar), Jesse's sixth son; A Field Servant of Jesse's (sp).

Chorus: A unison chorus of altos and tenors sings the part of YAWEH (Jehovah, God, the Lord) – low tessitura for altos. This group sings the Biblical texts of God's commands to Samuel, but more often than not the line is wordless and written as a part of the orchestra. All tenors can double in this group except the Sons of Jesse.

Additional chorus women, mostly sopranos, form the mixed chorus in company with the Elders and Jesse's Sons (wives, grown daughters, etc.).

Chorus of Children – Jesse's grandchildren. Six to eight or more and all younger than Joab. A unison treble chorus and six or seven spoken parts including Jonadab, the "It-Boy" in the game of Blind Man's Bluff.

Orchestration: fl, ob, cl, bsn, hrn, 2 trp, 2 trb, perc, str

Dance: Some simple choreography in the children's games.

Synopsis: Yaweh approaches Samuel concerning the disobedience of Saul, who has captured King Agag and not destroyed him as well as the spoils of Amalek. Samuel therefore informs Saul that his kingdom will be taken away from him. Samuel calls for Agag and kills him in Saul's presence. Samuel's pupils are gathered discussing the execution of Agag. Samuel enters and admonishes them for their babbling and idle tongues. He dismisses them in deep dismay and finally himself goes to the hills to pray, overcome with grief because of Saul. Yaweh tells Samuel to go to the house of Jesse and there he will be told which of Jesse's sons he is to anoint as the next King of Israel. At the home of Jesse, the children are playing games. Samuel arrives and tells Jesse of Yaweh's message.

Act II opens with Samuel in prayer before the altar of God. Finally, he asks Jesse to bring all his sons before him. As the sons pass before Samuel, Yaweh says no to all the sons. Samuel asks Jesse, "Are all your sons here?" Jesse replies that the youngest is tending the sheep and after all, he's only a boy. David is sent for and finally appears before Samuel. Yaweh reveals to Samuel that this is the chosen one. Samuel anoints David King of Israel.

Material: From the composer or WTS.

Notes: May be performed in either a house of worship or theatre. Numerous stage directions in the VS.

LESLIE BRICUSSE

Scrooge

Music by **Leslie Bricusse** (b. 1931 – American). A Christmas Musical Play with lyrics in English by the composer based on Dickens *A Christmas Carol*.

Musical numbers are simple and descriptive with ensembles in one and two parts. Composed with both adults and children in mind, but with emphasis on children. Considerable dialogue.

One act. Overture. Fourteen musical numbers. Sets may be as simple or detailed as desired. Best performed in an intimate theatre. Duration: 55 minutes.

Singing Roles: All roles are musically and vocally not difficult. SCROOGE (bs-bar), lengthy role; BOB CRATCHIT (bar); KATHY (a girl sop); TINY TIM (boy sop – top F4; 1st GENTLEMAN (bar); 2nd GENTLEMAN (bar); TOM JENKINS (bar); 4 URCHINS (mid-range); FEZZIWIG (bs); MRS. FEZZIWIG (alt); CHRISTMAS PRESENT (bs); MRS. CRATCHIT (alt).

Spoken Roles: Though spoken, these actors may be included in the ensemble numbers. SCROOGE'S NEPHEW (young man); 1st WOMAN; 2nd WOMAN; CUSTOMER; WOMAN; MARLEY'S GHOST; CHRISTMAS PAST; FAN; ISABEL; EBENEZER; 1st DAUGHTER (of Cratchit); 2nd DAUGHTER (of Cratchit); PETER; A BOY; BUTCHER; TOY SHOP OWNER.

Chorus: SA children's chorus; SB adult chorus.

Orchestration: Piano or Accompaniment tape package available.

Synopsis: On a cold Christmas Eve, Scrooge is busy at work. Fred, his nephew, and Bob Cratchit, his employee, wish him a merry Christmas. Scrooge derides the whole idea of Christmas as a humbug and rudely refuses Fred's invitation to dinner the next day. He then grudgingly allows Bob the next day off to celebrate Christmas. Later that night, Scrooge is confronted by the ghost of his deceased partner, Jacob Marley. Marley laments his perpetual state of sorrow because of his selfish and narrow way of life. He warns Scrooge that the Spirit of Christmas Past, Present and Future will each visit him this very night. Scrooge dismisses the message as a bad dream and goes to bed. The three Spirits indeed visit him, each presenting him with events and people he has and will encounter in his life past, present and future. Scrooge's dream is brought to a climax with the Spirit of the Future. In his dream, Tiny Tim dies. A funeral procession takes him to a deserted graveyard where inscribed on a tombstone are the words: "Ebenezer Scrooge, miser; who lived unloved and alone." He insists that the future is not predestined and he will change it. He swears he will honor the Spirit of Christmas throughout the year and that he will change his way of living.

Scrooge awakens with a feeling of lightness and joy realizing that he still has a chance to change and enjoy his last few years. He quickly runs to join his nephew's Christmas celebration, bringing with him an enormous turkey, and joy and goodwill to everyone he meets.

Materials: Production suggestions, accompaniment tape, advertising posters, T-shirt transfers, program covers, conductor's score, teacher's manual, director's handbook, and production guide available from JP. A collection of Vocal Selections is available from SSM.

Notes: Best produced in a theatre.

FRANK BRIDGE

The Christmas Rose

Music by **Frank Bridge** (1879-1941). A Christmas Opera with libretto in English based on a play for children by Margaret Kemp-Welch and Constance Cotterell.

Composed between 1919 and 1929.

Conventional harmonies with considerable chromaticism. Melodic. Much accompanied recitative. Not difficult.

One act, three scenes. Sc. 1: In the hills near Bethlehem; Sc. 2: On the road to Bethlehem; Sc. 3: Outside the Bethlehem Inn. Duration: 60 minutes.

Roles: MIRIAM (sop – sustained C5); REUBEN (m-sop); SHEPHERD I (ten); SHEPHERD II (bar); SHEPHERD III (bs-bar).

Chorus: SSSAAA – Offstage chorus of women's voices; SATB – a chorus of Peasants.

Orchestration: 2 fl, 2 ob, 2 cl, 2 bsn, 2 hrn, 2 trp, trb, timp, perc, hp, str

Synopsis: One night in the hills near Bethlehem, three Shepherds see an unusual heavenly light. They are told of a new-born King in Bethlehem and resolve at once to follow the star there to worship the child of prophesy and offer him their homespun gifts. In the same location, Reuben lies asleep while Miriam sits watching. Miriam, startled by heavenly singing, is told by an angel of the birth of the Messiah. Her wish to see Him is thwarted by the Shepherds who insist that the way is too dangerous. Remembering that the Angel had said good tidings were to all people, she and Reuben resolve to set out at once. On the way to Bethlehem, Miriam and Reuben lose their direction. Weary and lonely, Reuben sinks to the ground and urges Miriam to go on without him. Miriam protests and suddenly hears an invisible chorus of angels and sees a star to guide them. The Shepherds, Miriam, and Reuben arrive at the inn of Bethlehem. The Shepherds leave their gifts and return to their flocks. Fearful that they will not be allowed to see the Child because they no gifts, Miriam and Reuben sadly leave. Suddenly, Reuben sees a green shoot pushing through the snow. Their gift has been given to them: roses in the snow. They enter the stable to a chorus of Alleluias.

Material: GAL (E. C. Schirmer).

Notes: Suitable for either theatre or church performance. Intended to be performed by adults for grades 3-9. A touching and effective dramatization.

BENJAMIN BRITTEN

The Burning Fiery Furnace

Music by **Benjamin Britten** (1913-1976). A Sacred Opera with libretto in English by William Plomer, based on the Old Testament story of Shadrach, Meschach and Abednego from the Book of Daniel. The second in a trilogy, "A Parable for Church Performance" (see also *Curlew River* and *The Prodigal Son*), Op. 77.

Premiered by the English Opera Group at the Aldeburgh Festival, England, June 9, 1966.

Largely plainchant. Considerable dissonance often lacking distinct tonality. Style sustains the Noh-play tradition. Continuous action.

One act. Setting: Old Testament times, approximately 6th century B.C. in Babylon. Duration: approximately 64 minutes.

Major Roles: NEBUCHADNEZZAR (ten); ASTROLOGER and ABBOTT (bar); ANANIAS (Meschach) (bar); MISAEL (Shadrach) (ten); AZARIAS (Abednego) (bs); HERALD and LEADER OF THE COURTIERS (bar).

Minor Roles: CHORUS OF COURTIERS (3 ten, 2 bar, 2 bs); ANGEL'S VOICE (treble); FOUR ATTENDANTS (treble), also ACOLYTES.

Orchestration: fl (picc), hrn, alt trb, vla, cb (Babylonian dr), hp (doubling little hp), perc, chamber org (doubling small cym).

Synopsis: The play is introduced by the Abbot. Three young Israelites who have come to Babylon are being honored with the appointment of leadership over three provinces. At the same time they are necessarily given Babylonian names: Shadrach, Meschach, and Abednego. When, because of their own religious beliefs they refuse to eat Babylonian food, the Astrologer, not particularly fond of the three Israelites, convinces King Nebuchadnezzar that this is an insult to their land. A decree is announced, requiring all to fall down and worship the great golden image of the Babylonian god Merodak. When the three Israelites refuse to heed the decree, Nebuchadnezzar sentences them to the fiery furnace. They stand in the midst of the fire, unharmed, protected by a fourth figure, an angel of God. Nebuchadnezzar, convinced of the reality of the Israelites' God, frees the three men, is converted to their God, and at the same time punishes the Astrologer.

Material: GS (Eng, Ger, Fr). Production notes and set designs in VS. Further notes available from GS. Recording on Decca.

Notes: Vocally, stylistically, and musically, this work requires strong musicianship and highly skilled musicians. This work is designed to be performed in a church/cathedral with abstract settings or sets, props and costumes that merely suggest the environment.

Curlew River

Music by **Benjamin Britten** (1913-1976). A Sacred Opera with libretto in English by William Plomer, after the medieval Japanese Noh-play, *Sumidagaw* (The Sumida River) by Juro Motomasa. The first of a trilogy, "A Parable for Church Performance" (see also *The Burning Fiery Furnace* and *The Prodigal Son*). Op. 71.

Premiered by the English Opera Group at the Aldeburgh Festival, Oxford Church, Suffolk, England, June 13, 1964.

The entire composition has its roots in the Gregorian hymn *Te Lucis Ante Terminum*. A miracle story. Melodically based on chant, highly stylized acting and singing required, atonal tendencies, some bi-tonality.

One act. Setting: Beside a river in the Fenlands of England in medieval times. Duration: 71 minutes.

Major Roles: MADWOMAN (ten); FERRYMAN (bar); TRAVELLER (bar); SPIRIT OF THE BOY (treble); LEADER OF THE PILGRIMS and ABBOT (bs). Various characters of the drama are distinguished by varying tone colors and leitmotifs.

Minor Roles: CHORUS OF PILGRIMS (3 ten, 3 bar, 2 bs). THREE ASSISTANTS (boys – silent roles, who are Acolytes).

Dance: The movements of all must be stylized; the processional and recessional choreographed.

Orchestration: fl (picc), hrn, vla, cb, harp, perc, chamber organ. Various instruments are associated with specific characters.

Synopsis: Chanting as they enter, the Monks prepare for a Miracle Play. The Abbot addresses the congregation while the Monks are given masks and robes to portray the various characters in the drama. A Ferryman introduces himself, announcing that he is about to take pilgrims to a shrine across the Curlew River. A noise is heard in the distance and a mad woman approaches. She seeks her son who has been kidnapped. The Ferryman grants her passage, but only after she has entertained him with her wild singing about strange birds in the Fenland. The sail is hoisted. During the crossing, the Ferryman tells of a boy who perished as the slave of a brutal master. People now believe him to be a saint whose spirit can work miracles. Embittered, the Madwoman is certain this is her son. Reaching land, Madwoman throws herself before the child's tomb in tears. The accompanying travelers join her in prayer before the child's tomb. During the praying, the woman hears a child singing from the grave. The child appears and promises they will meet in heaven. Miraculously, the grief of the woman disappears, and she is released from her madness. The play is at an end. The Abbot and Monks discard their robes and masks, and recess, blessing the congregation in the singing of the hymn that was part of the processional.

Materials: GS (Eng, Ger, Fr). VS contains production notes and set design.

Notes: Musically and stylistically a difficult score requiring highly skilled musicians. Designed for performance in a church/cathedral.

Noye's Fludde – Noah's Flood

Music by **Benjamin Britten** (1913-1976). A medieval *Chester Miracle Play* with libretto in 16th century English, based on the *English Miracle Plays, Moralities and Interludes* and Biblical story in Genesis 5-9. Old English spelling has been retained in the score, but modern pronunciation should be used throughout with some specified exceptions. The *Chester Miracle Plays,* a collection of 25 short Biblical dramas, are said to have been written by Henry Francis, ca. 1375.

Premiered by The English Opera Plyers with the Chorus of Animals and Orchestra from East Suffolk schools at the Aldeburgh Festival, Oxford Church, June 18, 1958.

Melodious, tonal; considerable dissonance. Various musical forms found throughout such as waltz, march, free recitative. Free flowing style with much implicit symbolism, humor, and fun. Audience participation suggested.

One act. Setting: a bare stage except for an ark. Duration: 45 minutes.

Major Roles: THE VOICE OF GOD (sp), should have a rich, commanding voice, and be set up high and away from the stage; NOYE (bs-bar); MRS. NOYE (cont).

Minor Roles: SEM, HAM, JAFFETT (all boy sop); MRS. SEM, MRS. HAM. MRS. JAFFETT (all girl sop). These six characters should have well-trained voices and lively personalities. Jaffett may be a tenor and Mrs. Jaffett should be a bit older than the other wives. They should not be too young, perhaps between eleven and fifteen. With the right physical appearance, it is not impossible to use adults, though this is not the intent of the composer. MRS. NOYE'S GOSSIPS (all girl sop), older with strong voices especially in the lower register – strong actors; RAVEN, DOVE (child dancers).

Chorus: Children – CHORUS OF ANIMALS AND BIRDS; as many as possible. forty-nine species are referred to in the libretto. While fewer may be used, it is essential to have seven well-balanced groups. A fair number of boys in groups 1 and 2 may have broken voices. The *Kyries* should be sung in the character of the animal being impersonated. THE CONGREGATION joins in singing hymns throughout the score.

Orchestration: The orchestra is of two kinds, professional and children (amateurs). Professional: solo string quintet (2 vln, vla, vc, cb), solo treble rec, pia (4 hands), org, timp. Amateurs: 3 vln, vla, vc, cb, 2 descant rec, treble rec, bugles in Bb (four parts), 12 handbells in Eb (6 players), perc (6 players). Unusual needs include a wind machine, whip (clappers), slung mugs.

Synopsis: A somewhat humorous, entertaining account of the great flood and the man chosen by God to save mankind and the animal kingdom from extinction. After a congregational hymn, God speaks to Noye and tells him of the impending flood and commissions him to build an ark. The ark is constructed and he summons his family and two of every kind of animal into the ark. While Noye's sons and their wives willingly assist in the process, Mrs. Noye, slightly tipsy, refuses to leave her dear Gossips and must be forcibly carried aboard by her sons. The flood comes, destroying everything and everyone except those in the ark. At the appointed time, Noye sends a Dove and Raven to determine the appropriate time for disembarkment. When the land is dry, all depart from the ark. God sends His rainbow and covenants with Noah never to flood the earth again. All join in praising God for His great mercy.

Material: BH.

Notes: To be performed preferably in a church or large playing area but not a theatre. Large sanctuary and stage area needed. Costumes for animals may be as simple as masks or symbols, or complex animal heads or full costumes. Four property men can be used to help build the ark, move waves, hoist the rainbow, and assist in other odd production jobs. Specific instructions for the orchestra, cast, and production problems are included in the VS.

The Prodigal Son

Music by **Benjamin Britten** (1913-1976). A Sacred Opera with libretto in English by William Plomer, based on the Biblical parable in Luke 15. The third of a trilogy, "A Parable for Church Performance," Op. 81 (see also *Curlew River* and *The Burning Fiery Furnace*).

Premiered by the English Opera Group, Oxford Church, Suffolk, England, at the Aldeburgh Festival, June 10, 1968.

The score is quite translucent and exposed. The vocal lines are largely chanted with the score based primarily upon plainsong. Both music and acting are highly stylized. Dissonant, straying tonalities and atonal at times.

One act, three scenes. Sc. 1: The son's home; sc. 2: In the city; sc. 3: Reverse direction of sc. 1. Duration: 72 minutes.

Major Roles: TEMPTER and the Abbot (ten); FATHER (bs-bar); ELDER SON (bar); YOUNGER SON (ten).

Chorus/Minor Roles: CHORUS OF SERVANTS (3 ten, 3 bar, 2 bs); FIVE YOUNG SERVANTS, also ACOLYTES (5 male treble). These assume the multiple roles of Parasites, Servants, Distant voices, and Beggars.

Orchestration: alt fl (picc), trp in D, hrn, vla, cb, hp, perc, chamber org

Synopsis: A procession of Monks enter the sanctuary and assume the costumes of their characters. The Tempter announces he will break up the happy life of the rich man and his two sons. Despite the Father's warning to his sons, the Tempter is able to convince the younger son to request his inheritance in order to leave home. The understanding father gives in and they part. The Tempter joins the younger son and guides him to ruin as Parasites in the city strip him of all he possesses. The Tempter rejoices in his accomplishments until the younger son repents and returns home where his father welcomes him back. The elder son is jealous at the grand reception given his younger brother, but the Father is able to reconcile the two. The Tempter/Abbot reappears to pronounce the moral at the close of the opera as all recess.

Material: GS (Eng, Ger, Fr). Production, design and costume notes, and props list are included in the score. Recording on Decca.

Notes: Should be played in a church/cathedral with sets as simple as possible. A difficult score requiring highly trained singers in the major roles and professional instrumentalists.

The Rape of Lucretia

Music by **Benjamin Britten** (1913-1976). An Opera with strong religious and moralistic statements; libretto in English by Ronald Duncan, fashioned after the French play by Andre Obey, *Le Viol de Lucrece*, with occasional moments from Shakespeare.

Premiered in Glyndebourne, July 12, 1946.

Strongly dissonant, chromatic, difficult vocal lines, recitatives, set numbers, bordering on atonal at times. *Sprechstimme.* Tragedy.

Two acts with two scenes in each. Setting: 500 B.C., in Rome. Act I Prologue; sc. 1: The tent of the Generals in an Army Camp by the Tiber; sc. 2: a room in Lucretia's house in Rome, that same evening. Act II prologue; sc. 1: Lucretia's bedroom; sc. 2: the same room as in Act I, sc. 2, the next morning.

Major Roles: LUCRETIA (cont – E2-A4), wife of Collatinus, dramatically and vocally very demanding; PRINCE TARQUINIUS (bar – B1-G3, high tess, sustained, dramatic personality), son of the Etruscan tyrant, Tarquinius Superbus; MALE CHORUS (high lyric ten – top Bb3); FEMALE CHORUS (sop). The two chorus people are situated at either side of the stage in the fashion of a Greek chorus. They frame the tragedy but do not take part in it. Although the story is set in Rome in 500 B.C., they comment upon, explain, and even at times anticipate the story from a Christian perspective.

Minor Roles: COLLATINUS (bs), a Roman General, calm, noble character; JUNIUS (bar – E1-Gb3), a Roman General; BIANCA (m-sop), Lucretia's nurse; LUCIA (sop – top B4, high col passages), Lucretia's maid.

Orchestration: fl (picc, alt fl), ob (Eng hrn), cl (bs cl), bsn, hrn, perc, hp, string quartet, cb.

Synopsis: Lucretia, famed throughout Rome for her beauty and virtue, burnished the public image of her husband, Collatinus, a Roman General. Among the most envious were two fellow Generals, Junius and Tarquinius. Junius slyly incites Tarquinius to test Lucretia's chastity which Tarquinius accepts. Arriving at her home late at night while her husband is away, Tarquinius ravishes Lucretia by force. Collatinus together with Junius arrive the next morning only to hear Lucretia confess the events of the prior night. Collatinus wishes to forgive her, but, unable to live with her sin, Lucretia stabs herself saying, "Now I'll be forever chaste, with only death to ravish me." The Choruses conclude with their comments: "For this did I see with my undying eye, His warm blood spill upon that Hill and dry upon that Cross? Is this all loss? Are we lost? It is not all. For now He bears our sin...For us did He die...In His passion is our hope Jesus Christ, Saviour, He is all, He is all!"

Material: BH.

Notes: While this opera is more associated with secular repertoire, the message most certainly makes a strong Christian statement.

R. R. BROOME

The Finding of the King

Music by **R. R. Broome** (20th century British). A Nativity Play with text in English by F. C. Happold. Some Latin.

Premiered in Perse School, 1924, Cambridge, England.

Carols used are based on words and music of traditional or of 14th to early 17th century origin. Simple homophonic carols separated by dialogue. Comic.

One act. Prologue. Setting: Sc. 1: An Inn; sc. 2: The stable. Duration: 35 minutes.

Roles: Roles are undesignated but of medium range and may be sung by an all male, all female, or a mixed cast. Vocal balance in the larger ensemble sections should receive attention when casting. THE MESSENGER; THE INNKEEPER OF BETHLEHEM; A VAGABOND; GASPAR; MELCHIOR; BALTHAZAR; THREE SHEPHERDS; A SOLDIER; OUR LADY (mute); ST. JOSEPH (mute); THE VOICE OF AN ANGEL (sp).

Chorus: SATB – Chorus of Angels, Train of Attendants, Giftbearers, Heralds, etc.

Orchestration: Keyboard.

Synopsis: A Vagabond enters the inn requesting a place to spend the night. As he has no money and there is no room at the inn, the Innkeeper forces him to leave. Three Shepherds enter inquiring of the location of "a king." They tell an interesting story of a strange dream, bright lights in the sky, and a celestial messenger instructing them to go to Bethlehem, for a king is born this day. Dumbfounded, the Innkeeper is both amused and at a loss for words. Suddenly a Soldier enters asking for the location of a king – King Herod has ordered the search. The Innkeeper, more perplexed than ever, insists on being left alone and going to bed but is stopped by the entrance of three Kings and their entourage asking where the king is located. The Innkeeper is beside himself. As the stories from these various people begin to corroborate, and the Innkeeper continually asks "Why, why in my Inn?", a host of angels appear outside the window singing "Gloria in excelsis Deo." The entire group winds its way to the stable where the Child, the King lies in a cradle. As praises are sung and gifts presented, the Innkeeper finally concludes that this is no dream. He too falls to his knees in adoration.

Materials: OUP (© 1928).

Notes: Ideally suited for church performance and effective for young audiences. VS contains numerous stage and production suggestions.

RICHARD E. BROWN

The Gift of the Magi

Music by **Richard E. Brown** (b. 1947). A Christmas Opera with libretto in English by Nancy Grobe, based on the story of the same title by O. Henry.

Composed in 1985.

Twentieth century idioms mixed with traditional harmonic structures.

One act, three scenes. Setting: An American city, 1898. Della and Jim's apartment, a jewelry store, a hair salon. Duration: 25 minutes.

Roles: DELLA (sop); JIM (bar).

Orchestration: pia, brass quartet.

Synopsis: Della and Jim, a young married couple who are poor and very much in love, spend their Christmas Eve determining how, with their few saved pennies, they can afford to buy each other the Christmas gifts they have in mind. Jim adores Della's rich chestnut hair. Della knows how much Jim's gold watch means to him, a watch he received from his grandfather. She counts and recounts the one dollar and eighty-seven cents she has saved for Jim's present. Disappointed and at her wit's end, she decides to sell her hair.

Meanwhile, Jim, alone and wondering how to deal with their meager means, enters a jewelry shop determined to buy a set of combs for Della. Meanwhile, Della has entered a hair shop. As her hair is being cut, Jim exchanges his prized watch in order to buy the combs. Della quickly runs to buy a chain for Jim's watch from the same man who had just sold Jim the combs. Back in their apartment, Della is trying to make the most of her butchered hair when Jim comes in with a package... and just stares. As they exchange their presents, they realize that each present is now useless. Holding each other in a long embrace, they realize their love is all they have and need.

Materials: Unpublished. AMC and the composer.

Notes: Adaptable to either theatre or church performance.

DAVID WARREN BRUBECK

Beloved Son

Music by **David Warren Brubeck** (b. 1920). An Easter Dramatic Oratorio with text by Herb Brokering, based on the betrayal, trial, death and resurrection of Christ.

Premiered August 9, 1978, Minneapolis, MN. Commissioned by the American Lutheran Women's Convention.

Traditional harmonic texture with twentieth century influences; chromaticism, dissonances, but tonal and melodic. Occasional rhythmic complexities. Continuous texture with choral music throughout.

Three parts. Part I: Abba Father; Part II: Eli; Part III: Rabboni. Duration: 45 minutes.

Roles: JESUS (bar – top G3), lengthy and demanding role; MARY (sop).

Chorus: Two groups: SSAATTBB – commentators; SSA – commentators.

Orchestration: 3 fl (picc), 2 ob, Eng hrn, 2 cl, bs cl, 2 bsn, contra bsn, 4 hrn, 3 trp, 3 trb, tba, timp, 3 perc, hp, strings, pia/org.

Synopsis: The scene opens with Jesus praying in the Garden while his disciples, some distance removed, sleep. The soldiers approach; Judas identifies Jesus to the soldiers by giving Him a kiss. Jesus is arrested. A very short trial occurs as we hear the crowd cry "crucify Him." The scene shifts quickly to Golgotha where Christ hangs on the cross. He utters His final words as the crowd looks on and the women mourn.

Part three opens on resurrection morning. The women are approached by the risen Jesus. He instructs Mary to "Tell His disciples He is risen and will be with all until the end of time." A final hymn, *Jesus, Meet Us in the Center*, was presented at the premiere performance, intended only for that performance.

Materials: GS (Shawnee - © 1978).

Notes: While written as an oratorio, the use of pantomime artists and actors to portray the action is quite feasible. The composer's intent that this work receive some stage treatment is verified by his own stage instruction in the score. Best performed in a church/cathedral (theatre is feasible) with adequate space for orchestral forces.

La Fiesta de la Posada

Music by **David Warren Brubeck** (b. 1920). A Christmas Choral Pageant with text taken from Old and New Testaments adapted by Iola Brubeck; some original words by Iola Brubeck.

Premiered December, 1975, Honolulu, Hawaii. Commissioned by the Hawaii Bicentennial Commission.

Highly romantic sound with thick chordal textures and a touch of twentieth century harmonies. Mariachi instruments give it a truly Mexican sound.

Fifteen sections. Overture segues into the drama. Last number is only orchestra. Setting is around the nativity scene which can be constructed during the Overture. Duration: 40 minutes.

Roles: MARY (sop – top C5), who also assumes the part of a narrator; FIRST WISE MAN (bs); SECOND WISE MAN (bar – top G3); THIRD WISE MAN (ten – top B3).

Chorus: Solo SATB, SATB chorus and children's chorus unison.

Orchestration: three options: 1. 2 fl (picc), 2 ob, Eng hrn, 2 cl, bs cl, 2 bsn, contra bsn, 4 hrn, 4 trp, 3 trb, tba, timp, 2 perc, hp, hpsch, gui, strings. 2. "Mariachi" band (2 trp, 2 gui, hp, fl, 2 marimba, timp, perc, cb). 3. Reduced orchestra (2 trp, 2 gui, perc, cb, pia).

Synopsis: The chorus introduces us to the plot with a prophecy from the book of Isaiah. We move quickly to the Wise Men who are in search for the King of the Jews.

Having found Him, the villagers join them in a grand choral *Gloria*. Mary sings a wonderful setting of the *Magnificat*, followed by a choral lullaby. All again proclaim the power and glory of the newborn Son. The atmosphere changes to a festive one with children's games, dancing, juggling, all building toward the breaking open of the Piñata.

Materials: GS (SHP – © 1975). Recording by Columbia Mastersound 36662.

Notes: The VS contains historical information on the Posada celebration in Mexican tradition. Rather extensive staging, lighting, and costuming suggestions are included. Ideal for staging in a sanctuary with a simple stable setting in the chancel area.

The Light in the Wilderness

Music by **Dave Brubeck** (b. 1920). A Dramatic Oratorio with libretto in English by Dave and Iola Brubeck with selections primarily from the Gospels and Psalms – some original texts.

Premiered in its choral version, January, 1968, Chapel Hill, NC; symphonic premiere in February 29, 1968, with Cincinnati Symphony and Miami University A Cappella Singers.

Conventional style with twentieth century influences such as jazz, twelve-tone dissonance. Several improvisatory sections which are optional and may or may not be in the jazz idiom.

Two parts, 12 numbers or tableaus. The twelve numbers, except the opening two scenes in which Jesus faces the temptation of Satan, depict various settings in which Jesus is teaching his disciples and villagers. Duration: about 75 minutes with improvisation, 60 minutes without.

Roles: BARITONE soloist who sings the words of Jesus throughout (top G3); very long and extremely demanding role).

Chorus: SSAATTBB – some double chorus numbers. Chorus sings throughout, taking on the character of either disciples or followers of Jesus.

Orchestration: First version: org with optional 3 perc, cb, and pia. In the later version, the org became the basis for: 3 fl (picc), 2 ob, 2 cl, bs cl, 2 bsn, contra bsn, 4 hrn, 3 trp, 3 trb, tba, perc, hpsch, org, strings.

Synopsis: There is no continuing plot, but rather a series of individual scenes from the teachings of Jesus. The chorus responds by either reiterating His words, by asking questions, answering His questions, or commenting on His teachings. There is a continuing dialogue between Jesus and the crowds.

Materials: GS (SHP). VS includes org, perc, and cb; improvisation guide.

Notes: May be performed in either a church or theatre. Will require creative directing and design work.

GEOFFREY BURGON

The Fall of Lucifer

Music by **Geoffrey Burgon** (b. 1941). A Sacred Opera with libretto in English taken from the first play of the *Chester Mystery Plays* by Maurice Hussey.

Commissioned for the Silver Jubilee of the Tilford Bach Festival and premiered in England on May 13, 1977. American premiere by Drummond Chapel United Methodist Church, February 17, 1980.

Tonally centered, unexpected melodic leaps, stark harmonies, coloristic harmonies to depict "other worldly" sounds, heaven, hell, the demonic ego of Lucifer, the awesome, righteous rage of God and the eternal praise of heavenly angels. Recitative. Some spoken dialogue. Traditional choral ensembles.

One act, two parts: Heaven and Hell. Duration: 25 minutes.

Roles: GOD (bar – top G3 opt, high tessitura, vocally demanding); LUCIFER (ct ten), comfortable range; LIGHTBOURNE (ten – top B3), Lucifer's friend.

Chorus: SATB – Angels and Archangels.

Orchestration: fl, 2 vln, vc, cb, hp, org.

Synopsis: God speaks to the angels of his plan to create Heaven and the Universe to which Lucifer as Chief Angel responds with adoration. God proclaims that He will also create a deep and dark dungeon that shall have no ending: Hell. God asserts His love for the angels but warns them not to touch or assume His throne while He is gone. God appoints Lucifer as governor during His absence, however, no sooner has God left than Lucifer proclaims himself as "wondrously bright" as God. Lightbourne encourages Lucifer and claims that he will sit beside Lucifer and together they will surpass God. Lucifer reaffirms that he is not afraid of God. God suddenly returns, banishing Lucifer and Lightbourne to Hell. They sing of their folly and accuse each other of initiating the plan. Lucifer vows revenge against God by working to lead mankind astray. God sings of His great sorrow over His rebellious former angels. The choir of angels sing a final anthem of thanksgiving and praise to God.

Material: CHES (MMB). Performance tape available from Drummond Chapel United Methodist Church.

Notes: This piece works well within a worship service. Setting designed for church performance or concert hall. Simple or no sets required other than a chancel area and sanctuary stage.

PAUL BURKHARD

Die Zeller Weinacht – A Swiss Nativity

Music by **Paul Burkhard** (1911-1977). A Christmas Play with music; English text by the composer, translated from the original Swiss-German dialect by Eleanor Gurewitsch.

First performed in the church of Zell im Toesstal, Canton Zurich, Switzerland in 1965.

Simple harmonic structures, composed for young voices. Set numbers with considerable spoken dialogue. Continuous action.

One act. Duration: variable up to 50 minutes.

Major Roles: Should be played by singers ages 16-20. GABRIEL; MARY; HERODIAS. KASPAR, MELCHIOR, BALTHASAR, JOSEPH, HEROD, THE HERALD should be played by six senior boys ages 16-20.

Minor Roles: The remaining roles should be played by boys and girls from ten to fifteen, some of whom play more than one role. Junior Boys: 1st SERVANT, 2nd SERVANT, 3rd SERVANT, 1st SOLDIER, 2nd SOLDIER, 3rd SOLDIER, WAR MINISTER, POLICE CHIEF; 1st ANGEL/1st GIRL/1st INNKEEPER'S WIFE; 2nd ANGEL/ 2nd GIRL/2nd INNKEEPER'S WIFE; 1st STUDENT/1st INNKEEPER; 2nd STUDENT/ 2nd INNKEEPER; 1st SCHOOL GIRL/1st MAID; 2nd SCHOOL GIRL/ 2nd MAID; NEGRO FATHER/3rd INNKEEPER; NEGRO MOTHER/3rd INNKEEPER'S WIFE; NEGRO GIRL/3rd MAID; NEGRO BOY/3rd ERRAND BOY; 1st SHEPHERD/1st ERRAND BOY; 2nd SHEPHERD/2nd ERRAND BOY.

Groups and Chorus: Junior boys ten to twelve years old from 6-12 in number; Younger boys from eight to ten years old from 6-12; Girls of all ages from 12-40; Shepherds from eight to twelve years old from 12-24; Angels of all ages from 12-40; Children's Chorus, six to twelve years old from 20-50.

Orchestration: 3 trp, 3 trb, org, hpsch (or pia or elec org), lg and sm dr, rec solo, rec (played by several children).

Synopsis: A very natural and practical approach to the telling of the Nativity of Jesus. The work opens with a processional by the full cast. Amongst themselves, they decide who will play the various roles. The first encounter is Gabriel telling Mary she will have a child. The three wise men enter the scene posing as teachers and pastors to the children seating around them. A scene with King Herod and his police is followed by the announcement by the Angels to the Shepherds. Next, we move to the inn and the arrival of Mary and Joseph. Since there is no room, they are ushered to the barn. The miracle of Jesus' birth and His adoration bring this work to a close.

Materials: GS (Eng).

Notes: Performance photos, numerous stage directions, props, and costume suggestions are in the VS. A highly effective and moving work, especially if adequate numbers of children can be involved. The music is gracious, not difficult, and the dialogue is natural to contemporary speech. Few stage props or sets necessary as the decor of the church will suffice in most cases.

BOB BURROUGHS

David

Music by **Bob Burroughs** (b. 1937). A Musical Drama for children and adults with libretto by Sarah Walton killer, based on I Samuel 16-18 from Scripture.

Tonal, traditional harmony, simple melodic style. Continuous action.

One act, five scenes representing various events in David's life. Duration: ca 35 minutes.

Roles: DAVID (boy sop or young girl); SAMUEL (high bar, or ten with strong lower range); GOLIATH (bs).

Chorus: Children's choir, unison and SA

Orchestration: pia and fl.

Synopsis: The drama is based upon several of the most significant events of David's boyhood: the calling and anointing of David by the Judge Samuel; David playing his harp in the palace to calm the distraught King Saul; the friendship of David and Jonathan; David's fight with Goliath, and the victory celebration which followed the death of the Giant.

Material: BP.

Notes: Sets can be simple using furniture pieces. Adaptable to the stage area in a sanctuary. May be performed concert style. Adequate time for scene changes is problematic in that the music is continuous.

GORDON BUSH

The Visitation

Music by **Gordon Bush** (20th century American). A Music Drama for Christmas with libretto in English by Robert Lallamant and Gordon Bush.

Traditional harmony, accessible vocal ranges, musically simple, some polyphony in chorus parts. Continuous music and action.

One act. Setting: A medieval parish church on Christmas Eve. Duration: 15 minutes.

Roles: PRIEST (ten); MARY (sop); JOSEPH (bs).

Chorus: SATB – Villagers.

Dance: Villagers are led in a celebration dance by the Priest. Folk dancing.

Orchestration: org, Perc (8 hand bells, sm hand dr, tri, tamb).

Synopsis: After the parishioners process into the church singing a Latin *Hodie*, the Priest explains that many years ago during a bleak winter when people were without food, only a few people came to worship on Christmas eve. But to those who did, a miraculous visitation by Mary and Joseph was seen. Ever since, at precisely the same time each year, the same thing is witnessed – the miracle kept alive by the love of the villagers. That is what the congregation has come to witness tonight. Just then the candle is extinguished and Mary and Joseph appear. They sing of the nativity of the Christ Child. The villagers dance around them in reverent joy. The vision disappears and they sing of their awe at this miracle and that of Christ's birth and the love that keeps them both alive. The villagers then recess singing a Latin/English hymn.

Material: EBM (© 1974).

Notes: Intended for church performance and suitable as part of a worship service.

EUGENE BUTLER

God's Word in Their Heart

Music by **Eugene Butler** (b. 1935). A Sacred Musical Drama with libretto in English by William McElrath.

Premiered in 1973.

Tonal, conventional harmonic structures; some contemporary gospel sounds.

One act, three scenes. Time and place can be variable. Duration: ca. 30 minutes.

Roles: MISSIONARY (bar); FATHER (bs); MOTHER (sop); TINO (boy sop); MARA, LISA (2 girl trebles).

Children's chorus: Unison and SA – (5-8 treble voices) – neighbors.

Chorus: SATB – Narrators. May be off stage.

Orchestration: Piano.

Synopsis: A missionary spends a cold winter night in the cottage of a poor village family. He shares his faith, tells some Bible stories to the children and leaves a copy of the Bible with the family. Many long evenings are spent by the family and their neighbors reading and studying the rare book left by the traveling missionary. Several years later, the missionary passes that way again. He is surprised and delighted to discover that a large number of new believers have joined together as a congregation, memorizing scripture and worshipping God.

Material: BP.

Notes: Designed to be performed in a house of worship.

Samuel

Music by **Eugene Butler** (b. 1935). A Sacred Musical Drama with libretto in English by William N. McElrath, based on events in the life of Samuel as found in the Old Testament, I Samuel 1-3. The libretto is set in paraphrased modern English.

Composed in 1970.

Tonal and highly melodic. Contemporary and occasional "pop" sounds.

One act, five scenes. Setting: Biblical, in the country of Ephraim, in Canaan, during Israel's period of the Judges. Sc. 1: In the Temple at Shiloh (Eli's room must be visible); sc. 2: In Ephraim; sc. 3: Same as sc. 1; sc. 4: In the home of Hannah and Elkanah; sc. 5: Same sc. 1. Duration: ca. 50 minutes.

Major Roles: HANNAH (sop); ELKANAH (bar); ELI (bs). SAMUEL, five roles: 1. as a baby (a doll may be used); 2. age 3-4 (mute); 3. age 8-11 (boy sop); 4. age 11-13 (boy sop); 5. age 16-20 (mute).

Minor Roles: VOICE OF GOD (sp), off-stage, commanding voice needed; VOICE OF HANNAH'S THOUGHTS (sop), off-stage.

Chorus: SATB and Two-part Children's Choir – worshipers and narrator. The chorus may consist of an adult choir, a youth choir, a children's choir, or any combination of these groups. It is preferable to use an adult choir together with a children's choir.

Orchestration: pia, perc (cym, tamb, wood block).

Synopsis: The chorus begins by setting the stage for the story of Samuel's call by God. The first scene centers on Hannah's prayer in the Temple of Shiloh. Her dedication of Samuel takes place in Ephraim just prior to another trip to Shiloh to offer sacrifices. There Hannah gives her son, Samuel, to God's service. Samuel then receives a visit from his parents while the chorus occasionally interjects a prophetic narrative answering the cry of Israel for a successor to Eli. In Samuel's sleep, he hears the voice of God calling him to service. Eli, at the same time is assured by God that Samuel is the chosen successor and prepares to anoint him. The work concludes with jubilation and praise to God.

Material: BP.

Notes: Best performed in a house of worship with minimal scenery and lighting and a few props. The score may be performed by a choir and soloists who act their own parts or by a choir and soloists who only sing with acting done in pantomime. Historical accuracy with regard to certain props (ark, lamps, and costumes) should be given careful attention.

MARY ELIZABETH CALDWELL

A Gift of Song

Music by **Mary Elizabeth Caldwell** (1909-2003). A Christmas Opera with libretto in English by the composer, based on facts surrounding the writing and discovery of the tune *Silent Night*, and the family of its composer, Franz Gruber.

Premiered by the Pasadena Youth Music Council, Pasadena, California, December 3, 1961.

Traditional harmony with twentieth century harmonic idioms scattered throughout. Vocal lines are lyric. Melodically conceived. Through-composed with some arias and accompanied recitatives. Considerable comedy. Appealing to all ages, K-adults.

One act, three scenes with two Interludes. Sc. 1: Christmas time, 1853, in the living room of the Gruber home, Hallein, Austria. Interlude: outside the Gruber home. Sc. 2: A year later in the choir rehearsal room of St. Peter's monastery, Salzburg, Austria. Interlude: same as first interlude. Sc. 3: Same as scene 1, Christmas, 1854. Duration: 70 minutes.

Major Roles: KARL FRANZ (sop – top C5), 12-year old son of Franz Gruber, the composer - small, youthful girl with mature, yet young-sounding voice or a boy sop who has a high upper range; ANNALISA (sop – C5), his older sister, ca. 18 years old; PAPA FRANZ GRUBER (bar), mid-sixties; CHORMEISTER WILHELM (ten), youthful appearance; CHORMEISTER HERR DOKTOR GEHEIMRAT PROFESSOR VON SMALLPLATZ (bs-bar), Ambassador from the King of Prussia, comic character.

Minor Roles: MAMA GRUBER (m-sop); RUDI (sop), a choirboy, could be sung by a mature boy sop; PAGE (sp).

Chorus: SSA. Represents the Salzburg Boy's Choir. Boys preferable but mixed group can work provided they look and sound like a boy's choir, ages 8-16.

Orchestration: fl (picc), ob, 2 cl, bsn, 2 hrn, trp, timp, perc, hp, pia, strings. On stage, a period spinet which may be played from the pit.

Synopsis: Karl Franz, assisted grudgingly by his sister Annalisa, are packing Karl's bags in preparation for his year of study at the Salzburg school for choirboys. Having finished packing, Papa and Mama Gruber say their last farewell by asking Karl to sing "Papa's little song" for them. They join together as they always do at Christmas, in singing a moving setting of *Silent Night*. Scene 2 opens to a noisy choir room, filled with choirboys playing games, fighting, etc. Chormeister Wilhelm enters, regains order and announces that today they will have a guest from the King of Prussia. A Page enters and announces the entrance of Smallplatz. He of course requests that they sing for him, which they do. Secretly, he tells Wilhelm that the King has asked him to travel the land in search of the composer of a particular song which the King wants included in the national hymnal. Smallplatz hands Wilhelm a manuscript containing the tune *Silent Night*, which Wilhelm has never heard. The boys tease Smallplatz whom they consider to be an old obnoxious simpleton. Finally, the pranks and teasing go too far. Karl Franz is targeted as the leader of the pranks and punished by not being allowed to go home for Christmas. In his pouting and crying, he inadvertently begins to hum his Papa's song which Wilhelm overhears. Wilhelm asks Karl where he learned that song, and Karl explains that his Papa wrote it. Wilhelm immediately cancels the punishment and accompanies Karl to his home to meet Papa Gruber. Christmas is being celebrated in the Gruber home. Karl enters with Wilhelm and tells Papa the story. Papa, after searching for his manuscript, is unable to find it. Karl suggests that he write it down while they all sing it. In a grand finale, *Silent Night* is sung by all.

Material: BH. VS contains numerous production aids including a full set design.

Notes: Music is continuous which necessitates quick scene changes. In the proper setting, the singing of the finale can include the choirboys and the audience. Can be effectively performed in a theatre or church with a large stage.

In the Fullness of Time

Music by **Mary Elizabeth Caldwell** (1909-2003). A Christmas Music Drama with libretto in English by the composer, based on various scenes from the Nativity of Christ.

Premiered by the San Marino Community Church, San Marino, California, December 3, 1978, with the composer overseeing the production.

Conventional harmonic structures with twentieth century harmonic idioms scattered throughout. In Mrs. Caldwell's words: "I have combined elements of the traditional medieval mysticism and mystery plays of the Christmas story with contemporary chamber opera." Highly melodic lines for soloists while the chorus is given considerable chant. Set numbers. Much use of tableaus with little action necessary. Arias and ensembles. Music is continuous with organ improvisation connecting the scenes. The composer is currently revising, with more definition and guidelines, the improvised sections. Appealing to family but especially grade eight and up.

Major Roles: STORYTELLER (sp); GOD (sp); HEROD (bar – top F3), sinister, sarcastic; MERCHANT (bar – top E3), character actor who both sings and speaks; MERCHANT'S SON (boy sop – top Bb4); MARY (sop – top Bb4).

Minor Roles: FIRST WISEMAN (bs); SECOND WISEMAN (bar); THIRD WISEMAN (ten); FIRST SHEPHERD (bar); SECOND SHEPHERD (ten – top G3); THIRD SHEPHERD (boy sop – top A4).

Chorus: SATB. Other than the processional, the chorus remains stationary, commenting on the action. The choral music grows from simple Gregorian Chants to a six-part grand finale. All Latin texts are echoed in English in antiphonal style.

Dance: A Slave Girl in Scene II entertains Herod with her dancing.

Orchestration: Org, gong, chimes, finger cym, fl and ob are optional depending on the resources of the org.

Setting and Synopsis: One act with prologue, six scenes and a finale. Duration: approximately 55 minutes.

PROLOGUE
Procession of the choir singing *O Magnum Mysterium*.
Storyteller and God introduce the plan for the world.

SCENE I – THE WISEMEN'S TEMPLE
Three Magi have gathered to study the stars and consider the prophecy of a promised Saviour. They will impart all knowledge and wisdom to Him when He comes.
God's response
Choral chant: *O Dei Mirabilia*

SCENE II – HEROD'S PALACE IN JERUSALEM
Herod expresses boredom and scorn for the people he rules and for his Roman superiors. He also scorns the idea of a promised Messiah but enumerates the things he could teach Him: how to live in luxury, how to cheat the people and build great palaces from over-taxing the people. He promises to destroy any child that should be born in Bethlehem that might fulfill the ancient prophecy.
God's response
Choral chant: *Vieni, Vieni Emmanuel*

SCENE III – A STREET IN JERUSALEM
A street merchant tries to sell his jewels, rings, and fruit. His son, absorbed in an ancient scroll that tells of the promised Messiah, is severely scolded by his father for reading when he should be helping. As the father goes on selling his wares at another gate, the boy remains alone to ponder the thought that the Saviour will come and to pray for Him.
God's response
Choral chant: *Te Deum Laudamus, Gloria Tibi Domine, Sanctus*

SCENE IV – A HILLSIDE NEAR BETHLEHEM
Three shepherds are tending their flocks. They speak of the ancient prophecy of the coming of the Lamb of God even as they express concern for their own flocks.
God's response
Choral response: *Agnus Dei*

SCENE V – MARY'S ROOM
Mary sits quietly and hears God's voice announcing that she is to bear His Son. She sings the *Magnificat*.

SCENE VI – THE BETHLEHEM STABLE
God descends bringing the Christ Child to Mary. The entire cast gathers to observe and bring their gifts to the Child.
Choral response: *Hodie*

FINALE
Choral conclusion: *And Peace Shall Come to All*

Materials: From the composer. *Hodie* is published separately by FB.

Notes: Sets and staging should be uncomplicated. The appearance of God with the Christ Child can be awkward. A long descending stairway from a hidden area could work. A clever lighting design throughout the show is imperative. The entire work can be performed in front of a large multipurpose triptych and is most effective when staged in the sanctuary of a church.

The Night of the Star

Music by **Mary Elizabeth Caldwell** (1909-2003). A Christmas Opera with libretto in English by the composer. The plot focuses on the events surrounding the announcement of the birth of the Christ Child by the heavenly angels to the shepherds.

Commissioned by the Junior League of Pasadena and premiered on December 5, 1965 in the Pasadena Civic Auditorium, Pasadena, California.

Romantic harmonic style with considerable chromaticism and some dissonance. Melodic lines are vocally conceived but dissonance abounds in the lengthy middle duet section between Jonathan and Little Angel. Through-composed with arias for Jonathan, Little Angel, and Benjamin. Considerable comedy. Appealing to all ages, K-adult.

One act. Setting: During the time of Christ's birth, on a rocky field outside Bethlehem. Duration: 60 minutes.

Major Roles: JONATHAN (sop or boy sop – top Bb4 with opt G4), a young shepherd boy; LITTLE ANGEL (sop – top C5), same age as Jonathan; BENJAMIN (ten – top A#3), Jonathan's older brother in his early twenties, a shepherd.

Minor Roles: JACOB (bar – top F3), a shepherd; NATHAN (bs-bar – top E3), the oldest shepherd; ROMAN SOLDIER (bar), big and burly; SLAVE GIRL (m-sop – top A#4).

Bit Parts: TWO SLAVE CHILDREN (mute), boy and girl; THE ANGEL GABRIEL (sp).

CHORUS: SSAA – an invisible angel chorus.

Orchestration: FULL – fl (picc), 2 ob (Eng hrn), 2 cl, bsn, 2 hrn, trp, timp, perc, hp, cel, strings. REDUCED – pia, org, hp, cel, timp, perc (trp and fl are mandatory for the story line).

Synopsis: Three shepherds along with their younger brother Jonathan slumber around a fire, tending their sleeping sheep. Jonathan is awakened by the sound of music and wanders off in search of its source. Suddenly, an angelic choir is heard and Gabriel announces the birth of the Christ Child to the three shepherds. The three eagerly prepare for their visit to the Child and leave the sheep in the care of heart-broken Jonathan. As Jonathan guards the sheep, a little angel falls out of the sky and stumbles into Jonathan's camp. His wing is broken from a collision with another angel while playing hide and seek. Jonathan agrees to fix Little Angel's wing. Little Angel is intrigued by Jonathan's earthly flute while Jonathan so badly wants to hear the angels sing. The two barter, exchange gifts and Little Angel hurries off, leaving his halo behind, to catch up with the other angels at the stable.

No sooner has Little Angel departed than a slave girl and two slave children, in chains, run onto stage. Jonathan frees them and just as a Roman Soldier appears, finds a hiding place for them. The Soldier threatens to kill Jonathan if he does not reveal their hiding place. The Little Angel reappears in the sky and frightens the Soldier away. The older shepherds return and relate to Jonathan the wondrous story of the Christ Child's birth, making note that among the gifts they saw was a flute just like his. As dawn approaches, heavenly choirs fill the skies, the heavens glow revealing the figure of Little Angel waving to Jonathan. Jonathan cries out, "O thank you, angel!" and waves back to him as the *Gloria in excelsis Deo* rises to a climax.

Materials: TP. VS contains costume suggestions, a list of set and working props, production notes, set design ideas, and photos from the first production.

Notes: Gabriel and angels' chorus must sound ethereal, appearing in the distant sky; therefore, the use of scrim and scaffolding may be necessary. Also, an important working prop is Jonathan's little lamb, which must be believable whether it is real or a toy. Most effectively staged in a theatre, but conceivable in a house of worship with a large stage area.

Pepito's Golden Flower

Music by **Mary Elizabeth Caldwell** (1909-2003). A Sacred Folk Opera with libretto in English by the composer, based on authentic historical data of Mission Santa Inez in California, shortly after the disastrous earthquake of 1812, which damaged the Mission and destroyed the belfry tower and bells. The umbrella sequence is based on an incident told in the book *California Padres and Their Missions* by Saunders and Chase.

Premiered March 1955, at the Civic Auditorium in Pasadena, California. Sponsored by the Junior League, the Pasadena Board of City Directors, and the Pasadena Symphony Association. The premiere was greeted with such enthusiasm that a repeat performance was arranged for on March 27, 1955.

Traditional harmonic characteristics with some impressionistic and twentieth century stylings. Highly melodic. Through-composed with some spoken lines. Appealing to all ages, particularly youth.

One act, two scenes, separated by a brief orchestral interlude. Setting: sc. 1: On the patio of the Mission Santa Inez in 1812; sc. 2: Six months later. Duration: 53 minutes.

Major Roles: PEPITO (boy sop or m-sop – top A4), Mission Indian boy; ROSITA (sop – top Bb4), a young Spanish girl; THE PADRE (high bar – B2-G3, high tess - could be sung by a heavy ten), middle-aged and plump.

Minor Roles: CAPTAIN ALVARRO (bar), Spanish Sea Captain, Rosita's father; MANUEL, Mission Indian, sings only with chorus, no solos.

Chorus: SATB – Mission Indian adults; Children's treble voices who are Mission Indian children (6-10); Four Tulare Indians, tall and thin, may double as Mission Indians and sing with chorus in Fiesta scene.

Dance: Fiesta Dancers (Spanish), any practical number from 2 to 8; Indian Ceremonial Dancers, any practical number from 2 to 8. Mission Indian children should also dance during the Fiesta scene.

Orchestration: fl (picc), cl, ob, bsn, hrn, trp, perc, hp, strings.

Synopsis: The curtain rises on a lively ball game between the boys led by Pepito and the girls led by Rosita. The Padre calls them to midday prayers which are constantly interrupted by the mischievous doings of Pepito who is finally scolded by the Padre. He then confides to Pepito and Rosita that he is very sad because of the earthquake damage to the Mission and the loss of the bells. After the Padre goes into the Mission, Rosita tells Pepito of a treasure hidden somewhere near the Mission which, if they could find it, would enable them to buy new bells to surprise the Padre. Pepito is excited and confident that he can find the treasure.

Shouts are heard in the distance telling of the arrival of Rosita's father from Mexico and the six-months' supplies for which Padre has so long waited. Padre asks Pepito to bring in the supplies but under no circumstances may he touch any of them. Pepito obeys for the moment but temptation is too great, and in no time the opened bundles are scattered all over the patio with Pepito dressing in the Padre's nightcap and long white underpants. Suddenly, he hears the approaching voice of the Padre. He frantically looks for a hiding place and finally hides underneath the umbrella.

Padre enters announcing that the fierce Tulare Indians are at war and will most certainly attack the Mission. Everyone hurries into the church to pray and make preparations while Pepito, afraid to follow them, digs a hole to prop up the umbrella under which he plans to spend the night. While digging, he uncovers the old treasure box. Simultaneously, the Indians enter and attempt to raid the Mission. Rosita screams as they grab her. Pepito bravely grabs the umbrella, hoists up the white pants, and jumps into the midst of the astonished Indians who flee in confusion. Padre comes in and praises Pepito for saving the Mission. Pepito confides to Rosita that he found the treasure and they make plans for sending it back with her father to buy new bells in Mexico.

The stage is darkened for a moment to indicate a six-month interval. When the lights go up, a fiesta is under way, celebrating Padre's birthday. The bells arrive and are installed without Padre's knowledge. At an appropriate moment, Pepito signals madly to Manuel who begins the ringing of the new bells. There is much jubilation and the curtain falls on a joyous *Te Deum* sung in thanksgiving for the new bells.

Materials: GS (SHP). VS contains ideas and drawings for set designs, photographs, properties, and costumes.

Notes: Reviews of various performances indicate strongly favorable audience reception of this work. A delightful and uncomplicated opera to produce. Best played in a theatre unless the interior of a church is adequate in size and decor.

MARIO CASTELNUOVO-TEDESCO

Saul

Music by **Mario Castelnuovo-Tedesco** (1895-1968). A Sacred Opera with libretto in English by the composer based on the Biblical story of Saul and the tragedy by Vittorio Alfieri.

Composed 1958-60. Unperformed.

A tragedy in three acts.

Roles: SOP, 2 TEN, 2 BAR, BS (designated characters).

Chorus: SATB.

Orchestration: 3 fl (picc), 2 ob, Eng hrn, 3 cl (bs cl), 3 bsn (contra bsn), 4 hrn, 3 trp, 3 trb, tba, timp, perc, hp, strings.

Materials: Unpublished. See CWMC.

Song of Songs

Music by **Mario Castelnuovo-Tedesco** (1895-1968). A Scenic Oratorio with libretto in English and Italian by the composer, based on The Song of Solomon from Scripture.

Written in 1955 as Opus 172; premiered in 1963, at the Hollywood Theatre Arts Workshop.

Typically late Romantic textures with lush harmonies and vocally conceived lines. Duration: 75 minutes.

Three sections.

Major roles: SOP, TEN, BAR (designated characters).

Chorus: SATB

Dance: Dancers required.

Orchestration: fl, 2 ob, 2 cl, bsn, 2 hrn, 1 trp, perc, timp, hp, strings.

Materials: Unpublished. Score in LC. Informational source: CWMC.

Tobias and the Angel

Music by **Mario Castelnuovo-Tedesco** (1895-1968). A Scenic Oratorio with libretto in English and Italian by Nick Rossi and the composer, based on Tobit from the Apocrypha. Though designated as an oratorio, the work is undoubtedly intended for stage treatment since the score contains some stage directions.

Composed in 1965, premiered February 1, 1975, La Guardia Community College, New York.

Highly eclectic style typical of the late Italian Romantic composers, especially Puccini. Melodic and colorful.

Three acts. Duration: 120 minutes.

Roles: Eight designated characters: SOP, 2 ALT, TEN, BAR, 2 BS.

Chorus: SATB

Orchestration: 2 fl, 2 ob, 2 cl, bsn, 2 hrn, 2 trp, 2 trb, perc, timp, hp, strings.

Synopsis: The story of the youthful Tobias as he is guided by his companion who turns out to be an angel in disguise. See "Synopsis" under *Tobias and the Angel*, by Bliss.

Materials: Unpublished. See CWMC. LC holds a holograph reproduction in three bound volumes.

Notes: Best performed in a theatre or auditorium. Written for student musicians.

EMILIO DE' CAVALIERI

La Rappresentazione di Anima e di Corpo –
The Representation of the Soul and Body

Music by **Emilio de' Cavalieri** (1550-1602). A Monody or Morality Play. Agostino Manni was the probable librettist. The work is not an oratorio in the modern sense of the word, but is among the earliest plays with music composed for an oratorio (a meeting hall of the society of clergy).

Premiered in February, 1600, during carnival time in Rome, Italy.

Written in the monodic style of the Florentine Camerata, of which Cavalieri was a member. Contains elements of spoken narrative, much recitative, solos, ensembles, continuo, and orchestra. Toward the middle of the 17th century, works of this style became known as oratorios. The work incorporated verses from earlier *laude*, intended to be a part of an informal devotional religious service at the oratory of Saint Filippo Neri.

Three sections or acts with prologue. The Prologue opens with a chorus followed by a spoken dialogue (8 min). Act I is 18 min. Act II, 33 min. Act III, 30 min. Duration: 90 minutes.

Major Roles: Allegorical characters. ANIMA (Soul) (m-sop); CORPO (Body) (bar); INTELLETTO (Intellect) (ten); CONSIGLIO (Counsel) (bs).

Minor Roles: TEMPO (Time) (bs), an old man; ANGELO CUSTODE (Guardian Angel) (sop); VITA MONDANA (Earthly Life) (sop); PIACERE (Pleasure) (ct ten);

DUE COMPAGNI (his two companions) (ten and bs); MONDO (World) (bs); ANIMA DANNATA (Damned Souls) (1 or 4 bs); ANIME BEATE (Blessed Souls) (1 or 4 sop); ECO (Echo) (sop solo or a group of four); AUUEDUTO (Prudence) and PRUDENTIO (Caution) (sp), two youths.

Chorus: SSATTB. In the Introduction written by Allessandro Guidotti for the first edition of this work, instructions for the beginning state that the chorus must be on the stage, a part seated, a part standing and paying attention to the performance, sometimes changing position and executing movements. When they have to sing, they must stand to make up their gestures and then return to their places. And as the music for the chorus is in four parts, if so desired these could be doubled, four singing at one time, eight at another but only if there is room for them on the stage.

Orchestration: In the introduction to this work, instructions are given as to the instruments. Cavalieri considered it particularly important that the emotions of the characters be carefully considered. He suggested the use of a double lira, a harpsichord, a chitarrone or theobe, or an organ with a chitarrone. Using more modern instruments, the following orchestration is suggested but may be altered with considerable variations: Org, hpsch, hp, strings, gui, chitarrone, double reeds, bsn, recorders, corn, trb, timp, tamb, tri, cym.

Synopsis: The Prologue opens with a chorus followed by a prose dialogue between Prudence and Caution. Act I begins with Time reminding the audience that time flies, and every moment should be counted, for the final trumpet is about to sound. Intellect states that pleasure only brings more desire, while contentment may be won by embracing God in heaven. The debate now begins between Body and Soul. Soul wins the first round, lauded by the Chorus with dancing, playing instruments, and praising God in psalm-like phrases. Act II opens with Good Counsel denouncing life on earth as an unending war. Once again Soul and Body contest each other, with Soul gaining the upper hand. Even at that, Body wavers until Angel tears off World's rich garments and bares an ugly wretch. The third act opens with Intellect counting the blessings of Heaven and Good Counsel enumerating the pains of Hell. The Damned Souls of Hell and the Blessed Souls of Heaven alternately display their features. Body and Soul finally both agree that they should desire only Heaven. All glorify God with singing and dancing.

Materials: MOS; RIC. Recording: Archiv 2708 016; English libretto on the insert is by Polydor London.

Notes: Setting can be minimal or elaborate. Best performed in a theatre. This work is important to anyone interested in sacred music drama because of its place in history and its relationship to staged works with a sacred text. It merits study and investigation as a basis for sacred music drama.

GEORGE WHITEFIELD CHADWICK

Judith

Music by **George Whitefield Chadwick** (1854-1931). A Dramatic Oratorio ("Lyric Drama") with text by William Chauncy Langdon (1871-1947), based on the Apocryphal Book of Judith.

Premiered September 21, 1901, Worcester Festival, Massachusetts, and revived January 29, 1977, at Dartmouth College.

Highly romantic with considerable eclecticism in evidence, i.e., the borrowing of musical styles from a variety of late Romantic composers. The orchestration is perhaps the most interesting feature of the score. Melodic and lyric in style. Accompanied recitatives.

Three acts, fourteen scenes. Act I: Within the walls of the town Bethulia; Act II: Same; Act III: Just outside the walls of Bethulia. Duration: 2 hours, 10 minutes.

Roles: JUDITH (m-sop), lengthy and demanding role; HOLOFERNES (bar – top Bb3); ACHIOR (ten); OZIAS (bs), a Priest; SENTINEL (ten).

Chorus: SSAATTBB (some double choir sections) – Israelites, captive Hebrews, soldiers, camp-followers; considerable choral singing.

Orchestration: Full orchestra.

Dance: Ballet.

Synopsis: The widowed Israelite beauty, Judith, boldly goes to the enemy Assyrian camp, entices their chieftain, Holofernes, to dine alone with her. She gets him drunk, then beheads him with the sword he had given to her. Judith herself then bears the severed head back to the Israelite camp to present it to her leader, Ozias, and has it hung on the towers of Bethulia as a symbol of Jehovah's might.

Material: DAC has photo reproduction of first edition (1972); GS holds first edition (© 1901). Score and holograph both in LC.

Notes: A difficult score to stage due to the lengthy and numerous choruses. Concert version suffers from the lengthy ballet music and more dramatic scenes of Act II in particular. Best suited to theatre performance.

DAVID CONTE

The Gift of the Magi

Music by **David Conte** (b. 1955). A one act chamber opera in four scenes with text in English based on the classic O. Henry short story with libretto by Nicholas Giardini.

First presented in a workshop production with two-piano accompaniment on December 7 and 8, 1997, at the San Francisco Conservatory of Music by the Conservatory's Cantata Singers. The orchestral version was premiered by the San Francisco Conservatory New Music Ensemble on December 3, 2000.

Orchestral introduction, with staging suggestions, leads directly into scene one. All scenes are musically connected. Considerable use of accompanied recitative style and highly melodic. Tonally conceived with some dissonances; frequent rhythmic variations and metric changes, a result of his attempt to bring a natural inflection to his word painting. Through-composed.

One act with four scenes connected musically. All scenes set on Christmas Eve in Della and Jim's sparsely furnished apartment. Duration: ca 67 minutes.

Major Roles: DELLA (sop); JIM (high bar)

Minor Roles: MAGGIE (m-sop); HENRY (bs-bar); 3 MAGI (ten, bar, bs), two short off-stage ensembles

Orchestration: 14 players – fl (picc), ob, cl, bs cl, bsn, hrn, trp, pia, hp, 2 vln, vla, vc, cb. Accompaniment for two pianos also available from publisher.

Synopsis: Della and Jim are a young couple very much in love and devoted to each other. They share a small apartment, and because of their meager incomes they pledge not to exchange Christmas gifts. Secretly, both decide to sell their own most precious possession to buy what each thinks will make the other happy. Though Jim adores her long flowing tresses, Della decides to cut and sell her hair to a wig maker so she can buy Jim a chain for his pocket watch, a family heirloom given to him by his father. Meanwhile, Jim decides to buy Della an exquisitely elaborate comb for her hair. But of course, the only way he can raise sufficient money is to sell his father's watch. In scenes two and three, both Della and Jim confide their plans in their best friends who adamantly try to dissuade them, but without success. In the final scene Della and Jim, having completed their "shopping," meet at their apartment. They exchange their gifts realizing neither have any need of them. In a moving finale, they reaffirm their love for each other which they now realize is the greatest gift of all.

Materials: ECS

Notes: Very accessible score; most suitable to a small theatre or intimate performance space.

CARSON P. COOMAN

Thieves

Music by Carson P. Cooman (b. 1982). A Chamber opera (Opus 544) in one act with libretto by Mark Schweizer, loosely based on the biblical narrative of Christ's crucifixion.

First performed April 5, 2004, St. James Episcopal Church, Alexandria, Louisiana. Commissioned by St. James Music Press. Considerable choral music.

Music derived primarily from the hymn-like chorale appearing in various forms and sung by the chorus throughout the composition. Highly melodic with interesting harmonic movement and considerable chromaticism but within clearly established tonalities. Through-composed.

One act. Duration: ca. 20 minutes.

Roles: JESUS (ten or bs – octave adjustment necessary – appropriate suggestions are given in the score); WOMAN (m-sop); MAN (bar)

Chorus: SATB – the chorus responds to the action as a Greek Chorus and thus should not be a part of the action.

Orchestration: Piano alone; or fl, vc, and piano. These two versions have some slight differences, thus all singers/chorus should work from the piano/vocal score.

Synopsis: The work begins with a Processional of the three characters, Jesus bearing his cross with the Man and Woman following in modern dress. Jesus is helped into place in center stage while the Man and Woman take their places on either side of Him; they represent mankind. Throughout the work, Jesus iterates His "seven sayings of the cross," while the Man and Woman interject their personal commentary. Meanwhile, the chorus responds to the comments of all three characters. The Woman moralizes in positive if not selfish tones while the Man berates himself and everyone else. In the end the Woman triumphantly thanks God that she is not like "this miserable thief," while the Man pleads for mercy and forgiveness. Jesus concludes with his final words: "It is finished."

Materials: SJMP – piano/vocal score and parts available.

Notes: Best performed in a house of worship as the work is conceived for performance in a church context. It is well suited for presentation within a worship service, especially during Good Friday or Easter season. The work is accessible to a good church music program. This opera is being recorded for commercial release scheduled for summer 2006 (Zimbel Records), production by Christ Episcopal Church, Alameda, California.

CARSON P. COOMAN and SANDRA GAY

See the Promised Dawn Arise

Music by **Carson P. Cooman** (b. 1982) and **Sandra Gay**. A chamber opera for the church in one act with libretto by John Thornburg, Sandra Gay, and Carson Cooman. Text in English with some Latin. Story taken from the Bible, based on three moments taken from the Easter story of the Gospels.

First performed April 15, 2001 by the Webster Presbyterian Church, Sally Turner, director.

Traditional harmony throughout; fifteen set numbers with several short arias and some spoken dialogue. Simple and accessible musical textures and vocal lines. Several hymns and anthems for choir and congregation are inserted within the story line. An instrumental prelude and postlude can be used for staging. The work was conceived to be performed entirely with church participants as actors, soloists, choir members, and orchestral players.

Three scenes with continuous action. Duration: 35 minutes

Roles: MARY MAGDALENE (sop); SALOME (sop); JOANNA (alt); ANGEL (bar); THOMAS (bar); JESUS (bar); NICODEMUS (sp); JAMES (sp); PHILIP (sp); PETER (bar); NATHANAEL (sp); JOHN (sp); SOLOIST (sop)

Chorus: SATB

Orchestration: fl, ob, cl, hrn, trp, trb, timp, perc, org, vln, vla, vc

Synopsis: Scene 1 begins with Mary Magdalene, Salome and Joanna visiting the tomb of Jesus three days after his burial. An Angel appears telling them that Jesus has risen, and that they should immediately go tell his disciples. Scene 2 finds the disciples gathered for dinner and conversation. Suddenly Jesus appears in their midst, removing their doubts and disbelief that he has indeed risen. Scene 3 opens with the disciples and Peter on their unsuccessful fishing expedition. Jesus challenges them to throw their nets to the other side of the boat. When they obey, they catch more fish than they can handle. Jesus then asks Peter three time, "Do you love me?" The work concludes with a confirming congregational hymn and a triumphant choral "Alleluia" setting.

Materials: ZP – parts and vocal scores available

Notes: Most appropriate for presentation in a church. Prop and costume suggestions are noted in the vocal score. A musically simple and accessible work for Easter.

ROBERT CUNDICK

The Redeemer

Music by **Robert Cundick** (b. 1926). A Dramatic Oratorio with libretto in English by the composer taken from the Holy Scriptures: *Book of Mormon, Pearl of Great Price, Doctrine and Covenants*, and the Bible.

First performance April, 1978.

Post-Romantic. Conventional harmonies with twentieth century harmonic influences. Highly melodic. Set numbers, arias and choruses. Continuous texture.

Three parts, seventeen numbers. Orchestral Prelude and Postlude. Part I: The Prophecy; Part II: The Sacrifice; Part III: The Promise. Duration: 80 minutes.

Roles: PROPHET (bar – top G3); ELIZABETH (sop); ANGEL (sop); JESUS (bs); MEZZO-SOP SOLO; SOPRANO OR TENOR (narrative).

Chorus: SATB divisi – acts as a Greek chorus.

Orchestration: 2 fl, 2 ob, 2 cl, 2 bsn, 4 hrn, 3 trp, 3 trb, tba, timp, 2 perc, hp, strings.

Synopsis:
  Part I – The Prophecy
  Prelude
   I.   The Prophet calls for repentance
   II.   Announcement of the birth of Jesus
   III.   Elizabeth sings the *Magnificat*
   IV.   Christ shall be call the Son of God
   V.   How beautiful upon the mountains are the feet of him who bringeth good tidings
   VI.   The baptism of Christ

Part II – The Sacrifice
- VII. Jesus introduces us to His mission
- VIII. Prophecy of Christ's death
- IX. Prophecy of Christ's resurrection
- X. The crucifixion

Part III – The Promise
- XII. Hope for life eternal
- XIII. The Prophet calls for repentance
- XIV. "Behold, this is the way"
- XV. His Word shall not pass away
- XVI. Jesus speak of His second return – be ready!
- XVII. The invitation of Jesus: "Let him who is athirst, come and take the water of life freely."

Materials: BYU.

Notes: No sets necessary. Can be presented in a series of tableaus in either a house of worship or auditorium.

LUIGI DALLAPICCOLA

Job

Music by **Luigi Dallapiccola** (b. 1904-1975). A Sacred Drama (*sacra rappresentazione*) with text in Italian, based on events in the life of Job as recorded in the Old Testament Book of Job.

Composition premiered in Rome, October 30, 1950.

Musically avant-garde, mixed meter, single tone row series, Webern influenced, atonality; use of non-singing vocal effects and large skips.

Seven numbers or episodes, but continuous action and music. Duration: 35 minutes.

Roles: All singing roles are highly chromatic with atonal tendencies. STORICO (sp), the narrator; JOB (bs-bar – top G#3), extremely demanding role both dramatically and vocally. Friends of Job: ELIFIZ (sop); BALDAD (cont – low E2), low tess; ZOFAR (ten – top Bb3); 4 MESSENGERS (sop, alt, ten, bar).

Chorus: Two groups: mixed speaking choir and an SATB singing choir, representing the voice of God and the voice of Satan. Some rhythmic complexities.

Orchestration: picc, 2 fl, ob, Eng hrn, 2 cl, bs cl, bsn, contra bsn, 2 hrn, 2 trp, trb, tba, timp, perc, cel, pia, hp, xyl, vib, string. Second group: org, 2 hrn, 2 trp, trb

Synopsis: Episodic, including the trials and tribulations of Job, his conversations with God and Satan, and the attempted support and encouragement of his three friends.

Materials: EZ (BH).

Notes: A powerful work with strong dramatic potential. Difficult orchestral parts and vocal lines. Minimal or no sets required. May be best performed in a house of worship.

MELVIN L. DANIELS

Lazarus

Music by **Melvin L. Daniels** (b. 1931). A Sacred Opera with libretto in English by Jack Welch, based on Luke 10 and John 11-12 from Scripture.

Premiered Spring, 1989, by the Episcopal Church of the Heavenly Rest, Abilene, TX. Commissioned by the Abilene Christian University Research Council.

Tonal and modal; strongly influenced by twentieth century idioms.

One act, three scenes. Setting: sc. 1: Outside Mary and Martha's home; sc. 2: Inside their home; sc. 3: The tomb of Lazarus. Duration: 39 minutes.

Roles: JESUS (bs); LAZARUS (ten); MARY OF BETHANY (sop); MARTHA OF BETHANY (alt); VISITOR (bar); THOMAS (bar); JUDAS (ten); JOHN (bs-bar).

Orchestration: Piano

Synopsis: Jesus comes to visit Mary, Martha and Lazarus. Martha is especially eager to have every household detail in order, while Mary listens attentively to Jesus. In scene 2, we find Jesus and his disciples discussing a note just received from Mary and Martha asking them to come immediately as Lazarus is very ill. Jesus' disciples attempt to dissuade Him from going since the Jews in Judea are eager to kill Him. They nonetheless go, learning from Martha upon their arrival, that her brother is dead. She asserts that he would not have died if Jesus had been there. There follows then the teaching on the resurrection and the raising of Lazarus from the tomb. The third scene depicts Jesus dining with Mary, Martha and Lazarus. Mary anoints Jesus with expensive ointment while Judas complains about the waste. However, Jesus says that this anointing was done for His burial. He reassures them all, telling them not to be afraid for the tomb cannot hold Him.

Materials: AMC and the composer.

Notes: Best suited to church performance. Can be performed with only one set.

PETER MAXWELL DAVIES

The Martyrdom of St. Magnus

Music by **Peter Maxwell Davies** (b. 1934). Chamber Opera with text in English by the composer based on the novel *Magnus* by George Mackay Brown.

Commissioned by the BBC for the Queen's Silver Jubilee. Premiered June 18, 1977, at St. Magnus Cathedral, Kirkwall, Orkney.

The musical foundation of this work lies in Gregorian chant. The work is largely atonal with infrequent tonal centers. Many special vocal effects, wide leaps in the vocal lines, disjunct melodic structures in non-chant sections, and extreme chromaticism characterize this work. Orchestral interludes connect the scenes. The over-all effect is intense and dramatic.

One act, nine scenes. Setting: The twelfth century. Sc. 1: The Battle of Menai Strait; sc. 2: The temptations of Magnus; sc. 3: The curse of Blind Mary; sc. 4: The peace negotiations; sc. 5: Magnus' journey to the Island of Egilsay; sc. 6: Earl Hakon resolves to murder Magnus; sc. 7: The reporters; sc. 8: The sacrifice; sc. 9: The miracle. Duration: 75 minutes.

Major roles: One woman and four men, all of who sing multiple characters. All roles contain recitation, chanting, falsetto, shouting, *sprechstimme*, and other special vocal effects. 1. BLIND MARY, MARY O'CONNELL, THE GIRL INGERTH (m-sop – E2-A4, very low tess); 2. EARL MAGNUS, PRISONER, REPORTER I, MONK (ten – top G3, much chanting); 3. NORSE HERALD, KING OF NORWAY, KEEPER OF THE LOOM, POLICEMAN, HERALD OF EARL MAGNUS, REPORTER II, LIFOLF (the butcher), MONK (bar – F1-F#3, high tess); 4. WELSH HERALD, THE TEMPTER, HERALD OF EARL HAKON, REPORTER III, MONK, POLICEMAN (bar – F1-F#3), many special vocal effects as the Tempter; 5. EARL HAKON, MILITARY OFFICER, REPORTER IV, BISHOP OF ORKNEY, MONK (bs – D#1-E3).

Orchestration: fl/alt fl/picc, cl, bs cl, hrn, 2 trp, hpsch, hp (opt), cel, autoharp, gui, vla, cel, many voiced and unvoiced perc

Synopsis: Blind Mary, the seer, sings a Viking spinning song in which she sees in her fabric and spinning wheel the various aspects of war. The Battle of Menai Strait between the King of Norway and the Earl of Shrewsbury is in progress. During this battle Magnus first distinguished himself as a pacifist. The action then moves to Orkney and the quarrel between Hakon and Magnus, joint earls of Orkney, which culminates in the murder of Magnus by Hakon. For this the action moves forward to the present day, and the martyrdom takes place in a police cell in any contemporary totalitarian state. The action moves back to the twelfth century again. Blind Mary prays for sight before the tomb of St. Magnus, against the litany and chanting of the monks. She receives her sight and sees the audience present – "dark faces, blind mouths, crying still for sacrifice." She prays to St. Magnus to "keep us from a bedlam of sacrifice," prophesying just such a course of events, before she dismisses the audience to "carry the peace of Christ into the world."

Materials: BH.

Notes: This work is to be played in the round if possible, to a small audience seated on the floor in a circle. There should be no extraneous light. Productions in theatres or churches are possible, but should always be characterized by simplicity. The lighting must be very simple and intensely dramatic. The cast, when not participating in the action should sit on a bench, beside which the few props and costumes are arranged conveniently. No attempt should be made to hide the ritual of change or to hide the costumes and props. The VS contains suggestions on staging, props, and costumes.

ANTHONY DAVIS

X (The Life and Times of Malcolm X)

Music by **Anthony Davis** (b. 1951). A Biographical Opera on the life and personality of Malcolm X. Not a sacred opera per se, but deals with the beliefs and life of a religious Muslim leader. Libretto in English by Thulani Davis, story by Christopher Davis.

Premiered September 28, 1986, New York City Opera. The work was developed at the American Music Theater Festival, and had its first full-length production with orchestra in Philadelphia, PA, on October 9, 1985.

Abrupt and sharply contrasting musical styles. Contemporary in sound, intensely rhythmic, often lyrical and melodic. Non-Western, pop, jazz, African sounds, and classical influences are all in evidence. Frequent sections of improvisation are indicated in the orchestra parts.

Three acts. Act I, sc.1: Meeting place during Malcolm's childhood; sc. 2: Pool room; Act II, sc. 1: Prison cell; sc. 2: Harlem; sc. 3: At a rally; Act III, sc. 1 Harlem; an interlude in Malcolm's home; sc. 2: On the way to Mecca; sc. 3: Outside a hotel room, then in a private room. Duration: full length.

Major Roles: MALCOLM (in scene 1 he is a boy soprano; later a high bar – top A#3), must be a charismatic and possess a dominant personality, lengthy role, some spoken lines; REGINALD (bs-bar); ELIJAH (ten – top D4), spiritual advisor, very high range.

Minor Roles: LOUISE (sop); SOCIAL WORKER (m-sop); ELLA (m-sop), Malcolm's sister); STREET (ten – top Cb3), pool player, some scat singing; QUEEN MOTHER (sp and sop); GARVEY PREACHER (bar); BETTY (sop), Malcolm's wife; POLICE OFFICERS (ten, ten, bar); REPORTER (sp); 2 DAUGHTERS (silent), Malcolm's children; several solo lines taken from the ensemble.

Chorus: A specific number of voices comprise the ensemble representing Malcolm's followers, congregation, pilgrims, reporters. A group of children (silent) are necessary for the opening scene.

Orchestration: 2 fl (picc), ob, 2 cl (2 sax), bsn, contra bsn, 2 hrn, 1 trp, 2 trb, timp, 3 perc, pia, strings. Jazz band: fl, 2 cl, trp, trb, perc, vc, bs, pia, drums.

Synopsis: The opera opens to a scene involving Malcolm as a child with reflections on his impoverished childhood. The remainder of the plot deals with his conversion, travel to Mecca, and his rise to leadership among the Muslims.

Materials: GS.

Notes: To be performed in a theatre with ample technical facilities.

CLAUDE DEBUSSY

L'enfant prodigue – The Prodigal Son

Music by **Claude Debussy** (1862-1918). A "scene lyric" or religious drama/opera with libretto in French by Ernest Guiraud, based upon the New Testament parable found in Luke 15.

Premiered Grand Prix de Rome in 1884.

Romantic harmonic structures with hints of Impressionism. Considerable chromaticism and rhythmic complexity. Through-composed. Highly melodic. Demands strong singers.

One act. Setting: An embankment near a village on the Lake of Genezareth. Duration: 35 minutes.

Major roles: LIA (sop – C3-B4), Azaël's mother, requires sustained, dramatic singing; SIMÉON (bar – C2-F3), Azaël's father; AZAËL (ten), the prodigal son.

Chorus: STB, village neighbors. Involved in celebration scene but only minimal singing.

Orchestration: 3 fl (picc), 2 ob, Eng hrn, 2 cl, 2 bsn, 4 hrn, 2 trp, 3 trb, tba, timp, perc, 2 hp, strings.

Dance: One or more dancers with general folk dancing by villagers.

Synopsis: Lia is found mourning the absence of her son Azaël. He has taken his inheritance and left home preferring the "free" life style. Siméon, Azaël's father, admonishes her for giving in to grief and encourages her to join a group of villagers in their jubilation. Azaël has returned home secretly and from his hiding place, watches his former friends dancing and enjoying life. He laments his wasted life. Discouraged and sick, he falls to the ground. Lia finds him, at first not recognizing him, and rejoices in the return of her long-lost son. Siméon enters with some happy villagers, welcomes his son, and bids wine and the fatted calf brought in to celebrate Azaël's return. There is great rejoicing and thanksgiving to God.

Materials: DUR. English translation by Nita Cox. Other Eng translations available by Harold Blumenfeld, Mozelle Clark Sherman from SBTS, Marguerite Fattey, Henry Reese, and David W. Scott. A new reduced orchestration (13 piece chamber orchestra) and English translation by Philip Hagemann is available from Mr. Hagemann (Appendix C): Orchestration: fl, ob, cl, bsn, hrn, trp, trb, timp, strings. First production was held April, 1987, sponsored by the University of Southern Indiana.

Notes: Performable in a house of worship, but best set in a theatre. Sets can be sparse or elaborate.

VICTOR DE LISA

Moses, Prince of Egypt

Music by **Victor De Lisa** (b. 1924). A Sacred Opera with libretto in English by Emilia De Lisa based on the life of Moses as recorded in the Book of Exodus.

Completed in 1976.

Oriental in musical flavor, some dissonance, but nineteenth century in style. Arias, ensembles, set numbers; numerous orchestral interludes or "ballets".

Two acts, eight scenes. Overture. Setting: Egypt in 1250 B.C. Duration: 120 minutes.

Roles: PRINCE MOSES (dram ten – top Bb3); JETHRO (bar – top F#3); PRINCESS BETHIAH (dram sop); MIRIAN (m-sop); AMRAN (bs); JOCHABED (cont); ZIPHORA (sop); MENESET (bs); ARON (bar); TENOR SOLO.

Chorus: SATB.

Dance: Ten orchestral "Ballet" sections, some intended for dance, some for scene shifts.

Orchestration: fl, 2 ob, cl, bsn, 2 hrn, 2 trp, trb, timp, perc, str

Synopsis: The plot traces the life of Moses beginning with the discovery and rescue of Moses as a baby from the Nile by members of Pharaoh's court. Raised in the royal household as Pharaoh's own son, Moses soon becomes an important leader of the land. One day, God calls on Moses, commanding him to lead his people, the Israelites, out of slavery and Egypt and into a land God has reserved for them. Moses hesitatingly obeys. With much discouragement and testing, through Moses, God leads the Israelites through the Red Sea and forty years of wandering in the wilderness before they reach the promised land. Moses dies just short of entering that land, but God first allows him to see it from across the Jordan river.

Materials: AMC and the composer.

Notes: Somewhat of an episodic drama requiring creative staging and set designing. Best suited for theatre performance.

LYUBOMIR DENEV

Cain

Music by **Lyubomir (Lubo) Denev** (b. 1951). An opera-mystery with libretto by Lyubomir Denev based on Lord Byron's mystery play, set in English.

The world premiere was held in Sofia, Bulgaria on June 20, 2005.

Set numbers including arias, duets, recitatives, and ensembles. Shifting meters; atonality throughout. *Senza misura* at times. Some spoken lines and *Sprechstimme* in all parts. Extremely dissonant throughout. Vocal lines very difficult but are occasionally doubled in the orchestra.

Three acts: Act I – In front of Eden's gate – 41 min; Act II – The Abyss of space – 18 min; Act III – The Earth, close to Eden – 34 min. Duration: 93 minutes.

Major Roles: CAIN (dram ten – B1-B3); ADAH (dram sop – top C5), wife of Cain; LUCIFER (bs – E1-Eb3; bar – top G3; m-sop; sop – top Db5) – the role of Lucifer is composed for 4 singers, a group character with 4-octave range and polyphonic possibilities. The bass has by far the most singing.

Minor Roles: ABEL (lyric ten); ZILLAH (lyric sop), wife of Abel; EVE (m-sop – G2-G4); ADAM (bar)

Chorus: SATB – Choir of Phantoms; pre-recorded voices on a CD

Dance: One number would benefit greatly by using dancers.

Orchestration: fl, cl (bs cl), bsn, hrn, trp, trb, 2 perc, synth, str quintet

Synopsis: Adam, Eve, Abel, Adah, and Zillah are offering a sacrifice to God while Cain stands silently nearby, despondent over life as he views it. He doubts the wisdom and justice of the Creator who condemned Adam's offspring to eternal suffering because of the sins of their ancestors. Lucifer enters, addressing Cain and offering him the power of knowledge and to show him other worlds, the realms of death, all on one condition: "That thou dost fall down and worship me thy lord." Cain, seeking another path, decides to go with Lucifer despite his beloved Adah's objections.

Cain and Lucifer fly through the infinity of space and time. Visions appear before Cain's eyes. Unknown worlds, planets, beings, universes pass before him as he enters the Kingdom of Shadows and Phantoms, of times passed and worlds lost. He learns of death and immortality, of eternity and hell's abyss. Insatiable in his desire for knowledge, Cain wants to see Jehovah's and Satan's dwellings; but Lucifer refuses, telling him that in so doing he must pass through the gates of death. Confused and unsatisfied, Cain returns to earth.

Cain and Adah sing over the cradle of their son Enoch. Abel enters, enticing Cain to make a sacrifice together with him to God. Cain begrudgingly agrees, and the two brothers prepare their individual altars. Abel's altar flames with an imposing fire column to the sky, while the altar of Cain is destroyed by a whirlwind. Angered by the obvious rejection of his sacrifice, Cain destroys Abel's altar and in the process fatally wounds his brother. Inconsolable, Cain weeps over his brother's corps. Zillah, Abel's wife, enters, and in complete shock and anger, runs to summon the rest of the family. Eve, deeply angered, realizes that her firstborn son is a murderer. Together with Adam, they curse Cain and expel him from their home. Cain is repentant but not reconciled. Adah, still in love with Cain, shares her husband's fate. Together they retreat to the wilderness.

Materials: Score, parts, CD available from the composer – see Denev in Appendix C for details.

Notes: Best presented in a theatre. Works equally well as a concert or staged piece. All vocal part are extremely difficult melodically and tonally – near perfect pitch for the singers would be needed for complete accuracy. A double CD recording of the world premiere performance is available as a multimedia presentation and contains the full libretto, video-excerpts, photos, and the full piano-reduction vocal score.

PETER DICKINSON

The Judas Tree

Music by **Peter Dickinson** (b. 1934). A Sacred Music Drama with libretto in English by Thomas Blackburn, based on the Biblical character Judas Iscariot. Some Latin.

Premiered May 27, 1965, College of St. Mark and St. John in Chelsea.

Aleatoric with use of mixed idioms: jazz, tone clusters, modal tendencies, simple homophony in choral sections. Some rhythmic speech for chorus. Spoken dialogue.

Three parts. Setting: Part I and II: An undetermined locale; Part III: A Nazi Concentration Camp. See "Notes." Duration: approximately 55 minutes.

Singing Roles: NARRATOR (ten – top G#3); MATTHEW and other soloists (ten II).

Speaking Roles: JUDAS ISCARIOT; PONTIUS PILATE; A DOMINICAN MONK; A NAZI COMMANDANT; SIMON PETER.

Chorus: SATB – commentators. A semi-chorus of four male voices and a bs and sop soloist are all taken from the chorus.

Orchestration: hrn, 2 trp, 2 trb, timp, 3 perc, strings, pia, org.

Synopsis: Judas hanged himself because he could not bear the guilt he had incurred by betraying Jesus. The work opens with Judas lying prone in a state of complete withdrawal. He has no feelings or thoughts because of his fear of facing the reality of the betrayal. Pilate, a detached observer, comments on Judas' situation and suggests that "without contraries there is no progression," and, in his strange way, Judas also furthered the Kingdom of God.

In Part II, in order that Judas may break out of his coma, a priest performs over him those Rites for the Dying by which the church helps her people to be born from time into eternity. If Jesus was the incarnation of the grace of God, perhaps one can think of no more obvious exhibition of the dark side than the Nazi regime. In order to expiate his crime and take his place in the scheme of eternity, Judas must undergo an experience comparable to the crucifixion of his Master.

Materials: NOV.

Notes: Numerous staging and production suggestions in the VS. A timelessness of the lesson to be learned should be built into the overall design. Best suited for church performance.

HUGO DISTLER

Dance of Death

Music by **Hugo Distler** (1908-1942). A Sacred Choral Drama with text translated into English from German. Spoken dialogue based on the *Luebecker Totentanz* by Johannes Kloecking; choral verses from the *Cherubinischen Wandersmann* by Angelus Silesius.

Premiered in 1934. The new English edition (MFM) was premiered on October 19, 1967, at the Grosse Pointe Memorial Church, Detroit, Michigan.

Considerable counterpoint in the voices, lyric style, rhythmic and metric complexities. Mostly modal. Melodically infused with folk elements. Singing is all choral. Spoken dialogue.

One act. No sets required. Duration: 20 minutes.

Roles: All spoken: DEATH; PRESIDENT; BISHOP; DOCTOR; MERCHANT; SOLDIER; SAILOR; JUDGE; FARMER; YOUNG LADY; OLD MAN; CHILD.

Chorus: SATB – Greek Chorus but should be visible within the framework of the action.

Dance: The action should be stylized mime or choreography carried out by the non-singing characters.

Orchestration: A cappella with optional flute solo.

Synopsis: This choral drama evolved from a medieval round dance or morality play. Death confronts living characters inviting each to "dance with him." Each character, the President, Bishop, Doctor, Merchant, Soldier, Sailor, Judge, Farmer, Young Lady, the Old Man and the Child, when confronted by Death, question their own fate and reflect on their life's worth.

Materials: MFM (Malcolm Johns, editor; Eng translation by Brigitte Rauer).

Notes: This work was intended to be performed as part of a worship service. The music is written in a naive and earthy style of folk poetry. Historical and performance notes contained in the VS.

ROBERT DOWNARD

Martin Avdeich: A Christmas Miracle

Music by **Robert Downard** (20th century American). A Christmas Opera with libretto in English by the composer based on the short story, *Where Love Is, God Is Also,* by Tolstoy.

Premiered by Opera Colorado and the Denver Chamber Orchestra, December 15, 1985, in Denver, Colorado.

Tonally conceived but with considerable dissonance. Melodic. Through-composed with some arias and accompanied recitative. Serious drama.

One act, four scenes. A brief orchestral prelude. Setting: The shoe shop and home of Martin Avdeich in a small village not far from Moscow. Also visible is the street above Martin's basement shop. Time: The day before and the day of Russian Orthodox Christmas in late nineteenth century Russia. Sc. 1: Martin's shop the day before Christmas. Sc. 2: That same evening; sc. 3: Christmas morning and the next day; sc. 4: That night. Duration: 60 minutes.

Major Roles: MARTIN AVDEICH (bar), a shoemaker.

Minor Roles: OLGA ALEXANDROVNA POSOKOV (col sop – top D5, high tess with frequent melisma), young daughter of a wealthy merchant;. FYODOR NIKOLAYEVITCH (bs), a religious pilgrim. STEPANUICH (ten), a retired soldier and neighbor to Martin. LARINA SERGHYEEVNA (sop), from Central Asia, mother to a baby boy she carries in her arms; ANFISA (m-sop), an elderly peddler in the village; KOLIA (boy alt), a village boy.

Chorus: TTBB – Pilgrims; SATB – tavern comrades.

Orchestration: fl, ob/Eng hrn, hrn, timp, chimes, wood block, pia, vln I, II, vla, vc, cb.

Synopsis: On the day before Christmas in nineteenth-century Tsarist Russia, Martin Avdeich, an excellent shoemaker, receives a visit from an old friend, Fyodor Nikolayevitch, a religious pilgrim. Martin is still embittered over the loss of all his family several years ago. Fyodor leaves his worn Bible with his friend, urging Martin to seek comfort from its words. Although Martin finds the suggestion of little use, he is nonetheless drawn to the book. He reads that evening and after having fallen asleep, hears a voice telling him to expect a Holy Visitation on Christmas Day.

Martin receives four visitations. A retired soldier living next door is given a cup of tea before he braves sweeping the snow; a wealthy merchant's daughter comes for dancing shoes left the day before; a woman with a baby is given clothes, food, and money to continue her search for her soldier-husband; and an old apple peddler and a boy who would steal her apples are pacified and told to forgive each other.

Christmas Day is done, and Martin grieves he has not received the Holy Visitation. Out of the shadows, all his visitors materialize saying "It is I." They tell Martin to read where the Bible is open and he finds, "Inasmuch as ye have done it unto the least of these my brethren, ye have done it unto me." Martin realizes he has indeed received a Holy Visitation.

Material: TP

Notes: Suitable for opera workshop, school performance, effective in a church setting. Designed for Christmas performance, but lends itself to non-seasonal presentation as well. An alternative text is available from the composer.

THÉODORE (FRANÇOIS CLÉMENT) DUBOIS

Les sept paroles du Christ – The Seven Last Words of Christ

Music by **Théodore (François Clément) Dubois** (1837-1924). A Good Friday Dramatic Cantata with Latin text based on the seven last words of Christ on the cross taken from New Testament Scripture.

Premiered Good Friday, 1867 at Ste. Clotilde, Paris, France.

Late romantic textures with lush harmonies; vocally conceived lines.

Set numbers but continuous action in one section. Duration: 35 minutes.

Major Roles: TENOR, BARITONE, and SOPRANO solos. No character designations. The soloists share characters though in general, the tenor carries the role of narrator (Evangelist), the baritone the role of Christ, and the soprano, the role of Mary or as commentator.

Chorus: SATTBB. The chorus alternates between the role of a Greek chorus, commenting on the action, and the crowd as it witnesses and reacts to the events of Christ's crucifixion.

Orchestration: 2 fl, 2 ob, 2 cl, 2 bsn, 4 hrn, 2 trp, 3 trb, timp, gong, bs dr, hp, org, str

Synopsis: The work opens with a soprano solo calling all to observe the suffering Christ. The seven words then follow, each being elaborated upon with story line and commentary as to the feelings and actions of the people watching the crucifixion.

Materials: GS (Eng translation by Theodore Baker. OD publishes the work with an Eng translation by Isabella Parker.

Notes: Though this work was written for concert performance, it has often been successfully staged.

ZSÓLT DURKÓ

Mózes – Moses

Music by **Zsólt Durkó** (b. 1934). A Sacred Opera with libretto in Hungarian by the composer, based on the life of Moses of the Old Testament and the 19th century play by Madach.

Premiered May 15, 1977, by the Budapest Opera.

Avant-garde, atonal, frequently non-metered, aleatoric. Non-traditional vocal effects, wide vocal leaps, some *sprechstimme*. Motivic.

Three acts. Act I, sc. 1: Israel's bondage in Egypt – a square in front of Pharaoh's palace; sc. 2: The burning bush in the wilderness; sc. 3: Crossing the Red Sea. Act II, sc. 1: The Ten Commandments given in the wilderness; sc. 2: The Golden Calf. Act III, sc. 1: The thunderbolt; sc. 2: Joshua's departure to Canaan; sc. 3: The death of Moses. Duration: 130 minutes.

Roles: All roles vocally difficult. MOSES (ten – top B3), demands great vocal strength; ANYA (sop – top Bb4), Moses' mother; ABIRAM (bar – top G3); AARON (bs-bar – low Ab1), high priest; JOSHUA (ten); MIRIAM (sop – top B4); HUR (ten – top Bb3); VOICE OF THE LORD (electronically amplified).

Chorus: SSAATTBB – Children of Israel. Considerable divisi.

Dance: A choreographed dance (at times erotic) around the Golden Calf which should include the entire cast.

Orchestration: 2 picc, 4 fl, 2 ob, 2 Eng hrn, 4 cl, 3 sax (bar opt), 3 bsn, contra bsn, 6 hrn, 3 trp, 4 trb, tba, 7 perc, 2 cel, 2 hp, strings, 2 pia, org.

Synopsis: The work opens with a passionate confession by the mother of Moses. She is guarding a secret: her son, a brilliant leader in Pharaoh's empire, does not know that she is his mother and that he is about to attack his own people, Israel. At last she reveals her secret to Moses and that he is the brother of Aaron and from the blood line of Israel.

Moses goes to the wilderness and there encounters God, manifest in a burning bush. He is commissioned by God to lead Israel out of Egyptian slavery into Canaan. Moses obeys and leads Israel through the Red Sea which opens before their feet, just as the Lord had promised. Forty days later, the people are tired and discouraged. Moses prays in anguish to the Lord in behalf of his distressed people. Meanwhile, the people of Aaron, Abiram and Hur fight over the distribution of goods. The Ten Commandments are given by God to Moses. However, the people grow deranged and bitter, finally erecting a Golden Calf to worship. At the culmination of passion, the people drum an ecstatic rhythm, bursting with uncontrollable emotion and frenzy. Angered beyond control, Moses hurls the stone tablets down from the mountain side, knocking down the Golden Calf and banishing Aaron and Hur.

Forty years later we see Israel, a nation at the end of its tether. Moses turns to Joshua, ceremoniously handing to him the responsibility of leadership. Moses is left alone, musing on his past life. The orchestra sounds a farewell to this far-seeing, God-fearing prophet.

Materials: BH.

Notes: Enormous musical and technical demands, requiring highly professional resources to produce. Joan Chissell of the London *Times*, found the score "sanely exploratory and very thoroughly composed rather than a bag of theatrical tricks." Stephen Walsh of *Tempo* noted that Durkó is "remarkably successful in this marrying of subject [melodrama] and treatment" – music of "adequate scale and range – without falling into empty musico-dramatic tub-thumping."

LINDA EKMON and ELIZABETH FYFFE

The Nativity: A Mystery Play

Music by **Linda Ekmon** and **Elizabeth Fyffe** (20th century Americans). A Christmas Music Drama set after the medieval mystery plays. Text translated and adapted from old French carols by the composers.

Premiered Christmas, 1921 in West Newton, Massachusetts.

Medieval flavor, simple accompaniment, archaic in style. Homophonic and hymn-like throughout. Narration is from the King James version of the Bible.

Three acts. Act I: In the city of Bethlehem; Act II: In a field outside Bethlehem; Act III: At the stable. Duration: 60 minutes.

Roles: MARY (sop); JOSEPH (bar); NARRATOR (non-singing); ANGEL (sop); SHEPHERDS (medium range); THREE KINGS (bs, bar, bar).

Chorus: SATB

Orchestration: pia or org, string quartet or section (opt), no cb.

Synopsis: Mary and Joseph arrive in Bethlehem, finally resorting to settling in a stable since all the doors of the inn are closed to strangers. The scene shifts to the fields where the shepherds are told by heavenly angels to go to Bethlehem to find the Savior in the form of a baby. The third and final act occurs at the stable where the entire cast joins in praises to God for the newborn Christ Child.

Material: OD.

Notes: A very simple production with flexible staging and minimal sets and props. The VS contains numerous staging and production suggestions. Best performed in the Chancel of a church.

PETER EKSTROM

The Gift of the Magi

Music by **Peter Ekstrom** (b. 1951). A Music Theatre work with libretto by the composer based on the O. Henry play of the same title.

Commissioned by Actors Theatre, Louisville, KY, and premiered there December, 1981.

In a "pop" musical style, but with some musical sophistication.

One act, two scenes. Setting: Both scenes in Jim and Della's one-room apartment, New York City, on Christmas Eve, 1905. Duration: 30 minutes.

Roles: JIM (bar); DELLA (m-sop).

Orchestration: Piano only.

Synopsis: Jim and Della playfully role out of bed on Christmas Eve morning. After teasing each other about their poverty and lack of funds to buy each other Christmas presents this year, Jim leaves for work. Della, after counting her few pennies, decides to sell her hair to Madame Sofronia, whose ad she has seen. Later that afternoon, she returns home with a gold chain for Jim's treasured gold watch. When she hears Jim return from work, she quickly tries to conceal her short hair. Jim immediately notices her hair and just stares at her in amazement. He gives her his present with apologies since the gift of real bone combs for her beautiful long hair is now useless. Della gives Jim his gift which is likewise useless since Jim purchased the combs by selling his gold watch. They laugh over the coincidence and realize that what they have in each other's love is far greater than material gifts.

Materials: SF

Notes: Adaptable to church, but best performed in a theatre.

MYRON S. FINK

Jeremiah

Music by **Myron S. Fink** (b. 1932). A Religious Opera with libretto in English by Earlene Hamel Hawley.

Premiered May 25, 1962, in Binghamton, New York.

Conventional harmonic structures with twentieth century idioms, dissonances and chromaticism. Vocally conceived with predominant lyricism in the melodic lines. Recitative. Through-composed; some set numbers. Tragedy.

Four acts, six scenes. Act I, sc. 1 and 2: Inside the Stephens home. Act II: Inside a hotel and a street corner in a nearby town. Act III: The Stephens home. Act IV, sc. 1 and 2: Inside a church. Duration: 2 hours, 25 minutes.

Major Roles: JEREMIAH STEPHENS (bar – B1-G3, high tess, considerable dramatic intensity required; SAMUEL STEPHENS (ten – D2-C4, opt Bb3), lyric singing; REBECCA STEPHENS (spinto sop – D2-C5), requires considerable vocal power and dramatic ability; DEBORAH CARTER (m-sop – G#2-G#4), a school teacher who boards with the Stephens.

Minor Roles: SARAH (m-sop), a neighbor who appears only in Act I; AMOS (bs), appears only in Act IV; NAOMI (sop), a neighbor who appears only in Act I; A YOUNG WOMAN, TWO YOUNG MEN taken from the chorus in Act II; TWO MEN; A WOMAN.

Chorus: SATB – the church congregation, courting couples, townspeople.

Dance: Act II requires waltzing, round dancing, and square dancing.

Orchestration: 2 fl (picc), 2 ob, 2 cl, 2 bsn, 3 hrn, 2 trp, 3 trb, tba, 3 timp, cym, xyl (opt), hp, str

Synopsis: The opera opens with a troublesome quarrel between Jeremiah Stephens and his wife Rebecca. Distressed, Jeremiah, who is also a religious fanatic, goes to their boarder, Deborah Carter, for consolation and sympathy. Deborah and Samuel, Jeremiah's son, are in love, and when Samuel takes her to a nearby town, they are discovered by Jeremiah who emphatically denounces them. Rebecca, of course, tries to convince Samuel and Deborah to leave together. At one juncture, they study and discuss parts of the Song of Solomon, and fall into a frenzy of passion. Later, Deborah confesses her sin to the congregation but does not go so far as to reveal the name of her lover. Samuel is accused by the congregation who in turn suggests that it is his father who should be accused. Jeremiah accepts the accusation but will not accept their judgment. He prays to God for guidance and opens his Bible to the story of Isaac's sacrifice. Jeremiah, accepting this coincidence as his answer, strangles his son in defiance and victory.

Materials: From the composer.

Notes: Dramatically and vocally, a difficult opera to produce. Best set in a theatre or large auditorium.

Judith and Holofernes

Music by **Myron S. Fink** (b. 1932). A Sacred Opera with libretto in English by the composer, loosely based on the Apocryphal Book of Judith.

Composed in 1969.

Traditional harmonic structures with chromatic tonality; dissonance.

Three acts, four scenes. Setting: Israel around 600 B.C. Duration: 2 hours, 30 minutes.

Roles: JUDITH (sop); HOLOFERNES (dr bar), Babylonian General; BOGOAS (ten), his slave; BERIAH (m-sop), Judith's maid. Small Tenor, Baritone, Bass parts may be taken by chorus personnel.

Chorus: SATB – Amorites.

Dance: Eight to ten male dancers in Act II.

Orchestration: 2 fl, 2 ob, 2 cl, 2 bsn, 4 hrn, 2 trp, 3 trb, tba, timp, 2 perc, hp, strings. Offstage: 3 hrn, 3 trp, 3 trb.

Synopsis: Holofernes, General of the Babylonian army besieging Bethulia in Israel, is sorely troubled by a recurring nightmare in which a strange melody accompanies his death. He forces his slave, Bogoas, to swear to help him control his own destiny. Bogoas tells Holofernes that a woman, Judith, has come from the besieged city with an offer of help from the Israelite God. Holofernes agrees to meet her and, impressed by her courage, gives her a place in the camp and orders a feast. Judith and her maid, Beriah, plan their murder of Holofernes. Beriah sees that Judith is more interested in Holofernes and in her own fame than in doing God's will. Although Judith vows to kill Holofernes at the banquet, she is overwhelmed by his presentation of himself as commander and ruler. She sings for him and her song is that of his dream. He invites her to kill him with his own instrument. She cannot, and their mutual attraction overcomes them.

The next morning, Holofernes, angered by his weakness, is determined to use Judith to help him end a life which is odious to him. Over her protests, he gives her to Bogoas to abuse and torment. He swears he will not be a victim, but the author of his own fate. When Judith is brought back, she finds that she must kill him, but whether for hate or for pity, she cannot tell. The opera ends as she makes her choice.

Materials: AMC and from the composer.

Notes: Best performed in a theatre.

JOHN FRANCESCHINA

The Lord's A Wonder

Music by **John Franceschina** (b. 1947). A Musical Play adapted from the medieval morality and mystery plays with text and translation by the composer.

Premiered at the 41st International Eucharistic Congress in 1976, in Philadelphia.

The work is divided into four sections intended to be performed without an intermission. Duration: 85 minutes.

Roles: NARRATOR, MANKIND (male narrator who also sings); NOAH'S WIFE, FLESH, requires excellent acting; NOAH, WORLD, requires a good comic style; CHERUBIM, GOOD ANGEL; EVE; ABEL; ADAM; LUCIFER, CAIN, DEVIL.

Chorus: Entire cast.

Orchestration: The following orchestrations are available: 1. piano alone, 2. Pia, gui, cb, perc. 3. Woodwind I (fl/picc, cl), woodwind II (fl, cl, bs cl), pia, cb, strings, perc.

Dance: Stylized movement requires some choreography.

Synopsis: This work is a musical adaptation of plays from the medieval world, pageant drama that expressed the faith of a Christian people, firmly rooted in a joyful dependence upon God's mercy and love. The first three pieces are new translations of the *Wakefield Mystery Plays*: "The Creation," "The Killing of Abel," and "Noah," to which have been added music, lyrics and pantomime to enhance the spirit of the original. The final piece, *The Play of Mankind*, is an assimilation of three medieval plays, "Mankind," "Everyman," and "The Castle of Perseverance," in which the Old Testament conflict between good and evil is portrayed in universal terms.

As would be indicated by the plays upon which this work is based, the story line follows the titles of the four plays: the story of creation, the murder of Abel, and Noah and his family during the flood. The final section portrays in universal terms the Old Testament conflict between good and evil. Arthur Jones in the *National Catholic Reporter* (Oct. 23, 1981) summarized it this way: "The impact comes from two types of continuity: the dramatic continuity of professional choreography and direction, and the continuity of the story line: the continuing moral. From Lucifer's fall, to Cain's guilt, to Noah's faith, to mankind's temptation, the Old Testament is brought, alive and relevant, down to today."

Materials: VS for sale; parts on hire. From the composer.

Notes: Best performed in a theatre.

To the Ends of the Earth

Music by **John Franceschina** (b. 1947). A Sacred Music Drama (more a revue than a play) with libretto in English by the composer adapted from letters written over the past two hundred years.

Commissioned by the Paul VI Institute for the Arts in Washington, D.C. Not yet performed.

Traditional harmonies with some "pop" tendencies. Contrapuntal at times; uses ballad and hymn tunes appropriate to the historical setting. Considerable spoken dialogue.

One act. The stage should be an open space with a raked cruciform platform extending diagonally from up right to down left. Duration: approximately 80 minutes, though this could change as the score reaches its final form.

Roles: All roles are mid-range except Actress Three and Four which should be sung by sopranos. EVERYMAN (bar); ACTOR ONE (Andrew White, S.J., Fr. Junipero Serra's Father, Civil War Officer, Bishop Machebeuf, Polish Immigrant, Fr. Abbelen); ACTOR TWO (Isaac Jogues, Bishop Flaget, Plasterer, Irish Immigrant, Isaac Hecker, Fr. Peter Vay); ACTOR THREE (Fr. Junipero Serra, Papal Legate, Civil War Soldier, Chief Two Bears, Moulder, Bishop Tobias Mullen); ACTOR FOUR (Rev. Joseph Mosley, Maj. General David Stanley, Bishop John Lancaster Spalding, Italian Immigrant); ACTOR FIVE (Thomas Jefferson, Fr. Peter Cooney, Polish Immigrant, Hungarian Worker); ACTRESS ONE (sop) (Fr. Junipero Serra's Mother, Sister Blandina, Bohemian Immigrant, Mother Cabrini); ACTRESS TWO (Sister Eulalia, Italian Immigrant, Dorothy Day); ACTRESS THREE (Mother Clare Joseph of the Sacred Heart, Dona Junita Simpson, Irish Washerwoman); ACTRESS FOUR (Elizabeth Seton, Secretary of St. Vincent de Paul Society, Mother Katharine Drexel).

Chorus: SATB – a Greek chorus.

Orchestration: Not yet orchestrated.

Synopsis: The work consists of a compilation of letters written over the past two hundred years tracing the development of the Catholic religion in the United States. The letters are at times sung by their authors, at times by Everyman and at times by the chorus.

Materials: Unpublished. From the composer.

Notes: May be performed in a church or theatre.

DON FREUND

Passion With Tropes

Music by **Don Freund** (b. 1947). A Dramatic Oratorio with texts taken from the Evangelists and 40 other poets, philosophers, and playwrights.

Premiered in 1984, written in 1983.

Musical language cannot be categorized but follows the eclectic direction dictated by the use of so many different text authors. 72 set numbers. Duration: 2 hours, 30 minutes.

Roles: Two SATB quartets and a group of "Pop" singers.

Chorus: SATB

Orchestration: picc, 2 fl, ob, 2 cl, bs cl, sax, bsn, 3 hrn, 2 trp, 2 trb, tba, 2 perc, pia, strings. Woodwind quintet. Brass quintet. Gui, string quintet. Solo perc. Jazz ensemble: 2 sax, 2 trp, 2 trb, elec pia, elec bs, elec gui, dr.

Dance: Contemporary choreography is suitable in several places.

Synopsis: According to the composer, *Passion With Tropes* is a collage of various music, theatre, and music-theatre experiences, using a collage of texts about the Passion, religion, love, death, and the experience of human existence. It may be described as a theatre work about the experience of attending a performance of an oratorio (or, more specifically, a Passion). But the medium of the oratorio is supplemented or challenged by the invasion of other musical and dramatic media (chamber songs, pop songs, excerpts from plays, poetry recitation, philosophical declarations, sermons, processions, etc.) just as the telling of the Passion story is convoluted, supplemented, and challenged by a text collage using the writings of over 40 writers.

Materials: Unpublished. From the composer.

Notes: Best performed in a theatre.

CHARLES HUTCHINSON GABRIEL

Saul, King of Israel

Music by **Charles Hutchinson Gabriel** (1856-1932). A Dramatic Cantata with libretto in English by Willis B. Perkins.

Written ca. 1901.

Five acts, 8 scenes.

Roles: SOPRANO, ALTO, TENOR, BASS (designated characters)

Chorus: SATB

Orchestration: Full orchestra

Materials: Published by Fillmore Bros., Chicago. Score in LC, No. 8779490.

Notes: Though referred to as a cantata, this work is clearly intended to be staged since the score contains specific stage directions.

PAOLA GALLICO

The Apocalypse

Music by **Paola Gallico** (1868-1955). A Dramatic Oratorio with text in English selected and arranged from the Book of Daniel and the *Apocalypse* by Pauline Arhoux MacArthur and Henri Pierre Roche. The libretto was published in 1919.

Written in 1920. Premiered in New York November 22, 1922. The composition won a $5,000 prize from National Federation of Music Clubs in 1921.

Post-Romantic harmonies with a leaning toward twentieth century chromaticism. Not vocally conceived. Voices in both solo and choral writing are faced with difficult and at times non-vocal melodic lines.

Three sections and a Prologue: Belshazzar's Feast, Armageddon, Babylon, and the Millennium. Duration: 90 minutes.

Roles: NARRATOR (bs); A MAN (ten), needs strong low range; A SPECTRE (cont); SPIRIT OF DRUNKENNESS (bar); SPIRIT OF GLUTTONY (bs – low Fl); A VOICE (sop); SPIRIT OF IDOLATRY (cont); SPIRIT OF WAR (bar – many high F3); ANOTHER VOICE (cont); BABYLON (sop).

Chorus: SATB, TTBB, SSAA (double SATB choirs at times). A 4-part boy choir is called for but may be sung by women's voices.

Orchestration: Full orchestra

Dance: A dance of concubines and slaves in the Prologue.

Synopsis: The plot deals primarily with Biblical prophecy, foretelling future events as found in the stories of Belshazzar, Armageddon, Babylon and the Millennium. In the prologue, Belshazzar's Feast, we find the Babylonian Empire at the height of its sensuality and irreligion. The Narration sets the stage while Drunkenness,

Gluttony and Idolatry are made impersonations. Dining and dancing pervade until the handwriting on the wall halts everyone's activity. Part I, Armageddon, describes what war has been from the time of Cain and Abel. Then the seven vials are poured out, the sixth being poured out to gather all armies together before that great day of God Almighty. Part II, Babylon, is personified and described as the woman lacking in the maternal and creative instinct. She knows she has lost her hold over the souls of men. Nearly the entire section is sung by Babylon. The Millennium describes the beauty and glory of heaven when all believers will be there.

Materials: GS (© 1922).

Notes: While most of this work contains material worthy of dramatic treatment, several sections, the last two in particular, will require creative and innovative stage directing and perhaps choreography. Best performed in a theatre or large auditorium.

JOHN GARDNER

Bel and the Dragon

Music by **John Gardner** (b. 1917). A Children's Opera performed primarily by adults. Libretto in English by Timothy Kraemer based on the encounter between Daniel and Cyrus, King of Persia, from Scripture. The words in the final hymn are an adaptation of Psalm 115.

Premiered in December, 1973, in St. James' Norlands Church, London.

Conventional harmonies. Lyric and vocally conceived. Composed with children in mind.

One act, thirteen episodes. Setting: In the Winter Residence of Cyrus, King of Persia in Babylon during Old Testament times. Duration: 60 minutes.

Major Roles: CYRUS (sop or ten), King of Persia; DANIEL (m-sop or bar).

Minor Roles: COOK (cont); HABACCUS (sop or ten); CHIEF PRIEST (sp); ANGEL (sp).

Chorus: The DRAGON is acted by as many children as are available (non-singing). The SEMI-CHORUS is a story-telling, non-acting group. The CHORUS is an acting group of priests, their families and soldiers. The semi-chorus may sing with the chorus for added strength. Both chorus and semi-chorus may be SATB or SA in which case the tenor and bass lines are cut.

Dance: Not necessary though the Dragon would benefit from choreography.

Orchestration: fl, cl, hrn, trp, 3 perc, strings (4.2.2.1). Also available: pia duet, org, 3 perc (timp, glock, xyl, vib, cym, sus cym, gong, tri, tamb, sd dr, ten dr, bs dr), strings as above.

Synopsis: Cyrus, King of Persia, is entertaining the prophet Daniel at his Babylon Winter Residence. Episodes included in the drama include a confrontation between Daniel and the pagan god Bel, the destruction of Bel, the appearance of the Dragon, Daniel in the lion's den, the reactions of the citizens, a processional, all concluding with the audience participating in the final hymn taken from Psalm 115.

Materials: OUP. Chorus parts and audience part for final hymn are on sale.

Notes: The VS contains staging and production suggestions. Best produced in a house of worship.

DON GILLIS

The Gift of the Magi

Music by **Don Gillis** (1912-1978). A Christmas Drama/Opera with libretto in English by the composer, based on a story by O. Henry.

Harmonically traditional with some contemporary sounds; at times simple, no extreme ranges. Appealing to all ages, teens and up.

One act, five scenes. Sc. 1: The manger scene; Sc. 2: New York City apartment in 1905, Christmas Eve; Sc. 3: Jim's office; Sc. 4: Same as 2; Sc. 5: Same as I. Duration: 42 minutes.

Major Roles: STORYTELLER (male or female medium range – sings and speaks), commentary continues throughout the work; JIM (lyric bar or low ten); DELLA (sop), his wife.

Minor Roles: All spoken ad lib: SANTA, FLOWER LADY, NEWSBOY.

Chorus: SATB – Carol Singers; Nativity Players are in tableau during the first and last scenes (silent parts).

Orchestration: Two pianos OR piano and organ OR chamber orchestra OR wind ensemble.

Synopsis: The Storyteller introduces us to the nativity scene and the story of the gift of the Magi. Scene 2 shifts into a contemporary apartment where Jim and Della are involved in a struggle to make ends meet. First, we see Della, counting her pennies and finding she hasn't enough to buy Jim the watch chain for his beautiful old watch. She wishes on a star and immediately comes up with an idea. Next we find Jim in his office bemoaning his inability to afford the combs for Della's beautiful long brown hair. At last he too, comes up with an idea. They return home. Jim opens his gift and finds his watch chain and when questioned how she could have bought it, she reveals that she has sold her hair. When she opens her gift of the combs, she understands his dismay and finds that he has sold his watch to pay for the combs. As the setting shifts to the nativity scene, the Storyteller draws the moral that these gifts were much like God's gift to man, given out of selfless love.

Materials: CRES (© 1964).

Notes: No sets necessary, only simple props and furniture. The Storyteller verbally creates each scene. Imaginative lighting design is necessary. Best produced in a house of worship. A work easily performed by the average church choir program.

The Nazarene

Music by **Don Gillis** (1912-1978). A Easter Music Drama with libretto in English by the composer, loosely based on the resurrection of Jesus.

Premiered in 1970, Dallas Baptist College, Texas.

Tonal, quite chromatic, no key signatures, frequent meter changes. Declamatory vocal lines with large skips over traditional harmony. Some short arias but mostly ensemble and choral music. Spoken dialogue.

One act. Setting: The courtyard of the public house named "The Sign of the Skull," which stands just outside the walls of Jerusalem on the road to Golgotha; the morning of the resurrection of Jesus. Duration: 55 minutes.

Major Roles: EZRA (ten), a crippled beggar, 40ish; JOANNA (sop – top C5), daughter of Amos, mid 20s.

Minor Roles: REBECCA (cont), teenage sister of Joanna; AMOS (bs), owner of the public house, 50ish; MARY MAGDALENE (sop), a friend of Jesus; THE VOICE OF JESUS, spoken offstage.

Chorus: SATB – Nazarene mourners, offstage, unseen if possible. Considerable chorus throughout.

Orchestration: Keyboard or chamber orchestra.

Synopsis: In the courtyard of the public house, a cripple named Ezra and Amos' daughter Joanna, comment on the racket being made by the wailing of a group of Nazarenes next door whose master has been crucified. They talk of all the events of this spectacular execution including Jesus' torture at the hands of Roman soldiers which she, Joanna, and her sister Rebecca witnessed. Ezra begins to tell of the time in Bethlehem when he was only a child and a baby was born, when he is interrupted by Rebecca, who berates the Nazarenes for all their noise. Amos follows and, relating his experience at the crucifixion, gloats over his purchase of Jesus' robe from the soldiers. Mary Magdalene appears, half delirious with joy, babbling about how Jesus has risen from the dead. Amos calms her while Rebecca goes with her to tell the mourners the good news. Ezra then relates the story of how he knew Jesus in Bethlehem. One day he heard that Roman soldiers were coming to kill all the small boys, so he ran to tell Mary and Joseph who had already fled. The soldiers caught him there, beat him and slashed his legs so badly that he could never walk again. Joanna believes and goes off to be with the Nazarenes. Left alone, Ezra prays, hears Jesus' voice and is healed. He rises to join the group in following the risen Jesus.

Materials: BP (© 1970). Orchestra parts available on rental from DBC.

Notes: Suitable in either a church sanctuary or auditorium/theatre.

ALEXANDER GOEHR

Naboth's Vineyard

Music by **Alexander Goehr** (b. 1932). A Dramatic Madrigal with libretto in Latin and English by the composer, loosely based on I Kings 21 from the Old Testament. First in a "Triptych." The other two, *Shadowplay* and *3 Sonatas about Jerusalem*, are primarily secular in nature.

Premiered July 16, 1968 in London; commissioned by the City Arts Trust for the 1968 City of London Festival.

Contemporary idioms, avant-garde with difficult vocal lines containing large leaps and disjunct melodic structures. Humorous.

One act. Setting: King Ahab's palace. Duration: 25 minutes.

Roles: Three soloists (bs, cont, ten) sing offstage or to the side of the stage while three actors mime the parts of KING AHAB, QUEEN JEZEBEL, and the PRINCE.

Dance: The pantomime of the three actors must be stylized.

Orchestration: fl (alt fl, picc), cl (bs cl), trb, vln, cb, pia (4 hands).

Synopsis: King Ahab is weeping because he cannot buy Naboth's Vineyard. He refuses to eat any food placed in front of him. Jezebel schemes to get the vineyard for him and eventually accomplishes the task by lying. The Prince is a party to the deception. In the end, Ahab is forgiven by God, but the Prince and Jezebel both remain hardened in their sin.

Materials: SCH.

Notes: Musically, a difficult score. Best performed in a house of worship.

NOËL GOEMANNE

The Walk

Music by **Noël Goemanne** (b. 1926). A Dramatic Choral work with texts taken from Scripture, Liturgy of the Roman Mass, Zen teachings, Richard Wagner's *The Creative Force*, Dhammapada, Stephen Crane's *War is Kind*, and original texts by the composer. Texts are in Latin and English, while the speech choirs and narrators may use any other languages such as German, Spanish, etc. The texts are arranged to reflect on the Stations of the Cross as a guide to our walk in real life.

First performed in concert version, May 12, 1978; first staged performance (multi-media) March 30, 1980 at St. Andrew's Roman Catholic Church in Fort Worth, TX.

Highly aleatoric music, incorporating many musical idioms and styles. "Program Notes" of a performance on February 20, 1983, state: "The eclectic approach to this work utilizes all styles of music from ancient chants, through the choral style, to the more sophisticated style of superimposing free rhythms and metered rhythms, and is indeed very symbolic of the way we must walk through this anxious and confused second half of the twentieth century, much the same way Christ walked His Stations of the Cross some 2,000 year ago."

Six sections. Duration: 45 minutes.

Roles: NARRATOR (sp); BARITONE SOLO, most often representing Jesus; SOPRANO SOLO, most often representing the people of the world. Several other solos taken from the chorus.

Chorus: SATB – children's choirs, speech chorus, narrators.

Orchestration: org, pia, sn dr, timp, with optional gui, hp, 2 trp, (additional perc may be used).

Dance: Some stylized choreography.

Synopsis: The work moves through the Stations of the Cross, symbolic of the human daily walk. The main theme is to love one another as Christ loved us. We are to follow Christ's example by forgiving rather than crucifying one another with criticisms, prejudice, and rash judgments. The events occur through dance, pantomime, projections, etc., a truly multi-media production. The choruses comment on the activity, remaining in a stationary location.

Materials: MFM (© 1978).

Notes: A demonstration tape was made at the first performance by Arkansas Tech Un. in Russelville, Arkansas. According to the composer, the score serves only as a guide. Director and performers are encouraged to recreate this work as they conceive it. Some production notes are in the VS. No sets necessary. Should be performed in a church.

EDWARD M. GOLDMAN

David

Music by **Edward M. Goldman** (b. 1917). A Sacred Opera with libretto in English by the composer, based on the life of David as recorded in I, II Samuel and I Kings.

Completed in 1967.

Simple and conventional textures. Emphasis on melody. Continuous texture.

Three acts, thirteen scenes. Can be staged with one large unit set. Act I, sc. 1: The mountains; sc. 2: The King's palace; sc. 3: The hills of Judah; sc. 4: Outside the King's palace. Act II, sc. 1: The roof of the King's palace; sc. 2: Bath-sheba's home; sc. 3: King's palace; sc. 4: The gate of Jerusalem; sc. 5: The wilderness; sc. 6: The palace; sc. 7: The woods. Act III, sc. 1: The palace; sc. 2: Outside the palace; sc. 3: The palace. Duration: 75 minutes.

Singing Roles: GOLIATH (bs – low Fl); JESSE (bs-bar), father of David; DAVID (ten – top Bb3); SAUL (bar – top G3), King of Israel; JONATHAN (ten – C2-A3), his son; ABIATHAR (boy sop – E3-G4), son of Ahimelech; VOICE OF GOD and A MESSENGER (bar – top F#3); ABISHAI (bs); BATH-SHEBA (sop); NATHAN (bs

– F#1-Eb3); ABSALOM (bar – top F3); HASHAI (bar – top F3); JOAB (bs); CUSHI (bs-bar); ADONIJAH (ten).

Non-singing Roles: MICHAL, Saul's daughter; SAUL'S ARMOR-BEARER; ABISSHAG, David's attendant; ZADOK, the priest; SOLOMON.

Chorus: SATB.

Dance: Two handmaidens dance sensuously around Bath-sheba.

Orchestration: Pia or org.

Synopsis: David, a shepherd boy, kills Goliath, leader of the Philistines and enemy of Israel. Saul, King of Israel, becomes jealous of David's military renown and plots to have him killed – but Jonathan, Saul's son, warns David and escapes to the hills of Judah. There he leads a band of 400 discontented men against the marauding Philistines. David soon realizes that Saul is following him. He joins himself and his band to Achish, King of Gath, a Philistine. When the Philistines fight against Israel however, David and his men are not allowed in the battle. Jonathan and his brothers are slain, Saul is wounded and commits suicide, and David is anointed King over Israel.

David, having impregnated Bath-sheba, wife of Uriah, has Uriah killed in battle. Nathan, a prophet of God, foretells the rising of evil against David from David's own children. David repents, Bath-sheba's child dies; but two more sons are born, Solomon and Absalom. Fulfilling Nathan's prophecy, Absalom plots to kill David but is himself slain in battle.

In act III, David is old and near death. He chooses Abischeg, a virgin, to minister to his needs. Adonijah, son of Haggith and David, aspires to the throne, but Zadok, the priest, anoints Solomon King of Israel. David dies.

Materials: AMC and the composer. Originally published by Independent Music Pub.

Notes: Best suited to performance in a theatre facility.

WILLIAM ARTHUR GOLDSWORTHY

The Judgment of Sheba

Music by **William Arthur Goldsworthy** (1878-1966). Sacred Operetta with libretto in English by the composer, loosely based on I Kings 3:16-38 from Scripture. For all-female cast.

Highly melodic, conventional harmonies, some set numbers but continuous action. Accompanied recitative. Musically, not difficult.

One act. Setting: Biblical times, a throne room in the palace of Solomon. Duration: 30 minutes.

Major Roles: All voices are in medium range. QUEEN OF SHEBA (Dram sop), small range; MOTHER OF CHILD (sop); FALSE MOTHER (alt).

Minor Roles: LADY OF JUSTICE (alt); FIRST HERALD (sop); SECOND HERALD (sop); SLAVE (m-sop); EXECUTIONER (silent).

Chorus: SSAA – ladies of the Queen's court. The Queen's retinue may be added as non-singing characters. Considerable choral singing throughout.

Dance: Courtly dancing by the ladies of the court. A solo dance may be interpolated after the entrance of the Queen.

Orchestration: Keyboard.

Synopsis: The curtain opens to the ladies of the court singing and dancing a song of joy. The First Herald announces Solomon's decree that all cases involving women shall be tried by the ladies of the court, presided over by the Queen of Sheba. The Second Herald announces the Queen's approach, accompanied by her retinue. A song of praise is sung to her and a dance is given in her honor. She announces her desire to see justice done to all and calls for the first case. The Lady of Justice ushers in the two claimants of the child and the trial begins, culminating in the Queen's decision that the child's body shall be divided between the two claimants and the real Mother's relinquishing of her claim in order to save the child's life. The Queen stops the sword, then asks the False Mother to explain her lie. She gives as her excuse the fact that her own child had died, and since her husband loved it dearly and she was afraid to tell him of its death, she stole her neighbor's child in its place. She begs to be forgiven which the Queen grants and all join in a song of rejoicing.

Materials: CF (© 1935).

Notes: Suggestions on staging, stage set, properties, and costumes are included in the VS. Simple stage set and properties. Can be staged in either a house of worship or theatre.

EUGENE GOOSSENS

Judith

Music by **Eugene Goossens** (1893-1962). A Sacred Opera with libretto in English by Arnold Bennett, based on the Apocryphal Book of Judith.

Composed in 1927. First performed on June 25, 1929, Covent Garden, London.

Highly chromatic, tonal; Puccini-like in texture.

One act. Setting: In the camp of Holofernes toward evening. Duration: 63 minutes.

Roles: JUDITH (sop – top C5); HAGGITH (m-sop), her maid; HOLOFERNES (bs-bar – top G3), Assyrian commander; BOGOAS (ten – top A3), his chief eunuch; ANCHIOR (bar – top G3), an Ammonite.

Supers: Servants, Slaves, Soldiers, Heralds of Holofernes.

Dance: A dancing woman at Holofernes' feast.

Orchestration: Full orchestra. On-stage trumpets.

Synopsis: Judith and Haggith have entered the camp of Holofernes. Bogoas interrogates them and commands Haggith to be bound and taken away. Suspicious of Judith but intrigued by her beauty, he calls for Holofernes as Judith has requested. Holofernes is overcome by Judith's directness and beauty and orders everyone to leave him alone with her. Bogoas warns him against such action, but he insists that Judith will sleep with him tonight. Wine and food is ordered by Holofernes during which time Judith hides her knife beneath the bed. Holofernes orders dancers to entertain them. Meanwhile, Judith continues to fill and refill his wine glass while she herself refrains. The dancers are ordered to leave. The two fall onto the bed. With Holofernes now quite drunk and nearly asleep, Judith seizes the knife and kills him. She orders Haggith to place the decapitated head in her bag and they leave quickly as the curtain falls.

Materials: CHES

Notes: Best performed in a theatre facility.

FRANÇOIS-JOSEPH GOSSEC

La Nativité – The Nativity

Music by **François-Joseph Gossec** (1734-1829 - Belgium). A Christmas Dramatic Oratorio with text in French by M.P.G. de Chabanon, based on the events leading up to the birth of Christ.

First performed December 24, 1774, Paris.

Seven set numbers, accompanied recitatives, *stile galant* style. Traditional harmony. Melodic; predominantly choral.

One act. Setting: On a hillside at the time of Christ's birth. Duration: 35 minutes.

Roles: SHEPHERD (alt or ten), some coloratura passages; SHEPHERDESS (sop – top B4), melisma; A VOICE (ten), narrator and an angel; ONE MAGI (bar – top F#3).

Chorus: SATB – Shepherds. SSAT – angels.

Orchestration: 2 fl, 2 ob, 2 cl, 2 bsn, 4 hrn, timp, strings.

Synopsis: Late in the day the shepherds prepare for the night. As they sleep, restlessness pervades the camp. Timpani beats and flurries of flute scale passages tell us that something is about to occur. Even the narrator appears upset. Fear spreads to the shepherds as the atmosphere of uneasiness increases until finally they give way to a prayer for mercy. An angel consoles them and informs them that "a Saviour King is born." The "March of the Shepherds" follows as they go to Bethlehem to worship the Child. In the final number, the on and off-stage choirs join in celebration of Christ's birth.

Materials: ABI (© 1966 by Tetra Music Corp).

Notes: Ideally suited for church performance, especially if the off-stage choir can be easily concealed. English translation by Phyllis Mead. Though conceived as a concert piece, the theatrical quality lends itself to stage treatment. The premiere included some staging.

JACK GOTTLIEB

Sharing the Prophets: A Musical Encounter For Singers

Music by **Jack Gottlieb** (b. 1930). A Dramatic Cantata with text in English by the composer.

Written for the American Bicentennial in 1976. Copyright in 1976 by the Board of Jewish Education of Greater New York.

One act. Fourteen numbers with considerable dialogue both with and without underscoring. Some rhythmic speech. Mixed meter, but conventional harmonic structures. Not difficult musically or vocally. Some "pop" idioms. Duration: 40 minutes.

Major Roles: All roles are mid-range and undesignated as to voice part. THE SCOFFER (male or female); JEREMIAH (top F#3); AMOS; ISAIAH; THE HUCKSTER; JONAH (top F3); MICAH.

Minor Roles: THE ENTHUSIAST (male or female); OBADIAH; MALACHI; ZEPHANIAH; ZECHARIAH; HAGGAI; HOSEA; HABBAKUK; JOSHUA; EZEKIEL; EZRA; DANIEL; JOEL; NAHUM; SAMUEL; FOLK SINGERS (2 females); THE PROFESSOR (sp).

Chorus: SATB (several short solo parts may be taken from the chorus).

Dance: Characters: Sodium, Chloride, Pepper, Comb (male or female).

Orchestration: piano alone or orchestration: cb, perc, org (opt), sound-effect tape.

Synopsis: Inspired by the universal themes in the teachings of the Old Testament Prophets, this work is an affirmation of their relevancy today and for all times. In addition, it is a reminder of how the origins of American civilization are steeped in Biblical history. The teachings and personalities of the Prophets are brought into our contemporary culture and language with commentary from the chorus. There is no plot as such.

Materials: Published by BJE. Materials from GS or BJE.

Notes: This work has considerable performing flexibility and may be performed elaborately, as a theater piece, or in concert form, with or without dancers, or instrumental combo. The work provides a provocative and entertaining way in music for young people to explore contemporary spiritual values. As a staged work, directors are encouraged to work within the parameters of their facilities and the abilities of the performers. Production notes are included in the VS.

CECIL GRAY

The Temptation of St. Anthony

Music by **Cecil Gray** (1895-1951). A Choral Drama (Op. 33) with libretto in English by the composer, based on Gustave Flaubert's *La Tentation de Saint Antoine*. Translated from French by the composer.

Composed 1935-37.

Through-composed with accompanied recitatives. Atonality, partial tone rows, and frequent chord clusters. Vocal lines are linear but extremely chromatic and often devoid of tonal centers. Solos dominate the texture.

Four sections but should be performed as a single movement without any break or interval. Part 1: The monologue of Saint Anthony; Part 2: The choral section of the various Christian heresies; Part 3: The succession of the pagan gods and religions of antiquity; Part 4: A final monologue and choral epilogue. Duration: approximately 90 minutes.

Major Roles: All roles may be sung by twelve or more soloists. ST. ANTHONY (bs – F#1-Gb3), an old man – dramatically and vocally, extremely demanding; HILARION (ten), an old dwarf.

Minor Roles: QUEEN OF SHEBA (sop – top B4); THE INSPIRED ONE (ten); The Heresiarchs: ARIUS (bs), SABELLIUS (bs), MARCELLUS (ten), METHODIUS (ten), VALENTINUS (ten), PAUL OF SAMOSATA (ten), A VALENTINIAN (sop), A SETHANIAN (alt), AN APOLLINARIST (sop), A MERINTHION (sop), A THEODOTIAN (alt), HERMOGENES (ten); GYMNOSOPHIST (bar – A#1-Gb3); APOLLONIUS OF TYANA (ten); 1515 (alt - very low tess); THE BUDDHA (bar – top G#3); DEVIL (ten), some spoken lines; DEATH (alt); LUST (sop); CHIMAERA (sop); A DRAGON (sop); SPHINX (bs).

Chorus: SSAATTBB. Extremely difficult ensemble music.

Dance: No specific dance numbers exist, however, choreography would greatly enhance several sections.

Orchestration: Double orchestra thickly orchestrated.

Synopsis: St. Anthony, seated on the ground weaving mats, reflects on his past and what he could have become. Weak from fasting, he begins to see visions of other ways of life. The Queen of Sheba appears to him, inviting him to enjoy her and join her in a life of ecstasy. He rejects her and she departs. An old disciple of his, Hilarion, appears and admonishes St. Anthony for burying himself in solitude and self-pity. Hilarion then takes him into a world where live various Christian heresies. These Heresiarchs taunt him with their warped beliefs and philosophies. Next appear religions and cults of every nation, attempting to lure him into their webs. Finally the Devil himself appeals to St. Anthony. Exhausted and near suicide he manages to overcome even the Devil's temptation. Awakened from his vision, St. Anthony suddenly realizes that he has seen all of life and been victorious over its many temptations. He determines to give his renewed strength to everyone and everything around him.

Materials: CHA (1874).

Notes: Staging suggestions are numerous throughout the VS. This work is extremely difficult musically and must be undertaken only with well-trained musicians. Sets must be simple and symbolic as little time is allowed for changes. Best performed on a large stage.

PHILIP HAGEMANN

Ruth

Music by **Philip Hagemann** (b. 1942). A one-act chamber opera with libretto in English by the composer, based on events from the Old Testament book of Ruth and other Biblical passages.

First performance (concert version) was held in December 2001, by the Rockland County Choral Society, Suffern, NY. Other early performances include New York Singing Teachers Association, Composers Showcase, Rose Building, Lincoln Center (one scene) in May 2002. The staged premiere was given on October 17, 2003 at Southern Illinois University, Carbondale, IL; November 2003 at Trinity Church, Mt. Vernon, IN, and Epiphany Lutheran Church, Carbondale, IL.

Considerable chromaticism and straying tonalities are found during times of chaos and sadness while more traditional harmonies are used to paint those texts which are positive and express happiness or hope. Vocal lines are mostly lyric and vocally conceived though chromatic and only occasionally disjunct. Accompaniment frequently doubles the vocal line. A few arias and set numbers exist along with some accompanied recitatives; continuous music throughout. Female chorus sections are very dissonant and difficult – could be done with a small ensemble. Three short orchestral interludes separate the scenes.

One act with several connected scenes. Set in the lands of Moab and Judah in Biblical times. Duration: ca. 45 minutes.

Major Roles: NAOMI (m-sop – top A4), a woman of Judah; RUTH (sop – top B4), Moabite daughter-in-law of Naomi; BOAZ (bar – top F#3, opt. G#3), a prominent landowner of Judah

Minor Roles: ORPAH (sop), Moabite daughter-in-law of Naomi; A SERVANT OF BOAZ (ten – top C4), short role with high tessitura; AMNON (ten), another land owner of Judah

Chorus: Women's Chorus of SSA – sometimes acts as a narrator or "Greek Chorus," and at times women of Judah. Men's Chorus of TB portray villagers.

Orchestration: ob, bsn, hrn, hp, timp, perc, strings

Synopsis: Naomi and her two daughters-in-law, Ruth and Orpah, have lost their husbands. In her sorrow, Naomi tells Ruth and Orpah that she must return to Judah, her homeland, and instructs them to return to their Moabite families. Ruth in a show of deep love and loyalty to Naomi insists on accompanying Naomi to Judah with the well-known words of her aria "Whither thou goest, I will go." Arriving in Judah and in need of sustenance, Ruth works faithfully and relentlessly in the fields of Boaz, gleaning leftover grain. The unmarried Boaz is so impressed by the humble and remarkably loyal Ruth, that he pursues and takes her as his wife.

Material: From the composer – see Appendix C.

Notes: Best performed in a house of worship. The composer suggests that scenery be kept to a minimum using perhaps only a backdrop which suggests first the barren landscape and then a field of grain. Buildings are unnecessary with the use of minimal furniture. Lighting could greatly enhance the changes of mood and scenes. Musical interludes between scenes are brief and continuous, allowing for minimal scenery changes. This is a challenging score requiring well trained singers in the lead roles.

GEORGE FRIDERIC HANDEL

Athalia

Music by **George Frideric Handel** (1685-1759). Dramatic Oratorio with libretto in English by Samuel Humphreys based on the play *Athalia* by Racine.

Premiered in Oxford, July 10, 1733, Sheldonian Theatre. Written for Oxford University in gratitude for the honorary degree which he never accepted.

Many moments of full scoring and thick textures both from voices and orchestra. Accompanied arias and secco recitatives. Harmonically Handelian.

Three acts. Setting: The action takes place within the compass of one day in Jerusalem. Overture. Act I, sc. 1: In the temple at Jerusalem; sc. 2: In the Palace; sc. 3: Same as sc. 1. Act II: In Jerusalem. Act III: The same. Duration: 2 hours.

Roles: ATHALIA (sop), Queen of Israel; JOAD (alt – low tess), the High Priest; MATHAN (ten), a Baal priest; ABNER (bs), commander of the army; JOSABETH (sop), Joad's wife; JOAS (sop), a young boy and heir to the throne.

Chorus: SSAATTBB – Virgins, Attendants, Sidonian Priests, Priests and Levites, and Israelites.

Dance: Dancing during the celebration and festival scenes is not mandatory but certainly adds to the festivities.

Orchestration: 2 rec, fl, 2 ob, 2 bsn, 2 hrn, 2 trp, timp, strings, hpsch, org (opt).

Synopsis: Israel is gathered for a Jewish festival. The nation is oppressed under the tyranny of Athalia's rule. Joad together with the people offer a prayer for deliverance. In the Palace, Athalia reveals her haunting dreams in which a young boy dressed as a Jewish priest plunges a dagger into her heart. Assured by Mathan that it was only a dream, he suggests a visit to the temple to confirm her fears. The scene returns to the temple. Joad and Josabeth believe the time has come to tell the people that Joas is the true heir to the throne. Athalia enters the temple only to see the young boy of her dreams: Joas. She asks Joas who he is, and he replies, Eliakim, an orphan. Still suspicious, she announces her intention of removing him to the palace. The chorus comments "The clouded scene begins to clear." Joad prophesies an immediate overthrow and death of Athalia. Joad asks Joas who his model would be should he ever be king; Joas replies by naming David. Joad and Josabeth reveal to Joas who he really is. Athalia enters and on hearing of Joas' position, raises a cry of treason and orders his arrest. All desert Athalia, and Mathan declares that Jehovah has triumphed over Baal. The final chorus raises its voice in thanksgiving to Jehovah. We never are told of the fate of the tyrants.

Materials: NOV. OUP with an edition by Anthony Lewis. Orchestration includes 2 fl (or rec), 2 ob, 2 bsn, 2 hrn, 2 trp, timp, strings, hpsch.

Belshazzar

Music by **George Frideric Handel** (1685-1759). Dramatic Oratorio with libretto in English by Charles Jennens based on Scripture, primarily the book of Daniel.

Composed in 1745, premiered March 27, 1745, at the King's Theatre.

Set numbers with secco recitative. Choral music dominates. Typically Handelian in texture, dramatic in story line.

Two acts. Setting: Biblical times after the destruction of Jerusalem and defeat of the Jews by Babylon. Prologue with Overture: A triumphal procession before the Babylonian King; Act I, sc. 1: A private chamber in the Palace; sc. 2: The walls of Babylon; sc. 3: In the Persian camp; sc. 4: Daniel's dwelling; sc. 5: In the royal palace; sc. 6: Outside the walls of Babylon. Act II: The Palace of Belshazzar; Epilogue: Jerusalem rebuilt. Duration: 3 hours unless cuts are made.

Major Roles: BELSHAZZAR (ten), King of Babylon; DANIEL (male cont or ten), Prophet of Israel; NITOCRIS (sop), mother of Belshazzar; CYRUS (male cont or ten), King of Persia; GOBRIAS (bs), a Babylonia nobleman who aligns himself with Cyrus.

Minor Roles: ARIOCH, (ten), a Babylonian Lord; 3 MAGICIANS; A MESSENGER (bs).

Chorus: SATB – Babylonians, Jews, and a group of Medes and Persians. They may be a part of the action or act as a Greek chorus.

Dance: Depending upon the use of the chorus, considerable pantomime and stylized choreography may be employed.

Orchestration: 2 ob, bsn, 2 trp, timp, strings, hpsch, org.

Synopsis: The Babylonian army has attacked Jerusalem, destroying the Temple and carrying the Jews and their sacred Temple objects into captivity. The Babylonians stage a triumphal procession before King Belshazzar. Years pass and wickedness increases. Cyrus, King of Persia, holds the city in siege. Meanwhile, Nitocris seeks consolation from Daniel and his God for her beleaguered people. The Babylonians refuse to take seriously the threat of the Persians outside their gates, looking down on them from atop their walls with smug distaste. Gobrias, a Babylonian nobleman, angered by Belshazzar's actions, aligns himself with Cyrus and together with the Persian army, plan an attack on the indulged Babylonians. Meanwhile, Daniel, studying the writings of the prophets Jeremiah and Isaiah, learns of the promised redemption of the Jews and return to their land through the Persians and Cyrus. He calls his brethren together who rejoice in God's promise.

Belshazzar announces a feast to their chief god Sesach. A celebration is planned which horrifies the Jews. The Persians outside the walls advance and begin their attack. In the midst of Belshazzar's feast and orgy, handwriting appears on the wall. Wise men and soothsayers are sought but no one can decipher the message. Daniel is brought in and he interprets the words as God's warning of Belshazzar's imminent doom. The Persians invade slaying Belshazzar and conquering the Babylonians. In fulfillment of his promise to God, Cyrus frees the Jews and promises to help rebuild Jerusalem. In the Epilogue, the newly built Temple is dedicated with hymns magnifying God.

Materials: NOV.

Notes: There is no direct performing tradition for this work as a staged production despite Handel's and Jennens' numerous stage directions. This work is perhaps the most highly unified and organic drama Handel set to music, with stage directions in the autograph that are richer and more vivid than those for most of his other oratorios. The dramatic structure of the music as well as the events give rise to staged interpretation, causing one to feel that even Handel would have preferred the work to be staged. Certain cuts and a compressing of events are necessary for today's audiences.

Deborah

Music by **George Frideric Handel** (1685-1759). A Dramatic Oratorio with libretto in English by Samuel Humphrey, based on the Biblical account in Judges 4-5.

Composed in 1733; first performed March 17, 1733, King's Theatre in London.

The musical style is typically Handelian with secco recitatives, arias, and considerable choral music.

Three acts. Set in Biblical times approximately 1100 B.C. Overture. Act I, sc. 1, 2, 3: In Deborah's Palace; sc. 4: Israelite camp. Act II: Same as Act Ii sc. 1. Act III: Outside the Palace. Duration: 2 hours, 20 minutes.

Major Roles: DEBORAH (m-sop), Judge of Israel; BARAK (originally for a castrato, scored for m-sop), Israel's General; GENERAL SISERA (originally for alt, Handel rearranged the role for ten in a 1744 version); ABINOAM (bs), Barak's father; JAEL (sop), a Kenite.

Minor Roles: HERALD (ten); 3 ISRAELITISH WOMEN (sop, m-sop, sop), four small roles which may be cast from the chorus.

Chorus: SATB – Chief Priests of Israel, Chief Priests of Baal, Priests and Israelites, and Priests of Baal. The chorus actually sings approximately one-half of the total oratorio. Many supernumerary parts may also be taken from the chorus, especially if they are directly involved in the action.

Dance: Several sections, particularly the celebration should be choreographed.

Orchestration: 2 fl, 2 ob, 2 bsn, 3 hrn, 3 trp, timp, strings, 2 hpsch, 2 org.

Synopsis: The Biblical narrative is concise: the Judge of Israel, Deborah, has called upon Barak to gather an army of Israelites to free them from captivity under the Canaanites ruled by General Sisera. The Canaanites, better armed and larger in size, are defeated by Israel under the hand of Jehovah who sends a storm and flash flood to confuse and deter the Canaanite army at the River Kishon. Sensing defeat, Sisera flees on foot, taking refuge in the tent of Jael, the Kenite. Aware of the battle and knowledgeable regarding the just and kind Deborah, Jael sides with Israel. While Sisera sleeps in her tent, Jael drives a tent stake through his temples. With the Canaanite leader dead, Israel claims victory and praises Jehovah for His deliverance.

Materials: NOV

Notes: Due primarily to libretto and story line problems, this score will require considerable cutting or rearranging to be effective as a staged work. Still, it is a worthy consideration. Best produced in a large house of worship or theatre.

Esther

Music by **George Frideric Handel** (1685-1759). A Dramatic Oratorio with librettist uncertain; before 1732, it was attributed to Pope. The revised libretto of 1732 ascribes the additional texts to Samuel Humphreys. Others have also been credited with contributions. May have been partially based on Racine's play *Esther* and on the Old Testament book of Esther.

Premiered as a staged work in 1720; performed in its revised version May 2, 1732 at the Crown and Anchor Tavern in London.

Musical style typical of Handel with secco recitative, arias, and numerous choruses.

Six scenes (1720 version). Overture. Sc. 1: Haman's Palace; sc. 2: A celebration; sc. 3: The same; sc. 4: The same; sc. 5: King Ahasuerus' throne room; sc. 6: Esther's feast. The 1732 version divides these scenes into three acts and adds several scenes. Duration of both: full length.

Roles: ESTHER (sop); AHASVERUS (male cont or ten), King of Persia; MORDECAI (alt or ten); HAMAN (bs); HARBONAH (ten); OFFICER (ten); ISRAELITISH PRIEST (ten); 2 ISRAELITISH WOMEN (sop, alt).

Chorus: SSAATTBB – Persian Soldiers and Israelites.

Orchestration: 1732: 2 rec, 2 ob, 2 bsn, 3 hrn, 3 trp, timp, strings, hpsch, org.

Synopsis: Haman, King of Persia, determines to destroy the Jews. Meanwhile, the Jews are in celebration over Esther's ascension to the throne as Queen. When a messenger declares Haman's intentions, they turn to mourning. Esther inquires of her kinsman Mordecai why he is mourning in sackcloth and ashes. He replies that Haman's vengeance is directed against him personally. Esther consents to intervene by seeing the King. Esther approaches King Ahasuerus who offers her a petition of up to half of his kingdom. Esther merely invites the King to dine with her and Haman.

In the final scene, Ahasuerus again asks her to name her petition. She reminds him that Mordecai once saved him from conspiracy. Haman meanwhile has built gallows for the hanging of Mordecai. Instead, the King, learning of Haman's plot, orders Haman put to death on the spot. Esther ignores his plea for mercy and the people sing in praise of Jehovah.

Materials: NOV (1720 version with 1732 revisions in the score's Appendix)

Note: Since two versions (1720 and 1733) exist, it must be decided which to perform. Neither are dramatically cohesive works for staging due primarily to the libretto, but with certain cuts and adjustments, either can be made effectively stageworthy.

Jephtha

Music by **George Frideric Handel** (1685-1759). A Dramatic Oratorio with libretto in English by Rev. Thomas Morell, incorporating writings from Milton, Pope, Addison and others. Based on Judges 10-11 from Scripture.

Premiered February 26, 1752, at Covent Garden, London.

Music texture is typically Handelian with chorus playing a major role; numerous da capo arias, repetition of text and secco recitatives.

Three acts preceded by an Overture. Duration: 2 hours, 45 minutes.

Roles: JEPHTHA (ten), leader of Israel's army; IPHIS (sop), Jephtha's daughter; STORGE (m-sop), wife of Zebul; HAMOR (ct ten or cont), fiancé of Iphis; ZEBUL (bs), Jephtha's brother; ANGEL (boy sop).

Chorus: SATB and SA – Israelites. May be commentators or directly involved in the action.

Dance: At the wish of the director, stylized movement may be incorporated.

Orchestration: fl, 2 ob, bsn, 2 hrn, 2 trp, strings, hpsch, org.

Synopsis: The Israelites, oppressed by the Ammonites for many years, elect Jephtha to lead them from bondage. He accepts and in his zeal promises God that "What or whoe'er shall first salute mine eyes, shall be forever thine, or fall a sacrifice." Unable to secure peace by treaty, Jephtha goes to battle and returns victorious. Hearing of her father's victory, Iphis and her virgin train resolve to meet him when he and her betrothed, Hamor, return. Jephtha returns home and much to his horror, is met by his own daughter, Iphis. His friends and wife beg Jephtha not to carry through with his vow, but in his own conscience, he must. Iphis resigns herself to her fate. The scene closes with a climactic chorus telling of the mysterious workings of God's providence. Jephtha prepares to offer up Iphis. The priests appeal to God for guidance; an angel appears, stopping Jephtha. He declares that, rather than die, Iphis must live a life of celibacy and service to God. Jephtha and his friends each state gratitude for being spared this deed and rejoice at the termination of their troubles and peace for their country.

Materials: NOV

Notes: Best suited, with its large forces, to a theatre or large stage.

Joseph

Music by **George Frideric Handel** (1685-1759). A Dramatic Oratorio with libretto in English by Rev. James Miller whose book is titled *Joseph and His Brethren*.

First performance on March 2, 1744, in London, Covent Garden.

Musical textures and harmonies typical of Handel. Secco recitatives, arias, and numerous choral ensembles.

Three acts. Overture. Set in Egypt. Act I, sc. 1: In a Prison; sc. 2: A Room of State in Pharaoh's Palace; sc. 3: In a Temple – the marriage. Act II, sc. 1: Seven years later in Egypt; sc. 2: In Prison; sc. 3: Joseph's house; sc. 4: The same. Act III: The same. Duration: full length.

Roles: JOSEPH (male alt or ten), an Hebrew; PHARAOH (bs), King of Egypt; Brothers to Joseph: REUBEN (bs), SIMEON (ten), JUDAH (ten), BENJAMIN (sop); POTIPHERA (alt), High Priest of On; ASENATH (sop), daughter to the High Priest; PHANOR (alt), chief butler to Pharaoh, afterwards Joseph's steward.

Chorus: SATB – Egyptians and Hebrews.

Orchestration: 2 fl, 2 ob, bsn, 3 trp, timp, strings, hpsch, org.

Synopsis: Imprisoned in Egypt, Joseph bemoans his fate, not knowing why he has been placed there. Phanor enters with the news that Pharaoh, having heard of Joseph's ability in interpreting dreams, has summoned him. Joseph interprets Pharaoh's dream saying that there are to be seven years of plenty followed by seven years of famine. Joseph advises him to appoint someone to prepare the country for the famine. Pharaoh appoints Joseph. Meanwhile Asenath has fallen in love with Joseph and the marriage takes place.

Act II opens with more than seven years having elapsed. The famine has come and Joseph's administering of the food situation has won him great praise. However, Joseph longs for his native land and family. Meanwhile, Simeon, one of Joseph's brothers has been imprisoned. Joseph summons Simeon to visit with him. It slowly emerges that Simeon has been left by his other brothers as a hostage. Joseph inquires of the two youngest brothers. He is told that Benjamin is at home and Joseph was killed by a wild beast. Joseph leaves the room, emotionally distraught. Phanor announces the arrival of "the long-expected strangers." It is Joseph's brothers who plead with Joseph to help relieve the famine in Canaan. The act ends with the brothers praying for deliverance. Joseph fills their sacks with food and secretly places in Benjamin's sack a silver cup. The brothers leave. Asenath learns from Phanor that the brethren have stolen the silver cup. Guards are sent to arrest and return the brethren to Egypt. They enter in chains and are accused of stealing the sacred cup. Joseph proposes to retain Benjamin as a hostage while the other brothers return home to their father. Joseph, moved to tears, finally reveals his identity as their brother whom they sold into slavery many years ago. Joseph forgives them while Pharaoh announces that Joseph and his family shall have the best land in Egypt. An anthem of rejoicing concludes the work.

Materials: GPI. NOV issued vocal scores of all Handel oratorios except *Joseph* and *Occasional Oratorio*.

Notes: While this work contains some of the most detailed stage instructions of Handel's oratorios, it is also one of the most difficult to stage due primarily to the poor libretto. Handel was in many regards hampered by generalizations in the text, colloquialisms, and most important, key omissions from the plot which are clearly spelled out in the Biblical account. A successful staging of this work would require some cuts and creative revisions.

Joshua

Music by **George Frideric Handel** (1685-1759). A Dramatic Oratorio with libretto in English by Thomas Morell, based on the conquest of Canaan after Israel's forty years of wandering in the wilderness. These events are found in the Old Testament Book of Joshua.

First performance on March 9, 1748 at Covent Garden, London.

Musically typical of Handel's oratorios with secco recitative, arias, and considerable choral music. The march around Jericho and falling of the walls provides an opportunity for Handel to display rich textures which employ brass and drums in full array.

Three acts. Orchestral introduction which leads into Act I: Near Gilgal, on the bank of the Jordan River. Act II, sc. 1: Outside the walls of Jericho; sc. 2: The Passover celebrated; sc. 3: After the defeat of Israel by Ai; sc. 4: On the battlefield - the sun stands still. Act III: The hosts of Israel gathered. Duration: full length.

Roles: JOSHUA (ten), leader of Israel; CALEB (bs), leader of Israel's army; OTHNIEL (male cont or ten), younger brother of Caleb; ACHSAH (sop), Caleb's daughter; ANGEL (sop).

Chorus: SSATB – Israelites, Youths, Virgins.

Dance: Choreography for the march around Jericho and the "Warlike Symphony" is necessary.

Orchestration: 2 fl, 2 ob, bsn, 2 hrn, 2 trp, timp, sd dr, strings, hpsch, org.

Synopsis: The opening chorus proclaims the praises of Jehovah for His miraculous guidance through the Jordan River into Canaan. The people are instructed by Joshua and Caleb to erect an altar to Jehovah in remembrance of His providence. An Angel appears, ordering Joshua to attack Jericho for victory is certain. A trumpet sounds and the people prepare for war. Act II opens at the beginning of the seventh day of marching around Jericho. He orders the final trumpet blast and the march proceeds. In a powerful chorus, "Glory to God," the walls collapse. The Passover is celebrated. Caleb then dispatches men to Ai to test Ai's strength. They return defeated, however, Joshua sends them back. Othniel, in love with Achsah and spending too much time with her, is rebuked by Caleb and sends Achsah away. Othniel now obeys the orders to join the armies. A "Warlike Symphony" represents the attack. As the daylight begins to vanish preventing victory, Joshua orders the sun and moon to stand still. Jehovah is with him and the enemy are defeated. Act III opens with a chorus of thanksgiving. Joshua proposes to allot the conquered territory to the tribes of Israel. Othniel states that only the town of Debir remains unconquered. Caleb, growing too old and tired to lead an attack, offers his daughter's hand to the victor. Othniel at once volunteers and returns victorious. He is greeted as the conquering hero and claims his bride. All of Israel sings praise to Jehovah.

Materials: NOV

Notes: This work offers in addition to some of the finest musical moments, some of the most dramatic scenes in all of Handel's oratorios. Act II will present the biggest production challenge with several large shifts in scenery, time, and locale.

Judas Maccabaeus

Music by **George Frideric Handel** (1685-1759). A Dramatic Oratorio with libretto in English by Rev. Thomas Morell, based primarily on the first Book of Maccabees 2-8 (the original libretto lists this work as a "Sacred Drama.")

Composed in 1746, with the first performance on April 1, 1747 at Covent Garden, London.

Typical of Handel's oratorios with secco recitative, da capo arias, duets, trios, and numerous choruses. Considerable chorale style writing.

Three acts. Setting: A central location perhaps a courtyard outside the Palace. Judea, 165 B.C. Overture. Duration: full length.

Major Roles: JUDAS MACCABAEUS (ten), many long and florid arias; SIMON (bs), some coloratura passages; ISRAELITISH MAN (ten), this role may be sung by one or more singers; ISRAELITISH WOMAN (sop), this role may be sung by one or more singers.

Minor Roles: A MESSENGER (alto); A MESSENGER (bs); PRIEST (bar or ten); EUPOLEMUS (bs).

Chorus: SATB – Israelites who sing during more than half the oratorio. They may sing as commentators on the action or be involved on stage. If they are treated as a Greek chorus, a dance or mime group would be necessary to enact the choral commentary.

Dance: See "Chorus" above.

Orchestration: 2 fl, 2 ob, bsn, 3 trp, timp, strings, hpsch, org.

Synopsis: In the depths of despair, Israel mourns the oppression of their captivity. Simon suggests the appointment of Judas Maccabaeus as the leader of their army to free Israel from their bondage. Judas is summoned and agrees to serve. Between Part I and II, Israel is victorious over Appollonius of Samaria, and Syria has been defeated. Israel rejoices and praises their hero, Judas, who reminds them that they must not become proud by claiming the victory themselves, but must give credit to Jehovah. Their celebration is interrupted by a messenger, telling them of Gogias, Leader in Egypt, whose intent is to destroy Israel and desecrate their Holy places. Israel is admonished to leave their idolatry and worship Jehovah alone. Judas again gathers the armies of Israel and defeats Gogias. Part III tells of the conquest and Israel's offering of praise to Jehovah.

Materials: NOV

Notes: Though the characters are designated and considerable drama exists within the music and plot, this work must be carefully studied before any attempt at staging can be successfully explored. Of all the Handel stageworthy oratorios, this may be among the most problematic to produce as a staged work.

Samson

Music by **George Frideric Handel** (1685-1759). A Dramatic Oratorio with text in English taken from the poem *Samson Agonistes* by John Milton, based on the Scriptural story of Samson in Judges 14-16.

First performed on February 18, 1743, Covent Garden, London.

Secco recitative with many da capo arias and choral ensembles. Musical language is typical of Handel.

Three acts. Overture. Throughout the work, action alternates between the prison cell where Samson is kept, and the Palace Hall where a celebration is in progress. Duration: 2 hours, 30 minutes.

Major Roles: SAMSON (ten), long singing role with difficult acting as he is blind; MICAH (alto), Samson's friend; MANOAH (bs), Samson's father.

Minor Roles: DALILA (sop), Samson's wife; HARPPHA (bs), a giant of Gath; ISRAELITISH MESSENGER (ten); ISRAELITISH WOMAN (sop).

Chorus: SATB – Priests of Dagon, the Virgins, Israelites, Israelitish Virgins, and Philistines.

Dance: During the feast day celebration scenes.

Orchestration: 2 fl, 2 ob, 2 bsn, 2 hrn, 2 trp, 2 trb (opt); timp, strings, hpsch, org.

Synopsis: The scene opens to a prison, where Samson, having been captured by the Philistines, is suffering and enduring his existence. He has been blinded, shorn, and chained. Meanwhile in the Palace hall, the Philistines are celebrating a feast day in honor of their god, Dagon, whose image they worship. Samson is visited by his friend Micah and his father Manoah, who encourage him to keep his faith in God. The chorus of Israelites pray for him. Dalila appears, attempting to make amends with Samson but he will have no part of her. Samson gradually experiences his inner spirit growing and his physical strength returning. Harapha, the giant of Gath, comes to ridicule Samson and challenges him to a duel which Samson accepts. Part III opens to the continuing festivities of the Philistines. A terrible and appalling noise is heard, succeeded by wailings and cries for help. An Israelitish messenger arrives and relates the story of how Samson pulled down the Philistine temple, burying his enemies and himself in its ruins. A Dead March is heard; Samson's body approaches on its way to the tomb; Manoah, Micah, and the Israelites pay tribute to their hero.

Materials: GS and NOV

Notes: Production should be mounted in a large theatre or house of worship with a large chancel area.

Saul

Music by **George Frideric Handel** (1685-1759). A Dramatic Oratorio with libretto in English by Charles Jennens adapted from events in the Old Testament Book of Samuel.

First performance on January 16, 1739, at the King's Theatre, London.

Typically Handelian oratorio. Secco recitatives, Da capo arias, ensembles, and numerous choruses.

Three acts. Setting: In and around the Palace of King Saul, except the opening of Act III which occurs in Endor. Overture. Duration: full length.

Major Roles: SAUL (bs), King of Israel – difficult role, vocally and dramatically; JOHATHAN (ten), his son; ABNER (ten), Captain of the Host; DAVID (male alt or ten); APPARITION OF SAMUEL (bs), the Prophet; DOEG (bs), a messenger; ABIATHAR (bs); MERAB (sop) and MICHAL (sop), daughters of Saul; WITCH OF ENDOR (ten); AN AMALEKITE (ten); HIGH PRIEST (ten).

Chorus: SATB – Israelites

Dance: A Sinfonia in Act I is designed as a dance by "the daughters of Israel" for the victorious David. The first Sinfonia in Act II represents a lapse of time during which David and Michal are married. A wedding could be pantomimed during this Sinfonia. The Act III Sinfonia represents the battle on Mount Gilboa.

Orchestration: 2 fl, 2 ob, 2 bsn, 2 trp, 3 trb, timp, perc (carillons), strings, hp, hpsch, 2 org. (A larger orchestration is also available.)

Synopsis: After David's victory over Goliath, he is presented to Saul who gives to him his daughter Merab for marriage. David and Jonathan, King Saul's son, begin a close friendship. Saul grows jealous over David's popularity and in a rage attempts to kill David. Saul charges Jonathan with David's demise, but God has plans for David and protects him. Jonathan intercedes with Saul in behalf of David. Saul feigns reconciliation by making David leader of Israel's army as well as giving him his younger daughter, Michal. Saul's rage is renewed when David returns from battle victorious. Saul again attempts to destroy David and finally, in disguise, resorts to a consultation with the Witch of Endor. At Saul's bidding, the Witch conjures up the ghost of the prophet Samuel who recalls his former prophecies and declares that the day of reckoning is at hand. The battle on Mount Gilboa takes place during a Sinfonia.

Not long after, news of the death of Saul and Jonathan are brought to David. David is hailed the new ruler of Israel.

Materials: NOV

Notes: Some of the most intriguing moments for dramatic treatment occur in this oratorio: a javelin-throwing, Goliath's head brought on stage, the raising of the ghost of Samuel, the Feast of the New Moon, the scene with the Witch of Endor, and the Dead March.

Solomon

Music by **George Frideric Handel** (1685-1759). A Dramatic Oratorio with libretto in English (author unknown, though some feel it is the work of Thomas Morell) based on events in the life of Solomon as found in I Kings and II Chronicles.

Composed in 1748; premiered March 17, 1749 at Covent Garden, London.

Musical textures and harmonies typical of Handel. It is a work of great grandeur, heraldry and pomp, embracing a spirit of not only the dramatic but of religious significance. Secco and a few accompanied recitatives, ensembles, and many powerful double choruses.

Three acts. Overture. A Sinfonia introduces Act III. Act I: Outside the temple - the inauguration of Solomon's new temple. Act II: Inside Solomon's Palace. Act III: The interior of Solomon's temple. Duration: full length.

Roles: SOLOMON (male alt – while Handel had both a bass and tenor available, he chose to give this lengthy and powerful role to an alto, perhaps to provide a less naturalistic and more symbolic aura to Solomon. Certainly this work is far less realistic and much more symbolic than most of his other oratorios), King of Israel; ZADOK (ten), the High Priest; PHARAOH'S DAUGHTER (sop), Queen; NICAULE (sop), Queen of Sheba; A LEVITE (bs); FIRST HARLOT (sop); SECOND HARLOT (sop).

Chorus: Double Chorus of SATB – Priests and Israelites. Many double chorus numbers.

Dance: In the grandeur of this work with its processionals and celebrations, there is much room for choreography. The entrance of the Queen of Sheba and subsequent viewing of the new temple (a "masque" sequence) in the beginning of Act III provide wonderful opportunities for dance and pantomime.

Orchestration: 2 fl, 2 ob, 2 bsn, 2 hrn, 2 trp, timp, strings, hpsch, org.

Synopsis: It is the inauguration of Solomon's new temple. A chorus of praise and thanksgiving from all of Israel opens Act I. Solomon turns to his Queen, promising her a new palace. She sings of the ecstasy of married love, touching the emotional heartstrings of Solomon. He bids her follow him to the cedar grove where "amorous turtles love beneath the pleasing gloom." The chorus bids them farewell with "May no rash intruder disturb their soft hours." Act II opens with the people praising Solomon, who unhesitatingly credits the Lord, the King of Kings, with his wisdom. An Attendant announces the arrival of two ladies, both of whom claim the same infant as their own. Solomon makes the decision that the infant shall be bisected, giving half to each woman. The Second Woman comments on the prudent and wise judgment of the King, while the true mother cries out to spare him. She gains the verdict and the people join in praise of Solomon and Jehovah. In Act III Solomon receives the Queen of Sheba, showing her around the new temple. She is impressed and offers gifts of gold, gems, and spices. The Queen leaves while the people offer yet another anthem of triumph.

Materials: NOV

Notes: This work may be viewed dramatically from two different perspectives. One, that it is symbolic and therefore a work of pageantry and symbolism; two, that it makes a very profound statement which must be viewed practically and therefore realistically. To view *Solomon* as a non-dramatic work, however, is to miss the inherent grandeur which only a staged presentation could offer.

LOU HARRISON

Jephthah's Daughter

Music by **Lou Harrison** (1917-2003). A Music/Theatre Drama with text taken from Judges 11 of Scripture.

The first version of this work was conceived at Cabrillo College, March, 1963. First staged performance held at the Cornish Institute, Seattle, Washington, November 21, 1980.

An experimental theatre piece; aleatoric characteristics with Oriental influences. Continuous music and action.

One act, four sections. Duration: variable, up to 30 minutes.

Roles: NARRATOR (male or female); DANCERS (at least two), impersonate the characters of the plot.

Dance: Two stylized impersonations.

Orchestration: One to three flutes, perc (dr, tam tam, 3 gongs, tri, sus cowbells or marimba or dulcimer – anything that "twangs or jangles," or even Jahlataranga; sustaining instruments such as a shang, sho, org, or strings; drones.

Synopsis: Jephthah the Gileadite, a mighty man of valour, is driven out of his home because he was the son of an harlot. When the Ammonites threaten to destroy Israel, the elders of Gilead ask Jephthah to return and lead their army against the Ammonites. He consents on the condition that, if victorious, he be named their head. Jephthah then takes a vow before the Lord that if Jehovah would indeed deliver the Ammonites into their hands, "then whatsoever cometh forth of the doors of my house to meet me when I return in peace from the children of Ammon, it shall be the Lord's, and I will offer it up for a burnt offering." Jephthah is victorious, and returns home only to be greeted by his daughter, his only child. His daughter requests a two-month period of mourning. At the end of the two months, she returns home and Jephthah carries out the vow he had vowed.

Materials: COR.

Notes: All materials come in a Theatre Kit consisting of 4 rhythmic declamations for Narrator, 4 compositions for percussionist, 3 compositions for transverse flute, 2 chords, 2 drones, a selection of 4 colors, a design for an arch, and a recommendation for a mask and make up. Mr. Harrison's performance instructions are also included and read: "Any musical unit of the kit may be used singly, or in combination with any other, an any way, or at any time. Repeats may be ignored, or multiplied, in any order, at any time. Any unit may be used with itself as well—many flutes may be played in 'parallels' at any intervals, or in canons—chords may be 'piled up'—etc. The combined rhythms occurring between any units used together may be at any speeds—twice, one-half, etc., or free. Declamations may be used with any other units of music, thought it might be good to retain the order of their occurrence, since they tell a story. Declamations, too, may be repeated if wished."

Performance interpretation notes from the premiere 1980 production are as follows:
    Percussion piece #1 accompanied by the dancers interpretation of the story.
    Narration #1 accompanied by the notated rhythm being tapped out on claves.
        A background "drone" was supplied by tuning wine glasses to the pitches specified by Mr. Harrison and distributed throughout the audience.
    Percussion piece #2 (as above)
    Narration piece #2 (as above)
    Percussion piece #3 (as above)
    Narration piece #3 (as above)
    Percussion piece #4 (as above)
    Narration piece #4 (as above)
    Make up for the dancers was done in the traditional style of Cantonese opera

Best performed in an intimate theatre or house of worship. Minimal sets necessary. Sufficient stage area for dancers.

JONATHAN HARVEY

Passion and Resurrection

Music by **Jonathan Harvey** (b. 1939). An Easter Liturgical Drama with libretto in English adapted by the composer from the Benedictine Latin Church Dramas.

Commissioned by Martin Neary. First performance March 21, 1981, Winchester Cathedral.

Avant garde influences; mixed meter; atonality and modality both frequent. Considerable plainchant. Disjunct melodic lines with frequent large skips.

Prologue, twelve scenes. Prologue: Jesus with disciples at the Passover meal; sc. 1: Judas bartering with Caiaphas; sc. 2: On the Mount of Olives; sc. 3: The same; sc. 4: Jesus on trial; sc. 5: In the courtyard – Peter's denial; sc. 6: Judas' remorse and death; sc. 7: Jesus before Pilate; sc. 8: Procula's vision; sc. 9: Same as sc. 7; Sc. 10: Jesus ridiculed; Interlude: Procession to Calvary; sc. 11: Jesus' death; sc. 12: At the tomb. Duration: 100 minutes.

Roles: PRIEST (bar), narrator; JESUS (bar – top Gb3); JUDAS (bs); CAIAPHAS (bs); PETER (bar); ANNAS (bs); SERVANT GIRL (sop); PILATE (ten); PROCULA (m-sop), Pilate's wife; HER MAID (m-sop); THIEF (ten); GOOD THIEF (bs); MARY MAGDALENE (sop – top B4); MARY 2 (sop); MARY 3 (cont); ANGEL (sop); JOHN (ten); ANGEL 1 (sop – top 8b4); ANGEL 2 (cont).

Chorus: SATB – Soldiers, Priests, People of Jerusalem. Congregation sings responses throughout.

Orchestration: hrn, trp, ten trb, bs trb, tba, 2 perc, 7 vln, vla, 2 vc, 2 cb, large org, chamber org (opt).

Synopsis: After the manner of the medieval mystery plays, this work makes use of simple dramatic imagery in short scenes, dealing with the events surrounding the passion, crucifixion and resurrection of Jesus. The plot is connected with orchestral interludes giving adequate time for scene changes. The scene descriptions given above outline the plot accurately. The final scene is the longest, beginning with the mourning of the three Maries and concluding with an ensemble number in praise of Christ's resurrection. The congregation is included in this finale.

Materials: FM (GS).

Notes: Intended for performance in a cathedral/church. A powerful work with considerable dramatic potential.

PAUL HINDEMITH

Das lange Weihnachtsmahl – *The Long Christmas Dinner*

Music by **Paul Hindemith** (1895-1963). A Symbolic Opera in the form of a morality play, with libretto in English by Thornton Wilder, and a German version by the composer.

Premiered December 17, 1962 in Mannheim, Germany, with first performance in the U.S. at Juilliard School, NYC, March 13, 1963.

Dissonant quartal harmonies, but tonal and melodically conceived. Set numbers within continuous musical texture. One aria, two trios, a quartet, one sextet. Comedy and tragedy.

One act. Setting: In the dining room of the Bayard home, southern U.S. Three doors must be a part of the set. Duration: 55 minutes.

Roles: LUCIA (sop); MOTHER BAYARD (alt); RODERICK (bar); BRANDON (bs); CHARLES (ten); GENEVIEVE (m-sop); LEONORA (sop – high tess); ERMENGARDE (alt); SAM (high bar – top Ab3); LUCIA II (sop); RODERICK II (ten). Possible doublings: Lucia and Lucia II; Mother Bayard and Ermengarde; Roderick and Sam.

Orchestration: 2 fl (picc), ob, cl, bs cl, 2 bsn, contra bsn, hrn, 2 trp, 2 trb, tba, hpsch, perc, strings.

Synopsis: Ninety years are traversed in this work, representing in accelerated motion, ninety Christmas dinners in the life of the Bayard family. The transition from generation to generation through the birth of children, the aging process, and death all occur during the eating of one continuous Christmas dinner. Similarities and recurring actions are contrasted with the cultural differences between the generations. There is virtually no plot, but rather an overall theme of love, memories, and conflict in life's revolving cycle.

Materials: Published by SCH; materials from BEL (Eng, Ger). The San Francisco Opera Center and American Opera Workcenter have a video available conducted by Robert Baustian, directed by Dan Balestrero. Contact OPERA.

Notes: Best performed in an intimate hall with a stage.

JEROME HINES

I Am the Way

Music by **Jerome Hines** (1921-2003). A Sacred Opera with libretto in English by the composer based on Biblical history. The words of Jesus are taken directly from the King James version of the Bible, while liberties have been taken with the words of some of the other characters.

Composed in the early 1960s. Performed at the Metropolitan Opera House in 1968.

Musical style identifiable with 19th century Romanticism. Vocally conceived, melodic, some chromaticism, but harmonically conventional. Continuous texture with a few arias. Mostly soloistic, few ensembles.

Four acts, eight scenes. Act I, sc. 1: John the Baptist – early morning on the banks of the Jordan river; Sc 2: The Woman at the Well – noon at Jacob's well in Samaria. Act II, sc. 1: Eliakim and Magdalene – in the Temple at Jerusalem; Sc. 2: At Bethany – in a garden at Bethany. Act III, sc. 1: Judas' Monologue – a dark, lonely street in Jerusalem; Sc. 2: The Resurrection of Lazarus – the burial grounds outside Bethany. Act IV, sc. 1: The Betrayal – a deserted street in Jerusalem; Sc. 2: The Last Supper – the upper room in Jerusalem. Duration: 2 hours.

Major Roles: JESUS, THE CHRIST (bs), long and highly demanding role; JOHN (ten), a disciple; JUDAS (ten), the disciple who betrayed Jesus – demands outstanding acting; PETER (bar – top G3), outspoken disciple; MARTHA (sop); MARY (sop), the Mother of Jesus (Mary, the Mother and Martha may be sung by the same person); MARY MAGDALENE (m-sop); ELIAKIM (bar), the High Priest.

Minor Roles: JOHN THE BAPTIST (bar), must be a powerful voice and personality; SAMARITAN WOMAN (m-sop), may be sung by the same person singing Mary Magdalene; THOMAS (bs), a disciple.

Ensemble Roles: The following are disciples who sing as an ensemble. Voice classification should be assigned in order to achieve ensemble balance. ANDREW, MATTHEW, THADDEUS, JAMES THE GREAT, JAMES THE LESS, PHILIP, SIMON, BARTHOLOMEW.

Acting Roles: NICODEMUS, MELATIAH, MARTHA'S ATTENDANT, LAZARUS, A CHILD, 2 GUARDS.

Chorus: SATB – Village people (should include children as supers).

Orchestration: fl, ob, cl, hrn, timp, hp, org, pia, strings (orchestration by Ralph Hermann).

Synopsis: ACT I: Disciples of John the Baptist are in prayer led by John the Evangelist. Their prayer is interrupted by a crowd from a nearby town who have come to hear the Baptist preach and to see him perform the ritual of water baptism, symbolic of spiritual cleansing which is not in accordance with Jewish tradition. Jesus and His newly-acquired disciples leave Judea to return to Galilee through Samaria. While the disciples go into town to buy food, Jesus stops to rest at Jacob's well and there encounters a Samaritan woman who has come to draw water. ACT II: As the miraculous ministry of Jesus continues, the Sanhedrin in Jerusalem becomes increasingly concerned. Eliakim, a High Priest, is sent to investigate Jesus. He summons Mary Magdalene, a woman of ill repute, for questioning. Eliakim's report to the Sanhedrin has caused much consternation and thus it is decreed that any follower of Jesus be cast out of the synagogue. Jesus' mother and the disciples fear that His life is in danger. ACT III: Judas, not understanding Jesus or His purpose on earth, contemplates the day when Jesus might claim the throne of Israel and overthrow the Roman rule. When Lazarus is stricken with a serious illness, Mary Magdalene and Martha, her sister, send for Jesus to come and heal His beloved friend. However, He deliberately tarries until Lazarus has died. Then ignoring the warning of the disciples that the Judeans seek to kill Him, Jesus goes to Lazarus arriving four days after his burial. The miracle of bringing Lazarus back to life concludes the scene. ACT IV: People by the thousands throng from Jerusalem to see the man that Jesus had raised from the dead. The Sanhedrin, now enraged, decides that both Jesus and Lazarus must die. Disillusioned because Jesus would not assert Himself as King of Israel, Judas decides to force the issue through his own secret plan of betraying Jesus to the Roman authorities. On the first day of the Feast of Unleavened Bread, Jesus eats His Last Passover supper with His disciples.

Materials: CAI. To date, the composer and his organization, Christian Arts, Inc., have maintained rigid controls on all materials: VS, FS, parts. Information may be obtained from CAI.

Notes: A large-scale production requiring theatre facilities. The individual scenes can also be successfully performed out of context.

LEE HOLDRIDGE

Lazarus and His Beloved

Music by **Lee Holdridge** (b. 1944). A Sacred Opera with libretto in English by the composer, based on the writings of Kahlil Gilbran.

Completed in 1977.

Lyric, tonal with some twentieth century harmonic idioms and chromaticism. Accompanied recitatives, arias.

One act. Setting: The garden of Lazarus' mother, the day after the resurrection of Jesus. Duration: 45 minutes.

Roles: LAZARUS (dramatic ten – top Bb); MARY (sop – top C5 sustained), his sister; MARTHA (m-sop), his sister; MOTHER OF LAZARUS (m-sop); PHILIP (ten), a disciple; THE MADMAN (bs-bar – top F3), works as a Greek chorus making observations on the action but never acknowledged by the other characters.

Orchestration: 2 fl, 2 ob, 2 cl, 2 bsn, 4 hrn, 2 trp, 3 trb, tba (opt), timp, perc, hp, strings.

Synopsis: The story tells of Lazarus' anguished re-entry into the world of the living after having been raised from death by Christ. Lazarus has been missing all day, sending his sisters, Mary and Martha, and his mother into frenzied worry over him. Lazarus finally returns and pours out his heart to Mary. He tries to explain that he has experienced a world beyond this mortal world, a world of perfection, a world in which he found his beloved: his higher self...God. He explains that he had all this until he was called back to this worldly plane, an existence of despair. Suddenly Philip enters with incredible news: "He is risen." Overwhelmed with this news, Lazarus realizes that he too must make a sacrifice and go out and proclaim Jesus, even though he has already known perfection and truth. The others are stirred by Lazarus' transformation and wish him well, realizing he has a destiny they cannot stop.

Materials: CLM. Also AMC and the composer.

Notes: May be performed in either a theatre or church with adequate space.

GUSTAV HOLST

Savitri

Music by **Gustav Holst** (1874-1934). A East Indian Legend Opera with libretto in English by the composer, based on an Indian folk tale taken from the *Mahabharata*.

Premiered November 5, 1916, in London.

Melodic, infused with Eastern musical textures and contemporary techniques, but maintaining a relatively simple harmonic structure. Through-composed. Moralistic and serious drama.

One act. Setting: A wood at evening. Duration: 30 minutes.

Roles: SAVITRI (sop), demands strong middle-range voice and convincing acting; SATYAVAN (ten), her husband and a woodcutter; DEATH (bs).

Chorus: SSAA off stage. Can be performed without chorus.

Orchestration: 2 fl, Eng hrn, 2 string quartet, cb.

Synopsis: Death is heard approaching Savitri, informing her that he will come this very evening to claim her husband. Satyavan returns home after work only to find his wife lamenting and trembling in fear. Death appears and takes Satyavan, and much to the surprise of both Savitri and Death, she no longer has any fear. Death, in awe of Savitri's great courage, offers her a boon: she may ask anything of him except the life of Satyavan. Savitri asks for never-ending life and Death grants it. Savitri then informs Death that he must give life back to Satyavan since her life can only continue through her children with Satyavan. Death is thus tricked into returning her husband to life.

Materials: GS.

Notes: May be performed with minimal sets: a mound representing the outdoors and a ramp on which Death enters and exits. Creative lighting can add considerably to Death's scenes. Intended to be performed out doors or in a small auditorium where chorus, orchestra, and conductor are not seen by the audience.

ARTHUR HONEGGER

Jeanne d'Arc au bûcher – Joan of Arc at the Stake

Music by **Arthur Honegger** (1892-1955). A Dramatic Oratorio with libretto in French by Paul Claudel, based on various events in the life of Joan of Arc.

Premiered May 12, 1938 in Basel. First fully staged performance, Zurich, 1942.

Melodic, unexpected harmonic and rhythmic directions, Romantic harmonies with twentieth century idioms; through-composed; considerable spoken dialogue with and without underscoring.

Prologue for chorus and sop solo; sc. 1: The Voices from Heaven; sc. 2: The Book; sc. 3: The Voices of the Earth; sc. 4: Joan Given Up to the Beasts; sc. 5: Joan at the Stake; sc. 6: The Kings or The Invention of the Game of Cards; sc. 7: Catherine and Margaret; sc. 8: The Kings Sets Out for Rheims; sc. 9: The Sword of Joan; sc. 10: Trimazo; sc. 11: The Burning of Joan of Arc. Duration: 80 minutes.

Major Roles: JEANNE D'ARC (mostly spoken, a few sung lines in sop range); BROTHER DOMINIQUE (sp); VIRGIN (sop – high tess); PORCUS (ten – top B3); MARGUERITE (sop); CATHERINE (cont).

Minor Roles: A VOICE (ten); 1st HERALD (ten); CLERK (ten); A VOICE (bs); 2nd HERALD (bs); A PEASANT (bs); THE VOICE OF A CHILD (sop). The following spoken roles may be performed by one or more persons: THIRD HERALD; THE ASS; DUKE OF BEDFORD; JEAN OF LUXEMBOURG; HEURTEBISE; A PEASANT. The following spoken roles may be performed by one or more persons: THE USHER; REGNAULT DE CHARTRES; GUILLAUME DE FLAVY; PERROT; A PRIEST. THE MOTHER OF TONNEAUX (sp from the choir).

Chorus: SATB. Children's chorus in unison.

Dance: Several scenes will benefit dramatically from creative choreography.

Orchestration: 2 fl (picc), 2 ob, 2 cl, bs cl, 3 sax, 3 bsn, contra bsn, picc trp, 3 trp, 3 trb, bs trb or tba, 2 pia, timp, 2 perc, cel, Ondes Martenot, strings.

Synopsis: This work is a search of a departed soul for acceptance of its earthly destiny, and a story of the transformation of Joan's former temporal environment through her death.

Against the background of war-torn fifteenth century France, these two themes are explored and developed: personal fulfillment of "a girl called Joan," and the national significance of St. Joan's life and sacrifice. Joan is guided through her experiences first by St. Dominic and later by the Virgin Mary. Catherine and Margaret, the heavenly voices, send the peasant girl from Domremy to fight for her country at Orleans, to attend the coronation of her king at Rheims, to fall into political betrayal at Compiegne, and to suffer public trial and execution at Rouen. As in a dream, Joan revisits these scenes of her earthly life in a sequence that is outside the chronology of time. Actual events are vested in the masks of fantasy as well as with the feelings with which Joan experienced them. Her delivery by her allies into the hands of the enemy is a stylized game of cards. Her trial becomes an absurd diversion of animals. The reuniting of France is seen as a meeting between a long estranged husband and wife: the giant Heurtebise (representing the wheat-producing North) and Mother Wine (the South). Joan's personal acceptance of her death at the stake to become a "candle sweet to shed a ray at Mary's feet," and the general recognition of her sacrifice as "a holy flame to light all France" are the climax of the work, merging public and private achievement in the end.

Materials: SAL (Eng translation by Dennis Arundell).

Notes: Staging a collage of scenes and events which occur at random and not chronologically can create production problems if realism is sought. Simplicity can solve many problems. It is helpful to use a full stage scrim concealing high platforms up stage, behind which much of Joan's and Dominique's action takes place, including the final scene. The action of the remainder of events takes place on stage level. If an intermission is desired, a good place for such a break can be taken at rehearsal No. 56. Creative lighting design is helpful. Best performed in a theatre or auditorium with a large stage.

Judith

Music by **Arthur Honegger** (1892-1955). A Sacred Opera with text in French by Rene Morax, based on events in the life of Judith as found in the Apocryphal Book of Judith.

Premiered February 23, 1925, France.

Difficult rhythmic sections. Considerable polyphony, melodic. Twentieth century harmonic textures.

Three acts. Act I: Within the walls of Bethulia. Act II, sc. 1: The same; sc. 2: Holopherne's tent. Act III: A place in Bethulia.

Roles: JUDITH (m-sop – top A4), long demanding role; OZIAS (bar – top F#3), Governor; HOLOPHERNE (bar – top F#3); BAGOAS (ten); LA SERVANTE (sop); A VOICE (sop); A VOICE (ten); A SENTINEL and A SOLDIER (ten); A VOICE (bar).

Chorus: SATB – Attendants to Judith; Soldiers; double speaking chorus.

Orchestration: Two versions: 1) 2 fl, 2 ob, 2 cl, 2 bsn, 2 hrn, 2 trp, 2 trb, harmonium, pia, perc, strings; 2) 2 fl, 2 ob, 2 cl, 2 bsn, 2 hrn, 2 trp, 2 trb, perc, hp, pia, strings.

Synopsis: Judith and her maidservant have entered the camp of Holopherne, seeking an audience with him in behalf of her starving people, though her intent is to captivate his attention by seeming to side with him and advising him as to how he can take complete control of Israel. Bagoas interrogates the women and grows suspicious of their intent, but is taken with Judith's beauty and grants them permission to see his commander. Holopherne is likewise overcome with Judith's directness and beauty and orders his guards to leave that he may spend the evening alone with her. Judith, overcome only momentarily with the power and virility of Holopherne, kills him. She and her servant quickly leave with his decapitated head, returning to their own people with proof that the enemy now is theirs.

Materials: SAL.

Notes: Designed for theatre performance requiring ample production facilities and highly skilled musicians.

ALAN HOVHANESS

Pilate

Music by **Alan Hovhaness** (1911-2000). A Ballet Opera with libretto in English by the composer, loosely based on the Biblical character Pilate who presided at the trial of Jesus.

Premiered June 26, 1966, at Pepperdine College, Los Angeles.

Musical and harmonic colors show Eastern and Oriental influences. Vocal lines are chant-like. Considerable use of percussion in accompaniment. Tragedy.

One act. Setting: On a mountain. Duration: 30 minutes.

Roles: PILATE (bs); SILENT WINGS (cont), wears black wings and a bird mask with beak; CHORUS (bs); SACRED POVERTY (Vision of a Saint); MURDERER (Vision of a Murderer).

Dance: Silent Wings must be a capable dancer in both ballet and Oriental styles. Dance and pantomime is important.

Orchestration: 3 fl, 3 trb, 5 perc (block, gong, 2 vib, ten gong, bs dr, chimes, giant tam-tam).

Synopsis: Pilate flees to Mt. Pilatus after washing his hands of the death of Jesus. His conscience is torn between the crowd's cries of "Slay poverty and free the murderer," and what he personally felt. No longer able to bear the torture of his own soul, he frees himself from this bondage by throwing himself from the summit of Mt. Pilatus to the rocks below. A funeral chant is heard in the background.

Materials: CFP

Notes: Best performed in a small theatre.

EUSEBIA SIMPSON HUNKINS

Wondrous Love

Music by **Eusebia Simpson Hunkins** (1902-1980). A Nativity Folk Drama with libretto in English by the composer, inspired and partially based on old Appalachian Mountain Carols.

Traditional harmony. Melodically conceived. Pre-dominantly choral with few solo sections. Set numbers with narration between numbers and with underscoring. Original compositions and arrangements of carols alternate throughout the score.

One act, five scenes. Setting: First Christmas. Sc. 1: Carpenter shop; sc. 2: Mary's sewing room; sc. 3: Outdoors; sc. 4: A roadway; sc. 5: The stable. Duration: 35 minutes.

Major Roles: NARRATOR (sp); SOPRANO, ALTO, TENOR, and BARITONE soloists; ANGEL'S VOICE (sp); MARY'S VOICE (sp).

Pantomime Roles: MARY; JOSEPH; A YOUNG GIRL; 4 SHEPHERDS; 2 CHILDREN; FUGITIVE SOLDIERS; TRAVELERS.

Chorus: SSATBB

Dance: As desired in conjunction with director's overall concept.

Orchestration: pia, org (gui or autoharp opt).

Synopsis: The Narrator tells the story of the Nativity beginning with an introduction to both Mary and Joseph in their own environments (sewing and carpentry). The story unfolds with the trip to Bethlehem and the visitation to the stable by various people. The narration is spoken in simple Appalachian folk language as the singers and actors portray the various episodes surrounding the birth of Christ.

Materials: SATB and SSA by CF.

Notes: With the suggested scenery and props, this work may be performed in a sanctuary, or with larger sets, in a theatre. The setting may also be altered to rustic American times with the Narrator costumed as a village pastor, surrounded by his flock who simply watch the story unfold as he speaks and the action is pantomimed. A versatile score with several options for dramatic presentation. In its simplest form, the work may be sung without dramatic action. Some staging and lighting suggestions are in the score.

VINCENT D'INDY

La légende de Saint Christophe –
The Legend of Saint Christopher

Music by **Vincent d'Indy** (1851-1931). A Sacred Legend Opera with libretto in French after J. de Voragine's *Golden Legend*.

Composed 1908-15; premiered June 9, 1920, Academie Nationale de Musique et de Danse in Paris.

Late Romantic style with thickly scored textures; highly chromatic. Melodic and colorful.

Three acts, eight scenes. Prologue. Duration: approximately 100 minutes.

Major Roles: L'ENFANT JESUS (sop); LA REINE DE VOLUPTE/NICEA (sop – B#2-B4); AUFERUS/CHRISTOPHORE (ten – Bb3); LE PRINCE DU MAL/SATHANAËL (ten); L'HISTORIEN (bar – top F3), narrator; LE ROI DE L'OR/LE GRAND JUGE (bs – top F3); L'ERMITE (bs-bar – top F3).

Minor Roles: UN AMANT (ten); FIRST OFFICER (ten); SECOND OFFICER; A MAN (ten); UN IMPORTANT (ten); UN ARCHER; LE SOUVERAIN PONTIFE; UN MARCHAND (bs); UN EMPEREUR (bar); UN BOURGEOIS (bar); LE HERAUT (bs); THREE CELESTIAL SPIRITS (sop unison).

Mime Roles: LA DANSEUSE; LE CAPITAIN DES ARCHERS; LE BOURREAU.

Chorus: SSAATTBB of at least 92 singers.
SATB – small chorus of 44 singers.
Children's chorus unison – top Bb4.

Orchestration: 3 fl, 3 ob, 3 cl, 3 bsn, 6 hrn, 3 trp, 3 trb, 3 bugles, 2 timp, cel, pia, 4 hp, strings. Small stage ensemble.

Synopsis: See "Synopsis" under *The Legend of St. Christopher* by Horatio Parker.

Materials: GS (SAL - © 1918) (Fr)

Notes: Theatre performance only. Requires highly skilled singers, instrumentalists and production personnel. It is said that with this work, d'Indy attacked the politics of the Third Republic.

MARTIN KALMANOFF

Noah and the Stowaway

Music by **Martin Kalmanoff** (b. 1920). "A Musical Diatribe" with Biblical and moralistic overtones. Libretto in English by Atra Baer. The work has little bearing on the Biblical story of Noah – only the setting has been adapted.

Composition completed in New York, April, 1950. Premiered in New York City, February 18, 1951; first staged performance October 12, 1952, Provincetown Theatre, New York.

Highly melodic with some twentieth century dissonance. Tonally conceived but considerable chromaticism. Good for children as well as adults. Comic and lyric drama.

One act. Lengthy Overture which is musically descriptive of the destruction of civilization and which could be staged. Setting: 2010 A.D. on a modern ark (boat). Duration: 30 minutes.

Major Roles: STOWAWAY (ten or high bar – top F3); NOAH (bs-bar); MRS. NOAH (m-sop).

Minor Roles: MR. ELEPHANT (bs-bar); MRS. ELEPHANT (m-sop); MR. DOG (ten); MRS. DOG (sop); MR. DOVE (anything); MRS. DOVE (col sop); FIRST SNAKE (ten); SECOND SNAKE (ten); MR. TIGER (bar); MRS. TIGER (cont).

Orchestration: Keyboard.

Synopsis: Something catastrophic has terminated nearly all life on earth. Noah and his companions are the only living creatures who remain. Situated on a boat, they have the responsibility of starting a brave, clean, peaceful new world. They set out to do this with exuberance and in high spirits. There is genuine comradery between the people and animals alike until the appearance of a Stowaway. He seems to breed fighting, quarreling, and general disarray. When they are temporarily worn out by their fighting and there is a moment of peace, they inquire as to the Stowaway's name. He first tells them a strange story and then reveals to them that he is "Human Nature." The future of the world certainly now remains in doubt.

Materials: Unpublished. ASU.

BRYAN KELLY

Herod, Do Your Worst

Music by **Bryan Kelly** (Bristish). A Nativity Opera with libretto in English by John Fuller, loosely based on several scenes surrounding the birth of Jesus.

Conventional harmony with twentieth century influences. Some chromaticism. Twelve numbers with spoken dialogue and narration. Vocally not difficult. Comedy.

One act. Setting: From the annunciation to Mary until the flight into Egypt. Duration: 60 minutes.

Singing Roles: All roles are middle range and accessible. JOSEPH (ten); MARY (sop); HOTEL RECEPTIONIST (bar or cont); THREE SHEPHERD BOYS (trebles).

Speaking Roles: GABRIEL and SIMEON (narrators); FIRST GUEST; HEROD; THREE ASTROLOGERS; BRASS HEAD; FIVE SOLDIERS.

Acting Roles: TWO ANGELS; SECOND GUEST.

Chorus: SATB – angels who respond to and comment on the action (one ten solo).

Dance: One dance number for the animals in the stable (sheep, cows, a dove, cock, hen, and a donkey).

Orchestration: fl, timp, 3 perc (side dr, bs dr, cym, sus cym, triangle, glock, tamb, xyl, castanets, bells, gong), cel, pia duet, str.

Synopsis: Simeon and Gabriel control much of the dialogue as they ask many of the age-old questions of man. How can we be happy? Can things really be changed? How may man regain his freedom? The work opens with Joseph and Mary discussing her pregnancy. The next scene takes us to the hotel where several guests, including Mary and Joseph, encounter a greedy receptionist, who takes all their money and puts them in a stable. We now meet Herod in his throne room, depicted by the narrator as one "who is so unreasonable, that if he did not exist, it would be impossible to invent him." His astrologers enter, warning him of the birth of a child who will be a greater king than Herod. Herod commands that all children under two years of age be killed. Back at the stable, the animals dance before the Holy Family. Out in the field, three shepherd boys, bored by the long, dark night are intrigued by the new shiny star and follow it to the stable. The astrologers arrive and warn the young couple of Herod's insanity. The play ends as the young family march off to a new land and the chorus sings of its new found hope in the Redeemer.

Materials: NOV (© 1968)

Notes: Gabriel and Simeon should be dressed in Biblical costume with all other characters wearing modern dress. The work may be set in either contemporary or traditional period. Four acting areas are required: a stable, a hotel lobby, Herod's throne room, and two dais for the narrators. Best performed in a church or cathedral. Scenery may be minimal. The chorus should be seated on either side of the stage, and possibly also at the rear, though there should be access to the acting area from the rear as well as from the left and the right of the stage. Access from the audience is also advantageous. A good lighting system to focus on specific areas will assist the scene changes.

An avant-garde approach to the Nativity story. A blending of the contemporary with the ancient story may perhaps cause some discomfort to the audience, however, there is a powerful message, relevant to our contemporary lives. Numerous stage directions exist in the libretto; some in the VS.

EDGAR STILLMAN KELLY

Pilgrim's Progress

Music by **Edgar Stillman Kelly** (1857-1944). A Musical Miracle Play (Op. 37) with text in English taken from John Bunyan's book of the same name.

Premiered May, 1918, Cincinnati May Festival.

Highly Romantic style with considerable chromaticism. Musically difficult due to large forces required for production.

Three parts. Part I: Prologue, The City of Destruction, The Wicket-Gate, The Valley of Humiliation. Part II: Vanity Fair. Part III: The Delectable Mountains, The Crossing of the River, The Celestial City. Duration: 2 hours, 15 minutes.

Roles: CHRISTIAN (bar); FAITHFUL (bar); THE DREAMER (bar); MR. WORLDLY WISEMAN (bar); EVANGELIST (ten); HOPEFUL (ten); ATHEIST (ten); APOLLYON (bs); MR. MONEY-LOVE (bs); SHEPHERD BOY (boy sop); FIRST SHEPHERD (sop); ANGEL (sop); MADAM BUBBLE (dram sop). Some of the soloists may assume more that one part: Evangelist may also sing Hopeful and Atheist. Apollyon may also sing Mr. Money-love and Mr. Worldly Wiseman. First Shepherd may also sing Angel.

Chorus: Double choir of SATB – Voices of Doom, Neighbors, Vendors, Visitors at the Fair, Fiends, Heavenly Host, etc. Children's Chorus optional (celestial voices). Voices of the Spirit (altos). Considerable difficult choral music.

Orchestration: Full orchestra

Synopsis: The plot remains faithful to Bunyan's drama. The Dreamer narrates his dream in the form of a story in which Christian travels through life. Christian seeks to be freed from his heavy burden which he carries on his back. He eventually comes to the foot of the cross where in humility he kneels and finds that his burden rolls off his back. He meets Celestial Voices who guide him on his way. Christian is heard singing as he enters the Valley of Humiliation. Here he meets Apollyon, the devil, with whom he does battle. Victorious, he continues his journey to the City of Vanity Fair where he and his friend Faithful are cast into prison. Faithful is put to death for his beliefs but Christian escapes and finally after successfully crossing the River of Death, his journey ends in triumph at the gates of the Celestial City.

Materials: OD (© 1917)

Notes: Due to the large forces and the many scenes through which Pilgrim travels, this work is not easily produced as a staged work. Projections/multi-media may be helpful. Kelly has attempted to compose this work without the limitations of the oratorio tradition on the one hand or the paraphernalia of the opera on the other. The possibility of stage production was kept in mind by the composer. See also Kelly's *The Shorter Pilgrim's Progress.*

The Shorter Pilgrim's Progress

Music by **Edgar Stillman Kelly** (1857-1944). A Musical Miracle Play with text in English based on John Bunyan book of the same name adapted by Elizabeth Hodgkinson.

See *Pilgrim's Progress* by E. S. Kelly.

Premiered May 10, 1918, Cincinnati.

Duration: 60 minutes.

Roles: CHRISTIAN (bar); THE DREAMER (bar); EVANGELIST (ten); HOPEFUL (ten); FIRST SHEPHERD (sop); ANGEL (sop). Since all of the characters represented do not appear simultaneously, one baritone, one tenor, and one soprano may be used.

Chorus: SATB – Voices of Doom, Neighbors, Celestial Voices, Heavenly Host.

Orchestration: org and orchestra *ad libitum*

Synopsis: See Kelly's *Pilgrim's Progress.*

Materials: OD (© 1917, 1921).

Notes: This version was prepared for the use of church choirs and omits Vanity Fair (Part II) and certain passages in Part I of Kelly's *Pilgrim's Progress.* The work may be presented with organ and additional instruments *ad libitum*.

GERSHON KINGSLEY

God and Abraham

Music by **Gershon Kingsley** (20th century American). A Musical Theatre work with libretto in English by Robert Larimer, based on the Biblical account recorded in Genesis 20-22.

Composed in 1972.

Mostly conventional harmony with some atonality and contemporary "pop" sounds. Mixed styles; spoken dialogue in contemporary language. Rhythmic; continuous texture.

One act, two scenes. Scene 1: Abraham's home; sc. 2: In the mountains. Duration: 20 minutes.

Roles: GOD (bar – top Gb3); SARAH (m-sop); ABRAHAM (ten – top A3 sustained); NARRATOR (sop); VOICE (sp), narrative.

Chorus: SSATTB – Greek chorus commenting on the action.

Orchestration: fl, 2 cl, 2 sax, hrn, trp, trb, perc, Fender 6, pia, org, electronic tape (opt).

Synopsis: A series of confrontations face Abraham. A confrontation occurs when God asks Abraham to sacrifice his most precious possession, his son Isaac. Abraham cannot tell Sarah the truth when she asks where he and Isaac are going. Finally Abraham and Isaac arrive at the appointed place of sacrifice. God, at the moment before Abraham sacrifices Isaac, miraculously provides a lamb for the sacrifice.

Materials: BOU (© 1972)

Notes: Best suited for church performance. Requires only properties; no sets needed.

FREDERICK KOCH

The Shepherds

Music by **Frederick Koch** (b. 1923). A Christmas Opera with libretto in English by Seymour Reiter, based on the early fifteenth century *Second Shepherds' Play*, a revision by the anonymous Wakefield Master of his *First Shepherds' Play.* In the tradition of the mystery plays.

Written in 1984 and previewed in the home of the composer, Cleveland, Ohio. Not yet premiered.

Melodically conceived with considerable harmonic dissonance. Lyric in nature. Continuous texture; some accompanied recitatives. Not a difficult musical score.

One act, one setting. Prologue. Duration: 60 minutes.

Major Roles: All roles except Coll are mid-range and not demanding. COLL (bar – A1-G3), the oldest shepherd – wide range; GIB (bar), the second shepherd; DAW (ten), the youngest shepherd.

Minor Roles: MAK (bar), a sheep stealer; GILL (m-sop), his wife; ANGEL (sop); MARY (sop).

Chorus: SATB. They are stationary acting as a Greek chorus, commenting on the action.

Orchestration: fl, hp, tamb, bells, sm tam tam, string quartet.

Synopsis: In the Prologue, Truth, Mercy, Justice and Peace debate in heaven whether mankind should be saved or not. We learn that it is God's intention to bring man to redemption. The three shepherds, tending their sheep, find one of their lambs missing. They suspect Mak, and decide to pay him a visit. Meanwhile, Mak, who has stolen the lamb, and his wife Gill, who are poor and without food for their children, anticipate a stormy encounter from the shepherds. Mak prays for mercy. Gill tells him the Lord will have nothing to do with their likes. They hide the lamb in the baby cradle. The shepherds arrive in great anger, accusing Mak of stealing their lamb. Mak and Gill deny any wrong doing and ask the shepherds to leave as their baby is ill. Daw bends down to kiss the baby, only to discover their lamb. The shepherds will not be like their masters, who blame them for trying to thwart starvation. They forgive Mak and go on their way.

The three shepherds lie down on the moors to rest. An Angel announces to them the birth of Him who brings the world a new spring. They go to Bethlehem and celebrate the Child's birth. Mary sings that the Father of Heaven has lent his Son to the world to restore love and peace.

Materials: CF.

Notes: The playing area must be divided into two distinct settings. On one side is the cottage of Gill and Mak simply furnished – on the other side, the hillside moors. A good lighting design will facilitate this separation. Can be effectively played in either theatre or church. The complexity of sets will be determined by the performing facility.

LESLIE KONDOROSSY

Ruth and Naomi

Music by **Leslie Kondorossy** (1915-1989). A Sacred Opera with libretto in English by Shawn Hall and Richard L. Glass, based on the Biblical Book of Ruth.

Commissioned and premiered by the Church of the Master, Cleveland Heights, OH, April 28, 1974.

Free harmonies, highly chromatic, post-expressionism; simple melodic lines with some *sprechgesang*.

One act. Duration: 20 minutes.

Roles: RUTH (sop); NAOMI (alt); BOAZ (ten). Supporting roles include sop, alt, ten, bar.

Chorus: SATB; also a children's chorus.

Orchestration: recorder or picc, fl, ob, cl, hrn, timp, perc, strings, org or harmonium.

Synopsis: Naomi, a widow, is returning with Ruth, her daughter-in-law, to the village of her people, the Jews. Ruth is quickly discerned to be an outsider, a Moabitess, because of her strange sounding accent and foreign garb. Insults ruthlessly follow. Naomi bids her return to her own home town which Ruth refuses to do with a simple statement: "Do not bid me leave you. Your people are my people, your God, my God. Beside you in death let me lie." Boaz has observed this highly emotional scene and sides with Ruth, telling the people that she has been a faithful gleaner in his fields, at all times modest and devoted to her mother-in-law. He reminds them to observe the Jewish law by welcoming strangers with open hearts of love and mercy, which are more important than tradition. Boaz then accepts Ruth as his own wife.

Materials: Unpublished. AMC and the composer.

Notes: Intended to be performed in a house of worship as part of a worship service.

ROBERT EDWARD KREUTZ

Francesco: A Musical Biography

Music by **Robert Edward Kreutz** (1922-1996). A musical biography of the life of St. Francis of Assisi with libretto in English by Willard Jabusch. Some Latin and Italian texts.

Premiered in concert version at Orchestra Hall in Chicago by soloists from the Lyric Opera of Chicago, the Chicago Symphony and the William Ferris Chorale, Sunday, October 4, 1987. Kreutz was in the process of editing the work when he died in 1996. Notes about these changes are available from Juliana Bishop Hoch (see end of this entry).

Lyrical melodies pervade the entire work. Harmonic language is rich and varied using traditional harmony together with modern 20th century techniques throughout. Considerable use of modality along with jazz influences are present. Arias, choral sections and some chant-like singing are incorporated.

Opera in 3 Acts, between 1200-1226 AD. Act I has three scenes in Assisi; Act II has three scenes in Assisi; Act III, sc. 1 in Africa/Morocco, sc. 2 in Rome, sc. 3 & 4 in Assisi. Duration: 2-1/2 hours

Singing Roles: GUIDO (ten – C2-A3), troubadour; PAULO/PRIEST (bar), young man of Assisi; BISHOP (ten); CARLO/SULTAN MALID-AL-KAMIL (bs), Commander-in-chief of Saracon armies; LUIGI/PIETRO DI CATANIO (ten); PIETRO DI BERNADONE (bs), father of Francesco/UGOLINO, Cardinal; FRANCESCO (bar – B1-G3), St. Francis of Assisi; PICA (m-sop), Mother of Francesco/GIACOMA DEI SETTESOLI, Countess of Frangepane; BERNARDO (bs), beloved Friar; CATERINA (m-sop), Sister of Chiara; CHIARA (sop – D3-G4), St. Claire

Non-singing Roles: (speaking and non-speaking roles) LEO, the Priest; Friars: GILIO, GIOVANNI, JUNIPER, TEOBALDO, AGOSTINO, MASSEO, KNIGHT; A LEPER; CRUSADERS; FRENCH GIRLS; TOWN PEOPLE; 3rd ORDER NUNS; BONA, Maid to Chiara; ACOLYTES; DEACONS

Chorus: SATB utilized throughout the opera

Dance: Optional Ballet Dancers are used in Act I.

Orchestration: fl, ob, cl, bsn, hrn, 2 trp, 2 ten trb, timp, perc, pia, hp, cel, str: 8. 6. 5. 4. 2

Synopsis: The opera begins in Francesco's teenage years which were filled with frivolity through the time of his conversion. It continues through his trip to Egypt during the Crusades and his visit with the Sultan, mystic experiences, his final illness, and death.

Guido, the troubadour, acts as the narrator for the opera and begins Act I by telling about the memories of his friend, Francesco, St. Francis of Assisi. The action starts when Francesco, a teenager in Assisi, is always flirting with the pretty ladies. Suddenly an army of young men comes into town, signaling the fact that war is nearby. Francesco's father, Pietro Bernadone, is a tailor and asks his son to walk in his footsteps. The confused Francesco begins to feel that there is more to life than money. In Act I, Scene II, Francesco goes off to join the war, and his mother, Pica, expresses her remorse in song. Francesco's army is defeated, and he returns home gravely ill. After one year of recuperation, Francesco decides to throw a party. His friends realize that something very important has changed in him; he has found his spiritual center and "Lady Poverty". The guiding purpose of his life has become to give to the poor. Francesco embraces the poor, the hungry, and the sick in a poignant scene at the end of Act I where he kisses a leper.

In Act II, Francesco is brought to trial for being a religious fanatic and an ungrateful son. He tells his father that he does not need the gold or family business, the house or the horses to ride. All he wants is to live as the poorest of men and to imitate and follow Jesus Christ. In Act II, Scene IV, it is Palm Sunday, 1211 AD, and in a moving aria that ends Act II, Chiara chooses the love of God for her life. In Act III, Guido sings about the crusade adventures of Francesco. While on this trip which includes Porziuncola, Morocco, and Damietta, near the mouth of the Nile, Francesco becomes ill and hears about an abundance of unrest within the church in Italy. He decides to return to Rome, telling about his crusade struggles. Cardinal Ugolino shuns Francesco for his wild ideas. Francesco returns to Assisi to die, and the opera ends with Guido again singing about his friend, Francesco.

Materials: Scores, parts available in hand manuscript from the composer's estate – see Kreutz in Appendix C

Notes: Best performed in a theatre. The opera captures the powerful influence that Francesco, St. Francis of Assisi had on the men and women that knew him.

This entry was written by Juliana Bishop Hoch, author of a definitive study and analysis of Kreutz's life and music. Her study/dissertation is available – see Hoch in Appendix C for contact information.

EZRA LADERMAN

And David Wept

Music by **Ezra Laderman** (b. 1924). A Sacred Music Drama with libretto in English by Joe Darion, based on the story of David, Bathsheba and Uriah as found in II Samuel 11 in the Old Testament.

Commissioned by CBS News. First performance was given April 8, 1971, on CBS television, conducted by Alfredo Antonini, choreographed by Jose Limon. First staged performance was May 31, 1980 at 92nd Street "Y", New York.

Rhythmic complexities, considerable dissonance and chromaticism. Wide ranges with chanting and spoken lines for the singers. Recitatives are accompanied but mostly spoken or chanted on a given pitch. Arias, duets, trios.

Eleven sections but continuous texture. Duration: 50 minutes.

Roles: DAVID (bar – top G3), King of Israel; BATHSHEBA (m-sop – A2 to A4); URIAH (bs-bar – G#1-F3), husband to Bathsheba and David's army general.

Dance: See "Notes" below.

Orchestration: fl, ob, 2 cl, bsn, 2 hrn, trp, hp, pia, hpsch, 2 perc, str

Synopsis: When King David looked out over his palace patio and saw Bathsheba bathing on the roof of an adjoining house, he was so taken by her beauty that he swore he would have her. However, David was King of Israel and Bathsheba was married to Uriah, David's army general. Furthermore, adultery was punishable by death. It is a story that happened long ago as we find these three characters reflecting on the incidents of their lives. It is a reflection on a story of passion, murder, despair, retribution, and regeneration. It is a story of the conflicts and contradictions that constantly batter the human heart.

Materials: OUP

Notes: This work can be performed in a number of different setting: 1) fully staged as a dance work with orchestra in the pit and singers stationary; 2) in pantomime with dancers as the singers' alter egos; 3) fully staged as in an operatic version; 4) or as a concert piece.

Galileo Galilei

Music by **Ezra Laderman** (b. 1924). An Opera-Oratorio with libretto in English by Joe Darion. This work was copyrighted in 1967 by Joe Darion and Ezra Laderman under the title *The Trials of Galileo*.

Commissioned by Pamela Ilott, Executive Producer of Cultural Programming of the CBS Television Network, and first performed on that network in May, 1967 under the title *The Trials of Galileo*. The first staged performance under the new title, *Galileo Galilei*, was by the Tri-Cities Opera in cooperation with the State University of New York at Binghamton, on February 3, 1979.

Rhythmic complexities, considerable dissonances, straying tonalities with much chromaticism. Some spoken dialogue, mostly with underscoring. Vocal lines melodic, though chromatic.

Three acts and an Epilogue. Setting: In and around Rome, Italy, in the seventeenth century. Act I: In the study of Galileo in Arcetri; Act II: A conference room in the Vatican, later in the quarters of Cardinal Bellarmine; Act III: The Inquisition trial; Epilogue: Same as Act I. Duration: approximately 2 hours.

Major Roles: GALILEO (bs-bar – F#1-E3), extremely long and demanding role, requiring a superb actor and singer. Role includes rhythmic speech effects as well as chanting; THE FRIEND (m-sop), a Roman noblewoman; POPE PAUL (ten), requires agility; CARDINAL BELLARMINE (bar – top G3, high tess); THE INTERROGATOR (high ten – high tess), disjunct and chromatic lines. CARDINAL BARBERINI (ten), Pope Urban VIII.

Minor Roles: THREE PROFESSORS (ten); TWO JESUITS (ten, bar); TWO DOMINICANS (ten, bar – top F#3); TORTURERS (baritones – high tess); MARINA (m-sop), Galileo's mistress; Galileo's daughters: LIVIA (sop) and VIRGINIA (m-sop); TEN CARDINALS OF THE INQUISITION COURT (1st & 4th are tenors; others are silent).

Chorus: SSATTBB. The chorus should be dimly seen and perhaps cowled, giving the impression of an impersonal force, of disembodied voices, or of thoughts. Musically difficult ensemble.

Orchestration: 2 fl, 2 ob, 2 cl, 2 bsn, 2 hrn, 2 trp, 2 trb, tba, hp, org, 3 perc, timp, strings

Synopsis: Galileo is seated in his study, defeated, rejected, and blind. He is old and as he awaits death he contemplates his long and turbulent life. His astronomical discoveries have consistently been rejected by tradition-bound professors as well as the church. A Roman noblewoman known as The Friend is beside Galileo, comforting and protecting him. To her, he pours out his heart. She warns him that he cannot break down the walls of ignorance of the universities. The Anonymous Beast of Rome, the mob, assault him with their blind ignorance. He cannot conceal his findings. Act II opens to a meeting Pope Paul has called to consider Galileo and his discoveries. Distinguished church leaders find that Galileo's mind and work are a dangerous threat to the church and its doctrine. Bellarmine defends Galileo, stating that scientific truth can never hurt the church. The Interrogator requests that if Galileo is given over to him, he will never again trouble the church. Bellarmine summons Galileo, informing him that the Pope must be consulted on all discoveries before they are made public. Furthermore, he must stop his ill-treatment of women. A tableau of Galileo's ill treatment of women follow with brief scenarios of Marina, his mistress, his daughters, his tavern friends, and his faithful Friend. We are returned to his conversation with Bellarmine, in which Bellarmine warns him not to claim discoveries when he knows they are true, especially that the earth moves. Galileo angrily cries out "The earth moves" as the curtain falls.

In Act III, Barberini has become the new Pope, Urban VIII. He is angry with Galileo for not heeding the warnings of the church. He is given over to the Inquisition for trial. He is sentenced, imprisoned and finally placed under house arrest to his old home in Arcetri. In the Epilogue we are returned to Galileo's study during his final years. He has written all his discoveries into one massive book and begs his Friend to take the book to Holland and have it printed. She finally consents. Galileo, now blind, turns his face to the heavens and declares: "Let the world know what Galileo knows! If I am to be judged, let God judge me!" The chorus thunders a triumphant *Eppur se Muove* (the earth moves) as the curtain falls.

Materials: OUP.

Notes: Suggestions for performance: The stage area should be dark and consist of platforms with varying heights. Tables and chairs should be the only props. Lighting design should be creative and suggest the place, time, and mood. On the highest level upstage should be the chorus. The work can also be done in concert form.

JOHN LA MONTAINE

Erode the Greate

Music by **John La Montaine** (b. 1920). A Pageant Opera with libretto in English (some French and Latin texts) by the composer adapted from the Bible, Medieval Miracle Plays and the Latin Liturgy. Third and final opera of a "Christmas Trilogy." Two preceding operas were *Novellis, Novellis* (1961) and *The Shephardes Playe* (1967). The text for the libretto was constructed from the material found in the Corpus Christi plays of York, Wakefield, Chester and Coventry. The spoken words of the Narrator comprise the Christmas story as found in the King James Version of the Bible. At some points the chorus comments upon the universal significance of the action, using words from the Latin Liturgy. These three levels of language, culture and historical perspective are brought into interplay.

Commissioned by the Washington Cathedral; completed January 24, 1969, first performed, December, 1969.

Considerable use of modality, many rhythmic complexities, melodic but requiring mature voices, twentieth century harmonic idioms with considerable chromaticism. Continuous texture. Musically, not an easy score.

Two acts. Setting: during the time of Jesus' birth and after. Act I, sc. 1: The Palace of Herod the Great; sc. 2: The countryside near Jerusalem; Sc. 3: The Palace of Herod the Great. Act II, sc. 1: Bethlehem; sc. 2: Herod's Private Chambers; sc. 3: The same, The Manager, Hell's Mouth; Epilogue: The Countryside. Duration: 90 minutes.

Major Roles: NARRATOR (sp); HEROD THE GREAT (bar – top G3), a lengthy and dramatically demanding role with a high tessitura; LIGHTFOOT (ten), Messenger to Herod; JASPAR (ten), King of Tarsus; MELCHIOR (bar), King of Araby; BALTHAZAR (bs), King of Saba; MARY (sop); A YOUNG ANGEL (ten); GABRIEL (ten); COUNSELLOR I TO HEROD (ten); COUNSELLOR II TO HEROD (bar); DEMON FROM HELL'S MOUTH (ten). It is intended that the roles of Lightfoot, the Young Angel, and the Demon be sung by the same singer. The part of Gabriel may be sung by Jaspar.

Silent Roles: JOSEPH; Herod's Juggler and Tumblers; Attendants to Herod (mostly boys): Retriever of Herod's Sword, Cup-Bearer, Bearer of the Royal Fan, Falcon-Bearer, Custodian of the Books, Bearer of the Incenser, Bearer of the Bell; Knights, Custodians of Mace, Flail, and Ax; The Slayers of Innocents; JESUS (a young boy); A Child Angel.

Chorus: SATB and children serving as courtiers to Herod, shepherds, grieving women, and angels. At times they are involved in the action, at times they comment on the action as a Greek chorus.

Dance: The following may be dancers: Bearer of the Gold and attendant to Jaspar, Bearer of the Frankincense and attendant to Melchior, Bearer of Myrrh and attendant to Balthazar. Dancers are optional but some stylized choreography adds considerably to the environment.

Orchestration: 2 fl (picc), 2 ob (Eng hrn), 2 cl, 2 bsn, hrn, 3 trp, 3 trb, 2 perc (timp, sd dr, ten dr, bs dr, gong, cym, gong-chime, bell, tri, whip, ratchet, anvil, wind machine, earthquake), hp, strings. Additional instruments are optional. For Herod's Court Processional: bagpipe, cym, tamb, dr. For Herod's Processional: A cloche-rattle, cym, whip, anvil, ten dr, picc. Each of the three kings is attended by two instrumentalists, one played, the other mimed while played in the orchestra proper. For

King Melchior: a two-headed rustic hand-drum (played), a reed instrument (mimed); for King Jaspar: a tamb (played), a rec (mimed); for King Balthazar: a sus cym (played), a lyre (mimed).

Synopsis: Herod and his court enter in a brilliant procession of pageantry, with Herod proclaiming his own greatness with pompous words. The Wisemen enter from different directions through the audience, having been brought together by a common star. They greet each other and share their common goal: to find the prophesied King. Lightfoot presents them to Herod and they tell of their search for the new King. Herod cunningly sends them on their way, but asks them to return to him when they have found Jesus. When the kings arrive at the manger scene and present their gifts, an angel appears to them and warns them not to return to Herod. They leave, going their separate ways. Meanwhile, Herod calls his counselors to search for the prophecy concerning this new King. They read the prophecies. Enraged and hysterical, Herod grabs the books and tears them apart. Lightfoot returns and taunts Herod. Herod, now completely deranged, sends his knights out to kill all children two years old and younger. An angel appears to tell Mary and Joseph to flee. The opera ends with the Demon taking Herod into the fiery pit. In an epilogue, the Holy Family, passing through the countryside, exits through the audience.

Materials: FP.

Notes: Ideally performed in a large Cathedral. Sets should be minimal and simultaneously visible throughout the opera. The "Christmas Trilogy" traces the entire Christmas story in this way:
   NOVELLIS, NOVELLIS
      The Old Testament prophecy
      The Annunciation
      The Journey to Bethlehem
      The Birth of Jesus
   THE SHEPHARDES PLAYE
      The Shepherds in the Fields
      The Appearance of the Star
      The Journey to Bethlehem
      Rejoicing at the Manger
   ERODE THE GREATE
      Herod receives news of the Birth
      The Coming of the Three Kings
      The Flight to Egypt
      The Slaying of the Innocents
      The Death of Herod
      Joseph and Mary return with young Jesus to Israel

The Lessons of Advent

Music by **John La Montaine** (b. 1910). After a Medieval Miracle Play with text in English adapted by the composer.

Two traditional hymns are used, *O Word, That Goest Forth* from the seventeenth century, and *Adeste, Fideles* from the eighteenth. The remaining hymns and carols are original settings of texts, some as ancient as the early fourth century, some as recent as 1983. The composer has suggested that a dramatic performance follow the style of the Medieval Miracle Play.

Composition premiered December 4, 1983.

Harmonically tonal with modal tendency. Some twentieth century dissonances. Melodic and lyric.

Divided into eighteen lessons with Narration between most. Duration: 50 minutes.

Roles: NARRATOR (sp), a Prophet and Evangelist; TRUMPETER; DRUMMER.

Chorus: Double Chorus of SATB. Greek chorus. Though designed for double chorus, as many as four choruses may participate, two of which would be children.

Orchestration: ob, hp, gui, handbell choir (five octaves – a difficult part).

Synopsis: The readings from the Old and New Testaments range from the earliest prophecies to the Annunciation as found in St. Luke, while the carols touch, sometimes light-heartedly, upon the entire mission and meaning of Jesus on earth. The Narrator and accompanying drummer and trumpeter move about the edifice to announce each successive lesson – beginning in the West – the dark of the Old Testament, and moving to the East – the light of the New. At the close of the work, the participants may move to honor a Crèche placed appropriately, and thereby surround completely the auditors for the final hymn and alleluias.

Materials: FP.

Notes: An effective and musically rewarding work. Ideally performed in a church.

Novellis, Novellis

Music by **John La Montaine** (b. 1910). A Pageant Opera with libretto in English (some Latin) adapted by the composer from two medieval plays: *The Coventry Corpus Christi Play of the Taylors and Shearmen and Chester Corpus Christi Play of the*

Nativity. The words spoken by the narrator are from the King James Bible while the Latin words sung by the chorus are from the liturgy of the *Liber Usualis.*

First performance on December 24, 1961, at the Washington Cathedral.

Musical idiom is a response to the literary style of the mystery plays of the Middle Ages. According to the composer, the only guiding principle of the music has been that of appropriateness. Much of the music consists of modern elaborations or extensions of medieval musical materials. Some unaccompanied recitative sections; continuous texture. This is the least difficult of the "Christmas Trilogy," easily accessible, melodic.

One Act. Traces the Christmas story in four sections: The Old Testament prophecy, the Annunciation, the Journey to Bethlehem, and the Birth of Jesus. Duration: 50 minutes.

Major Roles: NARRATOR (sp); MARY (sop – C3-A4); JOSEPH (bs-bar – G#1-E3).

Minor Roles: GABRIEL (ten – C2-A3); FIRST PROPHET (bar); SECOND PROPHET (ten); JOSEPH'S ANGEL (boy sop – F3-F4), may be sung by Gabriel; SALOME (sop), a midwife; TEBELL (alt), a midwife; THREE ANGELS (silent roles), children.

Chorus: SSAATTBB. Greek chorus, sings in Latin.

Orchestration: 2 fl, 2 ob, Eng hrn, cl, 2 bsn, contra bsn, 3 trp, 3 trb, perc, timp, hp, hpsch, org (opt), strings.

Synopsis: Two prophets tell of the angels' message to the shepherds, the news of the Messiah's birth. Gabriel appears to Mary, telling her that she will be the Savior's mother, and that His name will be Jesus. When Mary breaks the news to Joseph, he bursts into a rage, but an angel appears to him in a dream, confirming her innocence. Joseph returns to Mary and together they travel to Bethlehem to pay their taxes. When they arrive, they are placed in a manger. Two Midwives are sought to assist and the Christ Child is born. The Prophets return to declare the fulfillment of prophecy and the chorus responds with an "Alleluia."

Materials: GS, later by FP.

Notes: See "notes" under La Montaine's *Erode the Greate.* Ideally suited for performance in a church. Minimal set requirements.

The Shephardes Playe

Music by **John La Montaine** (b. 1920). A Pageant Opera with libretto in English by the composer adapted from four medieval Corpus Christi plays from the towns of Coventry, Chester, Wakefield, and York. The words spoken by the Narrator are from the King James Bible. The Latin words sung by Chorus I are from the Latin liturgy of the *Liber Usualis*.

Commissioned and premiered by the Washington Cathedral, December, 1967; televised by ABC-TV. Paul Hume of the *Washington Post* called it "One of the loveliest moments in the history of music in the theater."

Dominated by modality; conventional harmonies with twentieth century idioms and chromaticism. Rhythmically intricate at times. Highly melodic. Continuous texture. Accompanied recitative and chanting. Two of the tunes come from sources contemporary with the plays: "On Wouldes have I walked full wylde," set to a tune by Guillaume de Machaut, and the Shepherd's Carol *As I outrode*, a free realization of one of the three songs used in the *Coventry Nativity Play*.

One act, three different scenes: Out in the fields, on the road to Bethlehem and at the Manger. Duration: 60 minutes.

Singing Roles: NARRATOR (sp, some chanting); HENKIN (bar – A1-F#3), 1st shepherd; HARVYE (bs), 2nd shepherd; TUDD (ten – F#2-A3), 3rd shepherd; TROWLE (boy sop – D3-G4), a shepherd boy; SOLO ANGEL (ten); MARY (sop).

Silent Roles: JOSEPH; ANGEL WITH LANTERN (small girl); CUSTODIANS OF THE OX AND ASS (two small boys – the animals are portable, but bigger than the boys); CUSTODIAN OF THE ZIMBELSTERNE (adult angel); CUSTODIAN OF THE FLOWER PETALS (teen-age girl angel).

Chorus: TTBB (Chorus I), SATB (Chorus II), TREBLE CHORUS (Angel's Chorus taken from Chorus I and II and added children (opt); all carry and play one finger cymbal. Later, as a part of the crowd, each child carries a tiny bell.

Dance: Peasant dancers required.

Orchestration: 2 fl (picc), 2 ob, Eng hrn, 2 cl, 2 bsn, 3 trp, 3 trb, hp, hpsch (opt), gui (opt), 2 perc (timp, sm dr, lg dr, lg gong, gong-chime, tri, tamb, bells), strings. Optional on-stage instruments for the angel orchestra: 2 ob, tamb, sm dr, drone on A, and a miscellany of others if desired – bagpipe, hurdy-gurdy, vielle, viola d'amore, any strings. For the shepherd's orchestra: cl, ob, bsn, tamb. Other optional musical props: a ram's horn (one note: F) and a portable Zimbelsterne.

Synopsis: The three shepherds gather around a fire after a day's work to discuss the day's activities. A little shepherd boy, Trowle joins them, bringing his little pet lamb with him. They say their evening prayers and settle down for the night. During the night they are awakened by a host of angels singing of the Messiah's birth. Frightened and confused they depart for Bethlehem. They gather villagers as they approach the manger scene. When they finally catch sight of the Christ Child, they are motionless. Then slowly the shepherds present their gifts of a flute, a spoon, a cap, and a little lamb from the youngest shepherd. Mary assures them of Christ's blessing and they depart rejoicing.

Materials: FP.

Notes: See "Notes" under La Montaine's *Erode the Great* for further notes.

STANLEY LEBOWSKY

The Children's Crusade

Music by **Stanley Lebowsky** (b. 1926). A Morality Play for the Young with text in English by Fred Tobias.

Musical themes by Palestrina. Many popular musical idioms and rhythms. Continuous texture with numbers tied together by narration and some underscoring.

Two parts, ten numbers. Setting: On the way to the Holy Land and before the King and Cardinal. Duration: 45 minutes.

Major Roles: STEPHEN (ten or boy sop), a French teenage peasant boy; THE KING (bs); CARDINAL (bar); NARRATOR (sp).

Minor Roles: May be taken from the chorus: SOPRANO SOLO, top B4; YOUNG BOY (bar); YOUNG GIRL (sop), top A4; BOY SOPRANO.

Chorus: SSAATTBB – the children and also commentary on the action. If the chorus is treated as a Greek Chorus, a group of children could be used as supernumeraries. Some Latin text and some unaccompanied sections.

Dance: One short dance number which is designed to be folk style or free ad lib movement by the cast.

Orchestration: pia alone or gui (acoustic and elec), bs (acoustic or elec), drums.

Synopsis: See Menotti's *The Death of the Bishop of Brindisi* for historical background. The Narrator and chorus establish the background for the Children's Crusade of 1212 A.D. Stephen, a young French boy, calls all who will follow him to reclaim the Holy Land, hoping to change the world with love. Numerous children follow him as they journey first to visit with the King and Cardinal, who reject the pleas of the children. They march on to Marseilles seeking someone who will transport them to the Holy Land. Finally a ship owner makes an offer and 2000 children triumphantly board ten ships. During the trip two ships were lost in a storm while the remaining children were sold into slavery. None reached the Holy Land. The world was not yet ready for their mission.

Materials: GS (© 1978)

Notes: As a theatre piece the possibilities are numerous. The composer has suggested the use of projected slides of medieval pictures and scenes, along with medieval costuming. The work may be performed in any period or style the director desires. The performers and musicians may be stationed on different levels or platforms enhanced by theatrical lighting. The entire work could be staged with dance, mime, strobe lights, or any form of mixed media conceivable. Best performed in a house of worship with production resembling a medieval morality play.

DAN LOCKLAIR

Good Tidings from the Holy Beast

Music by **Dan Locklair** (b. 1949). A Christmas Opera with libretto in English taken from the *Chester Miracle Cycle*. Edited and translated from the original Middle English by Suzanne Locklair.

Premiered December 21, 1978, First Plymouth Congregational Church, Lincoln, NE.

The work captures the flavor of early music in its use of modality, recorders, and chant-like expressions but infused with twentieth century devices. As the work progresses, the use of further chromaticism, polytonality, *sprechstimme*, bi-tonality and other non-traditional harmonic treatments become more in evidence.

One act. Duration: 50 minutes.

Roles: GABRYELL (ten); MARIA (sop); ELIZABETH (alt); JOSEPH (bs-bar); TEBELL (alt); SALOME (sop).

Chorus: SATB – Angels and Townspeople.

Dance: Some dance and stylized choreography needed.

Orchestration: rec (sop, ten), fl, ob, bsn, hrn, trp, strings, pia, 2 perc (chimes, sn dr, ten dr, bs dr, cym, tri, tamb, gong), org (ad lib).

Synopsis: Gabryell announces to Maria that she will bear the Christ Child. Excitedly she tells Elizabeth the good news. Together they sing the *Magnificat* unaccompanied. Joseph meanwhile makes plans to leave Mary since she has been gone from him for three month. Gabryell visits Joseph and convinces him that Maria is a part of God's plans. Maria returns home and the two travel to Bethlehem. Ready to deliver her child, Joseph seeks shelter and midwives to assist. The Child is born, and townspeople, angels and animals join in rejoicing.

Materials: SMC.

Notes: Designed for presentation in a church sanctuary, much like the early execution of the miracle plays. It is also designed to involve participation from the audience so that they too become a living part of the drama. Minimal property needed.

RUTH TAYLOR MAGNEY

The Gift of the Magi

Music by **Ruth Taylor Magney** (20th century American). A Christmas Music Drama with libretto in English by the composer, based on a story by O. Henry.

Premiered April 16, 1964, Minneapolis, MN.

Conventional harmonies, melodic. Comedy.

One act. Set in a large contemporary city. Duration: approximately 40 minutes.

Roles: DELLA YOUNG (sop), a young wife; JAMES YOUNG (bar), her husband; MADAME SOPHRONIE (cont), a hairdresser.

Chorus: SSA, offstage.

Orchestration: piano.

Synopsis: A young married couple, Della and James, live in a small apartment and struggle to make ends meet. Della counts her meager earnings and finds she does not have enough to buy James the watch chain for his beautiful old watch. James, on the other hand wants to buy Della combs for her beautiful long hair. Both independently come up with a clever solution. When they return home that evening with their gifts, James opens his gift and find his watch chain and when questioned how she could have bought it, she reveals that she has sold her hair. When she opens her gift of the combs, she understands his dismay and finds that he has sold his watch to pay for the combs. They both realize that they have given each other the greatest gift possible.

Materials: Unpublished. From the composer.

Notes: Suitable for either church or theatre performance.

DENISE MAINVILLE

The Christmas Troubadour

Music by **Denise Mainville**. A Christmas Operetta with libretto in English by the composer.

Tonal with conventional harmonies. Melodic and vocally conceived. Italian influences on vocabulary.

Three acts. Setting: the village square at Greccio, Italy. Duration: approximately 90 minutes.

Major Roles: FRANCIS; GIOVANNI; ADRIANO; VITTORIA.

Minor Roles: JACOPO; STEELA; MORICO; JUNIPER; A BEGGAR; FRIARS.

Chorus: SSA, representing village youths and peasants.

Dance: Required for the "Bird Ballet."

Orchestration: Keyboard

Synopsis: Francis of Assisi, the Little Poor Man, asks Giovanni De Vellita, a nobleman of Greccio, to have a replica of the stable of Bethlehem built in the village square so that he and all the people might come to a closer realization of the hardships suffered by the Christ Child at the time of His birth. While Giovanni and the village youths prepare for the Christmas Fiesta, Francis and the Friars recount tales of their trip to Rome. When Francis talks, even the birds listen and dance ("Bird Ballet"). Adriano Gurlandio, son of a rich silk merchant of Assisi, and boyhood friend of Francis, comes to Greccio for the Fiesta. While the villagers are gaily frolicking, Rinaldo brings the news of a royal party stopping at Greccio; and Vittoria, daughter of the reigning Doge, Pietro Ziani, comes to the square with her retinue. During his stay in Venice,

Adriano has met and fallen in love with the princess, but because of the differences in their life and station, has relinquished all hopes of claiming her for his bride. Vittoria, however, is searching for Adriano, who, hiding in the crowd hears the princess accept an invitation to attend the Fiesta.

In Act II, Adriano meets Francis, from whom he receives hope and counsel. Vittoria finally meets Adriano who reproaches her for seeking him. However, through the help of Francis, the two lovers are reconciled and through humility and love Vittoria finds a way to the heart of Adriano. Towards sunset, Francis and the Friars return from preaching. Francis tells of a misunderstanding between the Bishop and Governor of Greccio and how he wishes to effect a reconciliation. At midnight the village folk assemble in the village square for the Christmas Fiesta and Mass. The Bishop and Governor are moved to ask pardon of each other. Francis preaches the Christmas sermon at the stable, and a vision of Mary placing the little Christ Child in the arms of Francis is seen.

Materials: HF (© 1960).

Notes: Best performed in a theatre.

G. FRANCESCO MALIPIERO

La cena – The Last Supper

Music by **G. Francesco Malipiero** (1882-1973). A Passion with text in Italian by da Pierozzo Castellano de Castellani.

Composed in 1927.

Conventional harmony with some chromaticism. Through-composed. Highly melodic. Mostly ensemble.

One act. Setting: A large table in the Upper Room. Duration: 20 minutes.

Roles: ANGEL (bar), narrator; CHRIST (at different times SATB, 10 bs, or 10 ten); ST. PETER (bar); ST JOHN (ten); JUDAS (bs); 9 other disciples (mute).

Chorus: SATB – the voice of Christ.

Orchestration: Full orchestra.

Synopsis: Christ is seated with His twelve disciples preparing for their final meal together. Jesus suggests that Judas leave in order to take care of his "obligations." He then washes their feet, blesses the wine and bread and passes it to them all. Having finished the meal, they leave for the garden.

Materials: BIR (Eng translation by Anna Malipiero).

Notes: Best suited for church performance. Only a table and chairs necessary.

FRANK MARTIN

Le Mystère de la Nativité – The Mystery of the Nativity

Music by **Frank Martin** (1890-1974). A Scenic Oratorio with libretto in French based on the fifteenth century mystery play *Le mystère de la Passion* by d'Arnoul Greban.

Premiered December 29, 1959, in Geneva.

Uses twentieth century idioms; highly chromatic at times, some mixed meter. *Sprechstimme.* Set numbers. Requires large forces. See "Synopsis."

Three parts. Part I: The Annunciation; Part II: The birth of Jesus; Part III: Simeon, the Prophet. Duration: 105 minutes.

Roles: All, save one actor, play multiple characters. EVE and NOTRE DAME (sop); ELIZABETH and ANNA THE PROPHETESS (alt); GABRIEL and MELCHIOR (ten); SATHAN and YSAMBERT (ten); BELZEBUTH and RIFFLART (ten); ADAM and JOSEPH (bar); ASTAROTH (actor); PELLION and BALTHAZAR (actor); LUCIFER, ALORIS, JASPAR, LE PRÈTRE (bs).

Chorus: SATB – small chorus of 16-30.
SATB – large chorus of 50-100.
TTBB – chorus of 8-16.

Orchestration: 3 fl, 4 ob, 3 cl, 3 bsn, 4 hrn, 3 trp, 3 trb, tba, timp, perc, 2 hp, str

Synopsis: Follows the nativity story and mystery play faithfully beginning with the Annunciation and including the birth of Christ, the visit of the shepherds, the gifts of the three Magi and the fulfillment of prophecy concerning Simeon. Three levels of action occur throughout, each with its own corresponding musical texture. The bottom level is mostly atonal and deals with Satan, Hell and its devils. The top level represents other-earthly concepts including the angels, and is musically built in a simple harmonically traditional style. The middle level is musically between these two extremes and deals with earthly matters and people.

Materials: UE (Fr, Eng by George Barker – EAM).

Notes: Requires enormous musical forces but may be presented with minimal sets. Suitable to a large stage area in either a theatre or church/cathedral.

BOHUSLAV MARTINU

Griechische Passion – The Greek Passion

Music by **Bohuslav Martinu** (1890-1959). A Sacred Opera with libretto in German by the composer based on a novel by Nikos Kazantzakis.

Premiered June 9, 1961, in Zurich; American premiere April 4, 1981, Indiana University.

Conventional harmonies with materials derived from Greek Orthodox Liturgy, folk songs, accordion tunes, dances, and shepherd music. Vocally conceived with continuous texture and some dialogue. Considerable choral music since the plot revolves around the conflict of two large groups of people.

Four acts. Setting: in and around the small village of Lycovrissi on the slope of the Sarakina Mountains during the Turkish occupation of Greece. Act I: The village square on Easter morning. Act II, sc. 1: Near Katerina's garden by Yannakos's little house and stable; sc. 2: The fountain of St. Vassily in the village; sc. 3: In the mountains. Act III, sc. 1: Manolios's hut on the mountain slope; sc. 2: Katerina's house; sc. 3: A mountain road. Act IV, sc. 1: The village square; sc. 2: The mountain. Duration: approximately 120 minutes.

Roles: GRIGORIS (bs), the village Priest; PATRIARCHEAS (bs), an elder. **Villagers chosen for the Passion Play:** KOSTANDIS (bs), plays Apostle James; YANNAKOS (ten), plays Apostle Peter; MICHELIS (ten), plays Apostle John; WIDOW KATERINA (m-sop), plays Mary Magdalene; PANAIT (ten), plays Judas; MANOLIOS (ten), plays Christ. **Other villagers:** LENIO (sop – top Bb4), fiancée of Manolios; LADAS (sp), a miser; ANDONIS (ten), a barber; NIKOLIOS (ten), should play or simulate playing a flute; LENIO (sop); AN OLD WOMAN (cont). **Refugees who were driven from their village by the Turks and who settle on Mount Sarakina:** FOTIS (bar – top F3), Priest of the refugees; AN OLD MAN (bs); DESPINIO (col sop – top C5). NARRATOR (sp).

Chorus: Requires two large choruses of SATB representing the citizens of the village of Lycovrissi and the refugees whose village was destroyed by the Turks. Some non-singing children may also be added.

Orchestration: 3 fl, 3 ob, 3 cl, 3 bsn, 4 hrn, 3 trp, 3 trb, tba, timp, perc, hp, strings. On stage: accordion, flute-a-bec, harmonica, cl, vln, bells.

Synopsis: Priest Grigoris, who dominates the village, announces the cast who will perform the Passion Play in the village next Easter. As the villagers react in differing ways to the casting, a band is heard followed by refugees driven from their village by the Turks. They seek food, shelter and land on which to rebuild their village. As Priest Fotis tells their story, Manolios and Katerina receive them with compassion, but Grigoris orders the refugees away. Manolios advises them to camp on the mountain.

The remainder of the opera reveals the confrontation between the people of the village and the refugees on the mountain. Led by Fotis, the refugees plan a new village on the mountain. In the efforts to help the refugees, the attitudes of the participants of the Passion Play undergo a slow change from their normal village identities toward the roles they are to prepare.

Finally, as the village celebrates the wedding, not of Lenio and Manolios but of Lenio and Nikolios, Grigoris announces that Manolios has been excommunicated for blasphemy; Michelis, Yannakos, and Kostandis proclaim their support for him. Manolios proclaims his new found revelation, stating that the refugees cannot be ignored by decent people. His increasingly inflammatory language and the imminent approach of the refugees to defend him turns the villagers on him violently. They surround him crazed, and Panait stabs him. Both groups, subdued by the violence of the act in which they have participated, intone a *Kyrie*, each group from a different point of view. On Christmas Eve on the mountain, Priest Fotis and the refugees celebrate the birth of Christ and pray for Manolios.

Materials: UE (EAM). An English translation by Brian Large is available.

Notes: Cast and production crew of considerable proportions and professional technicians are required for this production. Requires a theatre for production.

What Men Live By

Music by **Bohuslav Martinu** (1890-1959). A Pastoral Opera with libretto in German based on Leo Tolstoi's *Pastoral*.

Premiered in 1935 in Hanover, Germany.

Highly melodic, traditional harmonies with some twentieth century chromaticism and dissonance. Accompanied recitatives. Spoken narrative.

One act, five scenes, but continuous texture. Setting: A cobbler's shop and the street outside one evening and the next morning. Duration: 50 minutes.

Roles: SPEAKER (sp), may be involved in the action; MARTIN AVDEITCH (bar – top F3), a shoe cobbler; AN OLD PEASANT PILGRIM (bs); STEPANITCH (bs), an old soldier; A WOMAN WITH CHILD (sop); AN OLD WOMAN (cont); A BOY (sp).

Chorus: SSATB – villagers. Several short solo parts within the chorus. If staged in the manner of a Miracle Play, the chorus should remain stationary.

Orchestration: 2 fl (1 opt), 2 ob, 3 cl (2 opt), 2 bsn, 2 hrn, trp, trb, perc, pia, strings.

Synopsis: Martin is told by voices to expect a visit from Christ the following day. He is encouraged by an old peasant friend to read his Bible and learn more about this visitor. As he reads and thinks, his anticipation grows. The next morning he rises early, eagerly watching for unfamiliar shoes to pass on the street outside his basement window. Only an old soldier, a poor woman with a starving baby, and an old woman appear. He befriends them and aids them, but all the while anxiously awaiting a visit from Christ. As the day nears its end and his hopes diminish, he suddenly is reminded by unseen voices that "as he had done it unto the least of these brethren, he had done it unto Him." Christ had indeed visited Martin, and the villagers join him in his praise to God.

Materials: BH (Ger, Eng)

Notes: May be performed in either a house of worship or theatre. While it is suggested that this work be produced in the manner of a miracle play, it can also be successfully staged realistically. VS contains numerous staging suggestions.

JULES MASSENET

Hérodiade – Herodias

Music by **Jules Massenet** (1842-1912). A Religious Opera with libretto in French by Paul Milliet and Henri Gremont (Georges Hartmann) after Flaubert loosely based on the Biblical account in Matthew 14.

Premiered December 19, 1881 in Brussels. Some revisions in 1884.

Chromatic and lush harmonic textures. Melodic; typical late Romantic operatic style.

Four acts, seven scenes. Setting: Galilee and Jerusalem around 29 A.D. Act I: Outer court of Herod's palace. Act II, sc. 1: Herod's chamber; sc. 2: A square in Jerusalem. Act III, sc. 1: Phanuel's house; sc. 2: The Temple. Act IV, sc. 1: A dungeon; sc. 2: The Great Hall in the palace. Duration: 2 hours.

Major Roles: HÉRODE (bar – C#2-Gb3, opt G3, high tess, requires both forceful and compassionate singing/acting; HÉRODIADE (m-sop – A2-Bb4, opt Cb5); SALOMÉ (sop – B2-C5); JEAN (ten – top Bb3, opt C4), the Baptist; PHANUEL (bs – G1-Eb3); VITELLIUS (bar).

Minor Roles: YOUNG BABYLONIAN (sop); HIGH PRIEST (bar); VOICE (ten).

Chorus: SSTTBB – Merchants, Priests, Levites, Jewish and Roman soldiers, Temple Attendants, Sailors, Overseers, Scribes. Many supers may be used.

Dance: A royal court dance before Hérode and Hérodias.

Orchestration: picc, 2 fl, 2 ob, Eng hrn, 3 cl, 2 bsn, alt sax, contra bs sax, 4 hrn, 2 corn, 2 trp, 4 trb, tba, timp, perc, 2 hp, string. On stage: nine parts.

Synopsis: Salomé is unaware that Hérodiade is her mother. Hérode is in pursuit of Salomé while Hérodiade is being condemned by the Prophet Jean for her evil ways. Salomé, meanwhile has been befriended by Jean and when she would seek his affection, he refuses her. In his bed chamber, Hérode longs for Salomé and rejects Phanuel's warnings of his wild and wasteful life style. Antagonized by Phanuel and Jean, Hérode appeals to the people to throw off the Roman yoke of power. Jean forceably declares to him that all power is from God. Meanwhile, Phanuel informs Hérodias that Salomé is her daughter. She is angered rather than pleased with this news. Back in the palace, Jean has been imprisoned with the priests insistence that Vitellius condemn him to death. Salomé, rejecting yet more advances from Hérode, joins Jean in his cell. Jean is taken by her devotion but advises her to save herself. The High Priest secretly offers Jean a pardon in exchange for his loyalties to Hérode against Rome. He refuses. While Hérode and Hérodiade entertain guests in the Great Hall, Salomé appears. Hérode will not listen to Salomé's pleas for Jean's pardon, but rather calls for the executioner who appears with a bloody sword after beheading Jean. Salomé, angered, turns on Hérodiade with a knife. Hérodiade reveals that she is Salomé's mother, whereupon Salomé kills herself.

Materials: TP (Heugel, Paris) (Eng, Fr).

Notes: An opera production of enormous proportions requiring professional musicians, technicians and mature singers. Performable only in a large theatre.

Marie-Magdeleine – Mary Magdalene

Music by **Jules Massenet** (1842-1912). A Dramatic Oratorio with words by Henry S. Leigh based on events in the life of Jesus as recorded in the Bible.

Premiered April 11, 1873.

Thick romantic textures with highly melodic vocal lines. Some set numbers, arias, ensembles and accompanied recitatives.

Three parts. Part I: An open area outside town. Part II, sc. 1: Martha's home; sc. .2: The Last Supper. Part III, sc. 1: Golgotha; sc. 2: At the tomb. Duration: approximately 80 minutes.

Roles: All roles highly lyrical; no range problems. MARY (sop); JUDAS (bs-bar); MARTHA (m-sop); EVANGELIST (ten), portrays both the role of narrator and the character of Jesus – should be sung by two voices in a staged version.

Chorus: Two groups of SATB – one for commentary and one for stage drama. They represent at various times villagers, youths, scribes, disciples, soldiers, executioners, and angels.

Orchestration: Full orchestra.

Synopsis: The crowd awaits the arrival of Jesus, their teacher. Mary arrives, despondent over her sinful past. Judas consoles her by pointing out that her present life is bright and joyous. Mary rejects his mocking of her anguish while the crowd of villagers taunt her by saying that she will soon return to her old way of life. Jesus arrives and consoles her, offering her forgiveness.

Part II opens with Martha and her retinue singing joyfully. Judas approaches Martha and warns her not to harm the Master when he comes to dine at her home. Insulted and angered, she sends Judas away. Jesus arrives and is welcomed by Mary and Martha. Mary speaks of her fear, yet believes His words of forgiveness. Jesus assures her that her faith has saved her. The scene shifts to where the disciples of Jesus are gathered. Jesus arrives, greeted by Judas. Jesus announces that one of them is a traitor, and then prays to the Father for mercy and the working out of His will.

Part III opens with Jesus hanging on the cross. The crowd of Pharisees, soldiers, and executioners jeer Him and finally disperse leaving Mary alone at the foot of the cross. Jesus breathes His last. Three days later, Mary sits by the tomb mourning when the risen Lord approaches her, telling her to go to His disciples and inform them of His resurrection. In a final triumphant scene, the Angels, disciples, and followers of Jesus join together in praise of their risen Lord.

Materials: TP (Heugel). Eng translation by Clifford W. Reims available. An earlier edition by Joseph Williams with Eng by H. S. Leigh.

Notes: Best performed in a theatre.

WILLIAM MATHIAS

Jonah

Music by **William Mathias** (1934-1992). A Musical Morality with text in English by Charles Causley based on the Book of Jonah, with additional texts from Matthew 12:39-41 and the hymn tune *Immortal, Invisible, God Only Wise*.

Commissioned by Guildford High School for Girls. Premiered in Guildford Cathedral on July 6, 1988. American concert premiere by the Philharmonic Orchestra of Indianapolis, April 2, 1989.

Frequent non-conventional harmonies, dissonances and chromaticism; tonal. Children's parts are often folk-tunes. Highly melodic and linear; colorful orchestration.

Seven set numbers but continuous action. 1: The Call to Ninevah; 2: The Voyage to Tarshish; 3: The Great Fish; 4: Jonah at Ninevah; 5: The Anger of Jonah; 6: The Green Tree and the Worm; 7: The Sign of Jonah. Duration: ca. 60 minutes.

Roles: JONAH (bar – A1-F#3), a Prophet of God; NARRATOR (ten – top Ab3); SHIPMASTER (ten); SPEAKER (sp), amplified – may be an adolescent girl or boy.

Chorus: SATB - Voice of God, Voice of the Whale and commentary. SA Children's Chorus – commentary and story telling. Both groups are stationary.

Orchestration: 2 trp, pia duet, timp, 2 or 3 perc, strings, org, pre-recorded tape (4 sections: calm sea, storm, whale sounds, cicadas and summer heat).

Synopsis: God calls upon Jonah to preach repentance to the wicked people of Nineveh. Jonah is incensed that God would ask him, a devout Jew, to lower himself to the level of Ninevah's Gentiles! He flatly rejects God's order and then deliberately catches the next ship going the opposite direction. While Jonah sleeps in the lower cabin of the ship, a furious storm erupts endangering the ship and its passengers. The Shipmaster wakens Jonah and begs him to call on his God to save them. When the storm persists, the soldiers cast lots to determine who is at fault for this adversity, and the lot falls upon Jonah. He confesses that he is running away from God and the only solution is for them to cast him into the sea. With great fear, they do so and the storm subsides. We next find Jonah in the belly of a whale. After three days and nights of this environment, Jonah readily agrees to obey God, whereupon God orders the whale to spit Jonah out on to dry land. Jonah doesn't waste a moment in getting to Ninevah where he preaches mightily concerning repentance and the ultimate destruction of their city. When God decides to spare Ninevah because of their repentant attitude, Jonah seethes with anger, accusing God of failing him. God then teaches Jonah the meaning of mercy and compassion. The Narrator next asks us to hear the words of Jesus concerning the sign of Jonah: as Jonah spent three days and nights in the belly of the whale, so shall the Son of Man be three days and nights in the heart of the earth. Jonah is a sign of redemption and resurrection. The entire cast and choruses conclude with the composer's setting of the hymn tune *Immortal Invisible, God Only Wise.*

Materials: OUP – purchase or rental of parts, FS, VS including the pre-recorded tape. A live-performance recording of the work is also available.

Notes: The roles of Jonah and Narrator require well-trained adult voices. The orchestra can be a combination of professional players and amateurs or students. The masque element may include a large or small group of children and/or adult performers and involves the imaginative use of movement, dance, costumes, and lighting. Ideally suited for church performance – also works well as a concert piece. A creative and delightful work.

WILLIAM MAYER

One Christmas Long Ago

Music by **William Mayer** (b. 1925). A Christmas Opera with libretto in English by the composer, freely adapted from *Why the Chimes Rang* by Raymond MacDonald Alden.

Premiered November 9, 1962 by Ball State Teachers College.

Traditional harmonies, recitatives, dialogue; vocally linear; not difficult.

One act, five scenes. Prelude with off-stage voices. Setting: A far-away Kingdom one Christmas Eve. Scene 1: Old Man's cottage; sc. 2: Three settings: homes of Countess, Sculptor, Rich Merchant; sc. 3: Snowy landscape outside town gate; sc. 4: Interior of the Cathedral; sc. 5: Snowy landscape. Duration: approximately 60 minutes.

Roles: OLDER BROTHER (boy sop or sop); YOUNGER BROTHER (boy sop or sop); COUNTESS (sop); BEGGAR WOMAN (m-sop); MINISTER (ten), can double with Sculptor; SCULPTOR (ten); PARSLEY THE PAGE (high bar – top F3); OLD MAN (bar – top F3), can double with Rich Merchant; RICH MERCHANT (bar); KING (sp).

Chorus: SSATTB representing Carolers, Choir, Congregation, and offstage sop.

Orchestration: fl (picc), ob (Eng hrn), 2 cl (bs cl), bsn, 2 hrn, 2 trp, trb, perc, pia (cel), Harmonium (opt), hp, strings. Orchestration for larger group also available.

Synopsis: Long ago there was a great cathedral whose bells were only rung when someone offered a very special gift at Christmas time. The bells, which rang of their own accord, had not been heard within human memory. Two boys on the way to the festival at the cathedral stop to visit an old man who tells them how his mother had once heard the bells ring. Later, the two boys come upon an old beggar woman who is half frozen. The older brother stays with the woman and sends the younger on ahead with their gift. Various royalty present their luxurious gifts expecting the bells to ring for them. The Countess gives all her jewels, the sculptor his own portrait, the rich man his gold, and the King his crown. As the boy enters the cathedral and moves toward the altar with his brother's silver coin, he is restrained by the attendants. During the ensuing struggle the ancient bells suddenly peal out. The Old Woman and the boy sitting together by the snowy roadside hear the bells too, faintly in the distance. When he wonders aloud who gave the gift that made them ring once more, the Old Woman answers, "Why, it might even have been you."

Materials: GAL (© 1963)

Notes: This work can be produced very simply or lavishly. The intimate scenes in the beginning should provide a stark contrast to the grandeur of the Christmas Festival in the Cathedral. Best suited for performance in a cathedral or church.

JOHN McCABE

The Lion, the Witch, and the Wardrobe

Music by **John McCabe** (b. 1939). A Biblical Allegory Opera with libretto in English by Gerald Larner, based on the book of the same name by C. S. Lewis. For children and adult voices.

Commissioned by the Manchester Cathedral Arts Festival with first performance in the Cathedral on April 29, 1969.

Mostly non-traditional in texture and harmony with some polytonality, irregular rhythms, chord clusters and frequent use of rhythmic speech mixed with lyrical lines. Considerable chromaticism within lyrically conceived melodic lines – very singable. Continuous texture.

Four acts. Act I, Prologue: Lamp-post in the forest; sc. 1: Interior of Tumnus' cave; sc. 2: Same as prologue. Act II, sc. 1: Interior of Tumnus' cave; sc. 2: Forest; sc. 3: Interior of Beaver's cave; sc. 4: Same; sc. 5: Courtyard of the Witch's palace. Act III, sc. 1: Spring forest; sc. 2: Stone table; sc. 3: A clearing in the woods. Act IV, sc. 1: Stone table; sc. 2: A night encampment; sc. 3: Stone table; sc. 4: Courtyard of the Witch's palace; Epilogue: Lamp-post in the forest. Best performed in a theatre or auditorium with large stage, though this work was premiered in a large cathedral. Duration: 75 minutes.

Roles: THE WITCH (sop); THE LION (bs-bar); SUSAN (sop/treble); LUCY (sop/treble); PETER (alt); EDMUND (alt); BEAVER (bar); MRS. BEAVER (sop); TUMNUS (treble), the Faun; MAUGRIM (bar); LEOPARD (bar); WOLF (bar); DWARF (treble). The roles of Maugrim, Leopard and Wolf can be performed by one singer.

Chorus: Mixed voices of adults and children representing Satyrs, Naiads, Dryads, Centaurs, Tigers, Dwarfs, Wolves, etc. Chorus parts are nearly always in unison or two-part.

Dance: No formal dance numbers but considerable choreography would be helpful in such scenes are the battle in Act IV.

Orchestration: 2 fl, ob, 2 cl, bsn, hrn, 2 trp, trb, timp, perc (sd dr, cym, sus cym, Chinese cym, sop xyl, bs xyl, sop glock, 3 bongos, Japanese Wind chimes, tom-toms, Chinese block), org, pia, strings. Piano may be used to strengthen the orchestra in addition to its duties as written in the parts.

Synopsis: Much Biblical symbolism can be detected in this story about a talking lion who saves his people by letting himself be sacrificed for another's crime, and being resurrected to reign his people forever. The enchanted land of Narnia is under the control of the White Witch who keeps the land in eternal winter. Lucy, Edmund, Peter and Susan find an entrance to Narnia through the wardrobe in the spare room of a house. The Witch fears the humans because of a prophecy which indicates her fall and death in connection with the appearance of four humans. Edmund comes under the Witch's control and is a traitor to his brother and sisters. Aslan, the lion, the rightful ruler returns to Narnia and helps the children. The Witch demands the traitor as her lawful right and hopes to destroy any chance for fulfillment of the prophecy. Aslan is accepted as a substitute and loses his life under her dagger. She thinks she has won, but Aslan comes to life again according to another prophecy. He helps the children defeat the Witch, restore all her captives, bring back the springtime, restore order in Narnia, and become the kings and queens of Narnia. Eventually they return safely to their original home.

Materials: NOV.

Notes: Best performed in a theatre or auditorium with large stage, though this work was premiered in a large cathedral. A creative set design is required in that scene changes must be accomplished in the time allowed by the music, which runs continuously between several of the scenes. Stage directions in the VS are written with a revolving platform or disc in mind, which will facilitate quick changes. Production notes are also printed in the VS.

HOWARD D. McKINNY

A Mystery for Christmas

Music arranged and composed by **Howard D. McKinney**. A Christmas Music Drama in the medieval manner with text adapted by the composer, based on the Shepherds and the Wisemen's visit to the manger.

In addition to the composer's original work, the music of Bach, Zipoli, Cornelius, Musculus and anonymous carols has been arranged and edited by the composer.

Traditional, mostly homophonic textures, and simple harmonic structures are used. In keeping with the composers wishes, both the music and drama should be kept simple.

One act. Setting: The manger scene. The aisles of the sanctuary should be used freely. Duration: approximately 40 minutes.

Roles: MARY (m-sop or part may be sung by an off-stage voice); GABRIEL (ten or sop); FIVE SHEPHERDS (ten, ten, bar, bar, bs – two-part); THREE WISE MEN (may be sung by 3 bar or by an offstage alto solo).

Chorus: SATB who are not a part of the action; Gabriel's six attendant angels (SSSAAA); twelve angels, two roles are quite small (non-singing).

Orchestration: No orchestration is available, however it is suggested in the composer's notes that in addition to an organ, three trumpets and a string quartet (or more) may be added to specific pieces and played directly out of the vocal score.

Synopsis: Shepherds in the countryside are surprised by the sound of trumpets and Angels announcing the birth of Christ the Lord. They hurry to Bethlehem and present their gifts. Wise Men from the East now enter the scene and present their gifts to the Child. Mary gives thanks with the words of the "Magnificat." All bow before their King and sing *Osanna in excelsis*. The drama is interspersed with chorales and carol tunes for the choir and audience alike.

Materials: JF.

Notes: Except for the numbers indicated for solo voices, it is the suggestion of the composer that the music be sung in parts, unaccompanied if possible. The VS includes complete staging directions and suggestions for lighting and costumes. Should be staged in a church/cathedral.

KIRKE MECHEM

The King's Contest

Music by **Kirke Mechem** (b. 1925). A Dramatic Cantata with text in English adapted by the composer from the Apocryphal Book of I Esdras 3-4.

Originally a chamber work titled *Zorobabel*, commissioned by the Amphion Foundation in Berkeley, CA. The version for large orchestra was first performed in the San Francisco Opera House June 16, 1974.

Twentieth century influences with non-conventional harmonic progressions but Romantic in nature. Some mixed meter. Melodic and lyric. Through-composed. Recitatives accompanied but at times hints of Bach are heard.

One act. Setting: In the palace of King Darius. Duration: 27 minutes.

Roles: NARRATOR (m-sop); THREE GUARDS OF THE KING (bar, bs, ten who is also ZOROBABEL); THE KING (bs – may be sung by the bs or bar Guard).

Chorus: SATB divisi. The chorus acts as the Grand Jury, questioning and disputing, and helping the Narrator tell the story.

Orchestration: Chamber version: 2 vln, 1 vla, 1 vc, 1 cb, perc (opt). Larger orchestra version: 3 fl, 3 ob, 3 cl, 3 bsn, 4 hrn, 3 trp, 3 trb, 3 tba, timp, 4 perc, hp, strings.

Synopsis: After a banquet in the palace of Darius, King of Persia, three young Guards attempt to win the King's favor and the coveted prize by naming the strongest force on earth. The Guards answer in turn: Wine, The King, and Women. Each one is given an opportunity to argue his point of view with support from one of the orchestral choirs: slightly drunk woodwinds accompany the baritone (Wine); the bass (The King), by brass (piano in the chamber version); the strings help the tenor (Women) represent the charms of women. Zorobabel, the tenor, is declared the winner. But he turns to the crowd and says that there is a power stronger than all these things: Truth. Without it, the others are all wicked.

Materials: GS.

Notes: May be fully or partially staged in either a house of worship or theatre. From the composer: "Each of us can interpret this truth as we choose, which may explain the universality of the story. Since truth, to many people, has always meant 'God's truth,' this originally secular tale found its way into the Apocrypha of the Old Testament. But like all ageless stories, the parable has a universal message: it speaks to that better, more human self within each of us - the feelings we know instinctively are true and right. And although the biblical story is often deliberately naive or told with tongue in cheek, it makes its point dramatically, with wit and charm. The music aims at nothing loftier than conveying these qualities."

ÉTIENNE NICOLAS MÉHUL

Joseph

Music by **Étienne Nicolas Méhul** (1763-1817). A Sacred Opera with libretto in French by Alexandre Duval, based on the Biblical story of Joseph and his brothers as found in Genesis 38-48.

First performed February 17, 1807, Opéra-Comique, Paris.

Typical late Classical *opéra-comique* style with early Romantic tendencies. Set numbers, spoken dialogue with some accompanied recitatives. Melodic.

Three acts. Setting: Acts I and III in Joseph's palace in Memphis, Act II in an open area by the wall of Memphis. Overture and two entr'acte. Duration: full length.

Roles: JACOB (bs – top G3, high tess), an old sheepherder in Hebron; Sons of Jacob: JOSEPH (ten), SIMEON (ten), BENJAMIN (sop), RUBEN (ten), NAPHTALI (bar). UTOBAL (bar), Joseph's counsel; AN OFFICER (sp).

Chorus: SSATTBB – Young ladies, the seven sons of Jacob, Egyptians, Soldiers.

Orchestration: 2 fl (picc), 2 ob, 2 cl, 2 bsn, 2 hrn, 2 trp, 2 trb, tba, timp, str

Synopsis: Having been abandoned as a young boy by his brothers, Joseph, now a high government official, laments the loss of his homeland and father. An Officer announces the arrival of strangers. They are Jacob's sons who have come to seek refuge in Egypt to escape the famine. Joseph recognizes his brothers but reveals it only to Utobal, his counsel. Joseph then offers them all asylum in Egypt. In Act II, Jacob and his family have arrived. Joseph meets Simeon and later Benjamin, both of whom express their grief over the death of their brother Joseph. The royal chariot arrives for Joseph, revealing to the brothers that they have been befriended by the powerful Cleophas (Joseph's adopted political name). Later, Joseph calls his family to the palace where Simeon confesses his part in the crime many years ago to do away with their brother, Joseph. Jacob, not having known of this until this moment, curses his sons. Joseph then reveals his true identity to them and a joyous hymn of thanksgiving concludes the work.

Materials: CFP (Ger, Fr). English translation by Copeland available from the BBC.

Notes: Best suited to performance in a theatre.

FELIX MENDELSSOHN BARTHOLDY

Elias – Elijah

Music by **Felix Mendelssohn Bartholdy** (1809-1847). A Dramatic Oratorio with text adapted from events in the life of Elijah the Prophet as recorded primarily in the Books of I, II Kings.

Premiered in August 26, 1846, Birmingham, England.

Music is highly Romantic with flowing vocal lines. Set numbers, accompanied recitatives. Coloristic orchestration.

Notes: In order to better understand the following material, the author's personal comments relative to the staging of this work and perhaps all designated dramatic oratorios will be discussed at this juncture. Please understand these are suggestions only.

These comments on *Elijah* are predicated upon two factors:
1. Priority at the outset will be given to the dramatic flow and stage treatment.
2. All text and number references will be made from the edition published by G. Schirmer.

Elijah, normally presented in concert form, frequently has been staged. Three elements stand as obstacles when considering a staged version of this work: 1) Mendelssohn identified it as an oratorio and therefore in a puritanical sense must be presented in concert form; 2) the frequent lack of adequate interlude passages necessary for enacting and motivating action called for in the libretto; and 3) choral and solo sections in which no drama or action occurs, i.e., commentary material.

In order to overcome at least some of these obstacles, the following cuts are suggested:
1. No. 5 – "Yet Doth the Lord"
2. Nos. 6, 7, & 7A – These numbers could become a separate scene, however, they are short and add little to the dramatic flow.
3. No. 18 – "Woe Unto Them Who Forsake Him"
4. No. 32 – "He That Shall Endure." This number could be included if properly choreographed, though it is similar to No. 31.
5. No. 35 and the chorus of No. 36 – This is mostly commentary material and similar in that respect to the last half of No. 34.
6. No. 37 – "For the Mountains Shall Depart." Essentially, this repeats what was said in No. 36.
7. Nos. 40, 41, 42 – These numbers are primarily commentary and contain little action. After Elijah's dramatic disappearance, including these numbers could be anticlimactic, especially this late in the drama.

Two parts, six scenes. Setting: Samaria approximately 875 B.C., during the rule of King Ahab. It should be kept in mind that King Ahab was a highly skilled and active architect. Part I, sc. 1: Outside Ahab's Palace (Introduction – No. 4). Between the Introduction and No. 1, (the Overture), a period of three years elapses, moving from a time of prosperity to poverty as a result of drought. Sc. 2: Cherith's Brook (Nos. 6 – 7A); sc. 3: The Widow's home (Nos. 8 – 9); sc. 4: Mt. Carmel (Nos. 10 – 20). Part II, sc. 5: Outside Ahab's palace sometime later (Nos. 21 – 25); sc. 6: The wilderness (Nos. 26 – end). Duration: approximately 2 hours.

Roles: ELIJAH (bar – dramatically and vocally, a very demanding role), a Prophet of Jehovah; AHAB (ten), King of Israel; JEZEBEL (m-sop), Queen of Israel; OBADIAH (ten), servant of Ahab; THE WIDOW (sop); WIDOW'S SON (mute); THE YOUTH (boy sop), twelve-year old servant of Elijah; TWO ISRAELITE WIDOWS (sop, alt), who sing No. 2; ISRAELITE WOMAN (sop), who sings No. 21; A HEAVENLY MESSENGER (ten), who sings Nos. 27 & 39; AN ANGEL (alt), who sings Nos. 30 & 31; AN ANGEL (sop), who sings No. 33.

Chorus: SATB, divisi. The chorus may observe and comment on the action as a Greek chorus. SSA are angels in No. 28. Including the chorus directly in the stage action will be difficult since the choral music is so extensive, making memorization problematic, and many of the choral numbers require large forces. As a replacement for an on-stage chorus, select two groups of actors: one group of adults and children would represent townspeople and Israelites, while the second group would be experienced in dance and movement (see "Dance" section).

Dance: No dance numbers in the score, however, if the chorus assumes a Greek chorus posture, a group of dancers could replace them in pantomime, reacting to what the chorus is saying and assuming several different roles throughout the work:
1. Israelites in Introduction through No. 4.
2. Prophets of Baal in Nos. 10-16.
3. Israelites in Nos. 19A-20 and 21-24.
4. Several may appear as angels in No. 28.
5. The wind, sea, earthquake, and whirlwind in Nos. 34 & 38.

Orchestration: 2 fl, 2 ob, 2 cl, 2 bsn, 4 hrn, 2 trp, 3 trb, strings.

Synopsis: Elijah, the only Prophet of Jehovah who still follows His way, declares that because of Israel's disobedience to God, He will withhold rain from Israel for the next three years. Three years pass. Obadiah asks the people to confess, forsake their idolatry and return to God. Elijah, a man rejected by all but God and living in a land of famine, goes to Cherith's brook where the ravens bring him food. The Lord commands Elijah to go to the home of a Widow in Zarephath; there he will be taken care of. The Widow's son has just died. Through the prayer of Elijah, the son is revived to life. Elijah goes to King Ahab and is accused of causing this famine. Elijah challenges Ahab and the Prophets of Baal to a confrontation on Mt. Carmel. Elijah and Ahab will both build altars to their individual gods; the god who sends fire to consume the offering on the altar will be declared the true God. Much ceremony surrounds the offering to Baal, yet nothing happens. Elijah then prays once to Jehovah and fire descends from heaven. The Prophets of Baal are slain. Elijah then prays to Jehovah to send rain again to this parched land and He does so. Sometime later, Israel has again slipped into idolatry and Elijah, discouraged, goes to the wilderness asking God to take his life. He falls asleep and is ministered to by angels and the voice of God, renewing his spirit. God then sends a whirlwind and takes him to heaven.

Materials: GS.

Saint Paul

Music by **Felix Mendelssohn Bartholdy** (1809-1847). A Dramatic Oratorio with text adapted from events in the life of St. Paul as recorded in the Biblical Book of Acts, with commentary from other Books of the Bible.

Premiered in Düsseldorf, May 22, 1836.

Traditional harmony typical of the mid-Romantic period. Accompanied recitatives, arias, chorales, and many large choruses with fugal and canonic treatment.

Two parts. Overture. Part I, sc. 1: A meeting room in the church (Nos. 1 – 7); sc. 2: Outside the church (Nos. 8 – 12); sc. 3: On the road to Damascus (Nos. 13 – 18); sc. 4: House where Saul is staying in Damascus (Nos. 19 – 22). Part II, sc. 1: In the church (Nos. 23 – 28); sc. 2: A roadside (No. 28 – 31); sc. 3: In Lystra, the Temple (Nos. 32 – 42); sc. 4: On the shore by a ship (Nos. 42 – end). Duration: 2 hours.

Roles: SAUL/PAUL (bs), the Apostle; BARNABAS (ten), his traveling companion; ANANIAS (shared by a sop and ten, but could be sung by one); STEPHEN (ten); TENOR (narrator); SOPRANO (narrator); ALTO (narrator). The composer is not always faithful in giving all quotations of a designated character to that voice. Adjustments in this can be made as desired.

Chorus: SATB – considerable choral music throughout, responding to the actions in various roles: sometimes as Christians, Hebrews, Jews, Gentiles, or the Voice of God. In a staged production, it would be preferable to use a Greek chorus off-stage while small groups or pantomime groups developed the action.

Orchestra: 2 fl, 2 ob, 2 cl, 2 bsn, 4 hrn, serpent, 2 trp, 3 trb, timp, strings, org.

Synopsis: The persecuted church in Jerusalem prays for power to resist the fury of the Heathen. Stephen, a leader in the church, is accused of blasphemy and placed before the Council and High Priest. They reject Stephen's stand and call for his death.

He is dragged out into the streets and stoned. In his dying moments, he prays for his assassins. Some devoted church people give him a burial. Saul, who is present, gives his consent to Stephen's death and resolves to continue the persecution of Christians. For this purpose Saul travels to Damascus. Suddenly a bright light from heaven blinds him and a voice calls on him to turn from his ways and instead, proclaim the message of the Lord. He is led by his companions to Damascus where God has sent Ananias to pray with him and restore his sight. He is baptized and boldly preaches the Word of God. In Part II, Saul, now Paul, and Barnabas are selected by the Holy Ghost to preach the Gospel of Christ abroad. Their boldness stirs up jealousy among the Jews who plot to kill them. Paul and Barnabas, seeing that they are not accepted among their own people, the Jews, turn to the Gentiles with their message. In Lystra, Paul heals a cripple, and is hailed by the people as a god. Instead, Paul tries to turn their attention to the power of Jesus Christ. This excites the anger of both Jews and Gentiles, and they attempt to stone him. The Lord protects him and he escapes. He calls the Elders of the church in Ephesus together to bid them farewell as he returns to Jerusalem, ready to die for the Gospel. On the shore by the ship, Paul bids them farewell and challenges them to fight the good fight, for a crown of righteousness shall be given to all who believe and love His appearing. Together they offer praise to God.

Materials: GS. NOV.

Notes: Whereas many similarities between this work and Mendelssohn's *Elijah* exist, a dramatic treatment of this work does present more problems. Refer to the *Elijah* entry in this book for suggestions on dramatic treatment which can be applied to both works.

GIAN-CARLO MENOTTI

Amahl and the Night Visitors

Music by **Gian-Carlo Menotti** (b. 1911). A Christmas Miracle Opera with libretto in English by the composer inspired by "The Adoration of the Magi," a painting by Hieronymous Bosch.

Premiered on NBC-TV, December 24, 1951. Commissioned by NBC-TV Opera Theatre. Stage premiere on February 21, 1952, by Indiana University.

Vocal line declamatory with many accompanied recitative-like passages. Arias, ensembles. Highly melodic.

One act. Setting: The interior of a peasant's hut near Bethlehem and the fields outside during the time of the birth of Jesus. Duration: 50 minutes.

Roles: AMAHL (boy sop – top A4); HIS MOTHER (m-sop – top A4); KING KASPAR (ten), requires excellent acting; KING MECHIOR (bar); KING BALTHAZAR (bs); PAGE (bar].

Chorus: SATB – Shepherds involved in the action.

Dance: Three or more dancers who dance for the Kings – folk dancing typical of the culture.

Orchestration: 2 fl, ob, cl, bsn, hrn, trp, hp, pia, perc, strings. Two-piano arrangement also available.

Synopsis: The crippled shepherd boy, Amahl, tells his mother of a "gigantic" star gleaming in the night sky. She chides him for his lucid imagination and perpetual lying. After Amahl is finally in bed, three Oriental Kings knock at the door asking for a place to rest. Amahl and his Mother invite them in but as they have nothing to offer them, the Mother invites all the neighbors who bring food and gifts for the Kings. A dance and celebration follow. The neighbors leave and all settle down for a night's rest. While all are sleeping, the Mother awakens and is captivated by the thought of how much she could do for her crippled son if she only had a little of the gold which the Kings brought with them to present to the newborn Christ Child. She attempts to steal the gold but is caught by the Page and a struggle follows. Amahl and the Kings are awakened. The Kings in their kindness tell her to keep the gold for the Child they are seeking doesn't need it. Feeling guilty, the Mother gives it back out of love for the newborn King they seek. Moved with compassion, Amahl too wants to offer a gift and holds out his dearest possession, his crutch. As he presents it to the Kings to take with them, he is miraculously healed. Rejoicing, he follows along with the Kings to personally present his gift to the Christ Child.

Materials: GS. A staging guide is also available for rent.

Notes: Equally adaptable to church or theatre performance.

The Death of the Bishop of Brindisi

Music by **Gian-Carlo Menotti** (b. 1911). A Dramatic Cantata with text in English by the composer adapted from the events of the Children's Crusades in the thirteenth century. The historical reference to this work is from Adolf Waas, *History of the Crusades* (1956, Herder & Co., Freiburg, Germany).

First performance May 18, 1963, Cincinnati May Festival. Commissioned by the Cincinnati Musical Festival Association.

Colorful orchestration. Choral ensembles, solos, accompanied recitatives with declamatory vocal lines. Typical of Menotti's early style.

One act. Setting: In a castle in Brindisi, Italy, early thirteenth century. Duration: 30 minutes.

Roles: BISHOP OF BRINDISI (bs – top F3); NUN (sop).

Chorus: SATB divisi (townspeople); 2 and 3-part Children's Chorus. Both choruses should be unseen as they represent the Bishop's memories and hallucinations.

Orchestration: 2 fl, 2 ob, 2 cl, bs cl, 2 bsn, 4 hrn, 3 trp, 3 trb, tba, timp, perc, 2 pia, hp, strings.

Historical Background: In 1212, an approximately ten-year old boy named Nicholas began gathering children from throughout Germany for a crusade on the Holy Land. He believed he was called by God to gather children and lead them through the sea to Jerusalem to free the Holy Land. Through the help of adults who were moved by the faith and child-like determination of the children, they managed to cross the Alps and enter Italy, though with considerable loss of life. Some of them reached Brindisi, where the Bishop tried to prevent their continued travel. When the Bishop saw he could no longer prevent their departure by ship, he gave them his blessing. Those children who left by ship were captured by pirates and sold as slaves in the Orient; others who survived managed to return to their homes.

Synopsis: The Bishop is old and near death as memories and hallucinations of the many children sent to their graves fill his mind. While a Nun tries to comfort and reassure him, in a "flashback," he hears the voices of the children beg for help and mercy. Meanwhile, the townspeople rage in their displeasure with the Bishop, blaming him for allowing the children's departure and ensuing tragedy. In his dying moments, the Bishop prays for the eternal truth and answer, fearful that he may not gain heaven's gates. In a final chorus, the answer comes, giving him his eternal rest.

Materials: GS.

Notes: Simple set requirements. Adaptable to performance in either a house of worship or theatre stage.

The Egg

Music by **Gian-Carlo Menotti** (b. 1911). A Parable Opera with libretto in English by the composer based on church history and events surrounding the life of a hermit, St. Simeon Stylites.

Commissioned by the Washington Cathedral and first performed there June 17, 1976.

Some unaccompanied passages, declamatory recitative-like sections, arias, choral passages. Traditional harmony with typical Menotti departures into twentieth century devices. Highly melodic with natural vocal rhythms guided by word accentuation.

One act. Setting: An open area – fifth century Byzantine Empire. Duration: 50 minutes.

Roles: MANUEL (high bar – top G3 with many F3); SAINT SIMEON STYLITE (ten – top A3); THE BASILISSA (dram sop), Empress of Byzantium (Pride); SISTER OF THE BASILISSA (m-sop) (Envy); AREOBINDUS (bar – top F#3), favorite of the Basilissa (Lust); GOURMANTUS (bs), the cook (Gluttony); EUNOCH OF THE SACRED CUBICLE (ten) (Sloth); PACHOMIUS (bar), the treasurer (Avarice); JULIAN (mute), Captain of the Guard (Anger); BEGGAR WOMAN (sop).

Chorus: SSAATTBB – members of the Basilissa's Court.

Orchestration: fl, ob, cl, bsn, hrn, 2 trp, trb, 2 perc, hp, vln, vla, vc, cb, org.

Synopsis: Saint Simeon, a hermit, seeks the meaning of life. An angel brings him an egg that will reveal the secret of life's meaning to anyone who can open it. The hermit's nephew, Manuel, comes to ask him about the meaning of life. He finds the unopened egg which the hermit has discarded as useless. On the way home Manuel is captured by the Empress of Byzantium who represents the seven deadly sins. Neither the Empress, the embodiment of lust, nor any of the other seven deadly sins dwelling in her court can open the egg to learn its meaning. Finally Manuel and the egg are thrown out of the court and banished from the city. Manuel gives the egg in charity to a beggar woman whose baby is dying from hunger. She easily opens the egg with which she saves her child's life as well as discovering the secret: it will only open when it is given away. The Empress suspects treachery and orders Manuel killed. Simeon intervenes and reveals the larger secret of the egg: only by sharing one's blessing with the unblessed can one hope for salvation.

Materials: GS.

Notes: Ideally suited for performance in a cathedral/church but can be adapted to the theatre as well.

Martin's Lie

Music by **Gian-Carlo Menotti** (b. 1911). A "Church" Opera in the medieval tradition with libretto in English by the composer.

First performed at Bristol Cathedral in England as part of the Bath Festival, June 3, 1964.

Typical of early Menotti with declamatory recitatives based on the natural inflection and rhythm of the words. Through-composed, a child-like simplicity is projected in both the plot and music. Melodic and accessible.

One act. Setting: St. Isidore's Orphanage, a former convent, in fourteenth century England. Duration: 50 minutes.

Roles: NANINGA (m-sop – top G4), the housekeeper; MARTIN (boy sop), an orphan; FATHER CORNELIUS (ten – top Ab3), head of St. Isidore's; CHRISTOPHER (boy sop), friend of Martin; TIMMY (boy sop), friend of Martin; FUGITIVE (bar – top F3); SHERIFF (bs).

Chorus: Two-part treble chorus of orphans.

Orchestration: fl, ob, cl, bsn, hrn, 2 trp, trb, 2 perc, hp, vla, vc, cb.

Synopsis: Naninga is telling the orphan children a bed-time story. Before they are sent off to bed, it is determined that it is Martin's turn to sleep in the kitchen, a duty assigned each night to one of the children in order to keep the rats away from the food. No sooner is everyone in bed then Martin hears a desperate knock on the kitchen door. He opens it to reveal a fugitive looking for a hiding place. The man is an escaped prisoner, charged with being a traitor. After a few moments, the fugitive convinces Martin that he is his long lost father. Martin hides him just as the Sheriff enters in search of the man. The Sheriff threatens Martin with death if he will not reveal where the fugitive has been hidden. The Father tries his best to bring Martin to the truth as do all his friends, but Martin insists that he will never betray the man who is his father. The Sheriff applies more pressure but without success. Suddenly, Martin falls to the floor, dead. The pressure was too severe for a boy with a frail heart. Rather than reveal to the law the hiding place of a man he believes to be his father, Martin chose to take a stand and suffer for it. As the church bells begin to chime for Martin, the children sing a prayer for him.

Materials: GS.

Notes: Ideally suited for performance in a cathedral/church but adaptable to the theatre.

JAN MEYEROWITZ

Esther

Music by **Jan Meyerowitz** (1913-1998). A Biblical Opera with libretto in English by Langston Hughes based on events from the Biblical Book of Esther with influences from Racine's *Esther*.

Commissioned by the Fromm Music Foundation. Premiered by the University of Illinois, March 17, 1957.

Tonal textures with some twentieth century dissonances. Melodic and linear. Traditional arias, ensembles, accompanied, declamatory recitatives; difficult chromatic vocal lines. Continuous texture.

Three acts, sixteen scenes. Setting: Fifth century B.C. at the court of King Ahasverus in the Kingdom of Shushan. Duration: 90 minutes.

Major Roles: ESTHER (sop – top C5 sustained); MORDECAI (ten – top Bb3); AHASVERUS, (bar – top F#3), King of Persia; HAMAN (bar – top G#3), the Grand Vizier.

Minor Roles: VASHTI (m-sop), the Queen; ZARESH (sop – top Bb4), Haman's wife; ARIDATHA (light ten – top Bb3), their oldest son; DANIEL (bar – top F3), first Hebrew Sage; HISDA (ten – Bb3), second Hebrew Sage; ELEAZAR (bs), third Hebrew Sage; BIGHAM (bar), first guard; TERESH (bs), second guard; THE KING'S CHAMBERLAIN (bar); HAKAMAN (mute), the Executioner; A PUBLIC CRIER (bs-bar); TWO ASTROLOGERS (bar, bs); TWO SOLDIERS (mute); OLD MAN (bs).

Chorus: SSA – Esther's Handmaidens (at least nine); SATB – a small crowd.

Orchestration: fl, 2 cl, bsn, 2 hrn, trp, trb, timp, 2 perc, hp, strings. On-stage: hrn, 2 trp, trb.

Synopsis: As the Sabbath is ending, three Sages conclude the day's ceremony. Esther, the Queen, enters and requests that the Sages inscribe on their Holy Scrolls the story of how the Jews of Shushan have been saved from annihilation at the hands of Haman. As they begin to write, the scene shifts to an earlier time. During a feast, the King berates his courtiers for deserting the feast and upon asking them what is lacking, they reply, "Women." The King calls for his wife, Vashti, who is the most beautiful of women. When she refuses to come, the King orders his Executioner to kill her. The next day, an announcement is made to all the world that the King is seeking a new wife. All the lovely virgins of the land are to be brought to him for his selection. That night in the house of Mordecai, his niece whom he loves as his own daughter is made ready for presentation to the King. Anxiety fills the household – if she does not go, her life is in danger, and her faith is in danger if she must live at court among the heathen. Esther says she is not afraid to go, nor will she relinquish her faith even among those pagans.

In Act II, Esther with her handmaidens await the announcement. Esther is selected from among thousands of virgins the King has seen. Months later, the King prepares to leave for war. Two Sentries plot the King's death. Mordecai overhears them and sends a warning via Queen Esther. Meanwhile, Haman learns that Mordecai, a devout Jew and worshiper of God, will not bow before him. Angered, Haman plots his death. Each day in her royal chamber, Esther removes her queenly attire and in simple garb sings of her love of Jordan, of her own people, and of her faith.

Haman with his wife and son plot the destruction of all Jews. They prepare a decree ordering the massacre. Waiting until the King is in a drunken stupor, Haman convinces the King to sign the decree. That night Mordecai informs Esther of the new edict and asks Esther to intercede with the King. No one, not even the Queen, may go in to the King without being bidden – so Esther's intercession might mean her death. However, Esther says that for the sake of her people, she will go. Taken anew with Esther's beauty, the King is glad she has come and offers her whatever she wishes. She asks his presence, together with Haman's, at dinner in her garden. At the same time, the King remembers that he has wished to honor Mordecai and orders Haman to honor Mordecai publicly throughout the town. Distressed, Haman begs that anything but honor be granted this Jew whom he hates. The King however insists. At dinner in the garden, Esther reveals to the King that Haman's decree means her death too, for she is a Jew. Not knowing this, the King is angered and orders that Haman be hanged on the very gallows he had prepared for Mordecai. The King repeals the decree that her people might live. In the final scene, we see the Sages writing the end of the story on the Holy Scrolls, while Esther and her Handmaidens join in jubilation.

Materials: AMP.

Notes: Best performed in a theatre with facilities for the numerous scene changes. A number of the scenes can be played in front of the house curtain.

P. NAPIER MILES

Good Friday

Music by **P. Napier Miles** (1865-1935). A Sacred Music Drama with libretto in English by John Masefield.

Mostly non-traditional harmonic structures; tonal with some bi-tonality. Highly chromatic. Through-composed and melodic.

Two acts. Setting: A paved court outside the Roman citadel in Jerusalem. Duration: approximately 110 minutes.

Roles: PONTIUS PILATE (bs – low El); PROCULA (dram sop – top Bb4), his wife; LONGINUS (bar – top F3), a centurion; A JEW (bs – E1-F3), leader of the rabble; A MADMAN (ten – top B3), blind; A SENTRY (bs – top F3); JOSEPH OF RAMAH (bs); HEROD (ten); 1st CITIZEN (ten); 2nd CITIZEN (ten); 3rd CITIZEN (bar); SLAVE (bar).

Chorus: SSAATTBB – Chorus of Faithful, Celestial Chorus (off-stage), Soldiers, Servants, the Jewish rabble, Loiterers.

Orchestration: picc, 2 fl, 2 ob, Eng hrn, 2 cl, bs cl, 2 bsn, 4 hrn, 3 trp, 2 trb, timp, perc, hp, strings. Off-stage: picc, 2 fl, ob, Eng hrn, bsn, tri.

Synopsis: Having already tried Jesus and interviewed Him personally, Pilate agonizes over the decision he has made. The Chief Jew demands His death, while Pilate's wife cautions him, telling him of her last night's foreboding dream. The Chief Jew brings a document with new evidence of claims Jesus has made: that He is a King, come to set the Jews free which thus presents a threat to Roman rule. A Madman, one whom Jesus had befriended, enters to plead in behalf of Jesus, but is cast aside by the soldiers. A trumpet fanfare brings order to the unruly crowd. Pilate announces that Jesus will be crucified – now. The crowd is delirious with delight and the anticipation of blood.

Act II: Jesus has just been crucified. Pilate and Procula discuss ways of justifying their deed. Joseph enters and requests of Pilate the body of Jesus for burial. Pilate, surprised that Jesus is already dead, does not believe Joseph's "bewildering" report of the events surrounding His actual death and sends for Longinus. Longinus, severely shaken by the events, describes in detail the great drops of blood, the earthquake, the sheet of fire that blazed across the sky and the opening of graves at the moment of Jesus' death. Pilate, thinking Longinus a bit unbalanced himself, dismisses him. Herod's arrival is announced. Their conversation focuses on the need for the two of them to work together more closely and cast aside past indifferences. As they leave, the Madman, left alone on stage, declares that the pain now is over, and only the truth remains.

Materials: OUP (© 1933).

Notes: One set required. Best performed in a theatre though adaptable to a large chancel area in a church. An effective dramatization.

DARIUS MILHAUD

David

Music by **Darius Milhaud** (1892-1974). A Sacred Opera with libretto in French based on the events in the life of David as recorded in I-II Samuel and I Kings 1-2.

Commissioned by the Koussevitsky Foundation in the Library of Congress. Concert premiere June 1, 1954 in Jerusalem; stage premiere January 2, 1955 in Milano.

Episodic. Melodic, highly chromatic but tonal and linear; some rhythmic speech for chorus, quick declamatory vocal lines.

Five acts, twelve scenes. Act I, sc. 1: Near Bethlehem, the home of Jesse; sc. 2: King Saul's camp. Act II, sc. 1: In the hills; sc. 2: The cave of the Witch of Endor; sc. 3: The ruins of Kiklag. Act III: The throne-room at Hebron. Act IV, sc. 1: A public square; sc. 2: The King's palace overlooking Jerusalem; sc. 3: The Mount of Olives; sc. 4: Near Mahanaim. Act V, sc. 1: King David's bedroom; sc. 2: At the fountain of Gihon. Duration: 2 hours, 50 minutes.

Major Roles: DAVID (bar – top Gb3); JONATHAN (ten – top G#3); MICHAL (sop – top B4), Saul's daughter and David's wife; ABIATHAR (bar – top F3).

Minor Roles: SAMUEL (bs – top F3), the Prophet; JESSE (bar – top F3), David's father; JESSE'S WIFE (cont); ELIAB (bar), David's brother; ABINADAB (bar), David's brother; CHAMA (ten), David's brother; ABNER (bs); SAUL (bar – top F3), King of Israel; GOLIATH (bs), Philistine giant; ABISSAI (ten); ABIGAIL (m-sop); ABINOAM (m-sop), a servant; THE WITCH OF ENDOR (cont); L'AMALICITE (ten – top Bb3); JOAB (bar – top F3); BATHSHEBA (dram sop); NATHAN (bar – top F#3); ZADOK (bs), High Priest; AHIMAAC (ten), courier; SIMAI (ten); ABISHAG (col sop); SOLOMON (alt), the child; Four guards of David (sp).

Chorus: Double chorus of SATB – Israelites. Several small solo parts taken from the chorus.

Orchestration: 2 fl (picc), 2 ob, 2 cl, 2 bsn, 4 hrn, 3 trp, 3 trb, tba, timp, perc, hp, strings.

Synopsis: Jesse and his family are preparing for dinner when Samuel appears, selecting and anointing the boy David as the next King of Israel. David visits King Saul and as is his custom, sings and plays to sooth the King's troubled spirit. The ensuing demise of Goliath by the boy David, and subsequent adulations of David leads to Saul's enormous jealousy and hatred of him. Saul, in a fit of temper, attempts to kill David by hurling his spear at David, but Michal, his wife, leads David to safety.

When David escapes to the hills, Saul and his soldiers follow. At night as Saul is asleep in a cave, he awakens upon hearing David's voice. Grateful for sparing his life, Saul blesses David.

Desperate, unstable and disguised as a beggar, Saul requests of the Witch of Endor that she bring the Prophet Samuel's spirit to life in order to inquire regarding his future and fate. Samuel informs Saul that his throne will be given to David and that he will lose his life the next day. Several days later, David learns of the defeat of their army by the Amelekites and the death of Saul and his son Jonathan.

Act III records the next seven years' history of David's reign which is quickly narrated to us. Act IV opens with David's singing and dancing before the Ark and the response of the people with songs of praise to the King. We next hear that David and Bathsheba are found together by Nathan. David confesses his sins and asks God for forgiveness. A choral interlude announces the birth of Solomon, their second child. Years later, Absalom, also one of David's sons, attempts to take over as heir to the throne. Shortly thereafter, he is found dead. David announces that Solomon shall be his heir and gives him his blessing. All the people sing the praises of David and thanksgiving is offered to God.

Materials: IMP (Fr, Heb).

Notes: Requires professional musicians and technical personnel. A large-scale operatic production suitable only in a large theatre. An English translation by Aharon Ashmann is in the VS.

CLAUDIO MONTEVERDI

Il Combattimento di Tancredi e Clorinda – The Combat of Tancredi and Clorinda

Music by **Claudio Monteverdi** (1567-1643). A Dramatic Madrigal with libretto in Italian by Torquato Tasso, based on verses 52-68, Canto XII of *Gerusalemme liberata*.

Premiered in Venice at carnival time, 1624.

Simple secco recitatives predominantly in the monodic style. Harmonically simple. Soloistic but no arias.

One act. Setting: on the battlefield during the final crusade in 1099. Duration: 25 minutes.

Roles: TESTO (ten), the narrator; CLORINDA (sop); TANCREDI (ten or high bar). It is stylistically acceptable to have the two singers merely sing their parts while the drama is enacted by two Pantomime artists.

Orchestration: Four viole da braccio – soprano, alto, tenor, and bass – in modern terms, a single string quartet and hpsch. Malipiero version: string quartet, cb, clavicembalo (or pia, hp, cel).

Synopsis: *Jerusalem Delivered* recounts the final episodes of the First Crusade. Tancredi, a knight heading 800 horsemen, has fallen in love with a pagan warrior-maid whom he chanced to see at a spring. At the first assault upon Jerusalem he again encounters, unhelms and recognizes her, and offers her himself or his life. Before she understands, she is attacked from behind and wounded. He pursues the assailant. Meanwhile, she disguises herself and attacks the Christians' siege-tower. No one guesses her identity though Tancredi suspects her and rides after her. Here is where Monteverdi's action begins. Tancredi arrogantly challenges her to do battle with him and she accepts. As darkness falls the two foes draw their swords and slowly approach each other. Crudely they lunge at one another, darkness preventing the use of cunning or strategy. They drop their swords and butt one another with their helmets and shields. Three times Tancredi clenches Clorinda in his arms; three times she manages to free herself. They return to their swords, fighting until both are covered with streams of blood. Exhausted by their efforts the two knights momentarily withdraw from one another. At the first light of day, Tancredi inquires the name and rank of his rival. The request is refused by Clorinda. Incensed by her arrogance Tancredi draws his sword and the battle is renewed. Plunging his sword deep within her, Tancredi deals the fatal blow. Knowing that she is dying, Clorinda pardons her enemy and asks that she be baptized. Tancredi, moved by her plea, fetches water from a nearby brook. As he prepares to baptize her he loosens her helmet and is horrified to discover her true identity. Full of anguish and repentance, Tancredi ministers the holy rites, and Clorinda dies in peace.

Materials: OUP (Eng translation by Denis Stevens); GS/CHES (Malipiero version with Peter Pears translation); RIC (It); AMP (Ghedini version in It). Eng translations also by Dennis Arundell, Richard Hart, Karks Mosher, Evelyn Radford, T. Deacon.

Notes: Minimal sets. Best performed in an intimate setting.

DOUGLAS MOORE

The Greenfield Christmas Tree

Music by **Douglas Moore** (1893-1969). A Christmas Entertainment with libretto in English by Arnold Sundgaard.

First performance on December 8, 1962 at Bushnell Memorial Auditorium in Hartford, Connecticut.

Highly melodic and vocally accessible. Spoken dialogue. Some unaccompanied choral passages. Traditional harmonic textures with twentieth century influences. Through-composed. Folk elements and simplicity are maintained in keeping with the intended child-like story telling process.

One act. Setting: In a barn on a New England farm in 1873. Prelude. Duration: 45 minutes.

Roles: JOHN FROTHINGHAM (bs-bar), the guardian Grandfather. His Grandchildren: TOBY (sp), age 11; PRUDENCE (sp), age 8; SUSAN (sp), age 6. SAMUEL (sp), the hired man; BRITA (cont), Norwegian housekeeper; REVEREND FLOOD (sp); CHORAL LEADER (bar), the narrator; THE DONKEY (bs); THE COW (alt); THE GOAT (ten); THE SHEEP (sop). Speaking roles should be equally divided between high and low voices if possible since they all are asked to sing in the final ensemble numbers.

Chorus: SATB – neighbors and friends.

Dance: Some simple folk dancing during the decoration of the Christmas tree.

Orchestration: 2 fl, 2 ob, 2 cl, 2 bsn, 2 hrn, 2 trp, 2 trb, perc, hp, str

Synopsis: Due to the stern Puritan influence which frowned on all worldly show of decoration, most New England states did not introduce Christmas trees into the season until the middle 1800s. The action begins with the sound of neighbors caroling from outside the walls of the barn. They sing of the birth of the Son of God. The Choral Leader introduces us to John Frothingham admonishing his grandchildren that only a savage would worship a tree; Christmas trees are a foolish, heathen custom. The four grandchildren are terribly disappointed in that their father and mother, who have died since last Christmas, always decorated a tree for Christmas. But Grandfather will not have a tree in his house. After all, what would Reverend Flood say if he did! Samuel and Brita are saddened by the disappointment of the children but seem unable to sway John. John leaves and they all begin piecing together a tree from various items they find in the barn. The church bell strikes twelve midnight and Christmas day is born. Even the animals are excited and sing of the birth of Christ. Suddenly there is a knocking on the door of the barn. Voices outside encourage the children not to be afraid. They open the door and there stands a big brightly decorated Christmas tree brought in by Brita and Samuel. The children are overjoyed. At that moment Grandfather John enters the barn angered at the disobedience of the children, Samuel and Brita. He is about to lose his temper when Reverend Flood steps out from behind the tree and calmly tells John that this is the first Christmas tree in all of Massachusetts, and he should be proud it chose his place! Grandfather is finally convinced that the tree poses no threat and joins in the celebration. Throughout the story telling process, the chorus comments on the birth of Christ and His presence here below.

Materials: GS.

Notes: Costumes and sets should convey the feeling that this is a children's story book come alive before the eyes of the audience. Best performed in an intimate auditorium.

FRANK LEDLIE MOORE

The Perfect Choir

Music by **Frank Ledlie Moore** (1923-1999). A Choral Drama with text in English by the composer.

Composed in July, 1982.

Choral Comedy. Considerable dissonance. No meters, a-rhythmic with a strong feeling for anacrusis and metacrusis required. Unaccompanied (pitch pipe). Ten numbers including some choral recitative.

One scene. Setting: at the gate of heaven. Duration: 12 minutes.

Roles: BUS DRIVER (mute).

Chorus: SATB – the composer suggests three singers per voice part. Memorization of score necessary.

Orchestration: None, however, a pitch pipe is required and must be used as often as possible since it is very obvious that in the character of this choir, they would never allow themselves to be caught off pitch.

Synopsis: An overly-proud choir, having all met death in a tragic bus accident, arrives in disarray at the gate of heaven. Although in its pride the choir members are certain the gates will open the moment they sing, they do not. They try every kind of choral music but to no avail. In desperation, they attack their Bus Driver, accusing him of being their murderer. They sing of their assets and flawless characters, but still gain no entrance. They eventually give up and descend to the "other place" singing their own dirge. Meanwhile, the bus driver, curious about the latch on the gate, calmly unlatches the gate of heaven and walks in alone. The choir, hearing the click of the gate latch, look back only to see the gate close.

Materials: PL or from the composer.

Notes: While this work may be classified as more secular than sacred, its "celestial" theme and message on pride may be suitable for some church choral groups. Best performed in a concert hall. A highly entertaining work. The composer has written six other similar choral dramas, all secular. Stage directions all given in some detail in the VS.

WOLFGANG AMADEUS MOZART

Die Schuldigkeit des ersten Gebotes – The Obligation of the First Commandment

Music by **Wolfgang Amadeus Mozart** (1756-1751). A Sacred Opera with text in German based on Matthew 22:37-40.

Premiered March 12, 1767 in Salzburg.

Secco recitatives, seven arias (most da capo), one trio. Considerable melisma in most arias.

One act. Setting: no particular place or time. Duration: approximately 50 minutes.

Roles: A CHRISTIAN (ten or sop – top Ab4); CHRISTIANITY (ten – top Ab3); WORLDLY SPIRIT (ten – top D4), many coloratura passages; MERCY (sop), much melisma; JUSTICE (sop – top A4).

Orchestration: 2 ob, 2 bsn, 2 hrn, trb, strings, hpsch.

Synopsis: Christianity, in discussion with Justice and Mercy, expresses concern over the luke-warm sons of men and the success of the cunning Worldly Spirit who lures them away from the path toward God. Mercy sympathizes, saying that the first commandment, to love God with all your soul, heart and strength, seems to be too great a burden for mankind. Justice, also sympathetic, cannot himself free them from their guilt. Christianity decries that his own example seems to have no effect on their carefree hearts. Justice concludes that the will of humans must be respected, whatever that will may be. In the midst of this discussion, Christian has fallen asleep. Justice wakens him with words of impending judgment. He is deeply troubled by his dream. Worldly Spirit immediately addresses him with the solution: "Has not the Creator given us the earth and all life? Then laugh, have fun, let your uneasy mind make room for glorious debauchery." Christianity re-enters disguised as a doctor, declaring himself to be the greatest physician. He vows anew that all his efforts shall be to see humankind converted and serve God. Mercy and Justice join him in a trio, declaring their intent to assist, but mankind must first be willing to ask for it.

Materials: KAL (Ger). English translation available by Mozelle Clark Sherman, SBTS.

Notes: Adaptable to either theatre or cathedral/church performance.

THEA MUSGRAVE

A Christmas Carol

Music by **Thea Musgrave** (b. 1928). A Christmas Opera with libretto in English by the composer based on the story by Charles Dickens.

Commissioned by the Virginia Opera Association with first performance by them on December 7, 1979, in Norfolk, VA.

Highly soloistic with some ensembles. Extensive use of twentieth century techniques: some *sprechstimme*, highly chromatic and straying tonalities. Non-traditional textures with highly colloristic orchestration.

Two acts. Setting: Christmas Eve. Act I, sc. 1: Scrooge's house; sc. 2: Marley's Ghost; sc, 3: The Spirit of Christmas Past; sc. 4: The Schoolroom; sc. 5: A Party at Mr. Fezziwig's; sc. 6: Belle says farewell. Act II, sc. 1: The Spirit of Christmas Present; sc. 2: The Cratchits celebrate; sc. 3: The Spirit of Christmas Future; sc. 4: The Cratchits mourn; sc. 5: The Graveyard; sc. 6: Scrooge awakens; sc. 7: Finale. Follows the Dickens story faithfully. Can be staged in three playing areas if stage space is adequate i.e.: Area I: Bedroom, Charwoman, Laundress; Area II: Schoolroom, Spirit of the Future, graveyard; Area III: Shop, Mr. Fezziwig, Spirit Present, Cratchet's home, Coffin scene, Finale. Duration: two hours.

Roles: The minimum cast is twelve; however, in certain circumstances it may be appropriate to enlarge the cast. SCROOGE (bar – top G3, high tess), dramatically and vocally demanding; SPIRIT OF CHRISTMAS (dancer); FAN AND STARVING WOMAN (sop – top C#5, opt E5), also CAROLLER, LIZA FEZZIWIG, BELINDA CRATCHIT and LUCY (Rosie's younger sister); BELLA FEZZIWIG and LAUNDRESS (sop – top C5), also MARTHA CRATCHIT and ROSIE (Fred's wife); MRS. CRATCHIT and CHARWOMAN (m-sop – top A4), also CAROLLER, MRS. FEZZIWIG and AUNT LOUISE; BOB CRATCHIT and MAN WITH SNUFF BOX (ten – top B3), also MR. DORRIT; FRED (Scrooge's nephew) and MAN WITH RED FACE (bar – top F#3), also BEN (Scrooge as a young man); PORTLY GENTLEMAN and FAT MAN (bs-bar), also MR. FEZZIWIG and TOPPER; MARLEY'S GHOST,

JOE THE RAG and BONE MAN (sp), MR. GABRIEL GRUB and GREAT-AUNT ERMINTRUDE; PAPER BOY (boy, about 12 or 13), also DICK (Fezziwig's apprentice), PETER CRATCHIT and BERTIE (Rosie's young brother); MOLLIE FEZZIWIG (girl, about 11 or 12), also CAROLLER, HARRIET CRATCHIT and VICKIE (Rosie's young sister); TINY TIM (boy, about 9 or 10), also CAROLLER and SCROOGE AS A YOUNG BOY. Extra children may be added to the Party Scenes and Act II, sc. 3.

Chorus: SSATBB (Off-stage voices which may be sung by characters not on stage at the time) An optional children's chorus can be included at the end of the Finale off-stage. Some supers may be used.

Dance: One dancer, SPIRIT OF CHRISTMAS, is required. Folk dancing at Fezziwig's Christmas party.

Orchestration: fl (picc), ob (Eng hrn), 2 cl (bs cl), bsn (contra bsn), hrn, 2 perc, hp, pia, str

Synopsis: One cold foggy Christmas Eve, Scrooge is busy at work. Fred, his nephew, and Bob Cratchit, his employee, wish him Merry Christmas. Scrooge loudly derides the whole idea of Christmas and rudely refuses Fred's invitation to dinner the next day. He then grudgingly allows Bob the next day off to celebrate Christmas. Later that night Scrooge is confronted by the ghost of his deceased partner, Jacob Marley. Marley laments his perpetual state of sorrow because of his selfish and narrow way of life. He warns Scrooge that the Spirit of Christmas Past, Present and Future will each visit him this very night. Scrooge dismisses the message as a bad dream and goes to bed.

The three Spirits indeed visit him, each presenting him with events and people he has and will encounter in his life past, present and future. Scrooge's dream is brought to a climax with the Spirit of the Future. Tiny Tim is crushed and dies. A funeral procession takes him to a deserted graveyard where inscribed on a tombstone are the words: "Ebenezer Scrooge, miser; who lived unloved and alone." He insists that the future is not predestined and he will change it. He swears he will honour the Spirit of Christmas throughout the year and that he will change.

Scrooge awakens with a feeling of lightness and joy realizing that he still has a chance to change and enjoy his last few years. He quickly runs to join his nephew's Christmas celebration bringing joy and goodwill to everyone he meets.

Materials: NOV. Recording Moss Music Group (MMG 302)

ALFRED NEUMANN

An Opera for Christmas

Music by **Alfred Neumann** (b. 1928). A Christmas Opera with libretto in English by the composer based on the Biblical story of the birth of Christ.

Premiered by the Christ Congregational Church, Silver Spring, Maryland, December 3, 1961.

Vocal lines easily accessible. Considerable accompanied recitative; arias, duets, ensembles. One unaccompanied choral section. Accessible for the average church choir.

One act, two scenes with continuous music. Fanfare and Overture. Setting: sc. 1: Two thrones in center stage; sc. 2: The manger scene. Duration: 28 minutes.

Singing Roles: EVANGELIST (ten); TWO WOMEN OF BETHLEHEM (sop, alt); FIVE INNKEEPERS (ten, ten, bar, bs, bs); FOUR SHEPHERDS (sop, alt, ten, bs).

Pantomime Roles: MARY; JOSEPH; COURT JESTER; 2 STANDARD BEARERS; 2 (or more) PAGE BOYS; SEVERAL SHEPHERDS.

Chorus: SSAATB – multitude of Bethlehem. Children's choir in unison or 2-part. The adult choir should be involved in the processional and then take their place as in a Greek chorus, commenting on the action during the remainder of the work. The Children's choir should be involved in the action.

Dance: Children's circle dance in a folk style.

Orchestration: org, cel, 2 trp (may be used in the processional), 2 trb, timp, cym. If the instruments are not available, the organist or pianist can play all cues. If the celesta can be placed adjacent to the keyboard, the organist or pianist can play it where indicated.

Synopsis: Following a Fanfare and Overture, the Evangelist welcomes everyone to the House of the Lord and sets the scene as he does throughout the opera. A royal procession follows, with King Joseph, Queen Mary, trumpeters, heralds, jesters, etc. When they reach their thrones, their royal robes are removed and they are presented as ordinary people, alone and ignored. Today, we tend to idolize them and place them into a position of royalty – but this is not at all the way it happened. Everyone leaves stage and the Evangelist traces the journey to Bethlehem. The Innkeepers try to explain that they are not to blame for having no room in their inns. They did not know or recognize Mary and Joseph. The world knew nothing of the prophecies; surely they are not to blame. This is how it really was and still is today: the world continues to shut out the Christ Child. The Shepherds enter knowing of the prophecy and having been told of Christ's coming. They stand in contrast to the unknowing Innkeepers. The Evangelist asks the audience if they are like the Shepherds, when upon hearing the news of great joy, knock, seek and follow; or are they like the Innkeepers, blind to the good that can be done in the world. An unaccompanied prayer for forgiveness is sung. The Women of Bethlehem sing "Come to us, we now have room." The Holy Family once again makes its entrance to the manger on stage, this time in a humble, lowly manner as it really occurred. The choir and children welcome them with alleluias and a renewed understanding.

Materials: Originally published by BEL. Materials from composer.

Notes: Ideally suited for performance in a cathedral/church. It may be performed with or without staging, with simple or elaborate settings. Designed to be incorporated as part of a worship service. Detailed staging suggestions are contained in the VS. Simple yet effective drama.

An Opera for Easter

Music by **Alfred Neumann** (b. 1928). An Easter Opera with libretto in English, based on the events surrounding the death and resurrection of Jesus.

Premiered by the Christ Congregational Church, Silver Spring, Maryland, April 4, 1965. Composed in 1962.

Traditional harmony with occasional plainchant. Continuous texture. Choral sections mainly homophonic and hymn-like. Participation by the congregation in familiar hymns.

One act, five scenes. Overture. Sc. 1: Palm Sunday; sc. 2: The last supper; sc. 3: The trial; sc. 4: The crucifixion; sc. 5: The resurrection. Duration: 30 minutes.

Singing Roles: A WOMAN OF THE CONGREGATION (sop – top B4); TWO WOMEN OF THE MULTITUDE (alto, sop). The soloists and chorus seldom are involved in the action which is carried out by the pantomime actors.

Pantomime Roles: CHRIST; BARTHOLOMEW; JAMES, the Younger; ANDREW; JUDAS; PETER; JOHN; THOMAS; JAMES, the Elder; PHILIP; MATTHEW; THADDEUS; SIMON; TWO ROMAN GUARDS.

Chorus: SATB, double choir – the multitude. Children's choir (ad lib). The work is mostly choral.

Dance: Liturgical dance may be incorporated in the Overture leading into the procession of Jesus into Jerusalem.

Orchestration: org, 2 trp, 2 trb, timp, bells, cym. The organ, bells and cymbals work well alone if instrumentalists are not available.

Synopsis: Jesus makes his entry into Jerusalem as children and the crowd hail him King. A member of the congregation stands and accuses the crowd of being hypocrites, praising Him one moment and crucifying him the next. The crowd refutes the statement and goes on with praise to their King. The scene shifts briefly to the last supper, Jesus eating with His disciples. Jesus leaves the table and is taken by two guards to the trial, where He is accused by a lady calling out against Him from the congregation. A procession leads Jesus to Calvary, where He is crucified while the congregation sings *O Sacred Head Now Wounded*. As He dies, the crowd and audience call for forgiveness. In the final scene, the choir chants "Truly we shall be in paradise with Him, Alleluia."

Materials: From the composer.

Notes: Intended for performance in a cathedral/church. May be incorporated as part of a worship service. Stage directions in the VS. An effective work involving the congregation in the drama.

An Opera for Everyman

Music by **Alfred Neumann** (b. 1928). A Sacred Opera with libretto in English by the composer, based on the "Everyman" medieval story.

Composed August, 1963.

Considerable plainchant and recitative; melodic. Tonality and modality with some chromaticism; primarily conventional harmonic structures. Spoken narrative.

One act, seven scenes with continuous texture. Overture. Scene 1: Everyman summoned; sc. 2: Lullaby and Baptism; sc. 3: Children's Carol; sc. 4: Confirmation; sc. 5: Marriage; sc. 6: Everyman summoned; sc. 7: Conclusion. Duration: approximately 30 minutes.

Singing Roles: MESSENGER (sp), the narrator; GOD'S VOICE (sop, bs duet).

Pantomime Roles: EVERYMAN, appears as a baby, a small child, a 12-year old child, and a young man; DEATH; FELLOWSHIP; KINDRED; GOOD DEEDS; MOTHER, of Everyman; A PRIEST (minister); TWO PAGES.

Chorus: SATB – Death and narrative. Should be stationary and out of the area of action. Sings throughout the opera.

Orchestration: org, 2 trp, 2 trb, timp, sn dr, cym, blocks, bells, tri.

Synopsis: The Messenger appears and summons Everyman to give a reckoning of his life. God asks Death to find Everyman and take him on a pilgrimage through his life. Everyman's life is brought into view through a series of highlight events which include his baptism, his childhood, his confirmation, his wedding, and finally his funeral. At the conclusion of his life, the Messenger addresses the audience with admonitions to forsake pride and save Good Deeds. The final chorus states that man's chief end is to glorify God, alleluia.

Materials: From the composer.

Notes: Designed for church performance. May be incorporated as part of a worship service.

The Rites (Rights) of Man

Music by **Alfred Neumann** (b. 1928). A Sacred Opera Buffa with libretto in English by the composer. A tune by Ralph Vaughan Williams is included.

Premiered November 9, 1980, Christ Congregational Church, Silver Spring, MD.

Recitatives; traditional harmony with frequent key changes; some chromaticism. Continuous texture. Comic.

One act, three scenes with Prelude and Epilogue. Prelude: End of a worship service; sc. 1: The Minister; sc. 2: The Committee; sc. 3: The Trustees; sc. 4: Youth; Epilogue. Duration: approximately 30 minutes.

Roles: DEVIL (bs, alt duet or solo); CHRIST (sop, bar duet); MINISTER (bar – top F#3); A WIFE (sop); A HUSBAND (mute).

Chorus: SATB – the congregation; SSSAA – the Committee; TTBB – the Trustees; Unison or 3-part – Youth choir.

Orchestration: fl, ob, cl, bsn, hrn, 2 trp, trb, timp, perc, str, gui

Synopsis: This work does not necessarily reflect the problems of any one church, but is a caricature of what can and at times does happen in a church setting. The morning worship service concludes with the choir and congregation singing *God Be With You Till We Meet Again* followed by a choral Amen. Conversations, chit-chat, and "gossip" among congregation (choir) members follows as they leave the sanctuary. A brief dialogue between the Devil and Christ occurs in which the Devil argues that this group of people is just like any other club. Christ maintains they are the arms of God. The Minister in Scene 1 elaborates, to himself, on the conferences, meetings, and busy work which keep him from preparing his sermons properly. Meanwhile, a committee meets and discusses trivial matters regarding their next meeting. In another corner of the sanctuary, a wife calls to her husband to hurry home as the dinner is getting cold. The Minister comments on yet another meeting!! A group of Trustees has gathered to seek solutions to the mounting bills of the church. Meanwhile, a youth group discusses the boredom of the church and asks help of "someone." Eventually all these discussions are voiced together in one large ensemble. The Devil enters, observes and is indeed pleased with the confusion. Christ answers him: "Without some confusion, my work is just illusion. Surely, Devil, you can see, these are the arms of God. Strong my church will always be, for these are the rites of man." The full cast joins in the words of Christ, concluding that when His love has reached all men, His Kingdom will be at hand.

Materials: From the composer.

Notes: Ideal for performance in a sanctuary.

CARL NIELSEN

Saul and David

Music by **Carl Nielsen** (1865-1931). A Sacred Opera with libretto in Danish by Einar Christiansen, based on various events taken from the Biblical Book of I Samuel.

First performance November 22, 1902, Royal Danish Opera in Copenhagen.

Highly Romantic texture with occasional non-traditional harmonic movement and chromaticism. Melodic, through-composed.

Four acts. Act I: In the Temple; Act II: Saul's throne room; Act III: In a cave; Act IV: Night time in the house of the Witch of Endor. Duration: approximately 110 minutes.

Roles: SAUL (bs-bar – top F3), dramatically and vocally demanding; JONATHAN (ten); MIKAL (sop), Saul's younger daughter; DAVID (ten); SAMUEL (bs); ABNER (bs); WITCH OF ENDOR (alt); ABISAY (sop).

Chorus: SSAATTBB – Villagers, Soldiers, Priests, Young Ladies.

Dance: Act II victory celebration. Mostly folk style.

Orchestration: 3 fl, 2 ob, 2 cl, 2 bsn, 4 hrn, 3 trp, 3 trb, tba, timp, perc, hp, str

Synopsis: The Philistines are closing in on and ready to attack Israel. Saul can no longer wait for Samuel to offer the sacrifice; he offers it himself much to the objection of Jonathan. Immediately after the sacrifice is offered, Samuel arrives. Angered by Saul's hasty action, Samuel reprimands him. Because of his action, says Samuel, God will remove Saul as King of Israel. David arrives from tending his sheep and meets Mikal. Act II opens with David singing and playing for King Saul, calming his troubled spirit. When David offers to fight against the giant Goliath of the Philistine army, Saul at first objects but then realizing David has no chance of survival and seeing David's demise as personally advantageous, sends him with the promise of Mikal as bride if he returns with the head of Goliath. Soon word comes back to Saul that David has slain Goliath. The wedding festivities are under way, spoiled only by Saul's fierce anger and jealousy of David's heroism. While David sings to calm him, Saul hurls a spear at him, attempting once again to rid himself of this boy.

In Act III David comes upon Saul who is in a deep sleep. David removes Saul's sword from his sheath and then wakens him. Saul is grateful for the sparing of his life. Word arrives that the great Prophet Samuel has died. Saul, in disguise, seeks counsel of the Witch of Endor. He requests that Samuel's ghost be brought to life in order to learn his own future from the Prophet. Samuel tells him he will die. Alarmed and despondent, Saul falls on his own sword and dies. David is hailed as the new King of Israel.

Materials: GS (Hansen/Chester) (Ger, Dan, Eng by Geoffrey Dunn).

Notes: Best performed in a theatre.

CARL ORFF

Comoedia de Christi resurrectione –
A Comedy during Christ's Resurrection

Music by **Carl Orff** (1895-1982). An Easter Play with libretto in German and Greek by the composer. Latin, Greek and German languages sung; spoken dialogue in German.

Premiered in 1957, Stuttgart.

Reflective of Baroque musical features and Greek tragedy. Rhythmic, declamatory speech patterns with considerable repetition. Chant. Most action occurs during spoken dialogue.

One act. Setting: Before Christ's tomb. Duration: approximately 60 minutes.

Roles: SOP SOLO; BASS SOLO (top F3); TWELVE SOLDIERS (sp), guards of the tomb; THE DEVIL (sp).

Chorus: SSATTB – Angels, mourners; 3-part children's chorus – angels.

Orchestration: 3 keyboards, 2 hp, 4 cb, perc (timp, xyl, ten xyl, marimba, 2 glock, tri, cym, tam tam, dr

Synopsis: Women mourn at the tomb of Christ. Two different groups of six soldiers discuss in cursory manner, the events leading up to Christ's crucifixion. In their midst is the Devil, casually toying with their opinions on these events. The Devil derives great pleasure from their indifference, frequently breaking into insidious laughter as they pass the time with games and gambling. Suddenly, they turn their attention to the tomb, observing to their surprise and the Devil's horror, that the tomb entrance is open and the grave empty. A chorus of Angels declares that Christ is risen from death! Hallelujah!

Materials: SCH (AMP).

Notes: Best suited to theatre performance, though technically adaptable to a church. Minimal sets are required.

HAROLD JOHN OWEN

The Passion of Our Lord Jesus Christ According to Saint Mark

Music by **Harold John Owen** (b. 1931). A Dramatic Easter Passion with text in English taken primarily from the Biblical Books of St. Mark, Psalms and Roman Catholic Liturgy.

Composed in 1972 (Doctoral thesis). First performance March 28, 1973, Central Lutheran Church, Eugene, Oregon.

Non-traditional harmony, considerable dissonance and chromaticism. Narration, occasional use of chant, non-misura sections, rhythmic choral speech.

Two parts, nineteen section. Duration: 75 minutes.

Roles: JESUS (bs-bar); HIGH PRIEST (bar – top F3); PILATE (2 ten); NARRATOR (sp).

Chorus: Double choirs: Chorus I (SSAA), Chorus II (TTBB). Frequently *a cappella*. Predominantly choral work. Choirs should remain stationary throughout, seated in the audience facing the action.

Orchestration: 2 fl, 2 ob, 2 cl, 2 bsn, 2 hrn, 2 trp, 2 trb, perc, timp, 5 celli. Thinly orchestrated; very soloistic.

Synopsis: The story of the Passion of Our Lord beginning after the last supper as Jesus takes his disciples to the Mount of Olives. The work concludes with Christ's last words and His death on the cross. The plot remains faithful to the St. Mark version.

Materials: Unpublished. USC, or the composer.

Notes: Harold Owen: "This work is written as a liturgical drama and is intended to be performed in a church setting. The 'congregation' is not only asked to be the spectators but to participate in the drama as the 'turba' or crowd.... The chorus is the representative of the people of the congregation and is seated in the front pews facing the altar. In the chancel area sit the players of the drama with their instrumental 'retinues': Jesus, with five celli before him, sits in front of the altar facing the people. On the left is Pilate (performed by two tenors standing back-to-back) with the brass and percussion. On the right and facing them is the High Priest and the wood winds. The narrator stands in the pulpit facing diagonally across the length of the church.... The part played by the people has been kept simple but direct.... It is hoped that the people will feel that the chorus is expressing their thoughts and emotions, much like the chorus of Greek antiquity."

RICHARD OWEN

A Fisherman Called Peter

Music by **Richard Owen** (b. 1922). A Biblical Opera with libretto in English derived primarily from the Bible based on the New Testament call of Apostle Peter.

Commissioned and premiered by Drew Church, Carmel, NY, 1965.

Considerable choral music. Accessible for good church choirs. Vocal lines follow speech patterns. Mid-range tessituras for soloists. Romantic in style.

Five scenes. Scene 1: By the bank of the Jordan River during the time of Christ; sc. 2: Simon's house; sc. 3: Capernaum on the shore of the Sea of Galilee; sc. 4: Simon's house; sc. 5: A hillside. Duration: 50 minutes.

Roles: SIMON, afterwards PETER (bar – top F#3); DEBORAH (sop – top B4), his wife; JOHN THE BAPTIST (bar – op F3); ANDREW (ten – C2 to Ab3), Simon's brother; DEBORAH'S MOTHER (m-sop); FIRST FISHERMAN (ten); SECOND FISHERMAN (bar); THE VOICE OF JESUS (sp).

Chorus: SSAATTBB – the crowd; TTBB – fishermen.

Orchestration: ob, trp, hrn, timp, vln, vla, vc, cb, org.

Synopsis: A multitude of people have gathered beside the river to hear John the Baptist preach of Christ's coming. Andrew pushes his way through the crowd and asks what he must do to be saved. John, Andrew and others leave to be baptized. Some of the crowd leaves, undecided as to the truth of his preaching. In their home, Deborah and her Mother prepare a meal. Simon and Andrew come in arguing, with Andrew attempting to convince Simon to go and hear this man Jesus. Simon is reluctant and disbelieves that he could possibly be the Christ. However, with the two women supporting Andrew, Simon finally consents to go. Scene three finds fishermen preparing to go out to sea. Simon, lost in thought, contemplates what he just heard Jesus say. Simon is questioned by the others, and he tells them of Jesus' message of love. The response is laughter. Left alone, he hears the voice of Jesus and follows the call to become a "fisher of men."

Deborah is home alone concerned about Simon's leaving his home and trade to follow Jesus. Simon tries to explain the call of Jesus to her. She tries to dissuade him but is finally convinced to come and hear Him herself. Together with the crowd, Deborah asks the Lord if He is indeed the Christ. As He teaches, they are all moved and many are convinced. After a dispute breaks out as to Jesus' identity, Simon boldly declares that He is the Christ, the Son of the living God. Jesus changes his name to Peter and bids him follow. As Peter starts to follow Jesus, Deborah nods her approval and the crowd sings a joyous chorus of praise.

Materials: GMC (© 1967).

Notes: Best suited to church performance. Imaginative lighting needed. The visual portrayal of the Voice of Jesus will require some creativity.

ALICE PARKER

The Martyrs' Mirror

Music by **Alice Parker** (b. 1925). A Sacred Opera with libretto in English by John Ruth, primarily based on the book of the same title. Some Latin (*Pange, Lingua*).

Premiered October, 1971, Lansdale, PA.

Renaissance in musical style; based on Reformation hymn texts and tunes. Simple, transparent texture. Ensembles, solos. Spoken dialogue. 26 set numbers.

Two acts. Setting: Switzerland (Austria or the Low Countries) in 1520-35. Duration: 90 minutes.

Roles: GEORG BLAUROCK (bar); CATHARINA BLAUROCK (cont), his wife; JAN WOUTERS (ten); MAYEKEN WOUTERS (sop), his wife; EXECUTIONER (bar); GEORG'S SON (boy sop); FRIEND (a child); MONK (sp); BAILIFF (sp); A NEW LEADER (sp).

Chorus: SATB – double chorus of believers, soldiers, friends, church dignitaries, neighbors, hostile crowd. A Men's quartet. Children's choir (mostly unison) – children of chorus members.

Orchestration: 2 rec, ob, bsn, trp, 2 trb, bs trb, perc, bells, harmonium, vln, vc

Synopsis: Early in the morning of a Festival Day, bells sound and a solemn procession honoring the Blessed Sacrament enters the sanctuary. Townspeople gather singing the *Pange Lingua*. At the fifth verse, all kneel except Georg, who, having read the newly-translated Bible, feels that this is not part of Christ's teaching! The Monk and Bailiff, representing the power of Church and State, enter with a flourish to read official mandates ordering the arrest and execution of all Anabaptists. Later in Georg's home, the family sings of their united strength and faith. Several children come for a Bible lesson, and their elders for a secret meeting. The Bailiff, having infiltrated the group, arrests Georg, Catharina, Jan and Mayeken. On the way to jail, Jan sings of his longing for martyrdom, following in Christ's steps. His wife yearns for her wee baby, left behind. Soldiers lead the family to jail cells. The martyrs discover that, although they cannot see each other, they can communicate by singing. When they are sentenced to die by fire on Market Day, Mayeken, realizing that she will never again see her child, accuses her husband of misleading her. She weeps as the martyrs are led away and the chorus prays for them.

On Market Day, children are playing and laughing in the Town Square. Soldiers enter, telling people to look and learn: the martyrs are being brought to the stake. Catharina reproves the men for teasing Mayeken; Georg tries to comfort her; the angry crowd taunts them all. When Jan sings of his great joy, the mood of the crowd shifts and they become unruly. Mayeken silences them with her song of new-found faith and tranquility. The martyrs ascend their own scaffolds, and Georg bids the Executioner begin. As he lights his torch, the action stops. The chorus sings of fire, its destructive, cleansing and regenerative power. A New Leader steps forward, blessing all martyrs. The entire congregation joins in the final hymn.

Materials: ECS.

Notes: Designed specifically for church performance.

Singer's Glen

Music by **Alice Parker** (b. 1925). A Church Folk Opera with libretto in English by the composer, based on the life of Peter Funk, his family, his music and his Mennonite church.

Composed in 1978, first performed April 1, 1978, Lancaster, PA. Commissioned by Hiram Hershey.

Set numbers, mostly shape-note hymn tunes taken from *Genuine Church Music* and arranged by Parker. Spoken dialogue connects numbers. Mostly ensembles, some solos. Musical language simple and hymn-like.

Two acts, Prologue, five scenes. Setting: A homestead in the Shenandoah Valley, Virginia, 1833 and 1842. Overture. Prologue: Winter, 1833, the Funk homestead; Act I, sc. 1: The same, Spring, ten years later; sc. 2: Later that day, inside the house; sc. 3: Inside the barn, set up for a singing school. Act II, sc. 1: Fall, 1842, inside the house; sc. 2: That evening, inside the barn. Duration: 115 minutes.

Roles: JOSEPH FUNK (bar); His children: HANNA (sop), TIMOTHY (ten), SOLOMON (bs), BENJAMIN (ten). BROTHER PETER (ten), the Bishop; AUNT MARTHA (m-sop); SUSAN RUEBUSH (sop); JACOB BAER (bar); THE OLD COUPLE and SUSAN'S PARENTS (ensemble).

Chorus: SATB – at least 20 plus the main characters. Four children with unchanged voices in Prologue.

Dance: Square dance with the singers.

Orchestration: fl, trp, trb, gui, pump organ (on stage), string quartet;

Background: Singers Glen is an actual town in Rockingham County, Virginia, named for the musical and publishing activities of Joseph Funk and his family. Born in Pennsylvania in 1779, he moved to the Shenandoah Valley in 1784. In 1816, his volume titled *Choral Music* was published: a collection of chorale tunes in two parts, with German texts. In 1832 appeared the first edition of *Genuine Church Music*, a collection of some 260 hymn tunes in three-part settings with English texts.

This opera tells of Joseph's life in relationship to his family, his music and his church. The hymns used throughout the opera are all from his three editions of *Genuine Church Music*, and the characters and situations are drawn from Joseph's life, notably from a remarkable series of letters he wrote to a married daughter. He was married twice, and the story begins with the death of his second wife, Rachel Britton, who died in 1832. Joseph was then 55, left with many children, a farm, occasional teaching positions and a passion for music.

Joseph Funk remained active in both music and church, seeing his hymnal through ten editions before his death in 1862, at age 84. There is no evidence that he left the Mennonite Church, however his children did. The tenth edition of the hymnal, now named *Harmonia Sacra*, was the first book to carry this imprint. The twenty-third edition of this book is still in print and in use today.

Synopsis: The Prologue finds Joseph a year after his hymnal was first printed, at his wife's funeral. His friends offer to help, but their counsel and that of Brother Peter is that he abandon his music and keep to the old ways.

Ten years later when the third edition of *Genuine Church Music* has just been printed, we find Joseph's children at work with him. Hannah keeps house, Timothy is a bookbinder and aspiring song leader, Solomon is learning the printing trade and Benjamin as the youngest helps everyone. The family plans a singing school to be held that night in their barn. Brother Peter visits to express his concern over the non-traditional upbringing of the children. Timothy and his girl share a quiet moment. Everyone then gathers for the singing school where Joseph teaches shape-note reading, faw-sol-law singing, and new and old favorite hymns.

Joseph opens Act II with a soliloquy, remembering his wife, thinking about his children and praying to God. The last scene is another singing school, with Timothy leading instruments and voices. As the young people begin dancing, the Bishop appears with a stern warning. Joseph defends his children but then is left to seek some kind of peace in the seeming conflict between his music and his church.

Materials: HIN.

Notes: Best suited for presentation in a house of worship or intimate auditorium. Numerous historical and production notes by the composer in the VS.

HORATIO W. PARKER

The Legend of St. Christopher

Music by **Horatio Parker** (1863-1919). A Dramatic Oratorio, Op. 43, with libretto in English (some Latin) by Isabella Parker.

Composed in 1897. Premiered April 15, 1898, New York Oratorio Society, Carnegie Hall.

Highly Romantic texture, reminiscent of mid-nineteenth century operatic styles. Through-composed, accompanied recitatives, arias, ensembles. Melodic. Frequent instrumental passages.

Three acts, nine scenes. Prologue (chorale); Act I, sc. 1: Before the King's Palace; sc. 2: A hall in the Palace; sc. 3: In the forest. Act II, sc. 1: A desert plain; sc. 2: At a cross. Act III, sc. 1: A hermit's cottage; sc. 2: Inside a cathedral; sc. 3: Hermit's cottage; sc. 4: A small hut on the river bank. Duration: Full length.

Major Roles: OFFERUS (bs – A#1-Fb3), the giant; THE QUEEN (sop – top B4); THE KING (ten – top Ab3); THE HERMIT (ten – top B3), the monarch, Oriens (The King and Hermit can double); SATAN (bar or robust ten – C#2-G3).

Minor Roles: THE ANGEL (sop – top B4), may be sung by the Queen; THE CHILD (boy sop).

Chorus: SSAATTBB – Soldiers, Maidens, Satan's legion, Worshippers, Angels.

Orchestration: Organ and full orchestra.

Synopsis: The King of Oriens enters the scene in great triumph heralded by his army and the people whom he rules. Meanwhile, the giant Offerus has been searching for the mightiest earthly monarch, that he might serve him. He now seeks to be the slave of King Oriens and is invited to serve. Offerus is presented to the Queen and made a servant of the Royal Court. The King and Offerus leave for a hunt in the forest. A deer runs across their path. The King is frightened, stating that this forest is haunted. Offerus, seeing a weakness in this King, decides to leave in search of a stronger King to serve.

In Act II, Offerus encounters Satan and perceiving his strength, decides to join his legions. As they march through the plains, they come upon the cross where the Lord of heaven died. Satan trembles and falters at the sight of the cross. Again Offerus must go on searching for a mightier monarch to serve.

Offerus comes to a Hermit's cottage in the forest and asks the Hermit to assist him in finding the Lord of Heaven who has caused even Satan to tremble. The hermit gladly takes him in and tells him of the Savior; then he shows him a cathedral where people worship this Lord. Back at the cottage the Hermit suggests that Offerus assist those who attempt to cross the dangerous river in the forest. That night, Offerus hears the voice of a child in distress. Offerus picks up the child and carries him safely across the violent river. Reaching the shore, Offerus learns from a heavenly choir that in his arms is the life of Christ, the Holy One. Offerus names the child Christopher. Angels sing of heaven's acceptance of Offerus' service and servant hood.

Materials: NOV. Recording: Vanguard VRS-1036/VSD-2021.

Notes: Best suited for performance on a large theatre stage. Numerous scenes may require extensive set changes. VS contains detailed stage directions.

THOMAS PASATIERI

Calvary

Music by **Thomas Pasatieri** (b. 1945). A Sacred Music Drama with text in English from the play by William Butler Yeats (1865-1939), based on the events surrounding the crucifixion of Jesus.

Premiered April 7, 1971, Thomas Episcopal Church, Bellevue, Washington.

Vocal line rhythmically complex at times; some spoken lines. Melodic. Some unaccompanied passages. Twentieth century influences with straying tonalities. Text is highly symbolic.

One act. Setting: Calvary on the day of Jesus' crucifixion. Duration: 33 minutes.

Roles: FIRST MUSICIAN (sop – C3-Bb4), narrates the story; SECOND MUSICIAN (sop – D3-A4); THIRD MUSICIAN (m-sop); CHRIST (bar – Bb1-G3); LAZARUS (bs); JUDAS (ten – Eb2-A3); THREE ROMAN SOLDIERS (bar, bar, bs).

Dance: A simple folk dance by the Three Soldiers.

Orchestration: fl, ob, cl, bsn, hrn, hp, vln, vla, vc.

Synopsis: The Musicians provide a narrative framework throughout, first setting the stage for the appearance of Christ at Mt. Calvary. Bearing His cross to Calvary, Jesus is confronted by an ungrateful Lazarus. By raising him from the grave, Jesus deprived him of the solitude of death. Then comes Judas who, realizing that Jesus is God, thought he could free himself of God's sovereignty by betraying Jesus. The Three Roman Soldiers, dice throwers who have no need of God, appear and make Judas hold up the cross while they nail Jesus to it, ending with a dance around the cross. Finally Jesus cries out in agony, "My Father, why hast Thou forsaken me?"

Materials: BEL (TP).

Notes: The text is highly symbolic, leaving interpretation at times open to question. Most suitable for performance in a cathedral/church. Production problem: hanging Jesus from and erecting a cross.

PETER PATENTE

Behold Your King

Music by **Peter Patente** (20th century American). A Dramatic Choral work for Christmas with text in English taken from Scripture.

Composed in 1964.

Considerable choral music; contemporary language.

Four scenes deal with Herod, Caesar Augustus and the Birth of Christ.

Roles: NARRATOR; BASS SOLOIST.

Chorus: SATB

Orchestration: 2 hrn, 2 trp, 2 trb, tba, perc, timp, Hammond org (registration suggestions included).

Synopsis: Several events surrounding the birth of Christ are dealt with. The two events which figure most prominently in the plot are King Herod's jealousy over the birth of a future king and the response of Caesar to the Birth of Christ.

Materials: Unpublished. LC (M2000.P293 B4). Score includes staging directions.

STEVEN PAULUS

The Village Singer

Music by **Steven Paulus** (b. 1949). A Folk Opera with libretto in English by Michael Dennis Browne, based on a story by Mary Wilkins Freeman.

Commissioned by the New Music Circle of St. Louis for the Opera Theatre of St. Louis; premiered June 9, 1979.

Antiphonal effects, tonal, melodic; mixed meter, dissonant.

One act. Setting: New England village around 1900. Alternately in Candace Whitcomb's cottage and in the church. Duration: 60 minutes.

Roles: CANDACE WHITCOMB (sop – top B4); *ALMA WAY (sop – top C#5); *MINNIE LANSING (sop); *JENNY CARR (m-sop); *NANCY FORD (m-sop), Candace's sister; *WILSON FORD (ten), Nancy's son, Candace's nephew, engaged to Alma; THE REVEREND POLLARD (ten); *TODD WILKINS (ten); *WILLIAM EMMONS (bar), choir leader; *BRENT FREEMAN (bs).
(*These singers make up the choir.)

Chorus: See under "Roles"

Orchestration: 2 fl, ob, 2 cl, bsn, hrn, perc, timp, hp, strings, pia, harmonium or elec org.

Synopsis: For forty years, Candace Whitcomb has been the leading soprano of her church choir. Her upper notes have become unreliable. The other choir members give her a surprise party and an album of photographs, and she, suspecting nothing, is touched by their tribute. When they have gone, she finds in the album a letter telling her she is no longer needed and that a younger soprano, Alma Way, has been engaged. The next Sunday, Alma embarks on her first solo. As her voice rings out, the people nod admiringly. Suddenly, above Alma's sweet voice, another hymn to another tune is heard. Candace's cottage is located immediately adjacent to the church, and Candace can now be distinctly heard playing on her organ and singing to drown out the voice of her rival. Later, the minister visits her but in vain. During the next service, the same battle is fought. In vain others visit with Candace. Suddenly, Candace takes seriously ill. She asks Alma to come to sing to her after a service. When Alma finishes, Candace, still with a holy and radiant expression remarks: "You flatted a little on 'soul'."

Materials: EAM.

Notes: An entertainment piece best suited for theatre performance. In addition to this work's entertaining and at times comic character, a poignant lesson is projected.

KRZYSZTOF PENDERECKI

Paradise Lost

Music by **Krzysztof Penderecki** (b. 1933). A Sacred Opera (*Sacra Rappresentazione*) with libretto in English by Christopher Fry based on John Milton's book of the same title.

Premiered November 29, 1978, Lyric Opera of Chicago.

Atonality dominates with the use of some serial devices. Eclectic but more conventional than many of his earlier works. Complex rhythmic schemes, some *sprechstimme*, frequent use of rhythmic speech patterns.

Two acts. Settings alternate: earth, heaven and hell. Duration: 150 minutes.

Roles: MILTON (sp); ADAM (bar – Bb2-A3), lengthy, high and demanding role; EVE (sop – top B4); SATAN (dramatic bar – G1-G3), demands strong actor and singer; BEELZEBUB (ten – top B3); MOLOCH (bs – low Fl); BELIAL (ten); MAMMON (bar – top Gb3); VOICE OF GOD (sp); DEATH (ct ten); SIN (m-sop – Bb2-Ab4); ITHURIEL and RAPHAEL (ct ten); ZEPHON (col sop – top C5); GABRIEL (ten – top C4); MESSIAH (bar); MICHAEL (ten).

Chorus: Double chorus of SATB (Greek chorus); Children's chorus representing animals.

Dancers: Considerable dancing and mime representing Adam, Eve, Cain, Abel, Panther, Gazelle.

Orchestration: Full orchestra with large percussion demands.

Synopsis: The plot deals with the fall of man, the triumph of Satan and the promise of salvation through the Messiah. Milton introduces the scene and takes us to the creation of Adam, his fall through disobedience and the loss of Eden. Satan and his angels enter at various times, inflicting on the world conflict, war and strife. After a brief encounter with Death and Satan, we journey with them through the chaos of Hell. A quick return to Eden finds Adam and Eve tending the birds and beasts. Satan, dismayed by their happiness, approaches Eve as she sleeps and plants in her mind the first seeds of disobedience. Gabriel and his angels drive Satan away, while God sends Raphael to warn Adam of Satan's message to Eve.

In act two, Eve strolls through Eden alone. Satan, seizing this opportune moment, tells her not to be afraid but to eat of the fruit of the forbidden tree, for "you will not die, but will know both good and evil." She eats, and heightened as with wine, she dances wildly. Adam joins her and together they dance until they fall asleep from exhaustion. God's voice is heard asking where can be found one who can pay the price of death for man's disobedience. Christ is heard offering to pay the price.

Adam and Eve hide as God approaches them. In the background, Satan and his host can be heard rejoicing in their victory over God's prize creation.

The Angel Michael shows Adam two visions of the effects of his original sin: Cain killing Abel and the warring of nations. With deep remorse and repentance, Adam and Eve are led out of Eden, but rejoice in God's promise to be with them in spite of their sin.

Materials: EAM.

Notes: A very large production with considerable demands on musicians and technicians alike. A staged version requires theatre facilities.

Passio et mors domini nostri Jesu Christi secundum Lucam – The Passion and Death of Our Lord Jesus Christ According to St. Luke – St. Luke Passion

Music by **Krzysztof Penderecki** (b. 1933). A Dramatic Oratorio with text in Latin based primarily on the book of Luke.

Premiered March 30, 1966, in the Muenster Cathedral on the occasion of its 700th jubilee.

Requires large forces. Avant-garde; mostly atonal; extremely difficult for singers and instrumentalists alike. Non-traditional vocal effects. Continuous texture. Spoken narrative.

Two parts. Part I: Jesus on the Mount of Olives, the Arrest, Peter's denial, and Jesus before Pilate. Part II: The Way to the Cross, the Crucifixion, Mocking Jesus on the Cross, *Stabat Mater*, Jesus' Death. Duration: 80 minutes.

Roles: SOPRANO SOLO (A2-C5 – requires considerable flexibility); BARITONE SOLO (B1-A3 – high tess), represents Jesus; BASS SOLO (low Fl), represents Pilate and Peter; NARRATOR (sp).

Chorus: Three separate SATB choruses who represent the crowd and comment on the action. A treble choir (SA).

Orchestration: 4 fl (2 picc, 1 alt), bs cl, 2 sax, 3 bsn, contra bsn, 6 hrn, 4 trp, 4 trb, tba, 4 timp, bs dr, 6 tom-toms, 2 bongos, vib, many other miscellaneous perc, hp, pia, harmonia, org, strings.

Synopsis: The plot follows closely the traditional form of the passion, beginning with the singing of a hymn. Jesus is heard praying on the Mount of Olives while His disciples sleep nearby. A multitude of people and soldiers, including Judas, approach Jesus and lead Him to the High Priest. Peter follows at some distance and when asked whether he is a follower of Jesus, denies even knowing Him. Meanwhile, Jesus is mocked and ridiculed by the people and finally sent to face Pilate. The People demand His crucifixion. He is given a cross to bear which He carries up the hill to Golgotha. There they crucify Jesus and place His cross between two crucified thieves. He is mocked as He speaks but a few words to His Father and to those who mourn His death.

With His mother and a few followers standing at the foot of His cross, He dies. The chorus concludes with a moving setting of Psalm 31:1-2,5.

Materials: EAM (Moeck Verlag).

Notes: A powerful work requiring a large space for the three choruses, large orchestra, and acting area. Highly skilled singers and instrumentalists mandatory.

EDMUND J. PENDLETON

The Miracle of the Nativity

Music by **Edmund J. Pendleton** (1899-1987). A Lyric Music Drama for Christmas with text in English (some Latin) by the composer, based on Scripture.

Premiered December 15, 1974, American Church in Paris, France. American premiere December, 1981, at Centenary College, Shreveport, LA.

Arias, recitative, ensembles, one spoken chorus.

One act, Prologue, seven scenes. Prologue: Choral; Sc. 1: The Annunciation; sc. 2: Joseph's doubt; sc. 3: Caesar's decree; sc. 4: The journey to Bethlehem; sc. 5: The announcement to the Shepherds; sc. 6: The birth; sc. 7: The Shepherds and Kings present their gifts. Duration: approximately 80 minutes.

Roles: MARY; JOSEPH; 2 ANGELS; THE ROMAN CONSUL; 3 INNKEEPERS; 3 SHEPHERDS; 3 KINGS; A SOLDIER.

Chorus: SATB.

Dance: Folk dance by the Shepherds.

Orchestration: Chamber orchestra.

Synopsis: Sc. 1: The Angel visits Mary, announcing to her God's plan for her to bear His Son. Overjoyed, she sings her hymn of thanksgiving, a *Magnificat*. Sc. 2: Joseph discovers Mary's pregnancy and reacts with serious doubts. Sc. 3: The Roman Consul reads Caesar's decree that all residents must come to Bethlehem to be registered. Sc. 4: Mary and Joseph travel to Bethlehem and search for shelter. Finding none other than a stable, they give thanks to God for such as they have. Sc. 5: An Angel announces the birth of Jesus to the Shepherds. Sc. 6: The Child is born. Mary sings a lullaby to the Child, followed by a duet of gratitude with Joseph. Sc. 7: The Shepherds arrive and dance and play musical instruments for the Child. The Three Kings arrive with their gifts. The Chorus concludes the work as they began it, with *Hodie Christus natus est*.

Materials: Published privately by ARSM; also CC.

Notes: Most suitable for performance in a cathedral/church where the entire sanctuary can be used for dramatic staging. Minimal properties needed.

DAVID PENINGER

The Door

Music by **David Peninger** (b. 1929). A Sacred Music Drama with text in English by the composer, conceived by William Treadwell.

Composed in 1972.

Originally designed to encourage congregational involvement in the "Youth Search for Meaning Week" at the First Baptist Church of Greenwood, SC. The musical setting hopes to point out a search that must inevitably go on within everyone and that it will help Bible study leaders and discussion group leaders face the impact of their responsibility.

Spoken dialogue, ensembles, solos, set numbers. Conventional harmonies in a folk idiom with some "pop" sounds. Melodic. Intended for high school voices.

One act. Prelude. Setting: A doorway in the present. Duration: 30 minutes.

Roles: All parts accessible by high school voices. THE STUDENT (ten); VOICE I (sop); VOICE II (alt); VOICE III (bar).

Chorus: SAB. The chorus parts duplicate the ensemble singing of the Three Voices. Additional voices may be added at the discretion of the director.

Orchestration: Organ or piano.

Synopsis: A student stands outside a door going through the motions of knocking. The Three Voices observe and discuss the probable reasons for the Student's persistence. Finally they gather enough courage to ask him. He replies that behind the door he hopes to find the answers to some of his deepest questions about life such as, "Who am I?" and "What's the purpose of life?" The Three Voices relate immediately and ask where he has looked for answers. He's tried everything – parents, friends, the church – and nothing has helped. The Voices tell him that they've been watching him

and thus far he's only been going through the motions of knocking and if he wants answers, then he should really knock and not just pretend. Voice III asks him if he intends to knock? The drama at this point has three options:
1. It may end here without the knock, and a discussion involves the cast and audience might follow.
2. The drama could end here with a blackout and three knocks being sounded in the darkness. The same type of discussion could follow.
3. The drama could go on to include the final number sung by the Voices and choir which asks the Student and/or audience, "Will you knock? Ask yourself. Will you follow Him?"

Materials: TP (1974).

Notes: Sets may be as simple as a free-standing door and three high stools. Different levels are recommended. Ideally suited to church presentation. Detailed stage directions are in the VS. A powerful dramatization for youth performance.

HANS PFITZNER

Palestrina

Music by **Hans Pfitzner** (1869-1949). A Music Legend with religious overtones; libretto in German by Felix Wolfes, based on the Council of Trent activities regarding Giovanni Palestrina.

Composed in 1916; premiered June 12, 1917 in Munich; American premiere May 17, 1982, Berkeley Symphony Orchestra, CA.

Highly chromatic with straying tonalities. Through-composed. Vocal lines disjunct at times. Thick textures.

Three acts. Setting: 1563, the final year of the Council of Trent. Overture. Act I: In Rome; Act II: In Trent (Palestrina's home) eight days later; Act III: In Rome fourteen days later. Duration: full length.

Roles: POPE PIUS IV (bs – low Fl); GIOVANNI MORONE (bar – Gb3), a Cardinal to the Pope; BERNARDO NOVAGERIO (ten – top C4), a Cardinal to the Pope; CARDINAL CHRISTOPH MADRUSCHT (bs), first Bishop of Trent; CARLO BORROMEO (bar – top F#3), Cardinal of Rome; CARDINAL OF LOTHRINGEN (bs); ABDISU (high ten – top Bb3, high tess); ANTON BRUS OF MUGLITZ (bs), first Bishop of Prague; COUNT LUNA (high bar – top Ab3), spokesman for the King of Spain; BISHOP OF BUDOJA (ten – top Bb3), Italian Bishop; THEOPHILUS (ten), Bishop of Imola; AVOSMEDIANO (bs-bar – top F3), Bishop from Cadix; GIOVANNI

PALESTRINA (ten – top Bb3; C4 opt), Kapellmeister from Rome; IGHIO (sop), his son, 15 years old; SILLA (m-sop – top A4), his pupil – a boy 12 years old; BISHOP ERCOLE SEVEROLUS (bs-bar – A1-F#3), Master of Ceremonies for the Council; FIVE KAPPELLSAENGER (bs, bs, ten, ten, low bs), from St. Maria Maggiore in Rome. Nine mute roles. Apparition singers: alt, ten, bar, bs, three sop.

Chorus: SSAATTBB.

Orchestration: 4 fl (picc), 2 ob, Eng hrn, 3 cl, bs cl, 3 bsn, contra bsn, 6 hrn, 4 trp, 4 trb, tba, 2 hp, timp, 3 or more perc, str

Synopsis: Silla and Ighio discuss the recent behavior of their master and father Palestrina. Since the death of his wife, he has not written one note of music. Borromeo and Palestrina enter. Borromeo confides to him that the Pope, before this Council concludes, wants to banish and burn all polyphony and return to Gregorian Chant. As a model of the "new" style, Borromeo asks Palestrina to compose a Mass. Palestrina declines the offer saying his genius is dead. Borromeo storms violently from the room, returning to the Council. Palestrina is visited in a dream by the apparition first, of old music masters so well known to him, and second by his wife, all telling him that he must write yet one more work. When morning breaks and while Palestrina sleeps, Silla and Ighio slip into the room noting music paper on which he has composed an entire Mass, apparently in one night.

Meanwhile, Borromeo arrives at the Council informing them that Palestrina has refused to write the desired Mass. Back in Palestrina's home, the master awakens. People are gathered in his room with an air of expectancy. Ighio informs him that they await the decision of the Pope, for at this very moment his new Mass is being sung before the prelates and Pope. The Pope and his retinue arrive declaring that the new Mass is sublime, likening it to the sound of angels. He blesses Palestrina as Servant and Son of the Pope. After all have left, Palestrina assures Ighio that he will now again be happy.

Materials: AF (© 1916), Ger. Eng translation by Ross Halper available.

Notes: A very large production suitable only for a theatre. Requires highly skilled musicians and production personnel.

GABRIEL PIERNE

The Children's Crusade

Music by **Gabriel Pierne** (1863-1937). A Music Legend in oratorio form with libretto in French (some Latin), based on the thirteenth century Children's Crusade.

First performance January 18, 1905, at the Concerts du Châtelet, Paris, France.

Accompanied recitatives, continuous texture. Harmonically, late nineteenth century Romanticism with considerable chromaticism, but strongly tonal. Some Impressionism in evidence.

Four parts. Setting: during the Crusades around 1212. Part I: The Forth setting – a public square in a Flemish town in 1212, at night; Part II: The Highway – a warm Spring morning on a highway; Part III: The Sea – on the shore of the Mediterranean near Genoa; Part IV: The Saviour in the Storm – on board a ship. Duration: approximately 115 minutes.

Roles: ALLYS (sop – top Bb4), youthful leader among the children; ALYAIN (sop – top Bb4), another leader; A MOTHER (sop); THE NARRATOR (ten – top A3); AN OLD SAILOR (bar); FOUR WOMEN (2 sop, 2 alt); VOICE FROM ON HIGH (bs), offstage.

Chorus: SSSAATTBB – villagers who watch and comment on the action. Since the chorus music is so extensive, a pantomime group could be used to portray the action of the chorus.

SSA – A children's chorus of 200 is suggested. When children are not available, their part may be sung by a special group of adult SSA with at least twenty to a part.

Orchestration: Full orchestra.

Synopsis: Alain and Allys hear a voice calling them to lead all children to Jerusalem to conquer the Holy City. Mothers plead with their children not to go. When they see their pleas are useless, they pray for the children's protection. The children are next seen happily skipping through the woods on their journey. At last they reach the sea, commenting on its vastness and power. There they find ships ready to take them to the Holy Land. The sailors set the ships out to sea. It soon grows dark and a vicious wind churns the waters. The ships begin to sink as the children hold hands, claiming they see their Lord. A voice from above calls them to come to Him. They sing of the joys of heaven and the end of earthly troubles.

Materials: GS.

Notes: An English translation by Henry Grafton Chapman is available. This work is dominated by choral music. Extensive mixed chorus and children's chorus necessitate a large stage area for performance. See additional notes under Lebowsky's *The Children's Crusade* and Menotti's *The Death of the Bishop of Brindisi.*

DANIEL PINKHAM

Daniel in the Lion's Den

Music by **Daniel Pinkham** (b. 1925). A Religious Music Drama with libretto in English taken from the Biblical Book of Daniel 6, the Apocryphal Book of Daniel, *Bel and the Snake*, Psalm 116, and a hymn by John Newton.

Premiered February 11, 1973, by the Pro Arte Chorale of Bergen County and the North Jersey Council.

Vocal line declamatory, speech patterns; occasionally unaccompanied. Twentieth century devices, dissonances, chromaticism, use of electronic tape, multi-media. Continuous texture.

One act. Setting: The Kingdom of Darius, Daniel's house, a lion's den. Duration: 25 minutes.

Roles: NARRATOR (sp); DANIEL (bar); HABAKKAK (bs-bar); ANGEL (ten).

Chorus: SATB – offstage.

Orchestration: 2 pianos, timp, perc (glock, tri, wood block, tamb, soft cym, crash cym, tam tam, sn dr, 3 tom-toms, bs dr), electronic tape.

Synopsis: The libretto follows the Biblical story faithfully. King Darius has made a decree that his kingdom must worship only the King for thirty days. When Daniel, a much loved Minister of the King, is found worshipping the God of Israel, jealous governors and ministers insist that he be punished by death in the den of lions. The King, with much remorse and regret, orders the deed be done. Meanwhile, an Angel appears to the Prophet Habakkak and takes him to Babylon to help deliver Daniel. Daniel is saved through the intervention of God who shuts the mouths of the lions. When the King learns of Daniel's state he is overjoyed and has Daniel taken from the pit. The evil governors and ministers are instead sentenced to death in the lion's pit. The King issues a decree that men shall fear and worship the God of Daniel.

Materials: ECS. Electronic tape available. LC (M2023.3. P56D3).

Notes: Minimal sets required. Best suited for presentation in a house of worship.

ILDEBRANDO PIZZETTI

L'Assassinio nella cattedrale

Music by **Ildebrando Pizzetti** (1880-1968). A Religious Opera with libretto in Italian adapted from the original text of the T. S. Eliot play by Monsignore Alberto Pizzetti.

Premiered March 1, 1958, Milan, Italy.

Melodic, with plainchant influences. Considerable chromaticism; non-traditional harmonic textures and rhythmic complexities. Lyric tragedy.

Two acts with an Intermezzo. Setting: The Canterbury Cathedral in 1170. Duration: 95 minutes.

Roles: ARCHBISHOP THOMAS À BECKET (bs – G1-E3) – requires a strong actor; A HERALD (ten); FOUR TEMPTERS (ten, bar, bar, bs); THREE PRIESTS (ten, bar, bar); TWO WOMEN (2 sop); FOUR KNIGHTS (ten, bar, bar, bs).

Chorus: SSATBB – Priests, Attendants, Women of Canterbury.

Orchestration: 3 fl (picc), 2 ob, Eng hrn, 2 cl, bs cl, 2 bsn, contra bsn, 4 hrn, 3 trp, 3 trb, tba, timp, hp, cel, perc, str

Synopsis: A quarrel over ecclesiastical authority between Archbishop Thomas à Becket and King Henry II has caused Becket to flee to France. He has been in exile for seven years. A group of women have gathered in the Archbishop's Hall to mourn his fate when a Herald arrives to inform them that Becket has returned to England. Becket is determined to defy the King as the conflict between the two has not yet been resolved. Becket arrives at the cathedral, reaffirming his faith in God. The Four Tempters attempt to dissuade him from carrying out his plan. On Christmas Day, Becket preaches a sermon on martyrdom. The service is interrupted by Four Knights sent by King Henry to warn Becket. Becket is unrelenting in his stand and is murdered at the altar by the Knights. Their vicious deed is rationalized by a statement prophesying its historical significance.

Materials: RIC. Eng translation by Geoffrey Dunn available.

Notes: May be performed in a cathedral provided adequate space is available for the large orchestra.

FRANCIS POULENC

Les Dialogues des Carmélites — *The Dialogues of the Carmelites*

Music by **Francis Poulenc** (1899-1963). An Opera with libretto in French by Georges Bernanos (adapted to a lyric opera with authorization of Emmet Lavery), inspired by a novel of Gertrud von le Fort and by a scenario of Rev. Father Bruckberger and Phillipe Agostini.

Premiered January 26, 1957, Milan, Italy.

Tonal with non-traditional harmonic progressions. Considerable speech-like declamation; chromatic but melodic.

Three acts, twelve scenes. Setting: April, 1789 in France. Act I, sc. 1: Library of the Marquis de la Force; sc. 2: Parlor of the Carmelite convent; sc. 3: Storage room of the convent; Infirmary of the convent. Act II, sc. 1: Chapel of the Carmelites; Interlude; sc. 2: Assembly room in the convent; Interlude; sc. 3: Parlor in the convent; sc. 4: Sacristy of the convent. Act III, sc. 1: Chapel; Interlude; sc. 2: Same as I, 1; Interlude; sc. 3: The prison; Interlude; sc. 4: Revolutionary Square. Duration: approximately 125 minutes.

Major Roles: BLANCHE DE LA FORCE (sop – top C5); MADAME LIDOINE (sop – top Bb4), second prioress; PRIORESS (cont – top A4), aged and feeble; MOTHER MARIE (m-sop – top Bb4, high tess); CHEVALIER DE LA FORCE (ten – top Bb3), Blanche's brother; SISTER CONSTANCE (sop – top C5), youthful.

Minor Roles: MOTHER JEANNE (cont), Dean of the Community; MARQUIS DE LA FORCE (bar), Blanche's father; SISTER MATHILDE (m-sop), FATHER CONFESSOR (ten); JAILER (bar); TWO OFFICERS (ten, bar); THIERRY (bar), a valet; M. JAVELINOT (bar), a physician.

Chorus: SSAATTBB – Policemen, Prisoners, Townsfolk, Officials, Guards. SSA – eleven nuns.

Orchestration: 3 fl, 2 ob, Eng hrn, 2 cl, bs cl, 2 bsn, contra bsn, 4 hrn, 3 trp, 3 trb, tba, timp, perc, hp, strings, pia

Synopsis: Serious revolution which threatens the French aristocracy seems imminent. Blanche de la Force, hoping to escape from the realities of life, joins the Carmelite convent. Prioress warns her that the convent cannot be a refuge for her; she must find peace and salvation within herself. The Prioress dies and is replaced by an outsider, Madame Lidoine. Meanwhile, Sister Constance tells Blanche of a premonition that they will die together. Messages from home urge Blanche to return to her father, but she remains steadfast in her commitment to the convent. The revolutionary leaders order all religious groups dissolved, threatening the continuation of the convent. Mother Marie confers with the nuns, deriving from them what appears to be a unanimous vow of martyrdom if necessary. The Carmelites are forced to depart from the convent. Blanche returns to her father's home to serve her family, rejecting Mother Marie's plea to remain with the sisters. The nuns are arrested and go to their execution singing. As the last sister, Sister Constance, is executed, Blanche appears. She mounts the scaffold to join her sisters in death.

Materials: RIC (Fr, Eng – translation by Machlis in BH). Eng translation by Jeanne Shaffer also available.

Notes: Numerous scene changes require theatre facilities for production.

RICHARD PROULX

The Pilgrim

Music by **Richard Proulx** (b. 1937). A Liturgical Music Drama in the manner of a medieval matins drama for Eastertide. Libretto is an adaptation by the composer of two twelfth century Sepulchre plays from Orleans, Fleury, and St. Quentin with additional texts from the *Sarum Antiphonary*, the *Liber Usualis* and two short poems of Christina Rossetti. The final hymn is a composite text from three early office hymns, generally a paraphrase of the *Victimae Paschali Laudes*.

Commissioned by the Friends of Music for the 1978 National Convention of the American Guild of Organists. Premiered June 29, 1978, St. Joseph Church, Seattle, WA.

Considerable plainchant with expressive lyrical melodies interwoven. In non-chant sections, dissonances and chromaticism pervade.

Six scenes, a Prologue, two Interludes, an Epilogue. Prologue: spoken Proclamation and Procession; sc. 1: Lament; sc. 2: Visit to the Spice Merchant; Interlude: Dawn; sc. 3: The Angel Appears; sc. 4: The Christus and Mary Magdalene; Interlude: The Search; sc. 5: Peter and John meet Mary Salome; sc. 6: The Sepulchre; Epilogue: Procession. Duration: 50 minutes.

Roles: HERALD (sp); MARY MAGDALENE (sop); MARY JACOBI (cont); MARY SALOME (m-sop); SPICE MERCHANT (bar – top F3), can be doubled with Peter; PETER (bar), the older Apostle; ANGEL (ten), can be doubled with John; JOHN (ten – some florid passages), the younger Apostle; THE CHRISTUS (bar).

Chorus: SSATTBB – Monastic choir, chanting and commenting on the action.

Orchestration: fl, ob, hrn, perc, timp, strings (3.3.2.2.1), Zimbelsterne (carried in procession), positiv org, Flemish handbells

Synopsis: Prologue: A proclamation is read by a Herald, greeting the audience. A festive procession follows, singing praises to the Lamb that was slain.

Scene I: The three Marys mourn and discuss the crucifixion. Their best efforts are providing spices and ointments for their blessed friend.

Scene II: The Marys exit; the music becomes more festive and dance-like as the Spice Merchant sets up shop. He gives his sales pitch, excitedly explaining his various spices and their range of prices. The Merchant is moved by the Marys compassion for their Lord and finally offers the best he has – free. The women depart.

Interlude: A Plainsong/Alleluia by the choir while the sepulchre is set in place.

Scene III: At the tomb the Angel greets the women and proclaims the resurrection of their Lord. Mary Salome runs to find Peter and John. The choir sings a madrigal explaining the meaning of Easter. Mary Magdalene and Mary Jacobi linger in the garden, wondering where their Lord might be. The Angel reappears, consoling them.

Scene IV: The Gardener (Christus) appears with concealed features and addresses Mary Magdalene, questioning why she weeps. Someone has taken her Lord, she says. The Christus reveals His identity and then departs. Mary turns to the audience and asks all to rejoice with her.

Interlude, Scenes V & VI: Mary Salome, Peter and John appear at different parts of the building. They run to each other. Peter goes into the tomb, reappearing with a shroud. He hands the linens to Magdalene who quietly places them on the High Altar, returning in place to form a tableau at the tomb.

Epilogue: All acclaim their risen Lord. A final hymn is sung, followed by a processional out of the sanctuary.

Materials: GIA.

Notes: Intended for presentation in a cathedral/church.

L. NATALIA RAIGORODSKY

The Promise of Peace

Music by **L. Natalia Raigorodsky** (b. ca. 1938 – USA). A Dramatic Oratorio with libretto in English by the composer, based on various New Testament passages.

Premiered in 1982 by the Opera Theatre of Washington (D.C.).

Traditional harmonic structure. Primarily a dramatic choral work.

Five scenes. Duration: 30 minutes.

Roles: Three soloists who narrate the action.

Chorus: SATB.

Dance: While the work does not call for dancers specifically, the premiere used eleven dancers to depict the action.

Orchestration: fl, ob, cl, hrn, trp, 2 trb, timp, strings. Reduced orchestration for fl and org.

Synopsis: This work dramatically portrays five incidents in which Christ miraculously healed the sick.

Materials: Unpublished. From the composer. The composer has slides which accompany the work.

Notes: Suitable to either a cathedral/church or theatre stage. Does not work well as a concert piece.

LICINIO REFICE

Cecilia

Music by **Licinio Refice** (1885-1954). A Legend Opera with libretto in Italian by Emidio Mucci.

Premiered February, 1934, Teatro Reale del'Opera, Rome, Italy.

Post-Romantic in the style of Puccini. Melodic, with lush harmonic textures. Arias, accompanied recitatives, through-composed.

Three acts. Setting: Rome.

Roles: Requires mature well-trained singers. CECILIA (sop); VALERIANO (ten), husband of Cecilia; TIBURZIO (bar), brother-in-law of Cecilia; LA VECCHIA CIECA (m-sop); IL VESCOVO URBANO (bs); AMACHIO (bar), governor of Roma; UN LIBERTO (ten); UNO SCHIAVO (bs); L'ANGELO DI DIO (in Act I, a small sop chorus; in Act II, a sop).

Chorus: SSSAAATTTBB – requires large ensemble.

Orchestration: 3 fl, 3 ob, 2 cl, 3 bsn, 4 hrn, 3 trp, 3 trb, tba, timp, perc, cel, 2 hp, str

Materials: RIC (It).

Notes: Requires professional singers, orchestra, and large theatre production capabilities. Suitable for performance only in a theatre.

OTTORINO RESPIGHI

Lauda per la Natività del Signore – *Laud to the Nativity*

Music by **Ottorino Respighi** (1879-1936). A Sacred Music Drama with text in Italian attributed to Jacopone da Todi with an English version by Harold Heiberg, based on the Biblical nativity story according to Luke.

Composed in 1930.

Conventional harmonies with frequent hints of sixteenth century Italian madrigal and Monteverdian styles. Melodic; full choral textures with several a cappella passages.

One act. Sc. 1: On a hillside outside Bethlehem; sc. 2: At the manger. Duration: 25 minutes.

Roles: ANGEL (col sop – top C5 sustained pianissimo), some melisma; VIRGIN MARY (m-sop); THE SHEPHERD (ten); JOSEPH (silent).

Chorus: SSAATTBB – Angels, Shepherds. The chorus should not be visible to the audience; their parts should be performed by dancers and mimes.

Dance: Dancers and mimes enact the parts of the Angels and Shepherds.

Orchestration: 2 fl (picc), ob, Eng hrn, 2 bsn, tri, pia – 4 hands

Synopsis: A brief orchestral prelude introduces the Angel who announces to the shepherds that the Saviour has been born in Bethlehem. A chorus of angels now joins in the story-telling and the shepherds respond with joy hastening to the City of David. At the manger, the shepherds comment that the crudeness of the manger is no place for the Saviour of the world. Mary sings a lullaby which is echoed by the angels and shepherds, at first soft and hushed, then building into a climactic ensemble of "Glory, praise and honor to Thee, Father Almighty." An *a cappella* section on the text "Peace on earth, good will toward all men of good will," brings the work to a calm and worshipful conclusion as all kneel before the Christ Child.

Materials: RIC, No. N.Y. 1944 (It, Eng) (c. 1958).

Notes: Best performed in a church/cathedral. The simple yet colorful orchestration and vocal elements make this an easily accessible and rewarding work.

Maria Egiziaca

Music by **Ottorino Respighi** (1879-1936). A Mystery Play, also described by the composer as a "concert triptych," with libretto in Italian by Claudio Guastalla.

Premiered in semi-staged form in Carnegie Hall, New York, March 16, 1932; fully-staged premiere in Venice, August 10, 1932.

Highly stylized concept. Conventional harmonies with recitatives, arias and ensembles. Vocal lines simple and often chanted with suggestions of monody and Monteverdian textures, reminiscent of early *sacra rappresentazione*. Two orchestral interludes.

Three episodes. 1: The harbour of Alexandria; 2: The Church of the Holy Sepulchre in Jerusalem; 3: The cave of the hermit Zosimus. Duration: ca. 70 minutes.

Roles: MARIA (sop); PELLEGRINO (bar), the Pilgrim; ABBOT ZOSIMO (bar); IL MARINAIO (ten); UN COMPAGNO and THE LEPER (ten); UN'ALTRA VOCE and UN ALTRO COMPAGNO (bar); THE BEGGAR and THE BLIND WOMAN (m-sop); L'ANGELO (sop); UNA VOCE DI MARINAIO (sop); ALTRA VOCE DI MARINAIO (m-sop).

Chorus: SATB. The chorus should be stationary responding as a Greek chorus.

Orchestration: Full orchestra.

Synopsis: Mary leads her life as a courtesan in the city of Alexandria. One day she overhears a sailor sing of the joys of sailing the seas and asks whether she may accompany him on his voyage. A Pilgrim traveling to the holy land approaches the ship. He invites her to come along if she can pay her own fare. Maria explains that she is a tramp and that her body will pay for the trip. Delighted with the prospect of merry making, the sailors welcome her on board, while the Pilgrim warns of God's displeasure with her behavior. Restless and searching, she goes to Jerusalem where in front of the church of the Holy Sepulchre, she is refused entrance by an angel. However, the door opens to a believing leper, beggar and a blind woman of simple faith. Overcome with guilt, she falls on her knees at the Temple's door, begging forgiveness and asking for salvation. An angel's voice is heard, supported by voices from within the Temple, assuring her of eternal rest.

In scene three, we see Mary in the cave of Zosimus receiving her last communion after spending forty years in repentance in the desert. In a quiet and moving finale, she is received into heaven.

Materials: RIC (c. 1931) (It, Eng). Recorded on Bongiovanni GB 2008/9 and Hungaroton/Conifer HCD31118 (text, notes and Eng translation included).

Notes: Intended by the composer to be performed before a single set consisting of three painted wings prescribed in the score. Suitable for either church or theatre performance.

HERMANN REUTTER

Saul

Music by **Hermann Reutter** (1900-1985). A Lyric Drama, Op. 33, with libretto in German after the drama of A. Lernet-Holenia, loosely based on I Samuel 28 of the Old Testament.

Premiered in Baden-Baden, 1928.

Avant garde and contemporary characteristics dominate. Highly chromatic, mixed meters, straying tonalities. Through-composed, spoken dialogue.

One act, four scenes. Setting: sc. 1: A modern family around the dinner table; Scenes 2-4: Hut of the Witch of Endor. Duration: approximately 45 minutes.

Singing Roles: SAUL (dram bar – many G3, high tess); THE WITCH OF ENDOR (sop).

Speaking Roles: MARSHALL, to the Right of Saul; MARSHALL, to the Left of Saul; SAMUEL; PEASANT; BOY.

Chorus: Only spoken (family members).

Orchestration: 2 fl (picc), 2 ob (Eng hrn), 2 cl (bs cl), 2 bsn (cont bsn), 4 hrn, 2 trp, timp, perc, pia, str

Synopsis: A family gathered around the dinner table, prays the Lord's prayer. They are interrupted by a Witch who changes the scenario to suit her own tastes. The family leaves. King Saul, in disguise, and his two Marshalls enter to consult with the Witch. Saul asks the medium to call up the Prophet Samuel from the dead that he may inquire concerning his own future. Samuel appears and informs Saul that his kingdom will be taken over by David. Most shocking is the prophecy that tomorrow he and his sons will all die. The Witch now recognizes Saul as the King of Israel. Saul, faint, is brought food to regain his strength. As he eats and stares into space, the curtain falls.

Materials: SCH.

Notes: A musically difficult but effective work. Suitable for presentation in either a house of worship or theater.

E. N. von REZNICEK

Holofernes

Music by **E. N. von Reznicek** (1860-1945). A Sacred Opera with libretto in German by Hebbel, freely based on the Apocryphal Book of Judith.

Premiered in Berlin, 1922.

Late romantic style, chromatic, highly melodic.

Two acts. Setting: Act I: In the town of Bethulia. Act II, sc. 1: In Holofernes' camp; sc. 2: As in Act I. Duration: 110 minutes.

Roles: HOLOFERNES (bs-bar – top F3), vocally and dramatically demanding; JUDITH (sop – top B4), requires excellent acting; OSIAS (bs), High Priest of Bethulia; ABRA (alt), Judith's maid; ACHIOR (ten), servant to Holofernes; THREE SERVANTS (ten, bs, bs); ASSAD (bs); DANIEL (ten), blind; GESANDTER VON MESOPOTAMIEN (bs); EIN TRABANT (bs); A WOMAN'S VOICE (sop).

Chorus: SSATBB – Priests and people of Bethulia, Assyrian soldiers, Priests of Baal, Servants of Holofernes.

Dance: Ballet number.

Orchestration: 4 fl, 3 ob, 2 cl, 3 bsn, 4 hrn, 2 trp, 3 trb, tba, timp, perc, str

Synopsis: Nebuchadnezzar, King of Babylonia, has sent his chief General, Holofernes, to demand obeisance from the surrounding nations, including the Hebrews from Bethulia. There he meets with resistance and a people dedicated to their own God. Holofernes wages a war of wits rather than arms by cutting off their water supply. Soon they are desperate. Their cries of surrender bring Judith, a widow of great beauty, out of seclusion where she has been since the death of her husband. Inspired, she asks for five days and the prayers of the people. Judith exchanges her mourning clothes for seductive gowns, oils and perfumes her body, and together with her maid, sets out for the enemy camp. Holofernes grants her an interview, apparently accepting her story that she has been sent by God to lead him to victory over the Hebrews without bloodshed. He is intrigued not only by her proposition but also by her bewitching beauty. Unexpectedly, Judith likewise is taken by his strength and virility.

Holofernes invites Judith to dine with him, courting her with gentleness and the best Assyria has to offer in entertainment. They go to bed together. Finally regaining her composure and sense of purpose, and while Holofernes sleeps, she kills him with her knife. Quickly she and her maid gather their belongings and leave for home. Back in Bethulia, Judith unveils the head of their enemy Holofernes. There is great rejoicing and a return of self-worth so long absent from the enslaved Hebrew nation.

Materials: UE (Ger) (© 1923).

Notes: Should be performed in a theatre.

PHIL RIZZO

Christ, the Man from Galilee

Music by **Phil Rizzo** (b. 1925). A Sacred Music Theatre work with libretto in English by the composer, based on events in the life of Christ taken from the four Gospels.

Commissioned by the National Endowment for the Arts, 1979.

Mixed musical styles; six jazz sequences separate scenes; singers accompanied by studio orchestra. Classical style singing required.

Four acts, six scenes. Setting: Judea in the time of Christ. Act I: Outdoors by the sea. Act II: In an open area. Act III, sc. 1: The Last Supper; sc. 2: The Garden of Gethsemane; sc, 3: Jesus before Pilate. Act IV, sc. 1: The path to Golgotha; sc. 2: At the foot of the cross. Duration: 2 hours, 10 minutes.

Roles: NARRATOR (sp); BLIND BOY (ten); PONTIUS PILATE (bs-bar); JUDAS ISCARIOT (bar); PETER (bar); JESUS (sp); MARY (sop), mother of Jesus; CAIPHAS (bar).

Chorus: SATB – Disciples, Scribes, Pharisees, Soldiers, Fishermen, Crowd. Small parts taken from the chorus as well as a group of eight voices.

Orchestration: 5 sax (1 fl, 2 cl, bs cl), hrn, 4 trp, 4 trb, perc, hp, cb, pia, gui.

Synopsis: A village fisherman, unable to attend the "Sermon on the Mount," asks a group of six villagers about the sermon. The group replies by quoting Christ's Beatitudes. The scene shifts to the blind boy who now can see because of a miracle performed by Christ. In Act II, the Narrator describes the actions and beliefs of the Pharisees who, in reality, were just religious hypocrites. Jesus approaches and condemns their actions. They plot to destroy Him. Judas confronts the authorities and agrees to deliver Jesus into their hands.

Act III begins with the Last Supper where Jesus tells his disciples that one of them will betray Him and that all of them will be scattered after He leaves. In the Garden of Gethsemane, Jesus spends His final hours with his disciples and in prayer to His Father. Soldiers, led by Judas, arrest Him and lead Him away. As foretold by Jesus, Peter denies ever having known Jesus when questioned by a young lady. Pilate interrogates Jesus and finally turns Him over to the people for crucifixion. In Act IV, Jesus is led down the path to Golgotha, carrying His own cross. Mary weeps as He is crucified. An instrumental "Storm Sequence" describes His death and leads directly into a final ensemble declaring His resurrection.

Materials: AMC and the composer.

Notes: Best suited for performance in a theatre but possible in a large chancel area.

RICHARD RODGERS

Two by Two

Music by **Richard Rodgers** (1902-1979). A Musical Theatre work with libretto in English by Martin Charnin, loosely based on Genesis 6-9 of the Old Testament.

Premiered November 10, 1970, Imperial Theatre, New York.

Spoken dialogue, traditional musical comedy style; 'pop' textures, much rhythmic speech. Comic.

Two acts. Setting: Before, during and after the flood. Act I: In and around Noah's home; Act II: An ark and atop Mt. Ararat (forty days and forty nights later). Duration: 2 hours.

Roles: NOAH (ten – Ab1-Ab3); ESTHER (alt), his wife; JAPHETH (ten), youngest son; SHEM (bs), oldest son; HAM (ten); RACHEL (sop), wife of Ham; LEAH (m-sop), wife of Shem; GOLDIE (sop – top C5), girlfriend of Japheth.

Chorus: None. Many supers – people and animals in pairs.

Orchestration: Woodwind No. 1: Fl/picc/cl/alt fl; Woodwind No. 2: fl/picc/cl/bs cl; Woodwind No. 3: ob/Eng hrn/cl; Woodwind No. 4: cl/Eb cl/fl; Woodwind No. 5: bsn/bs cl/bar sax/cl; 2 hrn, 2 trp (flugelhorn), 2 trb, 2 perc, org/cel, strings.

Synopsis: It is Noah's 600th birthday, and rather unexpectedly, God drops in to give him the assignment of building an ark. He works on God with every excuse imaginable, but to no avail. Noah calls his family and begins to explain. His eldest son, Shem, with his wife Leah leave their olive pickers unattended. Ham, his second son, leaves his gambling and sends for his estranged wife, Rachel. Japheth lives at home with nothing but his ideals and an oversized chip on his shoulder. After hearing Noah's story, his family has but one solution: "Put Him Away." However, conviction sets in when the family sees pairs of animals begin to assemble in the field. With the ark half finished, Japheth rebels and runs off; furthermore, he hasn't found a wife as yet. God then makes a small miracle happen: Noah is suddenly 510 years younger and filled with renewed energy, able to finish the ark alone. Japheth returns home followed by Goldie, a Golden Girl from the temple of the Golden Ram. A confusion of love affairs between the various children and their mates occurs, but everyone gets on board as the rain begins to fall.

Forty days and nights later, nothing has improved. Divorces and remarriages are in the making among the children. Noah, trying to forget the worsening situation goes on a drunk. When he awakens, he is again 600 hundred years old and none of the problems have been solved. However, the sun is out and the land is beginning to dry. Just then, Esther dies. The couples, slightly rearranged, leave the ark, each heading in a different direction and each expecting a child. Noah pesters God for a sign promising that He will never again destroy the world. Noah calls the terms and God agrees: He doesn't destroy the earth and we don't forget His name. A rainbow appears.

Materials: RHL.

Notes: Best suited for theatre performance.

GEORGE F. ROOT

Belshazzar's Feast or the Fall of Babylon

Music by **George F. Root** (1820-1895). A Dramatic Cantata with text in English by Gen. B. F. Edmonds taken from the Old Testament, primarily Daniel and Isaiah. All text sources are given in the VS.

Conventional harmonies; choral section mostly homophonic. Recitatives, some chanting, arias, ensembles. Use of King's English. Musically not difficult.

Ten scenes connected with narrative. Sc. 1: The Palace Hall; sc. 2: The queen's apartment; sc. 3: Jewish place of assembly; sc. 4: The walls of Babylon; sc. 5: The feast; sc. 6: Jewish quarter; sc. 7: Jewish place of worship; sc. 8: The interpretation; sc. 9: The camp of Cyrus; sc. 10: Within the city. Duration: approximately 45 minutes.

Roles: A READER (sp); BELSHAZZAR (bs), King of Babylon; NITOCRIS (sop), Queen; DANIEL (ten); JEWISH MAIDEN (alt); HANANIAH (bar); A LORD (ten); A LADY (alt); HIGH PRIEST (bs). Other small solo parts from the chorus.

Chorus: SATB – Jews, Chaldeans, and Soldiers.

Orchestration: Orchestra or keyboard.

Synopsis: The scenes quickly shift between the celebration in the King's banquet room, Daniel's place of worship, and the Queen's quarters. King Belshazzar is being praised at a large feast. Suddenly, words appear on the wall, the meaning of which is indecipherable. Daniel is called and indeed, with the help of Jehovah, he reads the meaning of the words to the King. The King is so grateful, he places Daniel second in command of his kingdom. There is great rejoicing and praises sung to the Lord God Almighty as the work concludes.

Materials: OD (© 1860)

Notes: Creative staging can make this work visually appealing. May be performed in a cathedral/church, but better on a stage with good technical facilities.

ANTON RUBINSTEIN

Der Thurm zu Babel – The Tower of Babel

Music by **Anton Rubinstein** (1829-1894). A Sacred Opera with libretto in German by Julius Rosenberg based on the Biblical account in Genesis 11.

Composed in 1869; premiered in 1870, Koenigsberg.

Traditional Romantic textures; considerable chromaticism. Melodic with accompanied recitatives. Solos all mid-range. Many choral ensembles; some folk elements.

One act. Setting: Before the tower of Babel. Duration: 45 minutes.

Roles: NIMROD (bs), King; ABRAHAM (ten – top B3), a shepherd; MASTER WORKMAN (bar); FOUR ANGELS (ssaa – children's voices).

Chorus: Three choruses of SATB – Semites, Hamits, Japhitides. Also Nimrod's followers, a crowd, angels, demons.

Orchestration: Full orchestra.

Synopsis: Before dawn the relentless Master Workman awakens the workers to continue building on the tower. It must reach the heavens before rest will be granted. Nimrod appears, pleased with his project and musing on how he shall undaunted soon stand in the presence of God. Abraham, overhearing his boasting, admonishes Nimrod and warns him to give up the tower, for what he is doing is sin. Incensed, Nimrod orders Abraham arrested and thrown into the fiery furnace, for no man insults Nimrod. Nimrod tells his workers to forget God and keep working. As they toil, they sing praises to Baal: "Worship him or else die," they cry. Angels suddenly descend to earth and full orchestral forces with highly dissonant textures and running passages describe the destruction of the tower and confusion of the people as each begins speaking in a strange tongue. The crowd gradually organizes itself into three distinct groups, departing for new homes in opposite directions. Nimrod repents his evil as the angels and people sing praise to the triumph of Jehovah, and the demons revere Satan, all claiming victory.

Materials: Originally published by S. Brainard's Sons (© 1879), Cleveland and Chicago (Eng – translation by Mrs. M. L. Nichols).

Notes: Suitable for either church or theatre performance. The destruction of the tower will require creative design and direction. A musically and dramatically powerful work.

CAMILLE SAINT-SAËNS

Samson et Dalila – Samson and Delilah

Music by **Camille Saint-Saëns** (1835-1921). A Religious Opera with libretto in French by Ferdinand Lemaire, based on the Biblical account in Judges 14-16.

Premiered in German December 2, 1877, in Weimar; in France in 1890.

Highly romantic in texture, chromatic, thickly scored; vocally melodic and demanding. Arias, recitatives, with some set pieces.

Three acts, four scenes. Setting: Palestine (Gaza), about 1150 B.C. Prelude. Act I: Public square in Gaza; Act II: Dalila's home in the valley of Sorek; Act III, sc. 1: Prison dungeon in Gaza; sc. 2: The temple of Gaza. Duration: 2 hours.

Major Roles: SAMSON (dram ten – E2-Bb3, high tess), requires considerable vocal strength, difficult acting; DALILA (m-sop – Ab2, F2 opt, to A4, B4 opt), requires strong actress and singer; HIGH PRIEST TO DAGON (bar – C2-F#3), high tess, demanding dramatically.

Minor Roles: ABIMELECH (bs), commissioner of Gaza; FIRST PHILISTINE (ten); SECOND PHILISTINE (bs); PHILISTINE MESSENGER (ten); OLD HEBREW (bs); A BOY (mute).

Chorus: SSAATTBB – Hebrews, Philistines, Priestesses, Priests.

Dance: Stylized dancing during the celebrations: Act I Dance of the Priestesses; Bacchanale in Act III.

Orchestration: 3 fl (picc), 2 ob, Eng hrn, 2 cl, bs cl, 2 bsn, contra bsn, 4 hrn, 2 trp, 2 corn, 3 trb, tba, 2 ophicleide (opt hrn or bsn), 4-5 perc, timp, 2 hp, strings.

Synopsis: In the public square in Gaza, Hebrews gather near the heathen temple of Dagon and pray to God for relief from their bondage to the Philistines. Samson rebukes them for their lack of faith in God and reiterates his own trust in God. Abimelech denounces the Hebrews and their God, whereupon Samson challenges him and exhorts his people to do battle against the Philistines. Abimelech attacks and Samson kills him with his own sword. The High Priest, seeing the power of Samson, leaves with those bearing Abimelech's body. Meanwhile, Dalila and her attendants celebrate the coming of spring. She remembers her earlier desire for Samson and invites him to come again to her dwelling. The High Priest informs her of Samson's victory and his unusual strength. She promises to defeat him that very night. In the gathering storm, Samson appears. She feigns disbelief at his constancy and demands that he show his love by telling her the secret of his strength. When he refuses, she threatens to deny herself to him and weeps.

He gives in to her, Dalila cries out and the guards rush in to capture and blind Samson, now shorn by Dalila of the long hair that held the secret of his strength.

In a dungeon, the sightless Samson pushes a grist mill, praying to God to take pity on his people, who should not have to suffer for his sins. Through the sounds of his suffering, one hears in the distance, the Jews castigating Samson for his weakness. In the Temple of Dagon, a celebration is in progress. Samson, led in by a child, endures taunts from Dalila and the Philistines. They humiliate Samson by forcing him to kneel down before Dagon. Samson whispers to the child to lead him to the two main pillars and then run away. He prays desperately for strength and with a mighty effort pulls down the pillars, crushing himself and the foes.

Materials: GS (Procter-Gregg English translation). FS, parts from HAL, MAP. Eng translations by Walter Ducloux and John McCrae also available.

Notes: This work requires full professional technical staff, musicians, and highly trained singers. Elaborate sets required; must be performed in a large theater.

KAREL SALOMON

David and Goliath

Music by **Karel Salomon** (1897-1947). A Miniature Opera with libretto in German by Albert Baer based on the Biblical Book of I Samuel 17.

Composed 1957.

Chromatic with occasional straying tonalities. Melodic and accessible for average singers. Light-hearted drama.

One act, three scenes. Scene 1: Bethlehem in front of Jesse's house; sc. 2: On a hill, near the camp; sc. 3: The field of battle. Duration: 36 minutes.

Roles: JESSE (bar), a sheepherder; ELIAB (bs – top F3), his firstborn; DAVID (boy sop or m-sop); GOLIATH (bs-bar – top F#3 – several florid passages), Philistine champion.

Chorus: Mixed unison (opt) – Israelites.

Orchestration: Ob, str

Synopsis: Jesse is worried over David's tardiness in returning from the fields. Greatly relieved when David finally does return, Jesse sends him with food and supplies to his older brothers who are camped with the Israelite army, preparing for war against the Philistines. David dreams and fantasizes of being in the midst of the battle as a mighty soldier. He arrives at the camp and hears the frightening sounds of Goliath as he hurls challenges and demeaning insults at the Israelites across the valley. David, intrigued by this giant and driven by the Spirit of God cannot resist Goliath's offer to do battle. He marches off to meet the giant, armed only with a sling and the "power of the Lord." The giant mocks "this funny little fellow," but before he is able to draw his sword, David has taken aim with his sling, striking Goliath in the forehead with a stone and killing him. The Israelite army rushes to join David in a victory celebration.

Materials: IMP (Ger, Heb, Eng). English translation by the composer; Hebrew version by Ephraim Dror.

Notes: Originally designed as an opera for marionettes, but can be performed as an ordinary opera. Suitable for presentation in a theatre or house of worship.

ERIC SALZMAN and MICHAEL SAHL

Noah

Music by **Eric Salzman** (b. 1933) and **Michael Sahl** (20th century American). A Music Theatre work loosely based on the Biblical account of Noah.

First performances: Pratt Institute, Brooklyn, NY and Washington Square Methodist Church, New York City, 1978; radio version, WBAI, New York City, 1978/79.

Two acts, three scenes. Setting: sc. 1: Atlantis City; sc. 2: On board the ark; sc. 3: The New Atlantis. Duration: 105 minutes.

Roles: PREACHER/GODTHEFATHER (bs-bar); NOAH (bar); MRS. NOAH (m-sop); LOVE GODDESS (sop); SHEM (ten), Noah's oldest son.

Minor Roles: May be played by students. MALE and FEMALE NARRATORS; 5 other members of Noah's family.

Chorus: Ten to twelve children for the ensemble – Inhabitants of Atlantis City, Animals, Inhabitants of the New Atlantis.

Dance: One or two featured dancers are desirable; a larger dance ensemble may be used.

Orchestration: A band of five, or a chamber orchestra.

Synopsis: The corruption of the Atlanteans – set forth in a series of pageant scenes – angers Godthefather who resolves to drown the city. Noah lives on the edge of town with his family and espouses a different ethic of traditional values and self-help. On one of his forays into town, he meets a local stripper known as the Love Goddess and discovers the coming fate of the city. While the Atlanteans jeer, he and his family build the ark. When the rains come, the Atlanteans are unable to cooperate to help themselves and each other. Noah must close the doors of the ark; even the Love Goddess drowns with the rest.

Noah, his family and the animals are safe but there is no land in sight. Godthefather appears to Noah on the deck of the ark and makes him dance his tango. Noah can escape His wrath and find a landfall but only if he signs the covenant. At first he refuses but then gives in. The New Atlantis, a kind of earthly paradise, is however not empty of inhabitants. Noah and his family take control and prosper. Noah celebrates his 600th birthday, but not all is well. The natives, supported by Shem, have rebelled. There is a confrontation between father and son; Shem accuses Noah of having betrayed his youthful ideals. Noah is stricken and gathered to his ancestors as the chorus sings of the ancient and modern themes of conflict, domination, power and rebellion.

Materials: Unpublished. Script, VS, audition tape from Mr. Salzman.

Notes: *Noah* was written and produced as a collaboration between a professional company and a school. Students played the seven smaller roles and formed the ensemble. The production took on the form of a medieval pageant play. The set consisted of a moveable "altar" which was transformed into the various locations of the story. Suitable for school, church or large theatre performance, in either a pageant or theatrical style. A free and unconventional interpretation of the Biblical account.

GREGORY SANDOW

A Christmas Carol

Music by **Gregory Sandow** (b. 1943). A Christmas Opera with libretto in English by the composer after the novel by Charles Dickens. Plot faithful to the original text with a few additions by the composer and poems by Christina Rossetti and Charles Mackay.

Commissioned by the Eastern Opera Theatre of New York; premiered by them in December 21, 1977, at the American Shakespeare Theatre in Stratford, CT.

Lyric drama with much comedy; tonal, melodic, traditional nineteenth century harmonic structures; considerable spoken dialogue. Musical style intended to fit the "old-fashioned" nature of the drama.

One act with numerous scenes. Designed to be performed with three playing areas. Setting: Scrooge's counting house with excursions in fantasy to other places; London around 1830. Duration: 75 minutes.

Roles: Designed to be performed by eleven people: an actor, seven adult singers (sop, 2 m-sop, 2 ten, bar, and bs), and three children (2 boys and a girl). The VS indicates the division of roles. The characters they play, in order of vocal appearance, are as follows:
EBENEZER SCROOGE (sp), requires strong actor; THREE CAROLERS (three children); SCROOGE'S NEPHEW (ten); TWO GENTLEMEN (bar, bs); BOB CRATCHIT (ten), Scrooge's clerk; MARLEY'S GHOST (bs); THE GHOST OF CHRISTMAS PAST (m-sop); SCROOGE'S FORMER SCHOOLMATES (actors); FEZZIWIG (bs); THREE OF HIS APPRENTICES (bar, 2 ten); MRS. FIZZIWIG (m-sop); SCROOGES FIANCÉE (sop), in her youth; HER HUSBAND (sp), from a later time; HER TWO CHILDREN (mute); THE GHOST OF CHRISTMAS PRESENT (bar); MRS. CRATCHIT (m-sop). Cratchit children: MARTHA (sop), PETER (boy sop), BELINDA (girl sop), TINY TIM (boy sop). SCROOGE'S NEPHEW'S WIFE (m-sop); HER SISTER (sop); TOPPER (bs); ANOTHER GUEST (ten); TWO POOR CHILDREN (mute), representing Ignorance and Want; THE GHOST OF CHRISTMAS YET TO COME (mute); THREE BUSINESSMEN (bar, 2 ten); THREE WOMEN (2 m-sop, sop); A BOY (sp).

Chorus: Taken from the characters, but may be supplemented by adult and children singers as desired.

Dance: Folk dancing.

Orchestration: fl, ob, cl, hrn, bsn, chimes, timp, 2 vln, vla, 2 vc, cb.

Synopsis: On a cold Christmas Eve, Scrooge is busy at work. Fred, his nephew, and Bob Cratchit, his employee, wish him a merry Christmas. Scrooge derides the whole idea of Christmas as a humbug and rudely refuses Fred's invitation to dinner the next day. He then grudgingly allows Bob the next day off to celebrate Christmas. Later that night, Scrooge is confronted by the ghost of his deceased partner, Jacob Harley. Harley laments his perpetual state of sorrow because of his selfish and narrow way of life. He warns Scrooge that the Spirits of Christmas Past, Present and Future will each visit him this very night. Scrooge dismisses the message as a bad dream and goes to bed. The three Spirits indeed visit him, each presenting him with events and people he has and will encounter in his life past, present and future. Scrooge's dream is brought to a climax with the Spirit of the Future. In his dream, Tiny Tim dies. A funeral procession takes him to a deserted graveyard where inscribed on a tombstone are the words: "Ebenezer Scrooge, miser; who lived unloved and alone." He insists that the future is not predestined and he will change it. He swears he will honor the Spirit of Christmas throughout the year and that he will change his way of living.

Scrooge awakens with a feeling of lightness and joy realizing that he still has a chance to change and enjoy his last few years. He quickly runs to join his nephew's Christmas celebration, bringing joy and goodwill to everyone he meets.

Materials: TP.

Notes: Set design and production suggestions are in the VS. Best performed in a theatre. A work which is easily accessible. "Mr. Sandow has concocted a consistently attractive score; its full measure of tunefulness extends to the inclusion of several real live Christmas carols and its many outbursts of folklike rhythmic buoyance reminded me of another work that has turned into a Yuletide staple, Menotti's *Amahl and the Night Visitors*. All in all, a happy holiday show and, judging from the rapt attention paid to it by the many children in the audience, one for all ages." –*New York Times*.

SIMON A. SARGON

Saul, King of Israel

Music by **Simon A. Sargon** (b. 1938). A Sacred Opera with libretto in English by the composer, freely adapted from the Books of I, II Samuel.

Commissioned by the Meadows Foundation. Completed in 1990. Southern Methodist University Opera Workshop gave the work a reading on May 3, 1990.

Some accompanied recitatives, arias, ensembles; through-composed; strong twentieth century influences within tonal textures. Melodically and vocally conceived.

Three acts. Setting: Palestine around 1100 B.C., during the twenty years reign of Saul, King of Israel. Prologue: A plain on the outskirts of the city of Ramah; Act I, sc. 1: The same, later; sc. 2: The same, later; sc. 3: A field near Saul's home in Gibeah; sc. 4: Samuel's home in Ramah twelve years later; sc. 5: Saul's royal tent in Carmel several months later. Act II, sc. 1: The hills near Bethlehem; sc. 2: The valley of Elah; sc. 3: The Hebrew camp near Elah; sc. 4: Interior of Saul's tent; sc. 5: A cave in the Judean hills; sc. 6: The Temple at Nob. Act III, sc. 1: Saul's camp near Mt. Gilboa eight years after the end of Act II; sc. 2: A cave near Endor; sc. 3: Saul alone; sc. 4: On the slopes of Mt. Gilead; sc. 5/Epilogue: David's camp in the wilderness. Duration: approximately 2 hours, 10 minutes.

Major Roles: SAUL (bs-bar – top F3), King of Israel. Lengthy role with many vocal and dramatic demands; NAMAN (m-sop), son of King Agag and spear bearer to Saul

– a boy of 15 in Act I; in Acts II and III in his early 20s; SAMUEL (bs – F1-F3), Prophet of Israel; JONATHAN (bar), spans from late teens to late 20s; ABNER (ten), cousin to Saul; DAVID (ten), spans from late teens to late 20s.

Minor Roles: AGAG (ten), King of Amalek; MALKIAH (sop – top B4), Queen of Amalek; AHINOAM (sop), wife of Saul; WITCH OF ENDOR (cont); AHIMELECH (bs), leader of Priests; MELCHISHUA (boy sop), 10-year old son of Saul; ABINADEV (alt), 12-year old son of Saul; TWO MESSENGERS (ten, bar); ELDER OF DAN (ten); EDLER OF JUDAH (bar); ELDER OF EPHRAIM (bar); ACHISH (bar).

Chorus: SATB with some divisi – Israelites, Soldiers, Priests of Nob, Maidens – involved in the action. A few small solos in the chorus.

Dance: A dancer impersonating Saul. A wild and frenzied religious dance by a group of prophets. A dance before the altar of God by Israelites. Dance of the Israelites celebrating their victory over the Philistines.

Orchestration: Not yet orchestrated – to be orchestrated.

Synopsis: Prologue: People clamor before Samuel demanding a king. Act I, scene 1: Samuel finds Saul informing him that God has chosen him to become King of Israel. He objects but is convinced through signs shown him by God. Scene 2: Saul is anointed King by Samuel before all Israel – they rejoice and celebrate. Scene 3: Israel is in bondage and under siege by the Ammonites. Saul, angered by their mistreatment of his people, gathers Israel and declares war on the enemy. Scene 4: Twelve years later, Samuel summons Saul to warn him of God's displeasure with his disobedience. To redeem himself, Saul must attack and destroy the entire tribe of Amalekites and their possessions. Scene 5: The sounds of war are heard in the orchestra. Amalek is defeated, but King Agag, his family and their choice flocks were spared. Samuel enters and, angered by Saul's disobedience again, slays Agag and his wife before Saul's eyes. He then informs Saul that, because of his continuing disobedience, God has taken his kingdom away and given it to another.

Act II, scene 1: Samuel anoints the young David as Saul's successor. Scene 2: The Israelites are at war against the Philistines. David, a young shepherd boy, courageously steps forward and slays their leader Goliath. Scene 3: A victory celebration follows in which David is highly honored. Saul's jealousy and anger grows toward David. Scene 4: Naman summons David, requesting that only his singing and harp playing can soothe Saul's troubled spirit. As David sings, Saul, in a fit of uncontrolled anger, throws his spear at David. Scene 5: Jonathan takes David to a cave where the two hide from Saul. Scene 6: David is being pursued by Saul. He seeks refuge and a weapon in the Temple. No sooner has he left, then Saul and his soldiers enter. When Priests refuse to reveal David's hiding place, Saul orders them killed.

Act III: Saul, utterly dejected, seeks advice from the Witch of Endor. The apparition of the Prophet Samuel is brought before Saul. Samuel tells Saul that tomorrow he and his sons will die. The next day, Jonathan, his beloved son, is killed in battle. Upon receipt of this news, Saul falls on his own sword. Naman brings news of these deaths and the defeat of Israel to David. David gathers Israel around him to mourn. The people then hail David as their new King.

Materials: Unpublished. Materials from the composer.

Notes: Numerous scene changes necessitate the technical advantages of a theatre, though a creative set design could make this work quite accessible.

LELAND B. SATEREN

Day of Pentecost

Music by **Leland B. Sateren** (b. 1913). A Choral Drama with text in English by Thomas W. Wersell, based on Acts 2:2-3 from Scripture.

Premiered Fall, 1974, by the Augsburg College Choir.

Rhythmic speech, aleatoric sections, free improvisation, non-traditional vocal effects. Some Latin from Liturgy.

One scene with five sections. Setting: Around 34 A.D., at the coming of the Holy Spirit or Day of Pentecost. Section 1: Sound; Section 2: Fire; Section 3: Sermon; Section 4: Faith; Section 5: Prayer. Duration: 20 minutes.

Roles: SOLOIST (sop or ten, or several singers).

Chorus: SSAATTBB.

Orchestration: *A cappella.*

Synopsis: A description, using voices in both traditional and non-traditional styles, of the events on the Day of Pentecost and the coming of the Holy Spirit. Included are the events of the five divisions of this work: the sounds people heard, the appearance of fire, the sermon that followed, multitude which believed after seeing God's gift, and the prayer of the people, praying for God's mercy upon them.

Materials: AUG (1975), or from the composer. Recording available from AUGC.

Notes: No sets required. Intended for presentation in a church. Chorus moves through the audience and involves them in the drama. Stage directions in VS.

"Involves contemporary choral devices, non-traditional notation, some improvisation, and movement of the choir off the risers and out into the audience." –Leland B. Sateren.

Here Comes Our King

Music by **Leland B. Sateren** (b. 1913). A Choral Drama with text in English by Thomas W. Wersell.

First performance Fall, 1979, by the Augsburg College Choir.

Non-traditional use of voices, contemporary choral devices, antiphonal singing.

Four sections. I. Messiah; II. Savior; III. Friend-Prayer; IV. King. No sets required. Duration: 20 minutes.

No soloists.

Chorus: SATB, divisi .

Orchestration: *A cappella.*

Synopsis: The singers begin by making a bold statement "Here comes our King! Messiah strong, God's love to bring, subduing wrong." Following this introduction, an aleatoric *Kyrie eleison* is sounded, interwoven with angry statements from the crowd who wanted Him crucified. A quiet prayer of "Our King and Lord, come soon" is uttered by the entire choir. A hearty antiphonal hymn of praise is sung, followed by a chorale of invitation, *Come, let us join our cheerful songs with angels round the throne.*

Materials: WAL (© 1979). Recording available from AUGC.

Notes: No sets required. Similar in style to the other listed Sateren Choral Dramas. Intended for church or concert performance. During the work, the choir may use body and arms gestures and move throughout the auditorium involving the audience in the drama. Stage directions in VS.

Meditations on the Seven Last Words

Music by **Leland B. Sateren** (b. 1913). A Choral Drama with text by John R. Milton, based on the Scriptures.

First performance Fall, 1978, by Augsburg College Choir.

Choral sections mostly homophonic and hymn-like. Solo sections are *non-misura* and chanted. Mostly conventional harmonies.

Seven sections corresponding to the seven words spoken on the cross by Christ. No sets required; stage props helpful. Duration: 13 minutes.

Roles: EVANGELIST (bar), represents Christ on the cross as well as the Evangelist as in the Baroque Passion settings.

Chorus: SSAATTBB – comments on the action.

Orchestration: *A cappella*

Synopsis: The Evangelist sings a paraphrase of each of Christ's seven words as He hangs on the cross. The choir responds to each word with commentary.

Materials: WAL (© 1978).

Notes: No sets required; stage props helpful. Intended for performance in a cathedral/church. Staging is minimal being confined to the Evangelist. However, actors could be used to pantomime the action. Staging suggestions and libretto are included with the VS.

Our Faith

Music by **Leland B. Sateren** (b. 1913). A Choral Drama with text in English by Rossiter W. Raymond and Herbert Brokering, based on the Gospel of John.

Commissioned by the Minnesota Composers Commissioning Program for St. John's Lutheran Church for the 100th Anniversary of that church on October 30, 1983.

Melodic, traditional harmony with some unexpected harmonic shifts. Accessible to average church choirs. Some non-synchronized choral singing. Audience is involved in singing one hymn.

One scene. No sets or props required. Choir involved in action requiring memorization of score. Duration: 20 minutes.

Roles: READER (sp); CRUCIFER (mute).

Chorus: SATB – mostly *a cappella*.

Dance: Twenty processional dancers.

Orchestration: 2 fl, 2 corn, 3 Orff instruments, org, string quartet. Some instrumentalists involved in the action.

Synopsis: The audience is introduced to the main musical theme by flutes located in the rear of the sanctuary. The choir processes singing. The Reader begins, reading from the opening verses of John. The choir picks up on the text, re-enforcing the Reader's story of John. Finally, the dancers and instrumentalists process, filling the sanctuary with their presence and sounds. The audience joins all the musical forces in a grand finale. The choir, orchestra and dancers begin to recess as the Reader concludes with "This is the victory that overcomes the world, our faith." The flutes echo the main theme from the rear of the sanctuary.

Materials: Unpublished. From the composer.

Notes: No sets or props required. Designed to be performed in a church as part of a worship service or sacred concert. VS contains full staging suggestions and diagrams.

ALESSANDRO SCARLATTI

Il primo omicidio – *The First Murder*

Music by **Alessandro Scarlatti** (1659-1725). A Sacred Entertainment (so designated on the title page of the printed libretto) with libretto in Italian (unknown), based on scripture taken from Genesis 4.

Completed January 7, 1707.

Set numbers, many *Da capo* arias, secco recitatives, frequent sinfonia. Traditional harmonic structures typical of the mid-Baroque. Vocal lines often highly florid.

Two acts. Duration: approximately 100 minutes.

Roles: The male alto indication represents the use of castrati by Scarlatti. VOICE OF GOD (male alt or ten); ABEL (male sop or ten), Abel's voice must take on a different color after his death; VOICE OF LUCIFER (bs); CAIN (male alt or ten); ADAM (ten); EVE (sop).

Orchestration: Strings, continuo.

Synopsis: Beginning with the birth of Cain and Abel to Adam and Eve, conflict between the two boys was in evidence. The plot deals with Abel's demise by Cain and the effects of Cain's guilt. The voice of Abel haunts Cain long after the murder.

Materials: EDS (c. 1968), modern edition by Lino Bianchi. First printed in 1706 by Antonio Bartoli in Venice as *Cain, the First Murderer.* Another printed libretto reads 1710.

Notes: This work is being included due in part to its stageworthy dramatic value, and also that, unlike other sacred "oratorios" of Scarlatti, the title page of both the 1706 and 1710 printed librettos list this work as "A Sacred Entertainment," a designation not assigned his other oratorios. While terminology for dramatic works during this period had not yet clearly been defined or delineated (i.e., opera, oratorio, cantata, *sacra rappresentazione*, etc.), it is clear that after Monteverdi, concert "oratorios" became, for a time, the most important dramatic expression, holding dominance even over opera and cantata. Other works worthy of stage treatment but listed only by Scarlatti as oratorios include *La Giuditta* ("The 'Naples' Judith"), *La Giuditta di Cambridge* ("The 'Cambridge' Judith") and *Agar et Ismaele* ("Hagar and Ishmael").

ARNOLD SCHOENBERG

Moses und Aron – *Moses and Aaron*

Music by **Arnold Schoenberg** (1847-1951). A Religious Opera with libretto in German by the composer, based on events as found primarily in the Old Testament books of Exodus and Leviticus.

Premiered in concert form in 1954; staged premiere in Zurich, June 6, 1957.

Twelve-tone, considerable *Sprechstimme*, continuous texture, highly declamatory. Musical and production aspects are all extremely difficult.

Three acts (Schoenberg finished only the first two but left a dramatic outline of the third). Setting: Egypt in the 17th Dynasty and the Valley of Canaan. Act I: The exodus from Egypt; Act II: In the wilderness mountains. Duration: approximately 120 minutes for the first two acts.

Roles: MOSES (bs-bar – F#1-C#3), mostly *Sprechstimme* which includes a top of G3; ARON (ten – B1-B3), requires near-perfect pitch – many wide leaps and disjunct lines; YOUNG MAIDEN (sop); YOUNG MAN (ten); EPHRAIMITE (bar); FEMALE INVALID (cont – low Ab2); MAN (bar); PRIEST (bs – top F3 opt); FOUR NAKED VIRGINS (2 sop, 2 cont); VOICE FROM BURNING BUSH (sop, boy sop, cont, ten, bar, bs).

Chorus: SSAATTBB – enormously difficult. Solo roles from the chorus: Seventy Elders (bs section plus supers); BEGGARS (6-8 cont, 6-8 bs); six voices in pit (sop, m-sop, cont, ten, bar, bs); twelve tribal leaders (TTBB). Many supers as Israelites are required.

Dance: Elaborate dances of the period and culture.

Orchestration: 3 fl (picc), 3 ob (Eng hrn), 3 cl, bs cl (Bb and A), 2 bsn, contra bsn, 4 hrn, 3 trp, 3 trb, tba, timp, perc (many), hp, pia, cel, 2 mandolin, strings. Stage: picc, fl, cl, Eng hrn, hrn, 2 trp, 2 trb, timp, bs dr, tamb, high and low gongs, cym, xyl, pia, 2 mandolin, 2 gui

Synopsis: Moses listens as God speaks to him out of the burning bush. He brings the message back to the doubting Israelites, convincing them through miracles which God has shown him. During the time which Moses spends with God in the mountains, the Israelites become impatient with their leadership. Aron gives in to the people and builds them a golden calf to worship. Three orgies, each one wilder and bloodier than the previous, are staged. Moses returns and seeing the debauchery of his people, destroys the calf and the stone tablets he has brought down from the mountains. Here ends the second act. In Act III, Moses confronts Aron who is now a prisoner. He accuses Aron of misinterpreting and misrepresenting God's commands. He is finally given his freedom, but dies almost immediately, signifying that the falsehood he represents is indeed self-destructive when placed in the presence of the truth of God represented in Moses.

Materials: SCH (BEL). VS has English translation by Allen Forte. English translation by David Rudkin also available.

Notes: Performable only with the largest companies of highly trained singers, instrumentalists, and technical personnel. An extremely difficult score.

HEINRICH SCHÜTZ

Historia der ... Auferstehungs ... Jesu Christi – The Easter Story

Music by **Heinrich Schütz** (1585-1672). A Dramatic Choral work with text in German based on the Biblical account of Christ's death and resurrection.

Composed in 1623; first performed in Dresden, 1623.

Traditional harmonic structures typical of Baroque practice. Set numbers, spoken narrative, secco recitative, vocally conceived, limited ranges. Fourteen short narratives provide continuity between the musical numbers (Butterworth ed.).

Roles: EVANGELIST (sp), narrator; MARY MAGDELENA (two voices – sop, alt); TWO ANGELS (sop, alt); THREE MARIES (sop, sop, sop); JESUS (two voices – alt and bar); THREE HIGH PRIESTS (ten, bar, bs); CLEOPHAS (ten); HIS COMPANION (bar); TWO MEN IN THE GRAVE (ten, ten).

Chorus: SSATTB – One double SATB chorus number. Short choral sections and smaller ensembles comment on the action which is revealed in the spoken narrative.

Orchestration: Four viola and continuo (original version).

Synopsis: The plot begins with the visit of the women to the sepulchre and ends with the resurrection.

Materials: CHA. This edition is arranged by Neil Butterworth. In order to provide more music for the full chorus, Butterworth has added two choral numbers from other works of Schütz. The original version (BAR) differs considerably from Butterworth's edition.

Notes: A versatile work with good potential for dramatic treatment. Suitable for performance in a cathedral/church. Accessible for most church choirs.

Historia der ... Geburt ... Jesu Christi – The Christmas Story

Music by **Heinrich Schütz** (1585-1672). A Dramatic Choral work with text in German based on the nativity story as found in Matthew 2 and Luke 2.

Composed and first performed in Dresden in 1664.

Set numbers, solos, ensembles. Secco recitatives. Traditional Baroque harmonic structures. Highly melodic with limited ranges. Spoken narrative (Butterworth edition).

One part with eight Intermediums. Various scenes could be staged at different locations throughout the auditorium. Manger scene should be on stage as the central focus. Duration: 40 minutes.

Roles: EVANGELIST (ten); ANGEL (sop – top A4), florid passages; THREE SHEPHERDS (alt, alt, alt or ten); THREE WISEMEN (ten, ten, ten or bar); HEROD (bs – top E3), some melisma.

Chorus: Predominantly SATB; Intermedium II calls for SSATTB (Angels). Wisemen and Shepherds may be sung by the choir, but in a staged version, soloists should be used.

Orchestration: Suggested in Mendel edition: 2 rec, bsn, 2 trp, 2 trb, org, cembalo, strings. Schütz did not indicate his exact orchestration, but rather gave permission to tailor the use of instruments to fit the occasion (See "Materials" below).

Synopsis: The Evangelist narrates the Christmas story from the Scripture and introduces the characters of the story as they appear. The Angels appear to the Shepherds announcing the birth of the Christ Child. The Shepherds respond with great joy. Meanwhile, the Wisemen come to Herod seeking the Christ. Herod calls the scribes together for counsel regarding this new king, then sends the kings on their way to find the Christ, demanding they return with the location of this new King. The Angel appears to Joseph, warning him to flee to Egypt for fear of Herod. Later, the Angel again appears to Joseph and Mary instructing them to return to Judea as Herod has died and it is now safe. The work ends with a chorus of thanksgiving.

Materials: GS (edition by Arthur Mendel with English translation by Henry S. Drinker). Elaborate remarks on performance styles and a history of the work are included in the VS. Also the Baerenreiter Ausgabe 1709. The Chappell edition is edited by Neil Butterworth and calls for Vln I and II, rec I and II, bsn, vc, and continuo.

Notes: Best suited for performance in a cathedral/church using the entire sanctuary and chancel for staging purposes. No sets required, only props for the manager scene.

MARK SCHWEIZER

Saturday, 29 A.D.

Music and libretto by **Mark Schweizer** (b. 1956). A dramatic dialogue for Holy Week in English loosely based on the limited scriptures relating to Pontius Pilate and his wife, Claudia Procula.

Composed for Lenten lunch series and first performed Lent 1997, St. James Episcopal Church, Alexandria, LA.

Tonal with frequent meter changes. Highly melodic. Occasional spoken lines; Considerable recitative – mostly chanted. Score utilizes four prominent motives which represent characters and situations. The hymn tune *Herzliebster Jesu* (Ah, Holy Jesus) and a quote from Benjamin Britten's *Canticle II – Abraham and Isaac* are found in the score.

One scene set in Biblical times after the trial of Jesus before Pontius Pilate. Duration: 21 minutes.

Roles: PONTIUS PILATE (bar); CLAUDIA PROCULA (m-sop), his wife

Chorus: SATB Greek chorus which comments on the action – very little singing. The opera could be performed without the chorus.

Orchestration: pia alone.

Synopsis: While the trial of Jesus before Pilate is found in all four gospels, his wife is only mentioned in the book of Matthew, where she sends a warning to Pilate, "Have nothing to do with that innocent man, for today I have suffered a great deal because of a dream about him." The plot of this drama focuses on the conflict between Rome and religion, or unbelievers and believers as represented by the Christian faith of Claudia and the patriotic commitment of Pilate to his country and to Caesar. According to tradition, Claudia is believed to have converted to Christianity shortly after the death of Jesus and became a prominent missionary in the early church. In this dramatic dialogue, Pilate represents more than himself. In a sense he becomes "Everyman" and is faced with the choice of accepting Christ or rejecting him totally. Claudia becomes the antagonist, pushing Pilate to a final decision. Ultimately, Pilate chooses the way of Rome and the world with the words "I know no sin but treason."

Materials: SJMP

Notes: A simple but emotionally effective drama for Holy Week. Best performed in a church – effective as a part of a worship service. Costumes and a few set pieces needed.

CHARLES KENNEDY SCOTT

Everyman

Music by **Charles Kennedy Scott** (1876-1965). A Morality Play with text in English adapted by the composer from the medieval play of the same title with some additions by Beatrice E. Bulman.

Composed in 1936.

Rich Romantic textures. Arias, mostly soloistic; continuous action. Unaccompanied plainchant and chant-style dominate vocal lines. Frequent meter changes.

Four acts. Act I: Summoning of Everyman by Death. Act II, sc. 1: Everyman's appeal to Fellowship; sc. 2: To Kindred; sc. 3: To Goods to go with him on his journey. Act III: Everyman's comfort by Good Deeds. Act IV: Everyman's ending. Duration: approximately 90 minutes.

Roles: MESSENGER (alt); GOD (bs); DEATH (ten – top Bb3); EVERYMAN (bar – top F3), lengthy and demanding role; FELLOWSHIP (ten); KINDRED (sop); COUSIN (cont); GOODS (bs); GOOD-DEEDS (sop); DISCRETION (m-sop); STRENGTH (bs); FIVE-WITS (sop); BEAUTY (ten); ANGEL (low ten); FOUR MONKS (ten, ten, bar, bs).

Chorus: Three groups: 6 sop, 5 alt, 4 ten, 4 bs (divisi) – Greek chorus; 9 women, 9 men – acting chorus; 4 sop, 4 m-sop, 4 alt – Angelic chorus.

Orchestration: fl, 2 ob, Eng hrn, cl, 3 bsn, trp, 3 trb, tba, hp, bells, org, str

Synopsis: God is displeased with Everyman's way of life and calls on Death to bring him to judgment. He replies to God that he will "strike Everyman," and that only Good-Deeds can save him from hell. In the distance the approaching voices of Everyman and his companions sing the Rabble Song. They burst on to the scene. When revelry is at its height, Death confronts Everyman with a trumpet blast. The crowd, frightened, disperses. Death tells him he must take the long journey from which there is no return. Everyman asks for time to clear his accounts but Death refuses – however, if any of his friends are willing to accompany him, Everyman may take them along. Everyman sings a song of lament.

Everyman appeals to Fellowship who is enjoying himself and others in a tavern. Fellowship assures Everyman that he will never forsake him and is ready to assist. Everyman explains his predicament whereupon Fellowship quickly deserts him. Everyman approaches Kindred and Cousin with some hope, but they too reject his pleas. Goods, when approached, laughs and scoffs at Everyman's distress. His last recourse is Good-Deeds. Sorrowfully and in a weakened state, she tells him what he must do before she can help him. She calls on Knowledge to be his guide. Confession comes and hears his desire to repent and joyfully do penance. He kneels and utters a prayer to God that his soul may be saved. Good-Deeds now has gained strength and can go with Everyman.

In Act IV, all of Everyman's friends have gathered to witness his death. The dread hour has come. One by one his friends leave him, not having the will nor power to follow where he goes – only his Good-Deeds go with him. Death blows his trumpet and Everyman dies. Soft alleluias come from the Angelic Choir growing to a brilliant and triumphant conclusion.

Materials: OUP.

Notes: Numerous staging directions, costume drawings, production notes, complete libretto and performance practice suggestions are in the VS. Best performed on a proscenium stage.

RICHARD JAMES SHEPHARD

Caedmon

Music by **Richard James Shephard** (b.1949). A Children's Opera sung by adults and children. Libretto in English by Mary Holtby, based on the life of Caedmon the cowman and the documented miracle that changed his life forever (recorded in detail by the Venerable Bede). Caedmon is remembered as the "father of English song," and lived in the 7th century.

Commissioned and premiered by the York Early Music Festival, York Minster, July 1994. American premiere was presented November 6, 1999 by Opera Sacra (see Appendix B), featuring the Western New York Children's Chorus.

Explores both nineteenth and twentieth-century harmonic influences including the use of twelve-tone techniques and polychords. Highly melodic; uses both originally conceived melodies and traditional English folk tunes.

One act. Setting: the Whitby Abbey, and a cow stable in 650-660 A. D. Duration: 60 minutes.

Roles: CAEDMON (bar – A1-E3 – some *Sprechstimme*); ANGEL 1 (sop – D3-G4); ANGEL 2 (sop – C3-G4; HILDA (sop – C3-Ab4); EDWIN (ten – D2-G3)

Chorus: Children's Chorus and SATB Chorus, divided as Monks and Nuns, Servants, Cows, and Learned Men.

Orchestration: fl, ob, bsn, 2 hrn, trp, org, perc, str

Synopsis: The plot details the life of Caedmon the cowman and the miracle that gifted him with the ability to sing. One night when the servants are gathered around the table for fellowship and music, the harp is passed from person to person. Caedmon, knowing nothing of poetry and song, leaves the table in shame as he has often done before, and retires to the stable where he has been assigned to care for the cattle. As he sleeps, a vision of angels appears to him, ordering him to sing. "You must be mad. I don't know how to sing. That's why I left the hall in disgrace and came back to my cows," he protests. The angels persist, and Caedmon, much to his surprise, sings in praise to God, using texts he has never heard before. The next morning Caedmon recites his text and his story to Abbess Hilda and the Learned Men, and all agree that he has received a Divine gift. The Abbess invites him to join the monastery, but being reluctant to leave his herd, Caedmon is allowed to continue caring for his cows as long as he comes to the chapel for the singing of the Divine Office. After a long life, during which Caedmon composed many songs based on Biblical texts, Caedmon is called home to heaven to sing God's praise eternally.

Materials: Unpublished. Materials available from the composer – see Shephard in Appendix C

Notes: Best suited to and designed to be performed in a house of worship. Creative staging is necessary to maintain continuous action during the change of settings.

This entry was written by Lisa Grevlos, author of a definitive study and analysis of Richard Shephard's life and sacred operas. Her study/dissertation is available – see Grevlos in Appendix C for contact information.

Good King Wenceslas

Music by **Richard James Shephard** (b. 1949). A Chancel opera in English with libretto by Mark Schweizer loosely based on and incorporating the well known hymn text by John Mason Neale (1818-1866). This carol is set to the 14th century tune "Tempus adest floridum," found in *Piae Cantiones* (1582). A second carol incorporated into the opera is "Thus Angels Sung," text by George Wither (1588-1667) and set to *Song 34* by Orlando Gibbons (1583-1625).

Premiered Christmas 1997 at First United Methodist Church, Hopkinsville, KY according to librettist, Mark Schweizer. St. James Press CD/DVD press release information of *Good King Wenceslas* states in the acknowledgment section that "Our thanks to Dr. Allen Henderson and the Austin Peay University Opera Workshop for their work in bringing these operas to life. The faculty and students in the voice, choral and orchestral departments have been invaluable both in the premieres and the recordings of these new works."

Tonal; conventional harmonies; melodic material is both original as well as derived from existing carols and hymns.

One act. Setting is the castle and surrounding grounds of Good King Wenceslas, 922-929 A. D. Duration: 30 minutes.

Roles: STEPHEN (treble – top F4), the page; MOTHER (sop); CHANCELLOR (ten – D2-A3); GOOD KING WENCESLAS (bs); ANGEL (sop); SHEPHERD GIRL (sop); KASPAR (ten); BALTHAZAR (bar); MELCHIOR (bar – top F3).
Mother/Angel and Chancellor/Kaspar may be sung by the same persons.

Chorus: SATB – parts need not be memorized and should be performed as a Greek chorus, outside the action.

Orchestration: Several instrumental adaptations are available: full orchestra, chamber ensemble, or piano alone. The opera was originally composed for a small instrumental chamber ensemble: ob, hrn, bsn, pia, perc (vib may be played on an electronic keyboard).

Synopsis: The story centers around a rude and spoiled young page, Stephen, who is celebrating his birthday. Good King Wenceslas summons Stephen and informs him that he will be embarking on a journey with the King to bring food, drink, and fuel to a poor peasant. Stephen grumbles and complains incessantly as he makes the journey with the King. The weather turns bad, and they soon lose their way in the storm. They find shelter, and as Stephen watches over the sleeping King, an angel disguised as an old woman appears to Stephen and tells him a story. A mystery play unfolds which reveals a story about selfless giving to the Christ child. Stephen's selfish heart is changed and he completes the journey in great joy with Good King Wenceslas offering "charity toward the upright."

Materials: SJMP – piano/vocal score and orchestra parts are available for purchase.

Notes: May be performed in either a house of worship or theatre, with or without sets, and is musically accessible for professional and amateur singers alike.

This entry was written by Lisa Grevlos, author of a definitive study and analysis of Richard Shephard's life and sacred operas. Her study/dissertation is available – see Grevlos in Appendix C for contact information.

St. Nicholas

Music by **Richard James Shephard** (b. 1949). A comic Christmas opera with libretto in English by Mark Schweizer, loosely based on the legend of *Tres Fillae* (three sisters), one of the oldest and most cherished legends of St. Nicholas. The opera also includes three well known carols: *Past Three O'clock*, a traditional London carol, *Poverty*, an old Welsh carol, and *Still, Still, Still* of Austrian origin.

Premiere in 1998 by Austin Peay State University, Clarksville, Tennessee.

Tonal, conventional harmonies, melodic material is both original as well as derived from existing carols and hymns.

One act. Setting is in the home of the three sisters, Sophie, Juliet, and Lucy; 1000-1100 A. D. Duration: 35 minutes.

Major Roles: SOPHIE (sop – top A4 with B4 opt); JULIET (sop – topA4 with B4 opt); LUCY (m-sop); ST. NICHOLAS (bar); TRAVELER (ten); TRAVELER'S WIFE (mute); SIR WILLIAM (ten). Traveler and Sir William may be sung by the same person.

Chorus: SATB – parts need not be memorized and should be performed as a Greek chorus, outside the action. Children's Chorus is optional.

Orchestration: Several instrumental adaptations are available: full orchestra, chamber ensemble, or piano alone. The opera was originally composed for a small instrumental chamber ensemble: cl, timp, perc (wood block, triangle), cel or elec kybd, pia, 4 trp (opt), 2 vln, vc

Synopsis: Three sisters, Juliet, Lucy, and Sophie are cleaning the house in preparation for Christmas. They are poor, having lost their father, but in the spirit of the season make their wishes. All three wish for husbands. They go to bed. St. Nicholas arrives and leaves three gold coins for them. Juliet awakens first and selfishly takes all of the coins to buy a dress for herself. St. Nicholas then leaves two more coins which Lucy takes in hopes of attracting a husband. At last, St. Nicholas leaves one coin for Sophie over which she rejoices in the knowledge that the money will keep herself and her sisters from going hungry.

There is a knock on the door. A man and his wife who are about to deliver a baby appear. They ask for food and shelter. Sophie tells them she has nothing to offer except one gold coin. They thank her and leave for the warmth of a nearby inn. The two sisters return from their shopping spree, discovering that Sophie also received a gold coin. Their jealousy turns to rage and they tear each other's new clothes. St. Nicholas, observing them, chastises the two girls for their greed. A knock at the door reveals Sir William, Sophie's long lost love. He has been searching for Sophie, having encountered a young couple with a new baby who told him that a young girl provided for their needs. Suspecting Sophie as the young girl, Sir William, having now found his Sophie, pledges to marry her. St. Nicholas entreats all to remember the true meaning of Christmas.

Materials: SJMP – piano/vocal score as well as full orchestra and chamber orchestra parts are available for purchase.

Notes: May be performed in either a house of worship or theatre, with or without sets. Easily accessible; enjoyable entertainment; light comedy.

This entry was written by Lisa Grevlos, author of a definitive study and analysis of Richard Shephard's life and sacred operas. Her study/dissertation is available – see Grevlos in Appendix C for contact information.

The Shepherd's Play

Music by **Richard James Shephard** (b. 1949). A Pastorale with libretto by Mark Schweizer in English, based on the biblical story of the Angel's announcement of Christ's birth to the shepherds. The Latin text, *Gloria in excelsis Deo,* is sung by the

Angels (chorus). This work is often performed between *Good King Wenceslas* and *St. Nicholas* to create a trilogy.

Premiered in 2000 by Austin Peay University, Clarksville, TN.

One act. A pastorale with continuous action. Setting is outdoors at the time of the birth of Jesus. Duration: 10 minutes

Roles: SHEPHERD 1 (ten – E2-A3); SHEPHERD 2 (ten or high bar – E2-F3); SHEPHERD 3 (bar – B2-D4); SHEPHERD 4 (ten or bar – D2-F3).

Chorus: SATB with a short sop solo section – parts need not be memorized and should be performed as a Greek chorus, outside the action.

Orchestration: fl, windchimes, string quartet or piano.

Synopsis: Three shepherds hear the angels proclaiming the birth of Christ and immediately leave their sheep to take their gifts to the Savior of the world. The fourth shepherd finds the sheep unguarded and scolds the three shepherds for their carelessness. The three shepherds exclaim their awe and amazement at hearing the angel's song and try to recreate the joyous sound. The angel chorus bursts in and beckons the fourth shepherd to come to see the wondrous sight. The three shepherds chime in and encourage the fourth shepherd to give the best gift of all, his heart.

Materials: SJMP – parts and vocal score available for purchase.

Notes: Works well in a house of worship though a theatre may be used, especially if all three works are being performed. May be performed with or without sets.

This entry was written by Lisa Grevlos, author of a definitive study and analysis of Richard Shephard's life and sacred operas. Her study/dissertation is available – see Grevlos in Appendix C for contact information.

FREDERICK SILVER

Exodus and Easter

Music by **Frederick Silver** (b. 1936). A Sacred Music Drama with libretto in English by Robert D. Hock.

Commissioned by the Department of Speech, Drama and Communication, Union Theological Seminary. Premiered February 16, 1966, Chicago, IL.

Twentieth century chromaticism; folk and "pop" musical elements. Contemporary language usage. Melodic. In the style of a musical theatre piece.

Three scenes and a Prologue. Setting: A playpen in the present. Prologue: Creation of the world; sc. 1: Warnings; sc. 2: Exodus and Easter; sc. 3: A call for action. Duration: approximately 35 minutes.

Roles: All roles are low to mid-range. THE CAPTIVE (female); THE POOR (male); THE BLIND (male); THE OPPRESSED (male).

Chorus: SATB – commentary.

Orchestration: Two pianos.

Synopsis: A brief Prologue describes the creation of the world. In scene 1, warnings are issued in the course of three numbers. The first, "Possessed," discusses the issues of four possessed people. Their problems include attitudes, the welfare system, negroes and white-washed churches. When facing deep troubles remain in control, is discussed in "Don't Loose Your Head." "Hangin' On" focuses on helping the poor who just barely survive from day to day. The first number in scene 2, "Exodus," informs the listener that it is possible to move from the darkness of sin to freedom. The solution is found in "Easter," which tells the story of Christ's life, death and resurrection. The final scene is presented in a quasi-militaristic setting. One number, "Look Alive," challenges the listener to become involved and be a witness of the Good News.

Materials: WMI. Performance rights from BAK.

Notes: Most suitable for performance in a church setting. Minimal sets and props needed.

Hannah

Music by **Frederick Silver** (b. 1936). A Religious Music Drama with libretto in English by Helen Kromer.

Premiere May 21, 1965, Veterans' Memorial Auditorium, Columbus, Ohio. Commissioned for the 177th General Assembly of the United Presbyterian Church.

Situation drama – a parable in music. Some chromaticism; highly rhythmic sections; melodic with mid-range vocal lines. Set numbers with dialogue, ensembles, solos. In the style of a musical theatre piece.

Two acts. Overture. Setting: The present in a medium-sized American city. Act I, sc. 1: The choir room; sc. 2: The Huckleby home; sc. 3: In the community; sc. 4: The bank; sc. 5: The church parlor; sc. 6: The Huckleby home. Act II, sc. 1: The Huckleby home; sc. 2: The choir room; sc. 3: The Huckleby home; sc. 4: The church; sc. 5: The community; sc. 6: The Huckleby yard; sc. 7: Anywhere. Duration: approximately 60 minutes.

Major Roles: HANNAH HUCKLEBY (sop), age 45; EUNICE HUCKLEBY (m-sop), paralyzed daughter of Hannah, age 12; ARCHIE MORDECAI (ten), bank employee, age 28; GRANDPA HUCKLEBY (bar), age 79; PAULINE PEABARKER BARNES (alt), age 60.

Minor Roles: SHERMAN COOPER (boy sop), age 9; SIMON SYOBI, age 29; MORGAN PRIOR, age 65; ALICE PRIOR (m-sop), age 63; MARABELLE ALLEN (m-sop), a school teacher, age 25; PETERS (ten), age 35; LUCY (m-sop), age 30; LEWIS (bar), age 40; THELMA (m-sop), age 35.

Chorus: SSATB – eight women including Frieda, Dorothy, Jane, Ruth, Lisa plus four men; two children (a boy and girl ages 9-11). Additional singers may be added.

Dance: Several dancers, both adults and teenagers are needed; folk and square dance styles.

Orchestration: Chamber orchestra.

Synopsis: The work opens with a church choir rehearsal. During the rehearsal, choir members begin complaining about Hannah Huckleby, a choir member some of them would like to see leave the organization. They take their problem to Pauline Peabarker Barnes, whom they all respect and admire. Pauline agrees to call on Hannah the next morning. Pauline befriends Hannah and her family, much to the dismay of the other choir members, after learning that Hannah is a widow with many more problems than anyone knows. The Ladies Association also tries to work with Hannah, but seemingly to no avail. Archie, a mild-mannered banker, is attracted to Eunice, Hannah's paralyzed daughter, but then turns his romantic interests toward Marabelle, a school teacher. Grandpa Huckleby suffers and seems to be near death. Gradually, the entire choir becomes friends with Hannah and her family, and join in celebrating Grandpa's surprise eightieth birthday party given him by the Ladies Association. They agree that the chief end of man is to glorify God and to enjoy Him forever. All seem to have learned a lesson.

Materials: WMI. Performance rights from BAK.

Notes: Best suited for performance in a theatre or auditorium with adequate stage space for the cast and chorus.

FAYE-ELLEN SILVERMAN

The Miracle of Nemirov

Music by **Faye-Ellen Silverman** (b. 1947). A Jewish Legend Opera with libretto in English (some Hebrew) by the composer based on a story by I. L. Peretz.

Doctoral dissertation, Columbia University, 1974.

Hebraic musical influences, chant-like passages; melodic, rhythmic speech with some spoken lines. Frequently atonal, rhythmic complexities; through-composed.

One act, eight scenes. Setting: In Nemirov, Poland around 1900, during Slichos (the penitential days between Rosh Hashanah and Yom Kippur). Duration: 30 minutes.

Roles: LITVAK (ten – top A3), an intelligent and cynical Jew from Lithuania; RABBI (bar), spiritual leader of Nemirov; MALKAH (m-sop), a sick Jewess; RIVKA (alt), mother of Seryll; SERYLL (sop); BERYLL (bs), husband of Rivka; CHAIM (ten – top A3), husband of Seryll; YOSHE (ten), Cantor of Nemirov; A BEGGAR.

Orchestration: fl, ob, cl, 3 hrn, perc, string quartet, pre-recorded tape (opt).

Synopsis: Seryll and Rivka are searching for the Rabbi who systematically disappears each day. A traveler, Litvak, is seeking night's lodging on his trip to Lithuania. The Rabbi finally appears and gladly offers him lodging as well as advice regarding his question of why man learns only to forget. Alone and awake after bedtime, Litvak listens to a recording of the *Talmud*, memorizing as he goes. The next morning the Rabbi is again absent. All conclude that he has ascended to heaven.

Materials: SMC.

Notes: Best performed in a theatre or synagogue. Few properties required. Some production notes in the VS.

STANLEY SILVERMAN

Up From Paradise

Music by **Stanley Silverman** (b. 1938). A Musical with libretto in English by Arthur Miller based on his book *The Creation of the World and Other Business*, and the Biblical account according to Genesis.

Premiered 1981, Musical Theatre Lab, Kennedy Center for the Performing Arts, Washington, D.C.

Traditional harmony with some operatic tendencies. Set numbers, spoken dialogue. Barbershop, Baroque classical styles, some chant-like passages. Comedy.

Two acts. Setting Act I: The Garden of Eden. Act II: years later around a dinner table. Duration: approximately 120 minutes.

Roles: All roles have operatic singing style mixed with "pop" style. GOD (bs – top F3); LUCIFER (ten); ADAM (bar); CHEMUEL (ten – top C4), Angel of Mercy; URIEL (high bar – top G3), Angel of Philosophy; AZRAEL (bs), Angel of Death.

Dance: Nearly all characters have dance sequences.

Orchestration: fl/picc/alt fl, ob/Eng hrn, cl/bs cl, hrn, bsn/contra bsn, pia, perc (bell tree played by pia, wind chime by ob, harmonica by ob, melodica by ob or actor). The three Angels should play instruments of their own capabilities. Abel and Cain play guitars (opt).

Synopsis: God approaches Adam, asking him to please lie down because He needs to remove a rib. Eve materializes and the Angels joined by Adam sing a rousing "Hallelujah" in barbershop harmony. Lucifer comes on the scene and discusses with God the magnificence of the woman. God warns him to leave the couple alone, to which Lucifer agrees. No sooner has God departed then Lucifer begins scheming. He approaches Adam and Eve convincing them to try a bite of the apple which God had forbidden them to eat. Immediately God appears and demands they leave the garden, but first put on some clothes! Lucifer appears and is questioned by God as to why he had deceived His most prized creation. He then tells Lucifer "to go to Hell," and Lucifer departs. Adam and Eve are given flocks to tend, suffering in their work, and pain in bearing children. Years later, around the dinner table, Adam and Eve chant a prayer before eating. Meanwhile, their two sons, Cain and Abel are offering their own sacrifices to God: Cain offers spinach while Abel offers mutton. God tries both and is reminded by Lucifer that He cannot possibly be just because everyone knows God prefers the taste of mutton to spinach. Cain, distraught over God's preference and in a heated argument breaks Abel's neck. Adam and Eve mourn the death of their son while Lucifer blames the injustice of God rather than human failing. Adam and Eve, fearful of the future, wonder how they can start anew.

Materials: SF.

Notes: Should be performed in a theatre. Some isolated lines and theology may be problematic in certain churches.

LARRY SITSKY

The Golem

Music by **Larry Sitsky** (b. 1934; Australian). A Jewish Legend Opera with libretto in English (some Latin and Hebrew) by Gwen Harwood.

Commissioned by the Australian Opera, Sydney; premiered in Sydney Opera House, 1992.

Twentieth century textures with complex harmonic and rhythmic structures. Straying tonalities. Discreetly conceals many Christian and Jewish hymn tunes and folk melodies. Non-traditional vocal effects, disjunct lines with large difficult skips. Continuous texture. Some chanting of Jewish prayers.

Three acts. Setting: Prague, fifteenth century. Act I, sc. 1: Prague ghetto outside Judah Loew's house; sc. 2: The Rabbi's dream; sc. 3: The banks of the Moldau, sc. 4: Outside Mordecai's house; sc. 5: In the Rabbi's house; sc. 6: In front of the Rabbi's house. Act II, sc. 1: Cardinal Silvester's room; sc. 2: The Golem's journey; sc. 3: Outside the Court House; sc. 4: Inside the Rabbi's house; sc. 5: A dark obscure place in town. Act III, sc. 1: A large court; sc. 2: The Rabbi's study; sc. 3: A lonely place; sc. 4: Street by the ghetto gate; sc. 5: The Rabbi's street; sc. 6: Jewish cemetery; sc. 7: The attic of an old synagogue. Duration: 2 hours, 45 minutes.

Roles: RABBI JUDAH LOEW (bs – E1-F3), spiritual leader of the Jewish community in a Prague ghetto; PERELE (sop), his wife; RACHEL (sop), his daughter; ISAAC (ten – top Bb3), Rabbi's son-in-law; JACOB (ten), disciple of the Rabbi; GOLEM (bar – top A3), named Joseph; MORDECAI MEISEL (bar – top F3), a rich Jewish banker; CARDINAL SILVESTER (bs-bar – top F3 sung, G3 *sprechstimme*); THADDEUS (ten – top B3), Roman Catholic priest; FLOREA (m-sop – low G#2), a gypsy, Meisel's servant; AN OLD BLIND WOMAN (sop); TWO SORCERERS (tenors); THREE RUFFIANS (tenors); SEPULCHRAL VOICE (ten); A GYPSY FIDDLER (ten – top C4), off-stage.

Chorus: TTBB – A chorus of Jews; SSA – A chorus of Christians; SATB – A chorus of gypsies. Off-stage chorus of SSAATTBB plays the following perc: handbells, maracas, sistra, hand cym, sus cym, gongs, anvils, Orff xyl.

Orchestration: picc, 2 fl, 3 ob (Eng hrn), 2 cl, bs cl, 2 bsn, contra bsn, 4 hrn, 3 trp, 3 trb, tba, 5 perc, hp, strings, cel, pia.

Synopsis: The subject of this work is a legendary occurrence in fifteenth century Prague, wherein the Rabbi of the Jewish ghetto, fearful of persecution, makes a Golem: an artificial being molded from the clay of the banks of the river Moldau. The appearance of the fearful Golem strikes terror in the hearts of both the Christians and the Jews, precipitating a series of events, many historically verifiable, which culminates in the destruction of the Golem by the same magical means through which it was first created. Many ideas are dealt with in this work: the matter of magic, both black and white, religious persecution and intolerance, and historical drama. A love story is woven through the fabric of all these events and ideas as the Golem, gradually acquiring human characteristics, falls in love with the Rabbi's daughter, Rachel.

Materials: SMC.

Notes: Requires large forces with highly skilled singers, instrumentalists and technical staff. Must be performed in a theatre.

THOMAS M. SLEEPER

Aceldama

Music by **Thomas M. Sleeper** (b. 1956). A dramatic opera with libretto in English by the composer. *Aceldama*, Greek for "field of blood," is very loosely based on the story of Cain and Abel from the Bible, referencing in particular the field where Cain slew Abel in the first recorded fratricide of the Judeo-Christian tradition. This tragedy is then taken through the ages to the Nazi Germany death camps and beyond. Other elements are fused from accounts of the Holocaust, Jewish texts, the Upanishads, the Arthurian legend, Dante's *Inferno*, the Faust legend, and other sources.

Commissioned by Joe Nicastri, artist. There has been no fully staged performance, only some concert performances of extracted suites. According to Sleeper, "If there was one I consider the "premiere" it would be with the Ruse State Philharmonic in Ruse, Bulgaria with the Danube Chorus December 1997. I also extracted a chamber suite lasting about 15 minutes for Soprano, Tenor (Adam) and 7 instruments that was used for performances in gallery spaces in conjunction with the exhibition of Joe Nicastri's "A Surplus of Memory" in Florida and New York."

Amidst Neo-Romantic tonality exists considerable dissonance, though quite melodic and lyrical. Highly effective orchestral colors and dramatic effects with three orchestral pieces for dramatic action or choreography. Some Latin. Some Sprechstimme. Continuous music and action.

One act in three parts with three different settings: The birth of Cain and Abel; 1940's – Adam and Eve's apartment; Auschwitz. The various scenes are enacted in and around these settings. Duration: 65 minutes.

Roles: ADAM (ten – top B3); EVE (sop – G#2-Ab4); CAIN (ten – top Bb3); NARRATOR (bar – top A3)

Chorus: SATB, at times a Greek chorus, at times prisoners. Some rhythmic speaking and whispering.

Orchestration: 2 fl (picc), 2 ob, 2 cl, 2 bsn, 4 hrn, 2 trp in C, 2 trb, bs trb, tba, timp, 3 perc (large battery of instruments), pia/cel, hp, str

Synopsis: Cain tries variations on the sacrifices from his crops but all attempts are rejected by God. Eve questions why God will not accept Cain's sacrifices. The answer comes in the form of a vision. Cain slays his brother Abel (and the House of Ahab, and the Ache Indians, and the Kurds and Armenians; Cambodians, Bosnians, Apache; Rwandans; Ukranians, etc., from generation to generation). A simple set of a 1940's apartment is revealed. Adam and Eve are packing for relocation. Eve believes they will be killed, but Adam believes in the future. His passionate plea with Eve is rejected by a flat "I cannot risk bringing another into this place, it is unclean." A train whistle is heard as the apartment is transformed into a concentration camp.

The chorus streams in from the back of the auditorium, portraying the Jewish prisoners as they arrive at the death camp. Cain is a Nazi guard. A selection of Lehar's *The Merry Widow* intended to pacify and deceive the murmuring prisoners can be heard. He complains of a wound that will not heal – a wound related to the death of his brother. The set changes once more to reveal images of the Holocaust. Off-stage voices grow in intensity: "*Auschwitz* – how long, O Lord, dost thou not avenge our blood on them that dwell on the earth," ending with three intoned wails of "*Aceldama!*" An over-powering voice demands, "Where is your brother? What have you done? The blood of your brother cries out to me from the ground!" This sound is cut off and we hear the *Dies Irae* offstage. Smoke from the ovens envelopes the stage as Adam searches for Eve. Adam encounters Cain/Amfortas, accusing him of atrocities; but Cain merely holds a mirror to Adam stating "I am you!"

Adam laments his lost soul (Eve), and recounts their relationship. In the final scene, an encounter between God (chorus) and Adam ensues. Accusations are cast as to who created and abandoned whom. Adam finally realizes that he is responsible for his own actions and that he has been given back his life, able to make choices and allowed to die. The opera ends in a powerful orchestral Postlude.

Materials: UP – parts available for rental, scores for purchase. Revised February 6, 2000

Notes: Best performed in a theatre. A musically and dramatically difficult work to produce. The fast paced time changes, multiple characterizations, segmented episodes within 64 minutes leave one a bit breathless and at times confused. Nevertheless, there are some very powerful moments both textually and musically. CD available: Albany Troy 541 Records.

DOUGLAS SMITH

Judith

Music by **Douglas Smith** (b. 1949). A Sacred Opera with libretto in English by Pauline Smolin, freely adapted from the Apocryphal Book of Judith.

Premiered September 4, 1982, Peterloon Festival, Cincinnati, OH.

Mostly nineteenth century sounds with twentieth century influences. Set numbers, use of electronic sounds. Episodic. *Sprechstimme*; some spoken lines. Continuous texture.

One act, three parts. Setting: 12th century B.C. Prologue: A square in Bethulia; Part I, sc. 1: The palace of Nebuchadnezzar; sc. 2: Same as Prologue; sc. 3: Holofornes' camp outside Bethulia; sc. 4: Same as Prologue. Part II: Same as I, 3. Part III: Same as Prologue. While the work is divided into scenes, the separation of scenes is best accomplished with lighting. Duration: 60 minutes.

Roles: NEBUCHADNEZZAR (bs), King of Israel; HOLOFORNES (high bar – top A3), his chief General; VAGAO (ten – top G#3), a servant to Holofornes; JUDITH (m-sop), a young widow of Bethulia; ESTER (sop – top Bb4), her handmaid; OZIAS (sp), civil leader of Bethulia; ELIACHIM, (bs-bar – top F3), Rabbi of Bethulia; WATCHMAN (bar), of Bethulia; NAOMI (sp), friend to Judith and Ester; A BABYLONIAN GUARD (bs).

Chorus: SATB – Hebrews of Bethulia.

Orchestration: 28 member chamber orchestra and pre-recorded tape (15 section DBX Stereo).

Synopsis: Nebuchadnezzar declares himself "God of the earth" and sends Holofornes to demand obeisance from the surrounding nations. Holofornes sets out on his mission, meeting with success until he arrives at Bethulia where he meets with determined resistance from the Hebrews who have been living in peace for a hundred years. Vagao and Holofornes find their water supply and cut it off. Finally mad with thirst, the Hebrews cry out to their leaders to surrender to the Babylonians. Their cries bring Judith out of seclusion. She reprimands them for their loss of faith and asks for five days and their prayers. She prays to God for strength, exchanges her mourning clothes for a seductive gown, oils and perfumes her body, and with her friend Ester, sets out for Holofornes' camp. Holofornes grants Judith an interview and apparently accepts her story that she has been sent by God to lead him to victory over the Hebrews without bloodshed. He invites her to dine with him that evening and she accepts. She succumbs to his desire and they sleep together. Insane with remorse from yielding to him, Judith insists that she is unclean but finally does what she came to do; she takes

Holofornes' life and decapitates him. Judith and Ester quickly leave camp, returning to her own people. Ester tells Judith that their army has defeated the Babylonians. They join the people in celebration as all give thanks to God that He alone is perfect.

Materials: Unpublished. From the librettist.

Notes: Equally adaptable for performance in a theatre or house of worship.

JOSEP SOLER

La tentation de Saint Antoine – The Temptation of Saint Antoine

Music by **Josep Soler** (b. 1935). A Sacred Legend Opera with libretto in French by Gustave Flaubert.

Composed in 1967.

Twentieth century harmonic influences, considerable dissonance and atonality. Rhythmic complexities, use of *sprechstimme*.

Two acts. Duration: 120 minutes.

Roles: L'INSPIRE (ten); SAINT ANTOINE (sp); TERTULLIEU (ten – top B3); BASILIDE (bs – low El); MANES (sop – top Bb4); HILARION (bs-bar – G1-sustained F3); LE REINE DE SABA (m-sop – top A4); LE GRIFFON (ten); LE BUDDHA (male), speech song, chanted and spoken; LE SADHUZAG (sp); LE DIABLE (bar – top G3); Une FEMME (m-sop – top Ab4); ISIS (sop – A2-C5).

Chorus: SATTBB

Orchestration: picc, 3 fl, 2 ob, Eng hrn, 2 cl, bs cl, 2 bsn, contra bsn, 4 hrn, 2 trp, 3 trb, tba, perc, 2 hp, strings, cel, vib, xyl, pia, glock, org.

Materials: SMC (© 1968).

Notes: Very difficult work both vocally and orchestrally. Production requires a well equipped theatre.

DAVID SOSIN

Esther

Music by **David Sosin** (b. 1951). A Sacred Opera with libretto in English by Sari Magaziner based on the Biblical Book of Esther.

Commissioned and premiered by the Children's Music Theatre of Long Island, March, 1977.

Traditional harmonic textures, neo-classical, Puccini-like in melodic contour. Continuous texture.

One act, nine scenes. Setting: The Court of Shushan in Persia, Biblical times. Duration: 50 minutes.

Roles: NARRATOR (sp); ESTHER and PARVINA, a dancer (sop); MORDECAI (bar); AHASHUERUS (ten – many A3); VASHTI (m-sop), his wife; SHULA (m-sop), a singer; RULA (m-sop), Esther's handmaiden; ZERESH (m-sop), Haman's wife; HAMAN (bar). The four m-sop roles may be sung by the same person.

Dance: One dance solo. Some "belly" dancing.

Orchestration: Piano.

Synopsis: Esther and her cousin Mordecai affirm their Jewish heritage. At the same time, King Ahashuerus has disposed of his disobedient Queen and is in the process of choosing a new one. Shula and Parvita sing and dance for him, but he is most pleased by the purity and simplicity of Esther, who is named the new Queen. Mordecai learns of a plot to kill the Jews and warns Esther, who is reluctant to emerge from her safe position. She would be in danger if her Jewish identity was revealed. She does eventually go to the King at the risk of her life, and the King agrees to a banquet given by Esther for the King and Haman. Haman, the evil advisor, who plans the Jews' destruction, schemes with his wife Zeresh. When he is brought to the King for advice on how to reward a hero, he details elaborate plans, thinking himself the recipient. Learning that Mordecai is to be rewarded for saving the King from assassins, he vows redoubled revenge on the Jews. At the banquet, Esther reveals her identity and exposes Haman, who is quickly disposed, being hung on the very gallows he had built for Mordecai. Mordecai is named the new advisor and a new joyous era begins.

Materials: Unpublished. AMC and the composer.

Notes: Suitable for performance in either a theatre or house of worship.

RICHARD STRAUSS

Salome

Music by **Richard Strauss** (1864-1949). An Opera with libretto in German by the composer, based on Hedwig Lachmann's translation of Oscar Wilde's play. Loosely adapted from the Biblical account recorded in Matthew 14.

Premiered September 9, 1905 in Dresden.

Complex harmonic structures with straying tonalities; considerable chromaticism and dissonance. Instrumentally conceived. Declamatory vocal lines, disjunct and often speech-like. Through-composed.

One act. Setting: A large hall in Herod's palace, Galilee, ca. 30 A.D. Duration: 90 minutes.

Major Roles: SALOME (dram sop – Gb2-B4), enormously demanding role both vocally and dramatically. Must be attractive and able to appear convincing in the Dance of the Seven Veils. HEROD (ten – A1-Bb3), neurotic King of Palestine; high intensity acting demands, often speech-like passages; bel canto not required. HERODIAS (m-sop – C3-Bb4), dark, harsh vocal qualities. JOKANAAN (bar – Ab1-F#3), the Baptist.

Minor Roles: PAGE OF HERODIAS (cont); FIVE JEWS (4 ten, bs); NARRABOTH (ten); TWO SOLDIERS (2 bs); SLAVE (sop); CAPPADOCIAN (bs).

Dance: Dance of the Seven Veils by Salome.

Orchestration: picc, 3 fl, 2 ob, Eng hrn, hecklephone, 4 cl, Eb cl, bs cl, 3 bsn, contra bsn, 6 hrn, 4 trp, 4 trb, tba, timp (2 players), 6 perc, 2 hp, cel, str. Stage: org. Reduced orchestration: 3 fl, 2 ob, Eng hrn, 2 cl, bs cl, 3 bsn, 4 hrn, 3 trp, 3 trb, tba, timp, 3 perc, hp, cel, str

Synopsis: Jokanaan has been imprisoned for speaking out against the sins of Herodias. Salome, daughter of Herodias, has taken a special interest in Jokanaan, a Prophet, who proclaims that the long awaited Messiah has come. Salome entices her lover Narraboth, a soldier, to grant her entrance to Jokanaan's cell. She begs Jokanaan to fulfill her lustful desires. He rejects and curses her. Meanwhile, Narraboth can bear her seductive behavior no longer and kills himself. In the midst of a celebration, Herod asks Salome to dance for him. She agrees but only on the condition that after the dance, she be given the head of Jokanaan. Herod, fearful and dismayed, cannot break the oath he made to her in front of his court. Salome lustily dances for him after which the bloody head of Jokanaan is brought to her on a silver platter. Insatiable and delirious, she kisses the dead lips of the head while Herod looks on in horror and Herodias with glee. Herod orders her crushed by the soldiers.

Materials: BH. Eng translations available by Josef Blatt, John Gutman, Tom Hammond, Alfred Kalisch, Sylvan Levin, Maria Massey-Pelikan, Polacheck, Alan Price-Jones.

Notes: Must be performed in a theatre with extensive technical resources. Requires highly trained instrumentalists, singers, and production personnel.

IGOR STRAVINSKY

The Flood

Music by **Igor Stravinsky** (1882-1971). A Sacred Music Drama with libretto in English arranged by Robert Craft. Primarily taken from the Book of Genesis, and the York and Chester Miracle Plays. In the manner of a miracle play.

Premiered June 14, 1962 on CBS-TV as *Noah and the Flood*. Staged premiere August 21, 1962, Santa Fe, NM.

Atonal, complex rhythmic and harmonic structures; difficult staging and production problems. Spoken narrative.

One act with short Prelude. Setting: Before and during the flood. Duration: 25 minutes.

Roles: GOD (2 bs simultaneously); LUCIFER, SATAN (ten); NOAH (sp); NOAH'S WIFE (sp); NOAH'S SONS (sp); NARRATOR-CALLER (sp).

Chorus: SAT – Greek chorus. Sings Latin *Te deum*.

Dance: The flood and the building of the ark sections are choreographed.

Orchestration: 3 fl (picc), alt fl, 2 ob, Eng hrn, 2 cl, bs cl, contra bs cl, 2 bsn, contra bsn, 4 hrn, 3 trp, 2 ten trb (alt trb), bs trb, tba, timp, xyl, marimba, cym, bs dr, cel, pia, hp, strings. Difficult and often soloistic; colorful.

Synopsis: The Prelude opens with a brief orchestral piece followed by a choral *Te Deum*. The Narrator and cast summarize the creation of the world, of man, and the fall of Lucifer. The audience is then told of Adam and Eve's dismissal from Eden, and how Satan is forced to crawl on his belly the remainder of his days. We are then taken to the time of Noah and God's command to build an ark. A choreographed orchestral section is devoted to the building of the ark. The animals enter the completed ark and with some persuasion from her sons, Noah's wife also enters. This flood itself is again a choreographed orchestral interlude. The storm subsides; God places a rainbow in the sky as His covenant with Noah.

Materials: BH (Ger and Eng)

Notes: Best performed in a theatre with ample pit space. Dramatic action is conducive to presentation in a house of worship.

PAUL O. STUART

The Little Thieves of Bethlehem

Music by **Paul O. Stuart** (b. 1956). A Christmas opera with libretto in English by Sally M. Gall loosely based on the manger scene with additional texts taken from Exodus, Judith, and the Psalms.

Premiered December 7, 1997 in Rochester, NY.

Highly melodic and lyrical. Conventional harmonies throughout; sparse accompaniment; some spoken lines. Set numbers with several arias, duets, trios, and ensembles. Original music with the addition of the carol tune, *Lo, How A Rose E're Blooming*. Dramatically conceived in the style of the Medieval passion plays.

One act, two scenes. The setting is the inn and the stable of Bethlehem, where the Holy Family is residing twelve days after the birth of Jesus (Epiphany). Duration: 55 minutes.

Major Roles: MARY (m-sop – low tess); JOSEPH (bar – top F3); INNKEEPER (ten – top Bb3); INNKEEPER'S WIFE (m-sop); SISTER (treble or sop); BROTHER (treble, sop, or boy sop)

Minor Roles: PEACEKEEPER (sp); RETINUE (treble or sop); FIRST KING (bar – top F3); SECOND KING (bar); THIRD KING (bar)

Chorus: SATB – Villagers. Children's Chorus – mostly unison

Orchestration: 10 players: fl, ob, 3 trp, hp, hpsch, 2 perc (3 cym, tamb, large, medium, and small toms, hand dr, finger cym), vc

Synopsis: Two young orphans, a brother and sister, are the talk of the village as they seem to be the center of mischief as well as of miraculous events. The neighbors refer to them as the "little thieves", and indeed the brother steals a favorite kerchief from the Innkeeper and food from his wife's kitchen. The Innkeeper is furious, but little does he know that these items are going to help the Holy Family. When the hostile Innkeeper finds that his kerchief has been miraculously changed from linen to a cloth of gold, all is forgiven. The servant of the three visiting Kings, Retinue, invites the little thieves to accompany him and his masters back to their homelands. However, in a moment of inspiration, the Innkeeper's Wife persuades the two orphans along with her husband to join in making a new family in Bethlehem.

Materials: VMM – all parts and scores available

Notes: Works particularly well in a house of worship provided there is adequate space for the inn, the stable, and the orchestra. A theatre would allow for a more elaborate set. Very accessible score, delightful and heartwarming – excellent work for all ages. A dissertation by Sandra Boysen on Stuart's operas is available (see Appendix C).

CONRAD SUSA

The Wise Women

Music by **Conrad Susa** (b. 1935). A Christmas mystery fable based on a "handed down" story adapted by the composer and set to lyrics in English by Philip Littell. The story is loosely based on the Biblical story of the three Wise Men.

Premiered in 1994 and commissioned by the American Guild of Organists for their Biennial National Convention held in Dallas, TX.

Uses both original and traditional hymns throughout the work. Set numbers with some arias and ensembles. Lyrical and melodic with traditional harmony and scattered dissonances. Choral and ensemble sections are typically well written and rich in texture. Recitatives are based on chant style.

One act with a Prologue and five scenes, but with continuous action. According to the composer, the work is designed to be presented in a church with the action placed as follows: The road in the church aisles; the encampment before the altar; the manger at the altar; and the heavens behind the altar. Duration: ca. 45 minutes.

Major Roles: THE STAR (3 sop: sop 1 – top B4; sop 2 – top G4; sop 3 – top G4); Three Wise Men: THE YOUTH (ten), THE HUSBAND (bar), THE OLD MAN (bs); Three Wise Women: THE MAIDEN (sop – top Bb4), THE GOODWIFE (sop), THE CRONE (m-sop)

Minor Roles: MARY (sop); JOSEPH (silent); BABY (silent – hopefully)

Children: Volunteers from the Congregation – do not sing

The Congregation: Sings Hymns Nos. 2, 5a, 11, 13 – both traditional and original hymns

Chorus: SSAATTBB – Shepherds and their Flocks
SATB chamber choir – Retinue of the Wise Men
9 solo voices SSA, AA*T, TBB or SSS, A*TT, BBB – Host of Angels
(* = Counter Tenor if possible)

Dance: One dance is required at the entrance of the Shepherds and their Flocks. This could be a simple folk dance by the characters, or a small dance troupe representing them.

Orchestration: In the Chancel: fl (picc), classical gui, hp, perc (vib, glock, Mark Tree, Bell Tree, cym, gong, tri, Tabor), Portativ Org
Grand Organ for the hymns
In various places: small handbell choir placed as needed
(The orchestra should move around as needed. The harp and vibes are part of the Nativity Scene, near the Angels. The conductor may move about as needed. Percussion in No. 5 are to be played by members of the chamber choir.)

Synopsis: The three-person Star enters from three different places and moves toward the altar inviting all to follow. The three Wise Men, three Wise Women, and their retinue follow the Star to the altar. There ensues a debate as to whether or not the Wise Women should accompany the Wise Men to the actual meeting with the King. The Wise Men find excuses why the Wise Women should not go with them: "Women's brains are smallest when their hearts are big with love;" "They will embarrass us;" "Do you remember when . . ." The Wise Men leave while the Wise Women decide it would be better if "The lion watches the gazelle: He will catch her! And the silent hawk the hare: She will catch him." Furthermore, the men insist they seek an adult king while the women are certain the monarch will be a baby. Disappointed and angry, the women lament their fates and retire. As the women sleep, the Holy Mother and Child appear to them in a vision, allowing them to see the baby before the men do.

The scene shifts to the manger scene with the Shepherds and their Flocks entering with singing and dancing. The Wise Men enter dismayed to find a baby instead of an adult king on a throne. Suddenly a mighty sound of thunder, fire, storm, etc. is heard, and the Angels appear. The Angels become terribly confused by the number 3: 3 Holy Family members, the little Baby is a trinity, 3 times, 3 Angels; 3 Wise Men; but where are their three wives? As the Angels finally break into a *Gloria in excelsis Deo*, ultimately joined by the entire company and congregation, the Star gathers children from the audience to come and see the Baby in the manger. The Wise Men leave; but suddenly the Wise Women appear to play with Mary and the Baby. Eventually, all become tired and fall asleep at the manger. Exhausted, the Wise Men enter, amazed to see their wives sleeping amid all the strangers. Humbled yet elated, they concede that their gifts were not enough to give their Lord! What is the adequate gift, they ask their wives? It is love, they reply, while the company echoes the obvious answer to the riddle. Satisfied, they all return to their homeland spreading the light of Christ.

Materials: ECS – parts and scores available

Notes: Designed to be played in a church, though the sanctuary must have aisles large enough for action, and a chancel/altar area large enough for the many chorus and principal characters. An entertaining work with a strong message and involvement of cast and audience alike. Several hymns and responses are sung by the audience. Solo roles are not difficult. Requires strong direction and production coordination.

DONALD SWANN

Baboushka

Music by **Donald Swann** (1923-1994). A Christmas Musical Legend with libretto in English by Arthur Scholey based on the Russian Legend of Baboushka (meaning 'Grandmother').

Premiered 1981 by the BBC.

Conventional harmonies with folk and some "pop" styles. Continuous texture; mostly simple strophic and modified-strophic forms. Melodic; requires "classical" vocal production.

One act. Setting: During the time of the birth of Christ in the home of Baboushka. Duration: ca. 35 minutes.

Roles: BABOUSHKA (m-sop – low E2, low tess at times). The three kings are all medium range: MELCHIOR (bs), BALTHAZAR (ten), CASPAR (bar).

Chorus: May be SSAA, SATB, children or a combination of these. The chorus should be large enough so that it will not be vocally too weak for its division into three sections later in the opera. When it divides, section 1 eventually processes off and may return as the three kings, servants and attendants. Section 2 becomes the villagers (four-part harmony). Section 3 remains the Greek chorus throughout and may be used to set up scenery as well. Supers may be used for the procession, Mary, Joseph, and other nativity-scene characters.

Orchestration: pia and sd dr. Optional orchestral score and parts which were used in 1981 and 1982 TV productions are available.

Synopsis: The chorus introduces us to the Christmas story by relating the shepherds' encounter with the angels. Baboushka enters through the audience with her basket of toys, interrupting the story of the shepherds. She is welcomed and encouraged to explain her unexpected appearance. As she does so, the entire cast begins to dramatize the action of her story. Villagers encourage her to come outside and look at the unusual star – however, she is too busy. Suddenly a procession followed by three kings is sighted, but again, Baboushka is too busy to pay attention. The kings come to her door, requesting a place to rest. She hesitatingly welcomes them into her home. Having rested, they invite her to join them in following the star to see the promised child of light. Again, she is too busy, her house is untidy and she has no gift – but she promises to follow soon. The kings depart. The next morning she is finally ready and leaves to find the child. When she arrives at the manger, it is empty. She is told of the angels' warning to Mary and Joseph of King Herod's threat and they have left for Egypt with the child. Baboushka realizes she is too late. Angels minister to her sorrow, telling her that if she will truly seek, He will be found in the good and the meek. She responds by saying that she will go seeking and making amends until the world ends. Baboushka leaves the auditorium with her concluding lines sung to the audience, "Is the Christ-child here? Tell me. I must find him... Is he here?" Thus, she leaves as she came, continuing to search and tell the story of her journey.

Materials: The composer. Drum part in VS.

Notes: Ideally suited for performance in a church/cathedral. VS contains detailed production and staging suggestions, full libretto and the drum part. A versatile work with many performance options.

Bontzye Schweig

Music by **Donald Swann** (1923-1994). A Yiddish morality musical with words in English by Leslie Paul, based on a story by Isaac Loeb Perez.

First performed at Edinburgh Festival, England, August, 1968.

Musically accessible for children and non-professional adults. Narrative. Melodic. Eclectic and somewhat cabaret in compositional style.

One act. Setting: The street of an East European ghetto; then heaven. Duration: 30 minutes.

Roles: NARRATOR (sp).

Pantomime Roles: BONZYE SCHWEIG; MARSHAL; FATHER ABRAHAM; PUBLIC PROSECUTOR; DEFENSE COUNSEL; SMALL BOY; CARRIAGE OWNER.

Supernumeraries: Police, Crowd, Ambulance men.

Chorus: A mixed group of adults and children representing children and angels – mostly unison, some two-part and rarely three-part.

Orchestration: Keyboard alone or Piano-organ arrangement available and trp or shofar.

Synopsis: Bontzye is a poor mid-European Jew who has suffered degradations and humiliations since childhood but has remained silent and unprotesting throughout. On his way from a delivery of sacks in an East European ghetto, Bontzye sees a runaway carriage careening through the streets. He seizes the horse's head and stops the carriage but is dragged under the wheels in the process. The rider of the carriage, a wealthy man, rewards Bontzye with an offer of a fine job, but Bontzye soon dies of his injuries. When he arrives in Heaven, the heavenly court decides to reward Bontzye with an eternal life of full celestial pleasures and privileges.

Material: GAL.

Notes: Minimal sets and props. Best suited for presentation in a theatre. Numerous and detailed stage directions are in the VS. Also works well as a concert piece.

Candle Tree

Music by **Donald Swann** (1923-1994). A Christmas Opera with libretto in English by Arthur Scholey, based on the legend of St. Boniface and the first Christmas tree.

Composed in 1981; premiered December 21, 1989, St. Botolph's, London.

Harmonically conventional with twentieth century dissonances, changing and mixed meters and some rhythmic complexities. Folk elements, melodic; frequent unaccompanied passages; plain-chant.

One act. Setting: The sacred grove of Odin. Duration: ca. 40 minutes.

Roles: BONIFACE (bar); HEADMAN (bs – low F#1); PRIEST (ten), of Odin; BOY (boy sop); MOTHER (cont).

Chorus: SSAATTBB – Worshipers of Odin; TB – Monks.

Orchestration: Rec (sop, descant, treble, ten, bs), bsn, wind noise, wood perc sounds, dr, sus cym, metal perc sounds, glock, tubular bells, hp, vla da gamba. It is suggested that all singers and instrumentalists be in costume and participate in the action, thus requiring memorization of parts which are all quite brief.

Synopsis: Gathered around the ancient sacred oak tree, the worshipers of Odin prepare to make a sacrifice of a small boy to their god. As they perform their rituals led by the Priest and Headman, a group of chanting Monks can be heard approaching, followed by Boniface. Boniface frees the boy and then challenges the people with the message that there is a living God they may worship – that both Odin and the oak tree they worship are dead and deaf. Incensed, they call on Odin to take vengeance on Boniface as he takes an ax and cuts down their "holy" oak tree. As the people see that Odin does not act, they are gradually swayed by Boniface's message of the living Christ. Boniface then asks his Monks to plant the new green and living tree they have brought along. He delivers the message of Christ's birth, death and resurrection by drawing parallels between the old tree and Christ's cross, and the new tree and His resurrection to new life; the people gradually join in planting the new tree. In a large final ensemble, in which the audience may participate, a folk carol is sung in praise of Christ and new life, symbolized in the "Candle Tree" they are planting.

Materials: Unpublished. The composer.

Notes: Works well in either a theatre or house of worship. Its message is conducive to inclusion in a worship service.

Perelandra

Music by **Donald Swann** (1923-1994). A Music Drama with libretto in English by David Marsh, based on the novel by C. S. Lewis.

Premiered in 1969, Swarthmore College in Philadelphia.

Mostly traditional harmonies with considerable chromaticism and twentieth century influences. Arias, accompanied recitatives, continuous texture except for occasional spoken dialogue. Highly melodic.

Three acts (an early version was in two acts). Time: Sometime in the future. Act I, sc. 1: Ransom's cottage; sc. 2: The cabin of Weston's spaceship; sc. 3: An island on Perelandra. Act II: The island. Act III, sc. 1: The island; sc. 2: The island; sc. 3: A cavern in the depths of Perelandra; sc. 4: The place of thrones. Duration: approximately 2 hours.

Major Roles: ELWIN RANSOM (high bar – top G3 sustained, high tess), a philologist and a symbol of Christ; EDWARD WESTON (bs – low F#1), a professor of science at the University of Cambridge and numerous other titles – ultimately Satan; LADY (sop), mother of her race.

Minor Roles: COLIN HUMPHREY (bs-bar), a physician; C. S. LEWIS (ten); THE KING (ten); SPIDER (bs-bar); A VOICE, could be taken from the chorus or be Ransom's voice amplified.

Supers: A Dragon and many other unusual but beautiful animals of Perelandra.

Chorus: SSAATTBB – commentators on the action from a stationary unobtrusive location.

Orchestration: 2 fl, 2 ob, 2 cl, 2 bsn, 2 hrn, 2 trp, 2 trb, timp, 2 perc, pia, hp, strings. Also one piano or two piano arrangements are available.

Synopsis: Ransom, having been taken away from earth by a force from outer space, has informed Lewis, his friend, that he will be returned to earth at a specific time and that he is to have a physician on hand for testing and verification. Thus, Humphrey, a physician, and Lewis await Ransom's return. Suddenly and mysteriously, he returns in the same glass coffin in which he was taken away. Humphrey notes the bleeding on Ransom's foot, a wound that somehow cannot be healed. Ransom then describes his trip to Perelandra as an exhilarating and beautiful experience in paradise. The scene changes to Weston's spaceship in which he is making last minute preparations for a landing.

The story now returns to Ransom's arrival on Perelandra, a place of floating islands. He meets Lady who offers him food. Weston arrives and promptly sets up his experiments. When a Dragon approaches, Weston panics and is about to shoot it when Ransom stops him, insisting that he must not bring death to Perelandra. Weston, angered, calls on his own force, claiming now that he will become both God and the Devil. He collapses in a spasm.

In Act II, Weston revives, but with a somewhat transformed personality. He proceeds to entice Lady to explore territory forbidden by Maleldil, her Father. She explains that Maleldil's love for her and the King make them free to choose whatever path they desire, but their love for Maleldil makes many paths impossible to choose. Meanwhile, Ransom tries his best to stop Weston's treachery and to dissuade Lady from following his evil and enticing suggestions. Weston explains to Lady that he has come to Perelandra to bring death and to make her wise. Ransom's attempts to save Lady grow weaker until he and Weston finally come to blows. Weston runs into the sea with Ransom in pursuit. In Act III, Weston and Ransom again do battle. Ransom at one point makes the sign of the cross, infuriating Weston. As they struggle, the chorus sings Ransom's name repeatedly as though urging him on. Ransom, seemingly lost, cries, "My God, my God, why hast thou forsaken me." Lady meanwhile has been in a deep sleep caused by Maleldil to prevent her from seeing the awful battle. The King explains to her that if Ransom fails to rid Perelandra of Weston, death will walk beside them all their days.

We next find Weston and Ransom in a cavern continuing to battle. Ransom is severely wounded having been bitten in the foot by Weston while Ransom has successfully pushed a huge boulder on Weston's head, sending him over a cliff into a sea of fire. Ransom returns to the King and Lady, informing them that the enemy is destroyed and Perelandra has been spared evil and death.

Materials: From GBAR.

Notes: Highly symbolic text but obvious in its intent and message. Lighting design of utmost importance. Should be played in a theatre. A powerful and highly effective drama.

The Visitors

Music by **Donald Swann** (1923-1994). A Chamber Opera with libretto in English by Arthur Scholey. A modern treatment of the Tolstoy tale concerning Martin, the cobbler.

Premiered in the Malthouse Theatre, Sussex, England, July 28, 1989.

Traditional harmonies, some folk elements; melodically conceived. Some unaccompanied solo passages with traditional arias, duets.

Two acts with prologue. Prologue: A room in a deserted house. Act I: In a hospital waiting room. Act II: The same. Duration: 75 minutes.

Roles: CHRISTOPHER COOPER (bs-bar – E1-F3); ANNA (cont – low G2), his wife; MARIA (m-sop), their daughter; RICHARD (boy sop – top F#4), her 10-year old son; DOCTOR (bar – A1-F#3); ANDREW (ten – top B3), Christopher's brother, requires a strong actor.

Orchestration: piano and perc (vib, tubular bells, glock, bs glock, woodblocks, sus cym, sn dr, xyl, bell tree, tam tam, military dr)

Synopsis: Andrew Cooper is a patient in a modern psychiatric hospital, following a tragic car accident in which his wife and son died but which he survived. He feels himself responsible for their deaths and has withdrawn into himself to the extent that he is unable, or unwilling, to communicate with or even recognize anyone. In the prologue, Andrew's brother, Christopher, has gone to Andrew's empty house to collect some family belongings. Beside Andrew's bed, he finds a copy of an old book of Tolstoy's stories. He recalls that the book was given to them both by their father when they were boys. He remembers that they once acted out their favorite story, that of the old cobbler, for their father, and that Andrew played the cobbler. Christopher decides to take the book to the hospital.

At the hospital, the Doctor encourages Christopher to read the story and suddenly there is a response from Andrew – but a strange one. Andrew responds in the character of Martin, the cobbler. In order to sustain this response, Christopher finds that he has to continue the scene in character, that of the priest and the roadsweeper. One by the one, Maria, Richard and Anna are drawn into the acting out of the story. Feeling their way into the characters, they discover parallels with their "real" world.

A lonely shoe cobbler, Martin, has just lost his wife and children, and after the loss of his son, despairs of God. Then in a dream, he hears a voice which says: "I will visit you tomorrow." He takes it to be the voice of Christ and spends all the next day at the window, looking for Christ to come. During the course of the day, he befriends an old roadsweeper, a destitute mother and her baby, and an old woman and a boy who has been caught stealing an apple from her. At the end of the day, he is once more in despair, believing that Christ has failed him. Again his vision returns, revealing to him the visitors he befriended during the day. The voice reminds him that Christ did indeed visit him in the people needing his love and help.

At the conclusion of the story, Christopher attempts to force a recognition of themselves as Andrew's relatives. This causes Andrew to break down and then relapse. The Doctor insists that they leave. When they have gone however, Andrew's plea, "Will they come again?" suggests the possibility of his eventual recovery.

Materials: Unpublished. The composer.

Notes: A musically accessible score with strong dramatic impact. Best performed informally or in an intimate auditorium.

ALEXANDER TCHEREPNIN

Le jeu de la Nativité – Nativity Play

Music by **Alexander Tcherepnin** (1899-1977). A Nativity Play with text taken from various sources compiled by the composer and including *Miracles de Notre Dame*. Original version for two sop, ten, bs, string quartet and perc. Revised to include chorus and full string orchestra.

Composed 1945. Commissioned by Madame Mathilde Amos. Premiered first postwar Christmas.

Conventional harmonic texture with some chromaticism and dissonance. Set numbers, through-composed.

One act, eight tableaus. See "Synopsis." Duration: 30 minutes.

Roles: ANGEL, ANGEL OF THE LAST JUDGMENT (sop – top Bb4); NOTRE DAME, MARY, THE VOICE OF A WOMAN, ST. THERESE DE L'ENFANT JESUS (sop); JOSEPH, ARCHANGEL MICHAEL, THE VOICE OF A MAN (ten); ARCHANGEL GABRIEL, THE SHEPHERD, ERNEST RENAN (bs).

Chorus: SSTB

Orchestration: perc (sn dr, cym, chimes), str

Synopsis: Scene 1: On the Road to Bethlehem. Mary and Joseph search for a place to spend the night. No shelter can be found until Joseph sees a stable where, in spite of the animals, it is a place for them to rest. Scene 2: The Stable. Mary gives thanks to God for the honor bestowed on her and places herself in His hands. The Angels sing praises to God. Scene 3: In the fields. A Shepherd, having been left alone for the moment, introduces himself to the audience. Night approaches and the Angel appears, announcing the birth of the Savior and then leading the Shepherd to the stable. Scene 4: The Stable. The Shepherd enters the stable and greets the Child, Mary and Joseph. The scene ends with an ensemble announcing to the world the birth of Jesus, our Saviour, and invites all mankind to rejoice. Scene 5: A Church during the French Revolution. A nude woman poses on the altar while a man invites the crowd to worship her as a symbol of nature. He claims Christianity is a fabrication of the priests while the drunken crowd cheers and dances. Scene 6: In Ernest Renan's library. Ernest Renan gives us a rationalistic interpretation of the life of Jesus, listing titles of "reliable" books about Jesus. He is interrupted and brought to silence by an orchestral fortissimo. Scene 7: In the convent. The Mystery of Love and Devotion are brought to us by St. Theresa. Scene 8: In a church. The play ends with the cast singing "Glory to God in the Highest."

Materials: CFP (© by M.P. Belaieff). Eng text by Edmund Pendleton.

Notes: Best suited for church performance. Offers a poignant message.

RANDALL THOMPSON

Nativity According to St. Luke

Music by **Randall Thompson** (1899-1984). A Christmas Musical Drama with libretto in English. Text taken from Luke 1 - 2 and a poem by Richard Rowlands (1565-1630).

Premiered December 12, 1961, Cambridge, England. Composed for the 200th anniversary of the dedication of Christ Church in Cambridge.

Highly melodic; declamatory vocal lines over conventional harmonic structures. Some modality. Arias, duets, quartet, 9 choruses.

Seven scenes. Setting: The age of Augustus; from the annunciation to Zacharias to the young boy Jesus at the Temple. Sc. 1: Zacharias and the Angel in the Temple; sc. 2: The Annunciation in a garden; sc. 3: The visitation in the house of Zacharias; sc. 4: The naming of John at the altar of the Temple; sc. 5: The Apparition in a pasture at night; sc. 6: The Adoration at the stable; sc. 7: The Song of Simeon in the Temple. Duration: 100 minutes.

Roles: ZACHARIAS (bar – F1-E3), a Priest and Censer of the Temple; ANGEL GABRIEL (ten – top A3); MARY (sop); ELIZABETH (cont – G2-G4, low tess), wife of Zacharias and cousin to Mary; ANNA (m-sop), a prophetess and aged widow; FIRST PRIEST (bar); SECOND PRIEST (bs); FOUR SHEPHERDS (boy sop, boy alt, ten, bs); JOSEPH (silent); SIMEON (bar – top F3).

Chorus: SATB – Angels, Shepherds and The Faithful.

Orchestration: fl, ob, cl, bsn, hrn, trp, perc (suspended cym, tri, tamb, church bells opt), timp, string quartet, cb, (additional strings are opt), org. Several long orchestral sections.

Synopsis: Zacharias comes to the Temple to pray. The Angel Gabriel appears and tells him his elderly wife is to bear him a son. Zacharias at first does not believe and is struck dumb because of his lack of faith. The scene shifts to Mary in her garden. Gabriel appears and tells her she is to bear the Son of God. She is frightened at first, but after Gabriel departs, she hurries to the house of Elizabeth to share the news. After John is born, Elizabeth and Zacharias take him to the Temple where he is named John in obedience to Gabriel's order. Zacharias regains his speech and stepping to the altar with Elizabeth and the child, blesses the Lord God of Israel. The scene shifts to the hillside, where the angel announces the birth of Jesus to the Shepherds. They hurry to the stable in Bethlehem to see the Christ Child. Mary sings a beautiful lullaby to the Child. The last scene returns us to the Temple where Simeon receives and blesses the Christ. The Holy Family and cast depart, singing Alleluias as they recess.

Materials: ECS.

Notes: Detailed staging suggestions in VS. Written for performance in a cathedral/church setting.

KARI TIKKA

Luther

Music by **Kari Tikka** (b. 1946). A biographical opera with libretto by Kari Tikka and Jussi Tapola based on events in the life of Martin Luther. Luther's hymn, *A Mighty Fortress is Our God*, is periodically woven into the musical fabric.

Premiered in Finnish, Rock Church, Helsinki, December 8, 2000. English language premiere: Central Lutheran Church, Minneapolis, October 25, 2001; German language premiere: Stadtkirche, Wittenberg, October 1, 2004.

Tonal with some dissonances; Neo-Romantic style dominates. Highly melodic vocal lines. Drama is intensified by highly rhythmic devises throughout. Some difficult ensembles.

Two acts, seven scenes – may be played on a unit set. Originally designed with specific churches in mind. The audience sings Luther's hymns between scenes. Duration: 125 minutes.

Roles: LUTHER (bs-bar – top G3), highly demanding role; SATAN (high col ten), in many guises; KATHARINA VON BORA (m-sop), Luther's wife; AVE VON SCHÖNFELD (sop); TENOR, in multiple roles; BASS, in multiple roles

Chorus: SATB – neighbors, parishioners

Dancers: Not required but highly effective if used as mimes throughout.

Orchestration: fl (picc), 2 ob, 2 bsn, 2 trp, 2 trb, 2 perc, str

Synopsis: Scene 1: Satan has summoned everyone to the medieval Dance of Death. Meanwhile, the Augustinian monk Martin Luther struggles to find a God of mercy. Scene 2: In his search and study of the Bible, Luther realizes that Christ has already destroyed Satan, broken the demands of the law, bound in chains the power of Death and Hell, and taken man's sins upon Himself. Scene 3: In the Leipzig disputation, Luther argues that the Pope has become the Antichrist. Excommunication from the church follows immediately for Luther. In his bold statement of 1521 in Worms, Luther refuses to revoke his theses: "Here I stand, I can do no other." Fearing both Rome and the people, Charles V declares Luther an outlaw. Scene 4: Secluded within the confines of Wartburg castle, Luther sets about to translate the entire Bible. Meanwhile, his colleagues incite people to rebellion and riot. Satan jumbles the ideas of the Reformation, setting off the bloody Peasants' War.

Scene 5: Having fallen in love with a runaway nun, Luther, now, an outlawed monk, marries Katharina von Bora in Wittenberg in 1525. Scene 6: Satan, disguised as

Erasmus of Rotterdam, continues to wreak havoc, declaring that man's free will should be fully exercised in his relationship to God. Luther's response is that we are saved by God's grace alone. Scene 7: In the final scene, Katie and Martin, now an old couple, reflect on the events of their lives. Satan again summons all to the modern Dance of Death, bringing us into the present day. The final scene includes a powerful adaptation/arrangement of *A Mighty Fortress is Our God*, sung by the entire company and audience.

Materials: FG – Parts, orchestra and piano scores available in English, German, and Finnish. DVD available at: www.ondine.net

Notes: Works particularly well in a house of worship setting with large acting space for a unit set. Theatrical lighting, period costumes, properties highly desirable. A powerful work, and in most aspects accessible, but professional soloists are needed.

STEPHEN TOSH

A Christmas Carol

Music by **Stephen Tosh** (20th century American). A Christmas Opera with libretto in English by Lloyd Severson, based on the novel by Charles Dickens.

Premiered by the University of Southern California Opera Theatre November 27, 1981, through grants from the National Opera Institute and the Opera Guild of Southern California.

Traditional harmonies with twentieth century influences. Stylistically, aleatoric. Chromatic. Recitatives, arias, ensembles. Melodic. Vocal lines tend toward high tessituras.

Two acts. Setting: London, England, 1885. Duration: 80 minutes.

Singing Roles: A number of singers may sing more than one role as indicated. SCROOGE (bar-ten); BOSTICTH, MARLEY, CHRISTMAS PRESENT (bar – top F#3); PEEPS, CHRISTMAS PAST (ten – needs strong low range); MRS. CRATCHIT, ELLEN, BEGGAR WOMAN (sop); MR. CRATCHIT, ADOLESCENT SCROOGE (ten); TINY TIM, BOY SCROOGE (boy sop); PETER, TOM (ten); MARTHA (sop); MARY (sop); MARK (boy sop); CHRISTMAS FUTURE (col sop); FEZZIWIG (bar and violinist – must play better than sing). Five roles taken from the chorus.

Speaking Roles: HARRY, THIEF, HAG

Chorus: SSATBB – Londoners; SA – Children

Dance: Folk dancing during the party scene.

Orchestration: Original orchestration for full orchestra. Composer's reduction as follows: fl, ob, cl, bsn, hrn, trp, trb, perc, 2 vln, vla, vc, cb, pia, hpsch, cel, org, hp

Synopsis: One cold foggy Christmas Eve, Scrooge is busy at work, paying no attention to the holiday atmosphere. When Bob Cratchit wishes him a Merry Christmas, Scrooge loudly derides the whole idea of Christmas and rudely refuses an invitation to dinner the next day; but he grudgingly allows him the next day off to celebrate Christmas. Later that night as he goes home, Scrooge is visited by the ghost of his deceased partner, Jacob Marley. Marley laments his perpetual state of sorrow because of his selfish and narrow way of life. He warns Scrooge that the Spirit of Christmas Past, Present and Future will each visit him this very night. Scrooge dismisses the message as a bad dream and goes to bed. No sooner has he climbed into bed than the three Spirits one by one pay him a visit. They present him with events and people he has and will encounter in his life past, present and future. Scrooge's dream is brought to a climax with the Spirit of the Future. Tiny Tim dies. A funeral procession takes him to a deserted graveyard where inscribed on a tombstone are the words: "Ebenezer Scrooge, miser; who lived unloved and alone." he insists that the future is not predestined and he will change it. He swears he will honor the spirit of Christmas throughout the year and that he will change.

Scrooge awakens with a feeling of lightness and joy realizing that he still has a chance to change and enjoy his last few years. He quickly runs to join his nephew's Christmas celebration, bringing joy and goodwill to everyone he meets.

Materials: Unpublished. From the composer or USC.

Notes: Best suited for performance in a theatre.

BRUCE TRINKLEY

Eve's Odds

Music by **Bruce Trinkley** (b. 1945). A comic chamber opera with libretto by J. Jason Charnesky, based on the biblical story of the "first sin", or the serpent's temptation of Eve and Adam.

Commissioned and premiered by Penn State University Opera Theatre. First performances were given on April 18 and 19, 1997 in the Pavilion Theatre on the Penn State University campus, conducted by Gregory Woodbridge and staged by Susan Boardman, Director of PSU Opera Theatre.

Tonality dominates though key centers tend to wander at times; traditional harmony throughout. Meter changes are frequent. Melodic and lyric lines for the singers are consistent. Several arias exist, but the music is through-composed. Accompaniment is supportive of the melodic material.

One act. The setting is the Garden of Eden, early in the morning of the second week. Duration: 45 minutes.

Major Roles: EVE (sop – top Bb4); SNAKE (bar – top G3), uses much hissing; ADAM (high bar or ten – top Ab3); LILITH (m-sop – Ab2-G4).

Minor Roles: GUARDIAN ANGEL (col sop – high Eb5); BAD ANGEL (m-sop).

Chorus: SSA – the chorus should always be visible but never directly part of the action on stage.

Orchestration: fl (picc), ob (Eng hrn), cl (bs cl, alto sax), bsn, 2 hrn, trp in C, trb, 3 vln I, 3 vln II, 2 vla, vc, str bs, keyboard (pia, cel, synth), 1 perc (bells, chimes, xyl, sn dr, wood block, sus cym, large and medium tam-tams, timp, bs dr).

Synopsis: A chorus of angelic voices sings a stately Alleluia. As they sing, they become more spirited and raucous, swaying in a wholly un-Anglican manner. Suddenly realizing their lack of dignity, they regroup and end the number in the best of High Church tradition! Eve appears, singing of the joys of this beautiful morning. She is suddenly joined by her friend, the Snake who has a sibilant problem with his esses! He sings a ballad about free will and assures Eve that the forbidden apple is not dangerous but will give her the very characteristics of God. Adam interrupts the conversation with his "naming song", explaining that he has had a very busy day naming everything he sees and feels, including the new word "danger". He doesn't know what it means, but he is certain that he and Eve will soon be in it. The Snake suggests that perhaps "danger" is the name of the new wardrobe that Adam has just built for Eve. The three play games by getting into and out of "danger" (the wardrobe)!

Unexpectedly, Lilith, Adam's first wife, enters, singing a habañera about her affair with Adam. Eve knew nothing about Lilith until now, and she flies into a rage and decides to eat the apple. Interrupting her, Adam exclaims that "he was waiting for the right moment" to tell her about Lilith. He then sings a love song and the couple is reconciled, ending the scene happily, but, the Bad Angel appears, tempting Eve further with her seductive "cha-cha-cha." The Guardian Angel appears just in time entreating (with her coloratura *cavatina* and *cabaletta*) Adam and Eve to strive for higher things. Pandemonium lets loose on stage until finally Eve shuts everybody up with her final decision to eat the apple. She does so! The chorus sings a blues of fate. Adam follows his heart, saying he will side with Eve, and he too eats the apple. Adam and Eve's eyes are opened and they name some new things: "nakedness", "eternity", and "maternity". They also go about inventing the middle class. As God is heard walking in the garden, the couple goes to face the unknown future. The chorus concludes with the statement: "God only knows."

Materials: Materials available from either the composer (Prof. Emeritus) or librettist at Penn State University, 226 Adams Avenue, University Park, PA 16803 (814) 237-2932. wbt1@psu.edu or jjc10@psu.edu

Notes: Can be presented in either a theatre or a house of worship. The production requirements are quite simple as are the musical and dramatic issues. This is a wonderfully funny and effective work.

ISAAC VAN GROVE

The Other Wise Man

Music by **Isaac Van Grove** (1891-1979). A Sacred Opera with libretto in English by the composer, freely arranged from the story of the same name by Henry Van Dyke.

Premiered July 14, 1959, Bentonville, Arkansas.

Continuous texture, traditional harmonies. Some set numbers, accompanied recitatives, melodic. Oriental and Hebraic influences.

One act, four scenes. Setting: Bethlehem and Jerusalem, covering from A.D. 1 to 33. Prologue; sc. 1: City of Ecbatana, Persia; sc. 2: By the walls of Babylon; sc. 3: A street in Bethlehem; sc. 4: Outside the Damascus Gate in Jerusalem. Duration: 65 minutes.

Roles: ARTABAN (ten – top Bb3, vocally and dramatically difficult – sings throughout), a wiseman of Magician Priesthood; STORYTELLER (bs), some spoken lines; ABGARUS (bs-bar), father of Artaban; ATOSSA (m-sop), mother of Artaban; ROXANA (sop), sister of Artaban; OLD HEBREW (ten or high bar); YOUNG MOTHER (m-sop); CAPTAIN (bar); WOMAN MOURNER (m-sop); PARTHIAN MAIDEN (sop); FIRST MACEDONIAN SOLDIER (bar); SECOND MACEDONIAN SOLDIER (bs); VOICE OF THE CRUCIFIXION (bar or ten), offstage – can double with Storyteller; SIX WOMEN MOURNERS (5 sop, m-sop).

Chorus: SSAATBB (in pit) – People of Bethlehem and Jerusalem. Interludes between scenes sung by chorus.

Orchestration: 2 fl, 2 ob, 2 cl, 2 bsn, 2 hrn, 2 trp, 2 trb, 2 perc, hp and/or pia, str

Synopsis: Artaban, one of the Magi, sells his belongings for three precious gems which he hopes to present to the newborn Babe in Bethlehem. He follows the star which will guide him to where the three Wisemen await him. On his journey, he meets an aged Hebrew who has been banned from the city to die. Artaban buys his freedom with one of his three gems. This delay has caused him to miss the Wisemen, so he hurries on to Bethlehem alone. Here, he encounters a young mother about to lose her baby to Herod's soldiers. He bribes a Roman Captain with the second of his gems to save the baby. Artaban loses his way and wanders for thirty-three years, seeking Jesus. He arrives in Jerusalem on the day of Christ's crucifixion, ill and nearly blind. Realizing the situation, he seeks to ransom Jesus with his remaining pearl, but instead gives it to Macedonian soldiers to save a young lady. At that very moment, a convulsion of nature erupts, mortally wounding Artaban. He drags himself to the foot of the Cross, crying that he has failed. He hears a Voice from above say, "Verily, I say unto you, inasmuch as thou hast done it unto the least of these my brethren, thou hast done it unto me." Artaban stretches wide his arms toward the cross, slowly sinks down and dies in peace.

Materials: Unpublished. Materials from IP.

Notes: Best performed in a theatre.

Ruth

Music by **Isaac Van Grove** (1891-1979). A Dramatic Cantata with libretto in English by Janice Lovoos, freely adapted from the Biblical Book of Ruth with some choral texts from the Psalms.

Composed in 1969 for and first performed by Inspiration Point Fine Arts Colony, Eureka Springs, Arkansas, 1972.

Considerable chromaticism with late nineteenth century style; some twentieth century rhythmic and harmonic devices. Accompanied recitatives, arias, ensembles. Melodic with continuous texture.

One act, two scenes. Setting: Era of the Biblical Judges. Scenes connected with narrative from the Storyteller. Scene 1: A graveyard in Moab; sc. 2: Harvest time on a threshing floor in Bethlehem. Duration: approximately 40 minutes.

Roles: STORYTELLER (bar or m-sop); NAOMI (m-sop), a widow from Bethlehem; ORPHA (sop), a Moabite widow and daughter-in-law to Naomi; RUTH (sop), a Moabite widow and daughter-in-law to Naomi; BOAZ (bs-bar), a prosperous farmer in Judea; ZIPPORAH (sop), handmaiden; FOUR HANDMAIDENS OF THE HOUSE OF BOAZ (sop, sop, alt, alt).

Chorus: SSA (men's voices may be added *ad libitum*) – a Greek chorus in stationary position.

Dance: REAPERS AND GLEANERS (boys and girls). Simple folk dancing.

Orchestration: 2 fl, 2 ob, 2 cl, 2 bsn, 2 hrn, 2 trp, 2 trp, perc, timp, str

Synopsis: The Storyteller asks the audience to hear the story of Ruth and narrates the background of the plot. Naomi, Ruth and Orpha weep at the graves of their husbands. As they leave, Naomi asks Ruth and Orpha to return to the home of their parents. Ruth pleads with Naomi to remain with her. Naomi agrees and as she has decided to return to the land of her birth, the two travel to Bethlehem. Naomi seeks out Boaz, a kinsman of hers, and introduces him to Ruth. As it is evening and all workers are exhausted from harvesting, Boaz retires, asking Zipporah to sing to him. Boaz falls asleep. Naomi meanwhile suggests to Ruth that she stay with Boaz and become better acquainted when he awakens. He is after all a widower and longs for a wife and family. Ruth hesitatingly agrees. When Boaz awakens, he tells Ruth that in his dream she was his wife and mother of his children. He goes on to explain that he has loved her since first seeing her. The two walk off together while the chorus sings praises to the Lord of heaven and earth.

Materials: Unpublished. Materials from IP.

Notes: Easily adapted to either church or theatre performance. VS contains detailed stage directions.

RALPH VAUGHAN WILLIAMS

The First Nowell

Music by **Ralph Vaughan Williams** (1872-1958). A Nativity Play with libretto in English adapted from medieval pageants by Simon Pakenham. The music for this work, Vaughan Williams last, is composed and arranged from traditional tunes with additions by Roy Douglas.

Premiered December 19, 1958, in the Theatre Royal, London.

Traditional harmonies, homophonic structures. Linear and vocally conceived. Some Latin. Set numbers; spoken dialogue.

One scene. Duration: 50 minutes.

Singing Roles: FIRST SHEPHERD (bs or bar); SECOND SHEPHERD (ten); THIRD SHEPHERD (ten or treble); SOPRANO SOLOIST; BARITONE SOLOIST.

Speaking Roles: CREATOR; GABRIEL; MARY; ELIZABETH; JOSEPH; CASPAR; MELCHIOR; BALTHAZAR.

Silent Roles: MARY'S TWO MAIDS; THREE ATTENDANTS for the Kings.

Chorus: SATB – angels

Dance: Shepherds dance

Orchestration: 2 fl, ob, 2 cl, bsn, 2 hrn, 2 trp, 2 trb, timp, hp, strings; or str and org (pia)

Synopsis: In the manner of the medieval play, this work in simple but vivid strokes tells the story of the birth of Christ. Events included are the Annunciation, the birth of Christ, the visit of the Shepherds and the presentation of the gifts by the three Kings.

Materials: OUP.

Notes: Intended for performance in a cathedral/church. Minimal sets, some properties needed. An effective and charming work with familiar carol tunes throughout.

The Pilgrim's Progress

Music by **Ralph Vaughan Williams** (1872-1958). A Morality Opera with libretto in English by the composer, based on Bunyan's allegory of the same name.

Premiered April 26, 1951, Royal Opera House, London.

Arias, ensembles, choral numbers. Modality. Some twentieth century influences with rhythmic complexities at times. Highly melodic.

Four acts, nine scenes with a Prologue and Epilogue. Act I, Prologue: In prison; sc. 1: Pilgrim starts journey; sc. 2: The House Beautiful; Nocturne: same. Act II, sc. 1: The arming of Pilgrim; sc. 2: Valley of Humiliation. Act III, sc. 1: City of Vanity Fair; sc. 2: Pilgrim in Prison. Act IV, sc. 1: At the edge of the Woods; sc. 2: The delectable Mountains; sc. 3: Entrance to the Celestial City; Epilogue: Same as Prologue. Duration: 2 hours, 15 minutes.

Major Roles: JOHN BUNYAN (bs-bar); THE PILGRIM (bar), vocally and dramatically very demanding; EVANGELIST (bs)

Minor Roles: PLIABLE (ten); OBSTINATE (bs); MISTRUST (bar); TIMOROUS (ten); THREE SHINING ONES (sop, m-sop, cont); THE INTERPRETER (ten); WATCHFUL, THE PORTER (bar); A HERALD (bar); APOLLYON (bs); TWO HEAVENLY BEINGS (sop, cont); LORD LECHERY (buffo ten); DEMAS (bar); JUDAS ISCARIOT (bar); SIMON MAGUS (bs); WORLDLY GLORY (bar);

MADAM WANTON (sop); PONTIUS PILATE (bs); MADAM BUBBLE (m-sop); USHER (buffo ten); LORD HATE-GOOD (bs); MALICE (sop); PICKTHANK (cont); SUPERSTITION (ten); ENVY (bs); A WOODCUTTER'S BOY (boy sop); MISTER BY-ENDS (buffo ten); MADAM BY-ENDS (cont); THREE SHEPHERDS (ten, bar, bs); THE VOICE OF A BIRD (sop); A CELESTIAL MESSENGER (ten); ANGEL OF THE LORD (sop). Eleven soloists are sufficient as a number of parts can be doubled.

Chorus: SATB divisi – represent various groups of people and angels throughout the work. Requires a large and vocally strong chorus.

Dance: The fight of Pilgrim with Apollyon requires choreography as does the Vanity Fair scene.

Orchestration: 2 fl (picc), 2 ob (Eng hrn), 2 cl, 2 bsn, contra bsn, 4 hrn, 2 trp, 3 trb, tba, euph, timp, perc (sd dr, ten dr, bs dr, cym, gong, tri, xyl, glock, bells), hp, cel, strings. The following may be omitted: contra bsn, stage trp, euph, cel.

Synopsis: Bunyan is in prison writing his final words of *The Pilgrim's Progress*: "So I awoke, and behold it was a dream." He stands and, turning to his hearers, reads from the beginning. A vision of himself as Pilgrim carrying a burden on his back appears. Evangelist directs Pilgrim to the Wicket Gate. Four neighbors rush out to warn him of the dangers on his journey to the Celestial City. Pilgrim first encounters the Cross. He kneels before it and his burden is removed. He is given a white robe and the great doors of the House Beautiful open. Pilgrim enters to rest. A trumpet sounds and Pilgrim's name is read from the book. He is armed for his journey.

In the Valley of Humiliation, he encounters strange creatures and does battle with Apollyon. Victorious but faint, he receives water of life from Heavenly Beings, a staff and key from Evangelist. At Vanity Fair he confronts all that the world has to offer. Pilgrim prays to keep his eyes from vanity but is imprisoned and sentenced to death by false witnesses. In prison, he cries out for help and remembers his key of Promise. As if by magic, the prison doors open and he resumes his journey. He encounters other tempting personalities but at last reaches the Delectable Mountains where he finds the Three Shepherds. The Shepherds anoint him in preparation for crossing the River of Death. In the darkness a distant trumpet sounds, and the voices from the Celestial City are heard singing. Darkness gives way to light as voices from the earth join the singing. Pilgrim is seen climbing the stairs to the City where he is welcomed by angels. The vision fades and Bunyan's dream is ended.

Materials: OUP.

Notes: Best performed in a large theatre due to numerous and difficult scene changes and the large cast. Effective as a concert piece as well.

The Shepherds of the Delectable Mountains

Music by **Ralph Vaughan Williams** (1872-1958). A Pastoral Opera with libretto in English by the composer, based on an episode in Bunyan's *The Pilgrim's Progress*. This episode was later incorporated by the composer into Act IV of his opera *The Pilgrim's Progress* (see entry), but may still be performed separately.

Premiered in 1922, London.

Melodic, considerable modality, traditional harmony, simple textures.

One act. Setting: A field at the foot of the Delectable Mountains. Duration: 35 minutes.

Roles: PILGRIM (bar); FIRST SHEPHERD (bar); SECOND SHEPHERD (ten); THIRD SHEPHERD (bs); A CELESTIAL MESSENGER (ten); VOICE OF A BIRD (sop), offstage.

Chorus: Women's voices offstage

Orchestration: 2 fl, ob, Eng hrn, 2 trp, hp, bells, str

Synopsis: Pilgrim, seeking the Celestial City, encounters Three Shepherds who invite him to rest with them. A Celestial Messenger arrives to take him to the Master. He pierces the heart of Pilgrim with an arrow sharpened by love and encourages him to cross the treacherous River of Death. The Shepherds anoint him and pray for his crossing. A heavenly choir welcomes Pilgrim and the Shepherds rejoice as he successfully reaches the Celestial City.

Materials: OUP.

Notes: Suitable for performance in either a house of worship or theatre.

GIUSEPPE VERDI

Nabucco

Music by **Giuseppe Verdi** (1813-1901). An Opera with libretto in Italian by Temistocle Solera based on Old Testament references to the Babylonian emperor Nebuchadnezzar, and his bondage of Israel.

Premiered at La Scala (Milan, Italy), March 9, 1842.

Early Verdian style with arias, accompanied recitatives, dominating melodicism. Considerable choral and ensemble music.

Four acts. Setting: 586 B.C., in Jerusalem and Babylon. Act I: In the Temple of Solomon in Jerusalem. Act II: Nabucco's palace in Babylon. Act III, sc. 1: The Hanging Gardens of Babylon; sc. 2: The banks of the Euphrates. Act IV, sc. 1: Nabucco's palace; sc. 2: the Hanging Gardens. Duration: 2 hours, 30 minutes.

Roles: NABUCODONOSOR (NABUCCO) (bar – top G3, high tess), King of Babylon; ISMAELE (ten), King of Jerusalem; ZACCARIA (bs – G1-F#3), Hebrew prophet; ABIGAILLE (sop – Bb2-C5, much melisma, vocally demanding, large skips), believed to be the eldest daughter of Nabucco; FENENA (sop), daughter of Nabucco; HIGH PRIEST OF BAAL (bs); ABDALLO (ten), old retainer of Nabucco; ANNA (sop), sister of Zaccaria.

Chorus: SSAATTBB – Soldiers, Levites, Hebrew virgins, Babylonian women, Magi lords of the Kingdom of Babylon, Populace.

Orchestration: 2 fl (picc), 2 ob (Eng hrn), 2 cl, 2 bsn, 4 hrn, 2 trp, 3 trb, tba, timp, 2 hp, perc, strings. On-stage band (opt).

Synopsis: The Hebrews bewail their defeat by Nabucco and call upon Jehovah to defend their holy Temple. Zaccaria enters with a prisoner Fenena, Nabucco's daughter, giving her into the care of Ismaele; then leading in a prayer invoking God's help against the Babylonians. When all have left, Ismaele and Fenena confess their love for each other, having met earlier. Fenena's sister Abigaille, together with a band of Babylonian soldiers disguised as Hebrews, suddenly enter the Temple. She offers Ismaele his freedom in exchange for his love, which he declines. The Hebrew priests rush into the Temple followed by Nabucco on horseback. Zaccaria seizes Fenena and threatens to kill her if Nabucco continues to profane the Temple. Ismaele snatches Zaccaria's knife, whereupon Nabucco orders the burning of the Temple.

Babylonia has taken many of the Hebrews as their slaves. Fenena has been appointed Regent by Nabucco, much to Abigaille's disgust. Abigaille has also learned that she is Nabucco's daughter only by adoption. When it is announced that Fenena is setting free the Jewish slaves, Abigaille agrees to seize the throne. Nabucco, returning from fighting, rushes in and retrieves the crown from Abigaille declaring himself to be the only god. A thunderbolt is heard and the crown is lifted from Nabucco's head by an unseen force and dashed to the ground.

Act III finds Abigaille seated upon the throne. Nabucco enters, distraught, and is surprised to find his throne occupied. Abigaille asks for his signature on the death sentence for all the Hebrew rebels including Fenena. Reluctant, he signs when taunted with being afraid of the Jews. Very shortly, trumpets are heard signifying confirmation of the death sentence. Meanwhile, Zaccaria chides the Hebrew slaves for lamenting. The Lord will set them free and will pour down His wrath upon Babylon, says Zaccaria.

Outside his balcony, Nabucco hears a crowd calling Fenena's name. He sees her in chains being led to execution. Falling on his knees, he prays in desperation to the Hebrew God for forgiveness, promising that the Temple of Judah will be rebuilt if God will only clear his mind of its confusion. His senses return and he convinces his guards to join him in saving Fenena. In the final scene, Nabucco rushes to interrupt the execution. He orders the Baal idol destroyed, and it shatters miraculously. He commands the release of all Jews and the erection of a new Temple. Abigaille, who has taken poison, is brought in. She asks Nabucco to bless the union of Fenena and Ismaele, implores God to forgive her, and dies.

Materials: RIC (It); Belwin-Mills (Eng translation by Tucker Hammond). Eng translation by Andrew Porter also available.

Notes: For theatre performance only. Requires highly skilled vocal and instrumental forces.

ANTONIO VIVALDI

Juditha triumphans – The Triumph of Judith

Music by **Antonio Vivaldi** (1678-1741). A Dramatic Oratorio (Sacrum Militare Oratorium) with libretto in Italian by Giacomo Cassetti, based on the Apocryphal Book of Judith.

Composed in 1716.

Conventional harmonies typical of late Baroque practice. Secco recitatives, da capo arias; melodic with some melisma in vocal lines.

Two acts. Act I, sc. 1: In the Temple of Bethulia; sc. 2: The camp of Holofernes; sc. 3: In Holofernes' tent. Act II, sc. 1: The same; sc. 2: The Temple of Bethulia. Duration: approximately 105 minutes.

Roles: JUDITH (m-sop), requires agility; ABRA (sop), her maid; HOLOFERNES (bar – some coloratura passages), Babylonian General; VAGANS (ten), servant of Holofernes; OZIA (bs), High Priest of Bethulia.

Chorus: SATB – Chorus of virgins (off-stage); Chorus of soldiers.

Orchestration: ob, mandolin (opt), 3 trp, timp, str, continuo.

Synopsis: An invisible chorus of virgins prays to the Lord in behalf of Judith who is going to Holofernes' camp. Ozia invokes the stars to be the death torches of the enemy. In Holofernes' camp, his soldiers sing of vindication and victory over the city of Bethulia, while Holofernes reminds them that arms are nothing if the heart of the soldier is not sound. Vagans announces the visit of a beautiful Jewish woman and her servant. Holofernes invites them to his tent. As soon as he sees Judith, he is struck by her beauty and asks her what she desires. She begs his clemency for Bethulia. His reply is guarded but hopeful. Holofernes orders his servant to serve the meal and momentarily leaves the tent. Abra comforts the frightened Judith and begs her to pretend with Holofernes; the destiny of Bethulia depends on her. From the city of Bethulia a chorus of virgins can be heard praying for Judith. The meal is served along with wine and words of love from Holofernes. He begs her not to repel his ardour. Holofernes, who has continued to drink more and more, falls back on the table and lies in a drunken sleep. Judith invokes God to give her strength. Then, taking the sword which is hanging in the tent, with one blow, cuts off the head of the tyrant. She calls Abra who rushes in and places the head in a bag. The two women flee. Vagans comes into the tent, finds Holofernes' headless body, and invokes the Furies to revenge this deed.

In the Temple at Bethulia, the High Priest announces the arrival of Judith. He invites all to praise the triumphant Judith. The chorus of virgins sings a hymn to the great woman, the glory of their country.

Materials: EDS, Rome (© 1949) (It).

Notes: Though Vivaldi titled this work an oratorio, some settings and stage indications are given in the VS.

JOHN WEBBER

The Nativity

Music by **John Webber** (b. 1949). A Liturgical Music Drama with libretto in English by anonymous authors with additional verses by Rembert Herbert. Based on the Chester Miracle Play of the same title.

Commissioned and premiered by St. James Church, Washington, D. C., December 24, 1981.

Considerable plainchant with modal texture. Audience joins in singing carols.

One act, five scenes. Setting: Time of Christ's birth. Scene 1: The Annunciation; sc. 2: An Angel with Joseph; sc. 3: At the Bethlehem Inn; sc. 4: In Bethlehem; sc. 5: In the stable. Duration: 30 minutes.

Roles: MARY (sop); GABRIEL (bar), an angel; JOSEPH (bs); AN ANGEL (ten); SALOME (sop), a midwife; TEBELLA (alt), a midwife.

Chorus: SATB – Commentators; should be stationary.

Orchestration: 2 fl, 2 cl, bsn, 2 hrn, perc, str quartet, org.

Synopsis: The Angel Gabriel appears to Mary informing her that she is to bear God's Son. Several months later, we encounter Joseph, lamenting and angry that Mary has been impregnated by someone other than himself. An Angel visits him, setting him straight on the facts. Together, Mary and Joseph leave for Bethlehem. Upon their arrival, due to the multitude of people, they are forced to find shelter in a stable. Joseph quickly finds two midwives as Mary is about to give birth. The three return to the stable, but alas, it is too late. Jesus has been born!

Materials: Unpublished. AMC and the composer.

Notes: Composed for church presentation

DAN WELCHER

Della's Gift

Music by **Dan Welcher** (b. 1948). A Christmas Opera with libretto in English by Paul Woodruff, based on O. Henry's *The Gift of the Magi*.

Premiered by the University of Texas Opera Theatre, February 26, 1987.

Highly melodic, mostly traditional harmony.

Two acts. Setting: Christmas, 1905. Prologue: Pantomime, a city street on Christmas Eve; Act I: Jim and Della's apartment. Act II, sc. 1: A jeweler's store and hair shop (split stage) off a city street; sc. 2: Same as Act I; sc. 3: Same as Prologue. Duration: 80 minutes.

Roles: DELLA (sop – top C5), some coloratura; JIM (bar); MRS. PURDY (m-sop), humorous landlady; MR. McCOOL (buffo ten), the butcher; JEWELER (ten); MME. SOPHRONIE (m-sop); SOLOMON (ten); SHEBA (m-sop). The two tenor and two mezzo-soprano roles may be sung by the same two singers, making a cast of four instead of eight.

Orchestration: fl (picc), ob, 2 cl, bsn, 2 hrn, 2 trp, trb, perc, pia/cel, hp, strings. Two-piano version available.

Synopsis: Della and Jim, a young married couple who are poor and very much in love, are window shopping when they encounter a rich man and his mistress. Struck by the contrast between money and poverty, Jim shows off the one thing he possesses that might inspire envy: his grandfather's gold watch. Back in their impoverished apartment, they laugh about the rich couple and in jest name them Solomon and Sheba. Jim adores Della's rich chestnut hair. She tries to convince Jim not to be envious of Solomon and not to wish for fancy trinkets. Jim leaves for work. She counts and recounts the one dollar and eighty-seven cents she has saved for Jim's Christmas present. Her counting in interrupted by the landlady and the butcher, both demanding payment of past bills. Della collapses in tears and decides to sell her hair.

Jim, alone and wondering how to deal with their meager means, enters a jewelry shop determined to buy a set of combs for Della. Meanwhile, Della has entered a hair shop. While Della's hair is being cut, Jim buys the combs. Della quickly runs to buy a chain for Jim's watch from the same man who had just sold Jim the combs. Back in their apartment, Della is trying to make the most of her butchered hair when Jim comes in with a package... and just stares. As they exchange their presents they realize that each present is now useless, as Jim has sold his watch to buy the combs for Della's hair. With the couple in a long embrace, the scene shifts back to the street. Solomon is flaunting his new watch (Jim's, purchased at the Jeweler's), while Sheba tosses the curls on her new wig. Jim and Della enter. Their love is all they have, easily eclipsing the purchased trinkets of Solomon and Sheba. Solomon delivers O. Henry's final lines: "Of all who give gifts, these two were the wisest. They are the Magi."

Materials: TP.

Notes: A charming and light-hearted work worthy of repeated performances. Best performed in an intimate auditorium/theatre. Highly suitable and adaptable for tour groups.

RONALD K. WELLS

Who is My Neighbor?

Music by **Ronald K. Wells** (20th century American). A Sacred Music Drama with libretto in English by the composer, adapted from various Scripturally based events of Jesus' ministry.

Premiered in 1971, Spartanburg, SC.

Traditional harmonic texture, choral numbers mostly homophonic. Some contemporary "pop" rhythms and sounds; some spoken lines.

One act. Prologue, five scenes. Setting: Undesignated places in and around Judea. Prologue: Christ and the young lawyer; sc. 1: The woman at the well; sc. 2: Blind Bartimaeus; sc. 3: Rich young ruler; sc. 4: Mary Magdalene; sc. 5: Christ with little children. Duration: approximately 60 minutes.

Roles: All roles accessible and mid-range. CHRIST (bar); LAWYER (bar); SAMARITAN WOMAN (sop – C3-G#4); BARTIMAEUS (ten); RICH MAN (bs); RICH YOUNG RULER (bar); MARY MAGDALENE (m-sop); YOUNG BOY (boy sop); PHARISEE (silent); SIMON (bs); TWO DISCIPLES (bar); SIX WOMEN (3 sop, 3 alt); OTHER CHILDREN (silent).

Chorus: SAATBB – stationary, they interpret and comment on the action.

Orchestration: 2 fl (picc), ob, 2 cl, 2 hrn, 2 perc, gui, vln I, II, III, vc, cb.

Synopsis: Each scene is preceded by and concluded with a choral number. In the Prologue, the young lawyer asks Jesus what the greatest commandment is, and he answers that the first is to love God with all your heart, soul and mind, and the second is to love your neighbor as yourself. The choir asks, "Who is our neighbor?" A Samaritan woman discovers Christ's water is a well of everlasting life. A rich man tells blind Bartimaeus to be quiet while a child leads him to Christ for the healing he requests and receives. Then a rich young ruler asks what he should do to inherit eternal life. Jesus tells him all he lacks is to give his riches to the poor and follow Me, but this is too great a burden. Mary anoints Jesus with oil and dries his feet with her hair. In the final scene, little children come to Christ and are almost turned away by His disciples before the Lord bids them come to Him and then blesses them. The chorus concludes the drama, declaring that one's neighbor is the woman at the well, beggars, rich men, humble women and children. The chorus suggests that we love indiscriminately.

Materials: CRES

Notes: Intended for performance without sets or props, however, a fully mounted production is quite possible and effective. The chorus ties the scenes together. Best performed in a cathedral/church. Accessible; not a difficult work.

WILMER HAYDEN WELSH

Faith and the Sewing Circle

Music by **Wilmer Hayden Welsh** (b. 1932). A Sacred Opera with libretto in English by Constance DeBear Welsh, loosely based on concepts taken from the story of Ruth and Naomi as recorded in the Biblical Book of Ruth, but set in a contemporary church. For female cast.

Composed in 1960.

Some twentieth century influences; dissonance, mixed meter. Mostly conventional harmony with continuous texture; tonal. Melodic with some chromaticism.

One act. Setting: A large room in which women can sew and perhaps set up a quilt. Duration: 25 minutes.

Roles: EVANGELIST (sp), the local Minister; VOICE I (cont – low E2); VOICE II (sop); VOICE III (sop).

Chorus: SSAA – women of the church's sewing circle.

Orchestration: Two pianos.

Synopsis: An instrumental prelude leads into the opening scene which finds the church's sewing circle gathered for an evening of sewing. As they sew and converse, a knock is heard at the door. The Evangelist (their Minister) has come to pay a visit. The ladies are immediately suspicious of his intent, but he assures them that he is there only to tell them a story and encourages them to continue their sewing while he speaks. Very casually, he begins to tell them the story of Naomi and Ruth and the wedding preparations for Ruth and Orpah. He asks the ladies to imagine they are in the final stages of sewing the wedding dresses. As he speaks they become involved in the scenario, drawing mental pictures of how the wedding must have occurred. They play out the wedding procession. The Minister compliments them, and then tells them how the young husbands of Ruth and Orpah died. Again, the Minister has the ladies imagine the mourning and the ladies who sewed the death shrouds. The Minister then relates how the husbands were buried and the emptiness of Naomi as she left for her homeland accompanied by the faithful Ruth. There Ruth met and married Boaz and bore him a son who became the ancestor of David and of Jesus. Throughout his story telling, the Minister challenges the ladies with the faith and love that existed between these Biblical characters. Could they somehow relate and sew love around their lives and faith into their souls? The ladies see the lesson and sing a joyful song to God for this application to their lives.

Materials: Unpublished. From the composer or DC.

Notes: Equally adaptable to church or stage performance. An effective dramatization of a relevant plot.

Judas Iscariot

Music by **Wilmer Hayden Welsh** (b. 1932). A Choric Sacred Drama with libretto in English by the composer, based on Biblical passages drawn from Psalms, Isaiah, Acts, the four Epistles and Old Testament sources dealing with Jesus' crucifixion.

Composed in 1977; first performed February 26, 1978, Davidson United Methodist Church, Davidson, NC.

Straying tonalities with non-traditional harmonic movements. Chant influences with free rhythmic and metric flow; many open sounds. Dialogue, set numbers; primarily choral.

Seven set numbers separated by dialogue. Duration: 55 minutes.

Roles: JUDAS (sp); READER (sp); WATCHERS AND WAITERS (two or more persons from the chorus reading dialogue).

Chorus: SATB. Several small solos taken from the chorus.

Orchestration: org, perc

Synopsis: Judas confronts his own feelings which are represented by a dramatic chorus (Watchers and Waiters). The action of the crucifixion itself is not seen but is reported by the Reader. The singing chorus offers Scriptural passages that comment, often in prophetic form, on the drama of Judas. At first Judas, who quotes Scripture pompously, relegates his betrayal of Jesus to the fulfillment of prophesy, thus justifying himself. He has done no wrong. As the chorus continues to confront him, he begins to see his fault, though he never anticipated that the betrayal would lead to the death of his hero – Yahweh would stop the process short of death. Judas responds with increasing despondency to each word Jesus utters from the cross. At last when Jesus dies, Judas can no longer bear it; he, along with Jesus, has been deserted by God.

Materials: Unpublished. From the composer or DC.

Notes: Moderate staging is required. The singing choir should not be included in the action. The Reader should be in the pulpit while Judas and the Watchers and Waiters carry out the drama. Ideally suited for presentation in a cathedral/church.

The Passion According to Pilate

Music by **Wilmer Hayden Welsh** (b. 1932). An Easter Dramatic Oratorio with libretto in English by the composer, based on the events of Christ's passion as found in the Gospels.

Commissioned by Trinity Presbyterian Church, Charlotte, NC; first performed by them March 28, 1971.

Set numbers or sections but continuous texture. Changing meters, some "pop" idioms, considerable chromaticism but tonal; Romantic texture with contemporary influences.

Drama carried out by pantomime; singers stationary. Improvised percussion. Contemporary language and textual idioms. Multi-media potential.

One act, eleven scenes. Setting: may be played either in Biblical or modern times. Simple sets requiring a pulpit and a series of platforms. Duration: 60 minutes.

Singing Roles: SOPRANO SOLO; TENOR SOLO; BARITONE SOLO.

Pantomime Roles: Minimum of 22 actors required. *MINISTER; *PONTIUS PILATE; *TWO GUARDS; *TWO MERCENARIES; *JESUS; BARABBAS; CARPENTER; SIMON OF CYRENE; WEALTHY LADY; BUSINESSMAN; PHYSICIAN; VIRGIN MARY; JOSEPH OF ARIMETHEA; NICODEMUS; FOLLOWERS OF JESUS; PEOPLE OF JERUSALEM. (*These characters must be played by the same actors throughout. The other characters may be played by actors who emerge from and return to the people of Jerusalem.

Chorus: SATB – A Greek chorus.

Orchestration: organ, perc. Percussion frequently improvises.

Synopsis: A silent processional brings the actors and singers to the stage area. The action begins with Pilate, his guards and mercenaries moving into position to begin the trial of Jesus. The action follows as is outlined in the eleven sections of the work:
1. Jesus is Condemned to Death
2. Jesus Receives the Cross
3. Jesus Falls Under the Weight of the Cross
4. The Cross is Laid on Simon of Cyrene
5. The Women of Jerusalem Lament for Jesus
6. Jesus is Nailed to the Cross
7. The Soldiers Cast Lots for Jesus' Garments
8. Jesus Dies
9. Jesus' Body is Taken Down from the Cross
10. Jesus' Body is Laid in the Tomb
Epilogue: The Challenge

Materials: Unpublished. From the composer or DC.

Notes: Designed for church performance. Elaborate stage and production directions in VS. Accessible for most church choirs; dramatically poignant. "Pilate's guilt lay in the fact that he did not care enough whether Jesus lived or died. Too many of us still do not care. This musical dramatizes some of the ways in which we show our lack of caring, and what we can do about it – if we want to." –W. H. Welsh.

Please Get Out of the Way While We Rehearse

Music by **Wilmer Hayden Welsh** (b. 1932). A Christmas Opera with libretto in English by the composer and Constance DeBear Welsh, loosely based on the presentation of gifts by the Magi to the Christ Child.

Written for the Davidson College Male Chorus (ca. 1969).

Choral intonations, some mixed meter, dissonance, considerable chromaticism, contemporary language; some plainchant; tonal.

One act. Setting: A rehearsal location with a manger scene. Duration: approximately 40 minutes.

Roles: DIRECTRESS (sop – top A#4), President of Ladies Aid for Jesus; NEW MELCHIOR (ten – top A3); NEW CASPAR (bs-bar); NEW BALTHAZAR (bs); OLD MELCHIOR (ten); OLD CASPAR (bs-bar – F#1-E3); OLD BALTHAZAR (bs – low F#1).

Chorus: TTBB who comment on the action.

Orchestration: Orchestra or Piano

Synopsis: A contemporary setting in which a rehearsal for a church pageant is in progress. The three kings are about to rehearse the presentation of their gifts to the Christ Child. While they wait to rehearse, they discuss their day's business activities and complain about the rehearsal schedules and various other inconveniences. "After all," they complain, "it's only a lousy little pageant." The Directress arrives and the rehearsal begins. As the kings approach the manger, they notice Joseph, Mary and the Child are missing. The rehearsal stops with more complaining and sarcastic remarks. The Directress explains that Mary and the baby are ill and Joseph's car won't start. After more complaining the rehearsal finally continues. Suddenly, three Old Kings enter the rehearsal and begin singing. The rehearsal again is stopped. The New Kings are amused and curious at the strangeness and message of these Old Kings. They sing of their gifts of gold, frankincense and myrrh. They explain that these gifts were not enough and if they did not give themselves to Him, they would be doomed. The three Old Kings are told by the Directress that they must be in the wrong rehearsal, but decide they will stay and watch. The rehearsal continues, but again the Old Kings intrude with their own story, explaining that after giving their gifts, they were never able to find their way back home. They plead with the New Kings to give of themselves to the Christ, not just material gifts. The Old Kings begin to leave, saying they must continue their search for people who will give their hearts to Him, for only then can the kingdom truly come and their searching cease. The New Kings suddenly realize the foolishness of their behavior and lack of dedication to the task they are undertaking in portraying the giving of gifts to Christ. The rehearsal continues with a new impetus.

Materials: Unpublished. From the composer or DC.

Notes: Designed for church performance. Projects a poignant and relevant message.

MALCOLM WILLIAMSON

Dunstan and the Devil

Music by **Malcolm Williamson** (1931-2003). A Legend Opera with libretto in English by Geoffrey Dunn, based on legendary encounters between the Devil and Saint Dunstan, Archbishop of Canterbury.

Premiered May 19, 1967, Cookham Festival Society, England.

Mostly conventional harmonic structures with some dissonance. Modal, melodic, plainchant. Thinly orchestrated.

One act, Prologue, four scenes. Setting: Glastonbury, Winchester and Rome in the 10th century. Prologue: Miracle of the candles in the Church of the Blessed Virgin Mary at Glastonbury, February 2, 925; sc. 1: Devil rises out of Hell; sc. 2: The Devil's first fight, Palace of King Athelstan, Winchester, A.D. 943; sc. 3: Vision of the Apostles, the Mons Gaudu near Rome; sc. 4: The tweaking of the Nose, Dunstan's cell at Glastonbury. Duration: 56 minutes.

Major Roles: DUNSTAN (ten – top Bb3); THE DEVIL (bs – F1-F3); THE LADY (sop – top B4); ALPHEGE (bar).

Minor Roles: HEORSTAN (bar); ST. PETER (ten); KEONDRUD (m-sop); ST. PAUL (bar); ST ANDREW (bs); OFFICER (ten).

Chorus: SATB – People of Glastonbury; SSSA – Angels.

Orchestration: Piano duet, timp, perc (sus cym, lg gong, sm gong, chimes, xyl, glock, tri, bs dr, sn dr, ten dr, maracas, bongos)

Synopsis: The parents of Dunstan, Heorstand and Keondrud, visit the Glastonbury church to receive a blessing on their unborn son. God blows out all the candles except that of the mother-to-be, Keondrud. Dunstan is thus predestined to a holy life. However, as a boy, he enjoys the things of this world. Uncle Alphege urges him towards a religious career but the Devil tempts him away. Then another miracle occurs when a large boulder, sent by the Devil, nearly lands on Dunstan as he is in prayer near Rome. Saints Peter, Paul and Andrew come down to earth and urge Dunstan to enter the monastery. While working on objects for the church, Dunstan is repeatedly tempted by the Devil, hoping to lure him into worldly pursuits. Finally, Dunstan in desperation, pursues the Devil, who assumes various animal forms, until at last he seizes the nose of the Devil, in disguise as a fox, with red hot pincers. The Devil is defeated at last while both Dunstan and God are glorified with an angels' chorus of alleluias.

Materials: BH (Josef Weinberger).

Notes: Intended for presentation in a cathedral/church.

The Red Sea

Music by **Malcolm Williamson** (1931-2003). A Sacred Opera with libretto in English by the composer. One choral section is in Hebrew. Based on Israel's crossing of the Red Sea as found in Exodus 12-15 of the Old Testament.

Commissioned by the Darlington Arts Society Patrons' Fund and first performed at the Darlington College of Arts, Devon, England, April 14, 1972.

Highly melodic, declamatory recitatives; arias, ensembles. Tonal with some modality and "Near Eastern" sounds. Occasional tone clusters in accompaniment; frequent dissonance. Continuous texture.

One act. Setting: Pharaoh's palace and the shores of the Red Sea. Duration: 45 minutes.

Roles: MOSES (bar – B1-F3); PHARAOH (bar – A1-Eb3); THE PILLAR OF THE CLOUD (sop – top Bb4); THE PILLAR OF FIRE (m-sop).

Chorus: THE WAVES OF THE RED SEA (female chorus – sop, m-sop); EGYPTIANS (male chorus – bar, bs); ISRAELITES (SATB).

Dance: The two Pillars and the Waves should be choreographed. The march of the Israelites and pursuit by the soldiers require some stylized choreography.

Orchestration: Intended to be played by any number of instruments regardless of timbre including the following: high melodic instruments (e.g., vln, fl, ob, trp, rec, etc.); middle melodic instruments (e.g., vla, cl, hrn, rec, etc.); low melodic instruments (e.g., vc, cb, bsn, trb, tba, rec, etc.); pitched perc instruments (bells, xyl, vib, metallophones, glock, chime bars, etc.); high unpitched perc, middle unpitched perc; low unpitched perc (e. g., gongs, drums); keyboard (e.g., pia and hpsch, or org, hp).

Synopsis: The Egyptians are gathered before Pharaoh's palace. Moses demands that Pharaoh release them from bondage. Pharaoh finally accedes to their demands after God's last great curse kills all their first-born sons. The Israelites, disoriented by freedom, ask Moses for a guide. The Pillar of Cloud and the Pillar of Fire guide them by day and night across the desert to the banks of the Red Sea where they pitch their tents. Pharaoh, meanwhile, has a change of heart and leads his soldiers after Israel to bring them back. Through a miracle of God, the waters of the Red Sea are parted, and Moses leads all of Israel safely across. No sooner have they reached the far shore then God closes the waves of the sea upon the pursuing armies of Pharaoh, drowning them all. The Israelites sing a chorus of joy, but Moses cautions them that they must earn the land that has been promised them. As he stands on the seashore addressing the Israelites, Pharaoh is seen on the far shore, weeping over the loss of his armies as well as his slaves, the Israelites.

Materials: BH (Josef Weinberger). Parts available for transposing instruments in Bb and F.

Notes: Best performed in a theatre or church with spacious chancel and sanctuary. Production problems include the visualization of the Pillars as they lead, and the Waves of the Red Sea as they drown the Egyptians. In all cases, dancers and appropriate costuming can aid in solving these problems. A guide to Hebrew pronunciation is included in the VS.

ALEC WYTON

The Journey With Jonah

Music by **Alec Wyton** (b. 1921). A Sacred Opera with libretto in English by Madeleine L'Engle, based on the Old Testament Book of Jonah.

Premiered in 1976, Ashville, NC.

Accompanied recitative, considerable chant. Mixed meter with strong twentieth century influences: chromaticism, non-traditional use of chorus, dramatic speech-song; all within a tonal and late-romantic style.

One act, six scenes. Setting: during the time of Jonah. Scene 1: Jonah's home in Gathhepher; sc. 2: On board ship; sc. 3: In the belly of the whale; sc. 4: In Nineveh; sc. 5: Jonah and the Turtle; sc. 6: Jonah and the Worm. Duration: 90 minutes.

Roles: TURTLE (sop); JONAH (bar – top F3), the Prophet; GOOSE (m-sop); OWL (alt), mostly spoken, some chanting; JAY (m-sop); CAT (sop). The Rat family: MOTHER (sop – top Bb4), FATHER (bs), THE CHILDREN (trebles), Huz, Buz,

Hazo. THE WHALE (ten, bar, bs – always as a trio); THE FISH (sop); THE WORM (ten).

Chorus: SATB – commentators, sometimes the voice of God. Aleatoric speaking at times. May include some children as supers.

Orchestration: pia, org, cel, perc, str, prepared tape

Synopsis: The Turtle, often speaking as the Voice of God, sets the scene, asking the audience to notice Jonah, who is sitting and speaking to the sky, seemingly in angry tones. The Goose, Owl, Jay and Cat join Jonah in a conversation regarding God's command to Jonah to go preach repentance to the people of Nineveh. Each animal brings its own bit of wisdom to Jonah, who finally tires of their chit-chat and leaves. Avoiding God's command, Jonah boards a ship bound for Joppa, the opposite direction from Nineveh. Also on board this ship is the Rat family discussing the joys and hazards of traveling on a ship. Suddenly their conversation is interrupted by Jonah who insists that the sailors throw him overboard in order to calm the treacherous sea, for it is his fault that the ship is about to sink. The sailors oblige him. In scene 3, a conversation between Jonah, the Whale and a smaller fish takes place in the belly of the Whale. After three days, Jonah can bear the conversation and environment no longer and pleads to be let out. The Whale obliges and vomits him out onto dry land. We next find Jonah preaching repentance to the people of Nineveh. Scores of them are repenting as reported by the Goose, Owl, Jay and Cat, who went on ahead, anticipating that Jonah would eventually make it to Nineveh. The Turtle reports that because of the numerous conversions, God has changed His mind and will now spare Nineveh. Jonah, anticipating the destruction of Nineveh as God promised, is depressed and angry that he came all this way only to have God change His mind. He goes to the wilderness, wanting to die. God causes a vine to grow up over night to shade Jonah from the intense heat. A Worm comes along and eats the vine. Jonah is again angered by the lack of shade and frustrated at not being able to understand the reasoning of God. He rises and starts his journey back to Gathhepher, conceding that Nineveh is in God's hands. He will return to whatever preposterousness God, in His incomprehensibility, sees fit to give him to do. The audience joins the cast reminding all to "hear the voice of the Turtle" (God).

Materials: Unpublished. From the composer.

Notes: Suitable for church performance. An opera with a uniqueness in its delivery of a story difficult to understand. An effective dramatization.

PHILIP M. YOUNG

Samuel: The Boy Who Talked With God

Music by **Philip M. Young** (b. 1937). A Sacred Music Drama for adults and children with libretto in English by the composer, loosely based on Samuel 3 from the Old Testament.

Premiered in 1981, First Baptist Church, Henderson, NC.

Simple traditional harmonic textures with mostly homophonic structures; many folk elements; ten set numbers connected with spoken dialogue. Rhythmic speech patterns. Contemporary language.

One act. Setting: Old Testament times in the House of the Lord in Shiloh. Duration: 40 minutes.

Roles: SAMUEL (boy sop); ELI (bar), the Priest; HANNAH (sp), wife of Elkanah; HOPHNI (boy sop), Eli's son; PHINEHAS (boy sop), Eli's son; LITTLE GIRL (sp); FIRST ISRAELITE; SECOND ISRAELITE.

Chorus: Mixed voices of Israelites – two-part, three-part and unison. A few short solos from the chorus (First Child, Second Child, Third Child, First Priest, Second Priest).

Orchestration: Piano alone or add fl, cb (or elec bs); tamb, hand dr, tri

Synopsis: A group of children including Samuel gather in the House of the Lord for the Holy Day services. They play and chit-chat about matters they have heard discussed among the adults, i.e., who will be their next leader. After a busy day of worship festivities, the children and adults leave for home while Eli and Samuel, who is Eli's helper, lie down to sleep. Samuel is awakened by a voice calling to him. Thinking it is Eli calling, he runs to him to inquire. Eli, saying he did not call, instructs Samuel in how to respond should the voice call again. The voice calls again and Samuel responds as Eli instructed him to do. The next morning Samuel relates to Eli that the voice of the Lord spoke to him, selecting him to set Israel free and lead them. All the people praise the Lord that they will again have a leader.

Materials: Unpublished. From the composer.

Notes: Vocally and dramatically, all parts could be sung by children though Eli, Hannah and some of the Israelites would be more believable if sung by adults. Best suited for performance in a house of worship. Minimal properties needed. Stage directions in the VS.

EUGENE ZÁDOR

Yehu

Music by **Eugene Zádor** (b. 1894-1977, in Hungary, moved to the U.S. after 1939). A Christmas Opera with libretto in English by Anna Egynd, based on legend.

Premiered by the Municipal Art Department, Bureau of Music, Los Angeles, CA, December 21, 1974.

Tonal, traditional with some chromaticism and unexpected harmonic modulations. A few sections of *sprechstimme*. Continuous action, through-composed.

One act. Setting: The first Christmas in the back yard of an old home in Bethlehem. Duration: 32 minutes.

Roles: YEHU (ten – top Bb3 with some sustained A3), Herod's soldier; RACHEL (m-sop), Yehu's mother; SIMON (bar), Yehu's father; ZURA (sop – top Bb4), a mute girl; SHARAH (sop – top Bb4), the neighbor; THE HERALD (bar).

Chorus: SSA. May be in the pit or observe the action from a distance.

Orchestration: 2 fl, ob, bsn, 2 hrn, 2 trp, trb, pia, hp, perc, str. May be substantially reduced if a second piano is employed.

Synopsis: A poor simple couple, awaiting the return of their son Yehu, offers lodging to two transients, Mary, who is pregnant, and Joseph. Some time later, Yehu, a soldier and a leper, returns home on command to complete a mission of infanticide. (The birth of Christ occurs offstage.) Yehu is unable to carry through with his orders to kill the Child. He suddenly discovers that his leprosy (a sign of his spiritual decay) vanishes. While an unseen celestial chorus sings of peace, love and harmony, a mute, secretly in love with Yehu, also miraculously regains the ability to speak. The family is reunited.

Materials: CF.

Notes: Most suited for presentation in a cathedral/church.

CARL ZYTOWSKI

The Play of Balaam and His Ass

Music by **Carl Zytowski** (b. 1921). A Church Opera with libretto in English (some Latin) by the composer, adapted from the medieval mystery plays, based on the Biblical account in Numbers 22-23.

Composition completed July 17, 1983. The first of three church operas titled "A Medieval Triptych" (see Zytowski's *The Play of the Three Shepherds* and *The Play of the Three Maries at the Tomb*).

Continuous texture. Thinly orchestrated. Vocal lines often chanted; modal tendencies; linear. Harmonically influenced by twentieth century devices. Mostly non-measured. In the manner of a medieval mystery play.

One act. Setting: on a hilltop in the land of Moab during the time of King Balaak. Duration: 35 minutes.

Roles: BALAAK (ten – top A3), King of Moab; BALAAM (bs-bar – E1-E3); ASINA (bar – Ab1-F3), Balaam's ass; THE ANGELUS (ct ten – Bb2-D3), an Angel of God.

Chorus: DEUS (speaking chorus; rhythmic speech), the voice of God; should number at least twelve, stationed in an upper gallery surrounding the audience if possible.

Orchestration: 2 trp, psaltery, hammered dulcimer, troubador hp, perc (4 tuned dr, 5 temple blocks, tri, sus cym, sm gong, whip, tamb, maracas, finger cym). See *The Play of the Three Shepherds* for optional instruments.

Synopsis: King Balaak, fearful of Israel, calls upon Balaam to curse Israel in exchange for wealth and position. Balaam is tempted but told by God not to curse His people. Nevertheless, Balaam sets out on his ass, Asina, to do Balaak's bidding. Asina, seeing and obeying an angel of the Lord which as yet Balaam cannot see, refuses to go. Three times Balaam abuses Asina but with no success. Suddenly The Angelus becomes visible to Balaam who kneels in repentance. Balaam prophesies the birth of the Messiah who will redeem all the world. Asina and The Angelus join Balaam in a song of praise to God Almighty.

Materials: Unpublished. From the composer or UCSB.

Notes: Written specifically for church performance. When performed as a triptych, the full work should be concluded with the singing of the *Te Deum* by the entire company.

The Play of the Three Maries at the Tomb

Music by **Carl Zytowski** (b. 1921). A Church Opera with libretto in English (some Latin) by the composer adapted from the medieval mystery plays; based on the Biblical account as found in Matthew 28, Mark 16 and Luke 24.

Composed in 1983; first performed April 22, 1984, at St. Michael's and All Angel's Church, Isal Vista, CA. The third of three church operas titled "A Medieval Triptych" (see Zytowski's *The Play of Balaam and His Ass* and *The Play of the Three Shepherds*).

Vocal lines chant-like, mostly non-metric; thinly orchestrated. Modal with twentieth century harmonic influences. Some rhythmic complexities. In the manner of a medieval mystery play.

One act. Setting: Before the tomb of Christ. Duration: approximately 25 minutes.

Roles: MARIA SALOME (sop – top C5); MARIA JACOBI (m-sop – top Bb4); MARIA MAGDALENE (cont – G2-E4); ANGELUS (two trebles – top A4), angels of God.

Chorus: SSA – should sing from offstage or from a balcony above the audience or stage area. They sing in Latin while the Maries sing an English translation.

Orchestration: Orchestra bells, psaltery, troubador hp, portative org, perc (tri, wood block, tamb, sm gong, sm bs dr). See *The Play of the Three Shepherds*, for optional instruments.

Synopsis: The work may begin with a procession to the tomb. The three Maries are seen mourning and reminiscing as they approach the tomb. They are concerned with the large stone in front of the tomb which prevents them from gaining entrance to honor the body of their Lord. When they arrive at the tomb, the stone is gone. Maria Salome enters the tomb and returns with news that two white-clad children (Angelus) are sitting within. The Angelus' approach them saying that Christ has risen. Maria Magdalene brings Christ's shroud from the tomb, proof that He is risen as He said He would. Together with the chorus and Angelus, all sing a hymn of praise to the living Lord.

Materials: Unpublished. From the composer or UCSB.

Notes: Written specifically for church performance. When performed as a triptych, the full work should be concluded with the singing of the *Te Deum* by the entire company.

The Play of the Three Shepherds

Music by **Carl Zytowski** (b. 1921). A Church Opera with libretto in English (some Latin) by the composer, adapted from the medieval mystery plays and based on the Biblical account as found in Luke 2. Additional text is derived from a carol from the time of Henry VI and from the plainchant *O magnum mysterium*.

First performed November 13, 1982, for the National Convention of the National Opera Association at Lewis and Clark College, Portland, OR. The second of three church operas titled "A Medieval Triptych" (see Zytowski's *The Play of Balaam and His Ass* and *The Play of the Three Maries at the Tomb*).

Modal, use of plainchant. Vocally accessible. Thinly orchestrated. Continuous texture. In the manner of a medieval mystery play.

One act. Setting: On a hillside near Bethlehem one night. Duration: 25 minutes.

Roles: FIRST SHEPHERD (bs-bar – A1-F3); SECOND SHEPHERD (ten); THIRD SHEPHERD (treble: boy sop or m-sop – Bb2-F4, A4 opt), some melisma; THE ANGELUS (ct ten and ten).

Chorus: Twelve male or mixed voices; 2-part and unison; playing the instruments where possible.

orchestration: alt rec, psaltery, hammered dulcimer, troubador hp, bells, perc (hand dr, sus cym, tamb, claves). Optional instruments: fl for rec, vln for psaltery, xyl for dulcimer, pedal hp for troubador hp.

Synopsis: A brief instrumental introduction is followed by the distant voices of The Angelus. The Shepherds hear the voices but complain how cold the night air is and decide to sing before going to sleep. As they settle down for night, The Angelus are heard again announcing the birth of the Lord and urging the Shepherds to go see the Child in Bethlehem. A bit confused at first, the Shepherds decide they should obey. They depart rejoicing and singing a *Noel* with The Angelus.

Materials: Unpublished. From the composer or UCSB.

Notes: Written specifically for church performance. When performed as a triptych, the full work should be concluded with the singing of the *Te Deum* by the entire company.

Thomas of Canterbury

Music by **Carl Zytowski** (b. 1921). A Church Opera with libretto in English (some Latin) by the composer, inspired by T. S. Eliot's play, *Murder in the Cathedral*. Text based on a fifteenth century Macaronic Carol with some Latin adaptations from an early hymn in praise of Thomas, a love song by the troubador Bernart de Ventadorn, texts from the opening service for Vespers, and the Introit for the Festival of the Holy Bishop and Martyr Thomas. In nearly every instance of Latin usage, the choir sings an English translation response. All male cast.

First performed June 6, 1981, by the University of California Santa Barbara, in the First Presbyterian Church, Santa Barbara.

Ceremonial in character. Vocal lines frequently chanted. Vocal lines often disjunct. Quite chromatic during dramatic moments. Motivic usage. In the manner of a medieval play.

One act with Prologue, six scenes, Postlude. Setting: Before the high altar. Prologue: December 29, 1170, Vespers service; sc. 1: Thomas as Chancellor; sc. 2: Thomas consecrated Archbishop; sc. 3: Thomas opposes the King; sc. 4: Thomas in Exile; sc. 5: The King is angered; sc. 6: The murder of Thomas; Postlude: Thomas, Saint and Martyr. Duration: 45 minutes.

Major Roles: JOHN OF SALISBURY (ten – Db2-Ab3), friend and secretary to Thomas – also narrator; THOMAS á BECKET (bar – A1-G3, high tess), Chancellor of England and later Archbishop of Canterbury; KING HENRY II (bs-bar – F#1-F3).

Minor Roles: A PRIEST (bs); FOUR KNIGHTS (ten, ten, bs, bs).

Chorus: TTBB – Monks of the Cathedral Church of Canterbury and Barons of England. Choir should be robed but not involved in the action. They also play percussion instruments.

Dance: The murder of Thomas requires highly stylized choreography.

Orchestration: Org (pipe org suggested), finger cym, claves, hand dr, castanets, tamb, bells (perc may be played by chorus)

Synopsis: A Vespers service is under way. Thomas makes his way through the church as a knocking is heard at the door. Thomas is urged to safety while the choir continues the service. John of Salisbury steps forward to relate to the congregation (audience) the events which have led to this day. A series of dramatic vignettes recall the friendship of King Henry II and his Chancellor Thomas á Becket, who through the King's influence was elected Archbishop of Canterbury in 1162. Thomas and the King quarrel over the prerogatives of the church, and Thomas, refusing to sign the

Constitution of Clarendon which would have established royal authority, is forced into exile in France. Thomas returns to England to popular acclaim seven years later. Henry expresses his wish to be rid of his adversary. Four Knights force their way into the church, calling on Thomas to submit. He refuses and is murdered before the high altar. The monks carry his body away, while the choir sings a hymn to the martyr Thomas.

Materials: Unpublished. From the composer or UCSB.

Notes: Intended to be performed in a cathedral/church.

ANONYMOUS EDITIONS, TRANSCRIPTIONS, ARRANGEMENTS

The Maastricht Easter Play

Edited, adapted, and translated into English by **Wilbur W. Hollman** and **Rev. David Morrison**. An Easter Liturgical Drama (twelfth century). The text is the interpolation of dramatic non-Biblical texts based on Scriptural events surrounding the resurrection of Christ into the seasonal portion of the Mass.

Original manuscripts discovered in 1947 in the Royal Library of the Hague. First known American performance in 1960, Cedar Crest College.

Highly melodic, modal texture. Simple and sparse accompaniment with chant-like melodic lines. Two thirteenth century motets have been inserted by the editor. Original instrumental compositions serve to introduce, sustain, and reflect the prevailing mood.

Four long and three short scenes. Setting should be the altar and chancel area of a church. Varied levels are suggested. Scene 1: The empty tomb; sc. 2: The lament of the women; sc. 3: The visit to the Sepulchre; sc. 4: The visit of Mary Magdalene; sc. 5: The two disciples; sc. 6: The pilgrims; sc. 7: Apotheosis. Duration: 35 minutes.

Roles: MARY MAGDALENE (cont or m-sop); MARY JACOBI (m-sop); MARY SALOME (m-sop); THE SAVIOUR (bs or bar); ANGEL AT THE HEAD (boy sop or sop); ANGEL AT THE FOOT (boy sop or sop); TWO DISCIPLES (bs or bar); Two Pilgrims: CLEOPHAS (bar or ten), THE OTHER PILGRIM (bar or ten); THE MERCHANT (ten). An all-female cast may be used with careful casting of character parts.

Chorus: SATB – Greek chorus.

Orchestration: Suggested instrumentation is org, vla, gui (lute), two rec or fl, bell chimes, handbells.

Synopsis: The three Marys mourn at the empty tomb when a Spice Merchant wanders by selling ointments. The ladies buy a few spices and return to the sepulchre where two Angels inform them of Christ's resurrection and instruct them to tell His Disciples. Mary Magdalene then encounters Jesus believing Him to be the gardener. Discovering Jesus' true identity, she runs to tell the others. Meanwhile, Jesus encounters the two Pilgrims, who do not know that He is Jesus. Jesus leaves them suddenly when they finally recognize who He is. The Disciples and women all join in a joyous *Te Deum* to conclude the work.

Materials: G. Schirmer.

Notes: Numerous staging, production and costume notes as well as historical information, Latin pronunciation guide and complete English translation of the text are included in the VS. The final *Te Deum* is optional in performance. Best performed in a cathedral/church.

Officium Pastorum – The Shepherds at the Manger

Transcribed and translated by **W. L. Smoldon**. A Christmas Music Drama (thirteenth century) from Rouen based on the Biblical account as found in Luke 2:7-10. Text in Latin but a singable English translation is given as an underlay.

Simple plainchant throughout. Solos and some ensembles. Modal; unison chorus, using rhythmic modes, but edited with bar lines.

One scene. Setting: The manger scene. Duration: 20 minutes.

Roles: THREE SHEPHERDS (basses – B1-E3); TWO MIDWIVES (sop); THE ANGEL (sop – D3-F4 or ten – D2-F3).

Chorus: ATTENDANT ANGELS (seven or more treble voices).

Orchestration: Org and chime bells.

Synopsis: The Angel appears to the Three Shepherds telling them of the birth of the Saviour. A host of Angels join in praising God. The Shepherds hurry to Bethlehem and there find Mary and the Child. The Angels and Midwives join the Shepherds in a song of joy.

Materials: OUP. VS contains bell and organ cues as well as historical notes, staging, production, costume and musical suggestions. A complete translation of the Latin is also included.

Notes: The announcement to the Shepherds could be staged at an appropriate location in the sanctuary away from the manger. Best performed in a cathedral/church. Ideal as a portion of a Christmas service or Mass.

Peregrinus – The Stranger

Translated and transcribed by **W. L. Smoldon**. An Easter Music Drama (twelfth century) from Beauvais based on the Biblical story as found in Luke 24:13-32. Text in Latin with a singable English translation given as an underlay.

Plainsong chant, mostly syllabic and unmeasured. Final *Magnificat*.

One scene. No set necessary except for a table and chairs. Duration: 30 minutes.

Roles: CLEOPAS (bs), a disciple; LUKE (bs), a disciple; CHRIST (bs); THOMAS (bar or bs); SERVITOR (mute).

Chorus: SATB – narrates and comments on the action.

Orchestration: Suggested instrumentation is org, hp, and chime bells.

Synopsis: The two disciples, walking along the road to Emmaus, discuss their crucified leader. A stranger joins them. They invite Him to share their evening meal. As He blesses the bread, they recognize Him to be Christ – He instantly disappears. They are left somewhat bewildered but nonetheless joyous with the realization that their Lord is alive. A *Magnificat* which includes the soloists and chorus concludes the work.

Materials: OUP. VS includes bell, hp and org cues as well as historical notes, staging, production, costume and musical suggestions. A complete translation of the Latin is included.

Notes: Ideally suited for a cathedral/church in which the entire sanctuary and chancel could be used for the drama.

Planctus Mariae – *The Lament of Mary*

Transcribed and translated by **W. L. Smoldon**. A Passion Music Drama (fourteenth century) from Cividale, Italy, based on the Biblical account as found in John 19:25-27. Text in Latin with English translation.

Plainsong chant. Soloistic with some ensembles.

One scene. Simple setting, requiring only a large crucifix. Duration: 25 minutes.

Roles: MARY (cont), the Mother of Jesus; MARY MAGDALEN (sop); MARY JACOBI (sop); JOHN (ten or bar).

Chorus: Mixed voices, mostly unison. Chorus should be relatively hidden from view as they narrate and comment on the action.

Orchestration: Suggested accompaniment is for organ and chime bells.

Synopsis: The three Marys and John are at the foot of the cross conversing about and lamenting the death of Jesus who hangs there dying. The Chorus, as onlookers, comforts the quartet with the words of the *Stabat Mater*.

Materials: OUP. VS includes cues for organ and bells; performance, production, staging and costume suggestions along with English and Latin libretto and historical data are likewise in the VS.

Notes: Best performed in a cathedral/church making use of the entire sanctuary and chancel for dramatic action.

The Play of Daniel

Edited by **Noah Greenberg** (1919-1966). A Liturgical Drama (thirteenth century) with text in Latin based upon the Biblical account as found in the Book of Daniel. Narrative in English by W. H. Auden.

First public performance since medieval times, January, 1958, by the New York Pro Musica.

In the style of medieval chant. Ensembles, solos, narration, much unaccompanied singing. Musically, not difficult; stylistically problematic, requiring research and study.

One act, nine scenes. Duration: 60 minutes.

Singing Roles: BELSHAZZAR'S PRINCE (ten); BELSHAZZAR (bs); TWO WISE MEN (bar); BELSHAZZAR'S QUEEN (sop); DANIEL (ten); KING DARIUS (bar); TWO ADVISERS (bar); FIRST LEGATE (bs); FIRST ENVIOUS COUNSELOR (ten or sop); SECOND ENVIOUS COUNSELOR (sop or ten); FIRST ANGEL (sop); HABAKKUK (bar); SECOND ANGEL (ten).

Non-singing Roles: FIRST MONK (narrator); SECOND MONK ; TWO LIONS.

Chorus: Suggested are eight sop, four ten, four bar, four bs. These numbers may vary.

Orchestration: In the Greenberg edition, all instrumentalists are involved in the action of the play. Sop rec, trp in C, ob, vla, gui, zither or autoharp, bell carillon or sm chimes, handbells in E, A, G, C, perc (played by various members of the court: sm dr, lg dr, tri, tamb, finger cym, sm cym, sleighbells, woodblock). While this orchestration adds a great deal of color, a good organ alone can also be effective.

Synopsis: A Narrator introduces the setting. A grand processional announces King Belshazzar while the princes and attendants sing his praises. As the celebration progresses, suddenly a hand appears and writes a message on the wall. The King, frightened, sends for his astrologers, none of whom are able to translate the writing. The King promises political authority over Babylon to any one who can decipher the meaning of the message. The Queen suggests that Daniel, a learned Prophet, be given the opportunity to translate the message. Daniel informs the King that according to the message, his kingdom is to be given into the hands of another. The King places Daniel in a position of authority. Belshazzar is killed, while Darius, King of Babylon, and his princes appear and take over the throne. Darius befriends Daniel, which creates jealousy among the princes and rulers of the court. They plot against Daniel. As a result Daniel is arrested for worshipping and giving his allegiance to Jehovah instead of Darius. Daniel is thrown into the pit of lions but is protected by an angel of God. When Darius sees the power of Jehovah in shutting the mouths of the lions, he commands the release of Daniel and the death of those princes who plotted against him. Darius then decrees that all must worship the God of Daniel. A *Te Deum Laudamus* concludes the work.

Materials: OUP. Recording: Decca DL 79402.

Notes: It is ideal if all playing areas can be located on or around the stage in order to prevent a break in the action. Originally conceived for performance in a cathedral – may be produced in an auditorium provided there are three points of entrance from the auditorium/audience onto the stage. The Latin text should not be a barrier to the performance of this work.

The English narrative and visual impact will clarify the message. Much opportunity for pageantry and color is allowed in this score. The VS contains the original stage directions along with the editor's introduction to Liturgical Drama, a translation of the Latin, notes on staging, costume suggestions and drawings, and a Latin pronunciation guide.

The Play of Herod

Edited by **Noah Greenberg** (1919-1966) with transcription and translation by **W. L. Smoldon**. A Christmas Liturgical Drama based on two plays, *The Representation of Herod* and *The Slaying of the Children*, both from the twelfth-century French manuscript known as the "Fleury Play-Book." Text is in Latin with English translation provided.

Originally performed by the men and boys of the choir school attached to the monastic church of Fleury. The New York Pro Musica production was first performed at the Cloisters, The Metropolitan Museum of Art in New York City, December, 1963.

Plainsong chant throughout; solos, ensembles in unison.

Two acts, five scenes. Major set requirements include a curtained manger with surrounding levels for the Angel Choir, and Herod's throne. Act I: The manager and Herod's throne. Act II: The slaying of the children. Duration: 75 minutes.

Singing Roles: ARCHANGEL (ten); TWO MIDWIVES (sop); THREE MAGI (bar); ARMIGER (bs); HEROD (bs); ARCHELAUS (bs), Herod's son; TWO COURIERS (ten); TWO SCRIBES (ten); JOSEPH (bar); RACHEL (m-sop).

Non-singing Roles: VIRGIN MARY; STAR BEARER, a child; TWO SOLDIERS; THREE GIFT BEARERS, three children.

Chorus: Angel choir (10 sop); Three Shepherds (3 alt); Holy Innocents (10 sop); Soldiers (6 bar and/or ten); Mothers/Consolers (5 sop and/or alt). The numbers may vary.

Orchestration: Suggested instruments are bell carillon, sop rec, vla, ob, ten dr

Synopsis: Act I begins with the nativity and adoration of the Christ Child while the Magi proceed to Jerusalem, following the star. King Herod sends a messenger to the Magi to inquire who they are and what their purpose is. They explain they have come from the East to seek a newborn king. Herod commands the scribes to find this prophecy. When they do, Herod becomes furious. He orders the Magi to return with news of the Child. The Magi find the Child, worship Him and offer their gifts to Him. The Magi depart, avoiding King Herod's court. In Act II, an Angel warns Joseph to flee to Egypt, for Herod is seeking the Child to destroy Him. The holy family departs. Herod discovers the Magi have journeyed home another way. Herod becomes angry and is about to kill himself when his messenger suggests he slay all young boys, for the Child may be among them. The children are slain while mothers watch. One mother, Rachel, sings a long lament, while watching her child being slain. Herod dies and his son rules in his place. An Angel announces to Joseph that Herod is dead and it is safe to return from Egypt.

Materials: OUP. Recording by Decca Dl (7) 10095/96.

Notes: Best performed in a cathedral/church. Considerable historical information, an English translation, production and performing suggestions are included in the VS.

The Play of Saint Nicholas

Reconstructed by **Frederick Renz**. A Liturgical Music Drama from the twelfth century based on the life and miracles of St. Nicholas as found in the four surviving dramatized *Plays of Saint Nicholas* (Manuscript 201 in the public library at Orleans, France). Text in Latin. English translation available.

Chant, non-measured with antiphons and responsories.

Four sections representing the four plays. Play 1: *Filius Getronis* (The Son of Getron); setting: three simultaneous settings – the throne of King Marmorinus, the City of Excoranda, the Church of St. Nicholas; duration: 30 minutes.
Play 2: *Tres Filiae* (The Three Daughters); setting: A room with window and an open space outside; duration: 23 minutes.
Play 3: *Iconia Sancti Nicolai* (The Icon of St. Nicholas); setting: The home of the Jew, the robbers' house; duration: 17 minutes.
Play 4: *Tres Clerici* (The Three Students); setting: A road, sleeping quarters, An inn; duration: 19 minutes.

Roles: Singers may assume roles in all or only one of the plays. **Play 1**: MINISTERS (2 ten, 1 bar); KING MARMORINUS (bar); ADEODATUS (boy sop), son of Getron; EUPHROSINA (ten), wife of Getron; CONSOLERS (2 male); GETRON (male); ST. NICHOLAS (male); TWO COURT MUSICIANS (bagpipe, sd dr); ADEODATUS'S MUSICIAN (Gittern); EUPHROSINA'S MUSICIAN (vielle); ST NICHOLAS' MUSICIAN (bell carillon).
Play 2: FATHER (bar); FIRST DAUGHTER (male); SECOND DAUGHTER (male); THIRD DAUGHTER (ten); SUITORS (ten); ST. NICHOLAS (male).
Play 3: MERCHANT (bar); FIRST THIEF (ten); SECOND THIEF (ten); THIRD THIEF (ten); ST. NICHOLAS (male).
Play 4: FIRST STUDENT (boy sop); SECOND STUDENT (male); THIRD STUDENT (male); INNKEEPER (male); OLD WOMAN (male); ST. NICHOLAS (male).

Chorus: School Children – a group of treble voices appearing only in Play 1. Entire ensemble appears at the end of each of the four plays.

Orchestration: Recent research seems to indicate only the use of organ and bells were admitted into the liturgy. This play being on the fringes of "religious" or "liturgical" may have included more instruments. Therefore the suggested instrumentation includes bagpipe, sd dr, gittern, several vielle, bell carillon, clay dr, gadulka, rebec, cornemuse, lyra, nun fiddle, Oud, rec, hp, org.

Synopsis: Play 1: Adeodatus is abducted by the King's armed ministers. After a year of mourning, searching and praying, the boy is miraculously returned to his parents, seemingly by St. Nicholas.
Play 2: The Father, a victim of misery and poverty asks counsel of his three daughters. Their counsel results in wealth and a husband for each. The final daughter's advice is to fear and love God. St. Nicholas appears, the giver of the gifts.
Play 3: Yet another miracle concerns St. Nicholas and a Jew who keeps the Saint's image hidden in his house and venerates it every day. He moreover is a wealthy man, and when he departs for a trip to the country, he leaves the image of St. Nicholas as guardian of his house, which he leaves unlocked. Thieves enter and steal all his property. After a short time, St. Nicholas miraculously restores it all to him, with the thieves returning the stolen goods.

Play 4: Three students request lodging of an old couple. The couple, in order to avoid poverty, decide to kill the three and claim their possessions. St. Nicholas arrives incognito requesting lodging and food. He tells the couple of their abominable deed. They confess and St. Nicholas, in the name of God, brings the students back to life. The work concludes with a joyous choral *Te Deum*.

Materials: From the composer. Recorded by Musical Heritage Society (MHS Stereo 824437).

Rachel

Edited by **Inglis Gundry**. A Christmas Medieval Music Drama based on the massacre of the innocents. Latin. English translation available.

Plainsong chant, solos and ensemble.

One scene, one set. Duration: 20 minutes.

Roles: ARMINGER (bar); THE ANGEL (alt); JOSEPH (bar); HEROD (bs); RACHEL (cont); CONSOLERS (m-sop, cont); THE INNOCENTS (treble).

Chorus: Mixed chorus.

Orchestration: Suggested instruments are 3 (or 2) trp (opt), 3 trb (opt), timp, org, str

Synopsis: Because of his jealousy and madness, King Herod orders the slaying of all boys under two, hoping thereby to rid the land of the supposed newborn King. Rachel, the mother of an infant, mourns as she watches her child murdered by the soldiers.

Materials: OUP. VS also includes *The Star*.

Notes: Minimal sets and properties needed. Intended for performance in a cathedral/church.

The Shepherds

Edited by **Inglis Gundry**. A Christmas Medieval Music Drama primarily based on the thirteenth century Rouen version. Latin text with English translation available.

Plainsong chant with solos and ensembles.

One scene. Duration: 10 minutes.

Roles: THE ANGEL (alt); THREE (or more) SHEPHERDS (ten, bar, bs); TWO WOMEN (or One Woman with non-singing Attendant – sop).

Chorus: Mixed voices as Choir of Angels – may be used as a Greek chorus or as a part of the action.

Orchestration: Suggested instruments include 2 rec, tabor, 3 (or 2) trp (opt), 3 trb (opt), org, str

Synopsis: The Shepherds attending their sheep are addressed by an Angel, telling them to go immediately to Bethlehem where Christ, the Saviour has just been born. They hurry to Bethlehem and worship the Child.

Materials: OUP.

Notes: Minimal sets necessary include a manger. Best suited to cathedral/church performance.

Sponsus – The Bridegroom

Transcribed, edited and translated by **W. L. Smoldon**. A Medieval Music Drama from the eleventh century, probably of the 'Mystère' type, based on the Biblical parable of the wise and foolish virgins as found in Matthew 25:1-13.

Plainsong chant, soloistic with unison ensembles.

One scene. Duration: 18 minutes.

Roles: GABRIEL (bar); CHRISTUS (bs), the Bridegroom; THE WISE VIRGINS (five sop or m-sop); THE FOOLISH VIRGINS (five sop – lighter tones than the Wise Virgins); THE OIL MERCHANTS (two bs); SOME DEMONS (mute).

Chorus: Choral group of four (male or female) in solo and in consort.

Orchestration: Suggested instruments are org, hp, ob (shawm), vla (rebec).

Synopsis: Ten virgins, five wise and five foolish, await the Bridegroom (Christ) before the wedding and feast. Gabriel appears, warning them to wait without sleeping. Meanwhile, the five Foolish Virgins fall asleep, even though they were warned against this. They awaken to see that their lamps have gone out, but that the Wise Virgins have brought extra oil for their lamps. They beg the Wise Virgins to share their oil but are denied and are told to ask the Merchants to sell them some. The Merchants refuse and refer them back to the Wise Virgins. When they return they find the Bridegroom has already come and left without them. They plead but because of their unpreparedness, they are cast into hell. The play may end at this point, or in either of two other ways: the singing of the *Te Deum*, or the cast and audience singing *O Come, O Come Emmanuel* as the entire cast exits through the audience.

Materials: OUP. VS includes cues for suggested instruments, performance, production, staging and costume suggestions together with historical information and an English libretto.

Notes: Text is at times in Latin, sometimes in a vernacular Romance dialect, and at times a mixture of the two. A singable English translation is given as an underlay. Due to the obscurity of the original dialect language, it is suggested that the English translation be used in performance. There is no evidence to support the original performance of this work within church walls. It may have been performed on the front steps of the church. Thus, this work may suitably be performed in an auditorium or even outdoors.

The Star

Edited by **Inglis Gundry**. A Christmas Medieval Music Drama based on the story of the Magi. Text in Latin with English translation available.

Plainsong chant with solos and ensembles.

One scene, two settings: a road in the country and the Manger scene. Duration: 25 minutes.

Roles: ARINGER (bar); HEROD (bs); ARCHELAUS (bar); SHEPHERD (bar); THREE MAGI (baritones); THE ANGEL (alt); WOMAN (m-sop).

Chorus: Mixed chorus

Orchestration: 2 rec, tabor, 3 (or 2) trp (opt), 3 trb (opt), org, str

Synopsis: The story focuses on the star and its guiding light to the manger of Jesus. The Magi are led by the star, first to Herod who insists that they return after visiting the newborn King to tell him of the Child's location. The Magi continue on their journey, still being led by the star, to the manger where they present their gifts to the Child and worship Him.

Materials: OUP. VS also includes *Rachel*.

Notes: Most suitable for performance in a cathedral/church.

Visitatio Sepulchri – The Visit to the Tomb

Transcribed and translated by **W. L. Smoldon**. An Easter Music Drama taken from the "Fleury Playbook" of the twelfth century. Text in Latin with English translation.

Plainsong chant. Single vocal lines and ensembles in unison.

One scene. Setting: The sepulchre. Duration: 30 minutes.

Roles: MARY MAGDALENE (sop); MARY SALOME (sop); MARY, Mother of James (sop); CHRIST (bs); FIRST ANGEL (bar); SECOND ANGEL (bs); JOHN (bs); PETER (bs).

Chorus: Unison – women, boys or men.

Orchestration: Org with optional parts for hp and chime bells.

Synopsis: The three Marys approach the sepulchre. Outside the tomb they see an Angel who tells them that Jesus is not here but is risen as He said He would. Mary Magdalene runs to tell Peter and John that Jesus lives. They immediately leave their tasks and hurry to the tomb. Mary Magdalene likewise returns to the tomb only to encounter the gardener, whom she finally realizes is the risen Lord. The Angels join with the Marys in rejoicing and singing the *Te Deum*.

Materials: OUP.

Notes: Most suitable for cathedral/church performance.

APPENDICES

APPENDIX A

SUPPLEMENTAL LIST

These are works in which segments or portions of the entire work are of a sacred nature and from which scenes may be extracted for performance or workshop purposes.

The list of "Christmas Carol" settings has been added as an informational item. Four representative works which are accessible and easily available have been selected from this list and have been annotated in detail in the main portion of this book.

Asmedai   **Josep Tal (b. 1910)**
   Libretto by Eliraz; premiered 1971, Hamburg. Jewish legend in the style of morality play. Twelve-tone. English translation by Alan Marbe available.

Behold the Sun   **Alexander Goehr (b. 1932)**
   Libretto by John McGrath and composer; premiered 1985, Deutsche Oper, Düsseldorf (SCH)

Billy Budd   **Benjamin Britten (1913-1976)**
   Libretto by Forster and Crozier; premiered 1951, Covent Garden (BH)

The Binding of Isaac   **Matthew Kenneth Peterson (b. 1984)**
   Libretto in English by Jason Zencka. Premiered April 30, 2006 at St. Olaf College, Northfield, MN. The plot is loosely based on the biblical story of the sacrifice of Isaac. It is about relationships: man and God, man and wilderness, husband and wife, parent and child – then ends with Isaac's scream as Abraham lifts the knife to sacrifice his own son. God's intervention and provision of a sacrificial lamb is omitted. One act with five connected scenes; traditional settings. Soloists: bar, m-sop, sop, treble; 8-part offstage chorus; 8-piece chamber orchestra. Duration: 35 minutes. See composer contact information in Appendix C for score and parts.

Cain and Abel   **Tsippi Fleischer (Israel)**
   In Hebrew; English translation has been performed in Germany. Ms Fleisher holds degrees in Semitic Linguistics, Hebrew and Arabic philology, Theory and Composition, an MA in music from New York University, and a Ph.D. in Musicology from Bar Ilan University in Israel. For contact information, see **Fleischer** in Appendix C.

Christus   **Anton Rubinstein (1829-1894)**
   Libretto by Bulthaupt; premiered 1895, Bremen

David et Jonathas   **Marc-Antoine Charpentier (1643-1704)**

    First performed in 1688 at Louis Le Grand College. Newly adapted by Timothy Nelson in 2005 for its American premiere in Baltimore, MD with the Ignoti Dei Opera Company, Timothy Nelson, Director. The opera is in five acts plus a prologue, and follows the Biblical love story of David, King of Israel, and Jonathan, future king of Israel. See Nelson in Appendix C.

Debora e Jaele   **Ildebrando Pizzetti (1880-1968)**

    Libretto by composer; premiered 1922, La Scala (RIC)

L'enfant prodigue **(1850)**   **D. F. Auber (1782-1871)**

    Originally published by Davidson

Golem   **John Casken**

    American premiere by Opera Omaha, September 15, 1990

Jepthe **(5 acts)**   **Michel Pignolet Monteclair (1667-1737)**

    Libretto by Pellegrin; premiered 1732

Job **(ca. 1980)**   **Curtis Finney**

    Libretto by J. Williams & J. Lange based on the Book of Job. Primarily choral work with organ accompaniment. Unpublished.

The Judgment of St. Francis   **Nicolas Flagello (b. 1928)**

    Libretto by Aulicino; premiered 1966, New York City

La Juive **(The Jew)**   **Jacques-François Halevy (1799-1862)**

    Libretto by Scribe; premiered 1835 (UE)

I Lombardi   **Giuseppe Verdi (1813-1901)**

    Libretto by Soler; premiered 1843, La Scala (RIC)

Mosè in Egitto   **Gioacchino Rossini (1792-1868)**

    Libretto by A. L. Tottola; premiered 1818, revised by Rossini in 1827 to "Moise et Pharaon" (BH)

Moses   **Anton Rubinstein (1829-1894)**

    Libretto by Mosenthal; premiered 1892, Prague

My Servant Job **(a Biblical opera)**   **Betty Jackson King (1928-1994)**

    Two acts; available from the composer (see Appendix C)

Nativity: A Canticle for the Child   **Norman Dello Joio (b. 1913)**

    Premiered in Midland, Michigan during the 1989-90 season.

Out of the Depths   **Samuel C. Yahres**
> Text from the Book of John; A Choral Passion Play. Narrator; designated characters; keyboard accompaniment. LC (M2023. 424092). Originally published by Ft. Vance Press.

Parsifal   **Richard Wagner (1813-1883)**
> Libretto by composer; premiered 1882 (GS, CFP, SCH, BREI)

The Promise (one act)   **Claude Bass (b. 1935)**
> A Christmas Opera for young people, sung by adults. Premiered in 1982 by Southwest Baptist Theological Seminary, Ft. Worth, TX. Available from the composer.

La Prophète   **Meyerbeer (1791-1864)**
> Libretto by Scribe; premiered 1849, Paris (BREI)

La sacra rappresentazione di Abram e d'Isaac   **Ildebando Pizzetti (1880-1968)**
> Libretto by Belcare; premiered 1926, Turin

Saul at Ein Dor (Saul at Endor)   **Josef Tal (b. 1910)**
> Libretto based on I Samuel 28; premiered 1957, Tel-Aviv (IMP). Includes Speaker and electronic tape.

Saul of Tarsus (two acts)   **Betty Jackson King (1928-1994)**
> Premiered in 1952 as an oratorio; available from the composer.

Sodom   **George Addison (cont. American)**
> Libretto by Mary P. Hansard; Master's thesis in 1979 from Louisiana State University. Mostly "pop" styles. AMC.

Suor Angelica   **Giacomo Puccini (1858-1924)**
> Libretto by Forzano; premiered 1918, New York's Metropolitan (RIC)

Der verlorne Paradies   **Anton Rubinstein (1829-1894)**
> Libretto by Schlönbach after Milton; premiered 1875, Düsseldorf

SETTINGS OR ADAPTATIONS OF DICKENS' "A CHRISTMAS CAROL"

A Christmas Carol   **Louise Averill**
> For Children; Waterloo Music Corp (WM)

A Christmas Carol   **Joseph Cohen**
> For children; St. Norbert College, West de Pere, Wisconsin

A Christmas Carol   **David Gray**
    2 acts; 2 hrs; NOV

A Christmas Carol   **Virginia Hagemann**
    For children; Theodore Presser

A Christmas Carol   **Peter Hart**
    For children; musical theatre; Dash Music in London

A Christmas Carol   **Bernard Herrmann**
    For children; a musical TV play; CBS-TV on 12/23/54

A Christmas Carol   **Thea Musgrave**
    See Title Index

A Christmas Carol   **Gregory Sandow**
    See Title Index

A Christmas Carol   **Malcolm Shapcott**
    Musical Play; Evans Plays in London

A Christmas Carol   **Stephen Tosh**
    See Title Index

A Christmas Carol   **Treharne**
    For children; 2 hrs duration; Frank Distributing Corp
    116 Boylston St., Boston 02116

A Christmas Carol   **F. W. Wadely**
    70 minutes; mostly choral; (BH – © 1938)

On Christmas Night   **R. Vaughan Williams**
    For children; 30 minutes; 2 soloists, chorus; OUP

Mr. Scrooge   **Martin Kalmanoff**
    1 act; for children; ASCAP

Scrooge   **Leslie Bricusse**
    See Title Index

APPENDIX B

PUBLISHERS AND DISTRIBUTORS

Numerous addresses and phone numbers of publishers and distributors have changed since the first printing of this book. Likewise, buyouts and consolidations have been and are on-going events. The internet seems to provide the most current contact information. Therefore, I am providing contact data that is either very basic or that may be more difficult to find. Though there are others, the following websites should be helpful in your search: Music Publishers' Association (www.mpa.org), National Music Publishers' Association (www.nmpa.org), Association of Independent Music Publishers (www.aimp.org), International Confederation of Music Publishers (www.icmp-ciem.org), Church Music Publishers' Association (www.cmpamusic.org), Prescribed Music List (www.uil.utexas.edu/muisc/pml_publishers.html), and Musical America (www.musicalamerica.com).

ABI   Alexander Broude Inc.

AF   Adolf Fuerstner

AMC   American Music Center
30 West 26th Street, Suite 1001
New York, NY 10010
212-366-5260
www.amc.net

AMP   Associated Music Publishers

ARSM   Ars Musica
110 rue Pierre-Demours
Paris, France
(also see CC)

ASCAP   American Society of Composers, Authors & Publishers
1 Lincoln Plaza
New York, NY 10023
212-621-6000
www.ascap.com

ASU   Arizona State University
Music Library
Tempe, AZ 85287
480-965-4267
www.asu.edu

AUG	Augsburg Publishing House P.O. Box 1209 426 South fifth St. Minneapolis, MN 55440-1209 800-328-4648 612-330-3300
AUGC	Augsburg College Music Department 731 21 Ave. S. Minneapolis, MN 55454 612-330-1265 www.augsburg.edu
BAK	Baker's Plays P.O. Box 699222 Quincy, MA 02269-9222 617-745-0805 www.bakersplays.com
BAR	Bärenreiter Verlag 224 King Street Englewood, NJ 07631 201-569-2898 maasturm@sprynet.com
BBC	British Broadcasting Corp. Broadcasting House Portland Pl. London W1A 1AA England (01) 580-4468 www.vvc.co.uk
BEL	Belwin-Mills Publishing Corp. (CPP/Belwin Inc.) 15800 N.W. 48th Avenue Miami, FL 33014 1-800-327-7643 305-621-1500
BH	Boosey & Hawkes 35 E. 21st Street New York, NY 10010 212-358-5300 www.boosey.com Stacy Frierson, Promotion Assistant Stacy.Frierson@boosey.com 212-358-5362

BIR	Summy-Birchard, Inc. 15800 N.W. 48th Avenue Miami, FL 33014 305-620-1500
BJE	Board of Jewish Education of Greater New York Music Department Nassau/Queens Center www.bjeny.org
BMC	Boston Music Co. CHANGED TO: Boston Scores Store 223 Newberry Street Boston, MA 02116 800-863-5150 or 617-236-5874
BMI	Broadcast Music, Inc. 320 W. 57th Street New York, NY 10019 212-586-2000 www.bmi.com
BOU	Bourne Co. 5 West 37th Street New York, NY 10018 212-391-4300 bournemusic@worldnet.att.net www.bournemusic.com
BP	Broadman Press 127 Ninth Ave. N. Nashville, TN 37234 615)-251-2000
BPC	Bartlesville Publishing Co. Box 265 Bartlesville, OK 74005
BREI	Breitkopf & Härtel Walkmühlsstrasse 52 D 65195 Wiesbaden, DE info@breitkopf.com www.breitkopf.com

BYU	Brigham Young University Music Library Provo, Utah 84602 801-422-4636 www.byu.edu
CAl	Christian Arts, Inc. Mr. Derek de Cambra, Artistic Director Long Island, NY
CC	Centenary College Hurley School of Music Shreveport, LA 71104-0188 318-869-5235
CF	Carl Fischer, Inc. 62 Cooper Square New York, NY 10003 212-777-0900
CFP	C.F. Peters Corp. 70-30 80th Street 718-416-7800 roger@c-fpeters-ny.com www.cfpeters-ny.com
CG	Carl Gerbrandt, Professor Emeritus of Opera and Voice University of Northern Colorado Home: 16474 Burghley Ct Platteville, CO 80651 970-785-2616 cjgerbr@hotmail.com
CHA	Chappell & Co.
CHES	Chester Music Ltd., London 7-9 Eagle Court London EC1M 5QD, England (also see MMB)
CLM	Cherry Lane Music Co., Inc.

COR	Cornish Institute Worlds of Music Office 710 Roy Street Seattle, WA 98102 206-726-5030 www.cornish.edu
COS	Central Opera Service (see OP)
CRES	Crescendo Music Sales Co.
CUR	Curwen
CWMC	"Catalogue of Works by Mario Castelnuovo-Tedesco" Nick Rossi, editor New York Public Library Lincoln Center New York, NY 10023 OR Mrs. Clara Castelnuovo-Tedesco 269 So. Clark Dr. Beverly Hills, CA 90211 213-657-0208 OR Library of Congress (LC) for photocopying
DAC	Da Capo Press Eleven Cambridge Center Cambridge, MA 02142 www.perseusbooksgroup.com/**dacapo**/home.jsp
DC	Davidson College Music Department Davidson, NC 28036 704-892-2000 www.davidson.edu
DBC	Dallas Baptist College P.O. Box 21206 Dallas, TX 75211 www.dbu.edu
DUR	Durand SA, France

EAM	European American Music Distributors Corp.
EBM	Edward B. Marks Music Corp.
ECS	E.C. Schirmer Music Company 138 Ipswich St. Boston, MA 02215-3534 617-236-1935 1-800-777-1919 office@ecspub.com www.escpublishing.com
EDS	Edizioni de Santis 1-00195 Roma Viale Mazzini, 6, ITALY
ESZ	Edizioni Suivini Zerboni (Gruppo Editoriale Sugar) 20138 Milano via Quintiliano 40 ITALY
FB	Fred Bock Music Publishers P.O. Box 570567 18345 Ventura Blvd., #212 818-996-6181 info@fredbockmusiccompany.com www.fredbockmusiccompany.com
FG	Fennica Gehrman P.O. Box 158 FIN-00121 Helsinki FINLAND www.fennicagehrman.fi
FM	Faber Music
FMD	Foreign Music Distributors
FP	Fredonia Press c/o John LaMontaine 3947 Fredonia Dr. Hollywood, CA 90028 323-851-3043

FPC	First Presbyterian Church Minister of Music 12 West 12th Street New York, NY 10011 212-675-6150
GAL	Galaxy Music Corporation
GEOF	Geoffrey Barlow The School House East Hoathly Lewes, East Sussex BN8 6EQ ENGLAND 082-584-677
GIA	GIA Publications, Inc. 7404 S. Mason Avenue Chicago, IL 60638 708-496-3800 custserv@giamusic.com www.giamusic.com
GMC	General Music Publishing Co. 145 Palisade St. Dobbs Ferry, NY 10522 914-693-9321
GPI	Gregg Press Inc. 1 Westmead, Farnborough Hants GU14 7RU ENGLAND
GS	G. Schirmer, Inc. 257 Park Avenue South, 20th floor New York, NY 10010 212-254-2100 schirmer@schirmer.com www.schirmer.com
HF	Harold Flammer, Inc.
HIN	Hinshaw Music Inc. P.O. Box 470 Chapel Hill, NC 27514-0470 (919) 933-1691 hinshaw@hinshawmusic.com www.hinshawmusic.com

HL	Hal Leonard Corporation 777 W. Bluemound Rd. Milwaukee, WI 53213 414-774-3630 nubick@halleonard.com
IMP	Israeli Music Publishers (see TP)
IP	Inspiration Point Fine Arts Colony P.O. Box 127 Eureka Springs, Arkansas 72632 501-253-8595
IUML	Indiana University Music Library Indiana University Bloomington, IN 47401 812-335-1582 www.indiana.edu
JB	Joseph Boonin, Inc. 831 Main Street Hackensack, NJ 07601
JF	J. Fischer & Bro.
JP	Jenson Publications (see HL)
JS	John Sheppard Music Press P.O. Box 6784 Denver, CO 80206 303-320-6838 www.shepherdpress.com (also see JB)
KAL	Edwin F. Kalmus & Co. Inc P.O. Box 5011 Boca Raton, FL 33431-0811 561-241-6347 efkalmus@aol.com www.kalmus-music.com
LC	Library of Congress Music Division Washington, D.C. 20540

MAP	Mapleson Music Rental Library 208 N. Broadway Lindenhurst, NY 11757 516-226-2244
MFM	Mark Foster Music Co.
MMB	MMB Music, Inc. Contemporary Arts Building 3526 Washington Avenue St. Louis, MO 63103-1019 314-531-8384 info@mmbmusic.com www.mmbmujsic.com
MOS	Moseler
NMTN	National Music Theatre Network 1457 Broadway, Suite 1111 New York, NY 10036 212-382-0984
NOV	Novello & Co.
OD	Oliver Ditson
OPERA	Opera 160 J Street Salt Lake City, Utah 84103
OUP	Oxford University Press Music Department 198 Madison Avenue New York, NY 10016 212-726-6000 hillb@oup-usa.org www.oup-usa.org
PL	Performer's Library 565 Broadway Hastings-on-Hudson, NY 10706 914-478-0923
PMC	Plymouth Music Co. 76 Spenser Drive Short Hills, NJ 07078 908-704-4546

RHL	Rodgers & Hammerstein Concert Library 1065 Avenue of the Americas, 24 th Floor New York, New York 10018 www.rnh.com
RIC	G. Ricordi & Co.
ROU	Rouart, Lerolle 29, Rue d'Astorg Paris, France (see also GS)
SAL	Editions Salabert
SBTS	Southern Baptist Theological Seminary School of Church Music 2825 Lexington Rd. Louisville, KY 40280 502-897-4115 www.sbts.edu
SCH	Schott Music International/European American Music 35 East 21st Street, 8th floor New York, NY 10010 212-871-0210 eamdllc@eamdllc.com www.eamdllc.com www.Schott-Music.com
SC	Smith College Music Department Northampton, MA 01063 413-584-2700 www.smith.edu
SF	Samuel French, Inc. 45 West 25th Street New York, NY 10010
SJMP	St. James Music Press Box 1009 Hopkinsville, KY 42241 877-822-0304 www.sjmp.com Mark Schweizer mark@sjmp.com

SHP	Shawnee Press, Inc. 1221 17th Avenue South Nashville, TN 37212 615-320-5300 km@shawneepress.com www.shawneepress.com
SMC	Seesaw Music Corporation Raoul R. Ronson, Pres. 2067 Broadway New York, NY 10023 212-874-1200
SSM	Stage and Screen Music, Inc. 17 W. 60th Street, 8th floor New York, NY 10023
SUM	Summy-Birchard, Inc. (see BIR)
SWAN	Swan & Co. Music Publishers, Ltd. 24 Great Pulteney Street Golden Square, London, W.I
TP	Theodore Presser Co. 588 N. Gulph Road King of Prussia, PA 19406 610-592-1222 presser@presser.com www.presser.com
UCSB	University of California at Santa Barbara Department of Music Santa Barbara, CA 93106 www.ucsb.edu
UE	Universal Edition, Inc. (see EAM or SCH) 212-358-4985 Hruschka@universaledition.com www.universaledition.com
UP	Uroboros Press uroboros@sleepermusic.com www.sleepermusic.com/Aceldama.html c/o Thomas Sleeper

USC	University of Southern California
Music Library
3550 Trousdale Parkway
University Park Campus
Los Angeles, CA 90089-0182
213-740-0183
music@usc.edu
www.usc.edu
VMM	VM Music, Inc.
P.O. Box 298
Pittsford, NY 14534
585-264-1705
p.stuart@frontiernet.net
info@equinoxsymphony.org
WAL	Walton Music Corp.
1028 Highland Woods Road
Chapel Hill, NC 27217
919-929-1330
writeus@waltonmusic.com
www.waltonmusic.com
WM	Waterloo Music Co., Ltd.
3 Regina St. N.
Waterloo, Ontario N2J 4A5
CANADA
519-886-4990
www.saterloomusic.com
WMI	Williamson Music, Inc.
1065 Avenue of the Americas
Suite 2400
New York, NY 10018
212-541-6968
www.williamsonmusic.com
WTS	West Texas A & M University
Department of Music
TX 79016
806-656-2016
www.wtamu.edu
ZP	Zimbel Press
1595 Plank Rd., Webster
NY 14580-9327
http://www.zimbel.com
info@zimbel.com

APPENDIX C

COMPOSERS, TRANSLATORS, EDITORS, RESOURCES

Many addresses and phone numbers of the following contacts have changed since the first printing of this book. The internet seems to provide the most current information in contacting individuals. Along with www.google.com, composers can be found in any number of websites. I have listed some of those below.

AIN, Noa (Miss)
917-957-3400
noaain@aol.com

BARAB, Seymour
1225 Park Avenue
New York, NY 10028
212-348-6802
www.seymourbarab.com

BASS, Claude L., Professor Emeritus
School of Church Music
Southwestern Baptist Theological Seminary
P.O. Box 22000
Fort Worth, TX 76122
www.swbts.edu

BINGHAM, Susan Hulsman
(Chancel Opera Company of CT, Inc.)
277 Willow Street
New Haven, CT 06511
203-562-0632

BOREN, Murray
801-422-3454
murry_boren@byu.edu
www.cfac.byu.edu/music

BOYSEN, Sandra
sboysen@frontiernet.net
Dissertation on Paul Stuart

BRANTLEY, Royal, Professor
West Texas A & M University
www.wtamu.edu
rbrantley@mail.wtamu.edu
806-651-2811

BROWN, Richard E.
224 Emherst Drive S.E.
Albuquerque, NM 87106
505-260-1110

CALDWELL, Mary Elizabeth
www.cco.caltech.edu/~dgc/mec.html

CHARNESKY, J. Jason
Penn State University
226 Adams Avenue
University Park, PA 16803
814-237-2932
jjc10@psu.edu
Librettist for "Eve's Odds"

COOMAN, Carson
2 Bayard Rd., #3
Pittsburgh, PA 15213-1918
carson@carsoncooman.com
www.carsoncooman.com
412-683-4447 -home
412-551-9966 - cell
614-748-4447 - fax
Composer, Organist, Editor

DANIELS, Melvin L.
ACU Station, Box 8274
Abilene, TX 79699
915-673-7423
Contact AMC

DENEV, Lyubomir
12 Solunska' St
1000 Sofia
Bulgaria
luboden@mail.bol.bg
www.lubodenev.com
Composer, Conductor

DE LISA, Victor
Renee Gate Rt. 6, Box 378
Mohegan Lake, NY 10547
914-528-6644
Contact AMC

FINK, Myron S.
10836 Charbono Pt.
San Diego, CA 92131
Contact AMC

FLEISCHER, Tsippi
7 Sderot Bat-Galim
Haifa 35012
Israel
OR
P.O. Box 8094
Haifa 31080
Fax - 009724 853-1605
Tel - 009724 853-4741
yakidolgo@walla.com
Composer

FRANCESCHINA, John, Professor
Pennsylvania State University
jcf@psu.edu
814-863-0789

FREUND, Don, Professor
Indiana University
dfreund@indiana.edu
812-332-9548

GOLDMAN, Edward M.
43 West 32nd Street
Bayonne, NJ 07002
201-436-4796

GREVLOS, Lisa
grevlos@augie.edu
Dissertation on Richard Shephard

HAGEMANN, Philip
35 Riverside Dr.
New York, NY 10023
212-724-0066
hagemannphilip@aol.com

HOCH, Juliana Bishop
1314 E. 18th St.
Loveland, CO 80538
970-593-0071
jbvoice@aol.com
Dissertation on Robert Kreutz

HOLDRIDGE, Lee
www.leeholdridge.com

KING, Betty Jackson
www.Bettyjacksonking.com

KONDOROSSY, Leslie
Contact AMC

KREUTZ, Robert E. Archive Library
c/o Mrs. Gina Kreutz Bartal
2460 W. Atlantic Ave.
Lakewood, CO 80228
303-987-9143

MAGNEY, Ruth Taylor
1100 Missouri Avenue
Deluth, Minnesota

NELSON, Timothy
lepetitprinceboi@hotmail.com
Director - Ignoti Dei Opera Company, Baltimore, MD
410-752-8558 (Theatre Project office)
Editor of Charpentier's *David and Jonathan*

NEUMANN, Alfred
c/o Christ Congregational Church
9525 Colesville Rd.
Silver Spring, MD 20901
www.christ-ucc.org

OPERA Sacra, Inc.
St. Joseph's Cathedral
50 Franklin Street
Buffalo, NY

OWEN, Harold John
c/o Central Lutheran Church
1857 Potter Street
Eugene, Oregon 97403
541-345-0395
clchurch-elca@qwest.net

PETERSON, Matthew Kenneth
100 E. Miller Dr. #62
Bloomington, IN 47401
mkp@indiana.edu

RAIGORODSKY, L. Natalia
R.D. 1
Muncie Valley, PA 17758
301-652-0620 or 717-482-2301
Organ composer

RENZ, Frederick, Director
Early Music Foundation
212-749-6600
info@earlymusicny.org

RIZZO, Phil
c/o 216-402-1176
www.angelfire.com/indie/philrizzo/main.html

SALZMAN, Eric
29 Middagh Street
Brooklyn, NY 11201
718-522-6138
esalzman@aba.org
www.kalvos.org/salzman.html

SARGON, Simon A.
3308 Dartmouth Avenue
Dallas, TX 75205
214-526-8084
ssargon@aol.com
www.simonsargon.com

SATEREN, Leland B., Professor Emeritus
Augsburg College
612-330-1265
www.augsburg.edu
5217 Windsor Avenue
Edina, MN 55436
612-920-8662

SCHWEIZER, Mark
mark@sjmp.com
St. James Music Press
Box 1009
Hopkinsville, KY 42240
270-885-8303
Composer, Editor, Publisher

SHEPHARD, Richard James
The Minster School
Deangate, York Y01 7JA
England
+44(0) 1904 557230
Richard@ogleforth.co.uk

SLEEPER, Thomas
sleeper@sleepermusic.com
mercurious@sleepermusic.com
Composer, Conductor

SMOLIN, Pauline, Professor Emeritus
University of Cincinnati
2328 Muriel Ct.
Cincinnati, OH 45229
513-721-6170
www.uc.edu

SOSIN, David
310 West 85th Street
New York, NY 10024
212-724-9536

STUART, Paul
585-264 1705
Music Director of The Equinox Symphony Orchestra
P.O. Box 298
Pittsford, NY 14534
paulstuart@equinoxsymphony.org
info@equinoxsymphony.org
p.stuart@frontiernet.net
p.stuart@gte.net
www.equinoxsymphony.org
Composer, Conductor, Publisher

SUSA, Conrad, Chair of Composition
San Francsico Conservatory
415-824-0452 - home

SWANN, Donald
www.donaldswann.co.uk

TIKKA, Kari
www.kolumbus.fi/kari.tikka/luther-ooppera
kari.tikka@kolumbus.fi
Publisher: Fennica Gehrman
PO Box 158
FIN-00121 Helsinki,
FINLAND
Composer and Conductor

TOSH, Stephen
Composer in Residence
Ensemble Monterey Chamber Orchestra
www.ensemblemonterey.org

TRINKLEY, Bruce
Professor Emeritus
School of Music
Penn State University
226 Adams Avenue
University Park, PA 16803
814-237-2932
wbt1@psu.edu
Composer and Conductor

WEBBER, John
1207 F. Street, NE
Washington, D.C. 20002
202-543-9469

WELSH, Wilmer Hayden, Professor Emeritus
Music Department
Davidson College
Davidson, NC 28036
www2.davidson.edu
Contact AMC

WYTON, Alec
25 Pound Street
Ridgefield, Connecticut 06877
203-431-9583

YOUNG, Philip M., Minister of Music
First Baptist Church
205 W. Winder Street
Henderson, North Carolina 27536
252-438-3172
fbchurch@ncol.net

ZYTOWSKI, Carl, Professor Emeritus
University of California Santa Barbara
www.music.ucsb.edu
OR
4013 Pala Lane
Santa Barbara, CA 93110

APPENDIX D

REFERENCES

BRUHN, Siglind. *Saints in the Limelight*, Hillsdale, NY (Pendragon Press), 2003 (ISBN 1-57647-096-2)

BUCKNELL, Peter A. *Entertainment and Ritual 600-1600*, London (Stainer and Bell), 1979

COLLINS, Fletcher, Jr. *The Production of Medieval Church Music*, Charlottesville (University of Virginia Press), 1972.

COLLINS, Fletcher, Jr. *Medieval Church Music-Dramas: A Repertory of Complete Plays*, Charlottesville (University of Virginia Press), 1976.

DEAN, Winton. *Handel's Dramatic Oratorios and Masques*, Oxford (Oxford University Press), 1959.

DOX, Thurston. *American Oratorios and Cantatas: A Catalog of Works Written in the United States from Colonial Times to 1985*, Volumes I & II, Metuchen, NJ, and London (The Scarecrow Press, Inc.), 1986.

DRUMMOND, John D. *Opera In Perspective*, Minneapolis (University Minnesota Press), 1980.

EATON, Quaintance. *Opera Production: A Handbook*, Minneapolis (University of Minnesota Press), 1961.

EATON, Quaintance. *Opera Production II: A Handbook*, Minneapolis (University of Minnesota Press), 1974.

Musical America International Directory of the Performing Arts, 825 Seventh Avenue, New York, NY 10019. An annual publication with an update on publishers addresses, artists, performing and arts organizations and libraries, among other arts information.

ROSSI, Nick. *Catalogue of Works by Mario Castelnuovo-Tedesco*, New York (New York City Library, Lincoln Center), 1977. (LC No. 77-79858)

SMOLDEN, William L. *The Music of the Medieval Church Dramas*, Oxford (Oxford University Press), 1980.

YOUNG, Karl. *The Drama of the Medieval Church*, Oxford (Oxford University Press), 1933.

APPENDIX E
WORKS FOR ALL-MALE OR ALL-FEMALE VOICES

MALE VOICES

The Burning Fiery Furnace (Britten)
Curlew River (Britten)
The Prodigal Son (Britten)
Thomas of Canterbury (Zytowski)

FEMALE VOICES

Baboushka (Swann)
Emma (Boren)
Faith and the Sewing Circle (Welsh)
The Judgment of Sheba (Goldsworthy)
The Maastricht Easter Play (Hollman & Morrison)
Piece Together (Bingham)
A Representation of the Book of Job (Blodgett)

APPENDIX F
WORKS ESPECIALLY SUITABLE FOR YOUNG AUDIENCES

Amahl and the Night Visitors (Menotti)
Baboushka (Swann)
Bel and the Dragon (Gardner)
Bontzye Schweig (Swann)
Caedmon (Shephard)
The Children's Crusade (Lebowsky)
A Christmas Carol (Sandow)
A Christmas Carol (Tosh)
The Christmas Rose (Bridge)
David (Burroughs)
David and Goliath (Salomon)
Della's Gift (Welcher)
The Door (Peninger)
Esther (Sosin)
Father of the Child (Barab)
La Fiesta de la Posada (Brubeck)
The Finding of the King (Broome)
A Gift of Song (Caldwell)
The Gift of the Magi (Gillis)
Good King Wenceslas (Shephard)
The Greenfield Christmas Tree (Moore)
Herod, Do Your Worst (Kelly)
Jericho Road (Aria)
Jonah (Mathias)
Jonah and the Whale (Argento)
The Journey with Jonah (Wyton)
The Lion, the Witch, and the Wardrobe (McCabe)
The Little Thieves of Bethlehem (Stuart)
Martin's Lie (Menotti)
The Night of the Star (Caldwell)
Noah (Salzman and Sahl)
Noah and the Stowaway (Kalmanoff)
Noye's Fludde (Britten)
One Christmas Long Ago (Mayer)
Pepito's Golden Flower (Caldwell)
The Promise (Bass)
St. Nicholas (Shephard)
Samuel (Brantley)
Samuel: The Boy Who Talked With God (Young)
Scrooge (Bricusse)

Sharing the Prophets: A Musical Encounter for Singers (Gottlieb)
A Swiss Nativity (Burkhard)
The Shephard's Play (Shephard)
Two By Two (Rodgers)
The Wise Women (Susa)

APPENDIX G

LISTING BY TEXTUAL SOURCE

Each work listed here will be found under its textual source. In the event that a libretto has been taken from more than one source, that work will be found either under the primary or most important source or under the "Other" category. Works have been listed here under general headings. Specific reference sources will be found in Paragraph 1 of the annotation entries.

In looking for a work under a specific textual source, also check "Medieval Plays/Dramas/Hymns" in this Appendix. While certain works are based upon these medieval sources, those sources in turn are often based on specific Scriptural texts or topics you may be looking for.

OLD TESTAMENT

Genesis

Abraham and Isaac (Boren)
The Binding of Isaac (Peterson)
Eve's Odds (Trinkley)
The First Murder (Scarlatti)
The Flood (Stravinsky)
God and Abraham (Kingsley)
Joseph (Handel)
Joseph (Méhul)
Noah (Salzman & Sahl)
The Sacrifice of Isaac (Bingham)
The Tower of Babel (Rubinstein)
Two By Two (Rodgers)
Up From Paradise (Silverman, S.)
The Wrestler (Adler)

Exodus

Móses (Durkó)
Moses and Aaron (Schoenberg)
Moses, Prince of Egypt (De Lisa)
The Red Sea (Williamson)

Joshua

Joshua (Handel)

Judges

Deborah (Handel)
Jephtha (Handel)
Jephthah's Daughter (Harrison)
Samson (Handel)
Samson and Delilah (Saint-Saëns)
Samson at Gaza (Alexander)
Yiphtah and His Daughter (Berger)

Ruth

Ruth (Ain)
Ruth (Berkeley)
Ruth (Bingham)
Ruth (Hagemann)
Ruth (Van Grove)
Ruth and Naomi (Kondorossy)

I, II Samuel

David (Burroughs)
David (Goldman)
David (Milhaud)
David and Goliath (Salomon)
And David Wept (Laderman)
Samuel (Brantley)
Samuel (Butler)
Samuel: The Boy Who Talked with God (Young)
Saul (Handel)
Saul (Castelnuovo-Tedesco)
Saul (Reutter)
Saul and David (Nielsen)
Saul, King of Israel (Gabriel)
Saul, King of Israel (Sargon)

I, II Kings

Elijah (Mendelssohn)
The Judgment of Sheba (Goldsworthy)
Naboth's Vineyard (Goehr)
Solomon (Handel)

Esther

Esther (Handel)
Esther (Meyerowitz)
Esther (Sosin)

Job

Job (Dallapiccola)
A Representation of the Book of Job (Blodgett)

Song of Solomon

Song of Songs (Castelnuovo-Tedesco)

Daniel

The Apocalypse (Gallico)
Bel and the Dragon (Gardner)
Belshazzar (Handel)
Belshazzar's Feast (Root)
The Burning Fiery Furnace (Britten)
Daniel in the Lion's Den (Pinkham)

Jonah

Jonah (Beeson)
Jonah (Mathias)
Jonah and the Whale (Argento)
The Journey with Jonah (Wyton)

Other

Cain (Denev)
Nabucco (Verdi)
Sharing the Prophets (Gottlieb)

NEW TESTAMENT

Matthew

Behold Your King (Patente)
L'enfance du Christ (Berlioz)
Hérodiade (Massenet)
The Obligation of the First Commandment (Mozart)
St. Matthew Passion (Bach)

Salome (Strauss)
Saturday, 29 A.D. (Schweizer)

Mark

Jericho Road (Aria)
The Passion of Our Lord Jesus Christ According to St. Mark (Owen)

Luke

A Conversation Between Mary and the Angel Gabriel (Bingham)
L'enfant prodigue (Debussy)
El Niño (Adams)
The Father's Love (Bass)
Laud to the Nativity (Respighi)
Nativity According to St. Luke (Thompson)
The Prodigal Son (Britten)
On the Road to Emmaus (Bingham)
St. Luke Passion (Penderecki)
The Shepherd's Play (Shephard)
Simeon (Bingham)
Song of Simeon (Arnold)

John

By the Pool of Siloam (Bingham)
Lazarus (Daniels)
Our Faith (Sateren)
The Raising of Lazarus (Bingham)
St. John Passion (Bach)
The Woman at Jacob's Well (Bingham)

Acts

Day of Pentecost (Sateren)
Saint Paul (Mendelssohn)

Other

The Awakening (Bingham)
Beloved Son (Brubeck)
The Birth of Our Lord (Bingham)
Christ, the Man from Galilee (Rizzo)
The Christmas Story (Schütz)
The Easter Story (Schütz)
La Fiesta de la Posada (Brubeck)

A Fisherman Called Peter (Owen)
I Am the Way (Hines)
In the Fullness of Time (Caldwell)
The Last Supper (Birtwistle)
The Last Supper (Malipiero)
The Light in the Wilderness (Brubeck)
The Little Thieves of Bethlehem (Stuart)
Marie-Magdeleine (Massenet)
The Miracle of the Nativity (Pendleton)
A Nativity in Threes (Barnard)
An Opera for Christmas (Neumann)
An Opera for Easter (Neumann)
The Passion According to Pilate (Welsh)
Piece Together (Bingham)
The Promise of Peace (Raigorodsky)
The Redeemer (Cundick)
See the Promised Dawn Arise (Cooman & Gay)
The Seven Last Words of Christ (Dubois)
Thieves (Cooman)
Who is My Neighbor? (Wells)

APOCRYPHA

Esdras

The King's Contest (Mechem)

Judith

Holofernes (Reznicek)
Judith (Chadwick)
Judith (Fink)
Judith (Goossens)
Judith (Honegger)
Judith (Smith)
Juditha Triumphans (Vivaldi)

Maccabaeus

Judas Maccabaeus (Handel)

Tobit

Tobias and the Angel (Bliss)
Tobias and the Angel (Castelnuovo-Tedesco)

LEGEND OR FOLK

American

The Greenfield Christmas Tree (Moore)
The Martyrs' Mirror (Parker)
Pepito's Golden Flower (Caldwell)
To the Ends of the Earth (Franceschina)
Singer's Glen (Parker)
Wondrous Love (Hunkins)

Eastern

Savitri (Holst)
X (The Life and Times of Malcolm X) (Davis)

Jewish

Bontzye Schweig (Swann)
Der Golem (Jewish) (d'Albert)
The Golem (Sitsky)
The Miracle of Nemirov (Silverman, F.)

Other

Aceldama (Sleeper)
Baboushka (Swann)
Caedmon (Shephard)
Candle Tree (Swann)
Cecilia (Refice)
The Children's Crusade (Pierne)
A Christmas Carol (Musgrave)
A Christmas Carol (Sandow)
A Christmas Carol (Tosh)
Dunstan and the Devil (Williamson)
The Egg (Menotti)
Emma (Mormon) (Boren)
Francesco: A Musical Biography (Kreutz)
A Gift of Song, Caldwell)
Good King Wenceslas (Shephard)
The Greek Passion (Martinu)
Jeanne d'Arc au Bûcher (Honegger)
The Legend of St. Christopher (d'Indy)
The Legend of St. Christopher (Parker)
The Martyrdom of St. Magnus (Davies)

Masque of Angels (Argento)
One Christmas Long Ago (Mayer)
Palestrina (Pfitzner)
St. Nicholas (Shephard)
Scrooge (Bricusse)
The Temptation of St. Anthony (Gray)
The Temptation of St. Antoine (Soler)
What Men Live By (Martinu)
The Wise Women (Susa)
Yehu (Zádor)

MEDIEVAL PLAYS/DRAMAS/HYMNS

Bethlehem – full-length version (Boughton)
Bethlehem – abridged version (Boughton)
The Christymas Playe (Boren)
Curlew River (Britten)
Dance of Death (Distler)
Erode the Greate (La Montaine)
Everyman (Scott)
The Fall of Lucifer (Burgon)
The First Nowell (Vaughan Williams)
The Glory Coach (Barnard)
Good Tidings from the Holy Beast (Locklair)
The Lessons of Advent (La Montaine)
The Lord's A Wonder (Franceschina)
The Maastricht Easter Play (Hollman & Morrison, ed.)
A Mystery for Christmas (McKinney)
The Mystery of the Nativity (Martin)
The Nativity (Webber)
The Nativity: A Mystery Play (Ekmon & Fyffe)
Nativity Play (Tcherepnin)
Novellis, Novellis (La Montaine)
Noye's Fludde (Britten)
Officium Pastorum (Smoldon, ed.)
An Opera for Everyman (Neumann)
Passion and Resurrection (Harvey)
Peregrinus (Smoldon, ed.)
The Pilgrim (Proulx)
Planctus Mariae (Smoldon, ed.)
The Play of Balaam and His Ass (Zytowski)
The Play of Daniel (Greenberg, ed.)
The Play of Herod (Greenberg, ed.)
The Play of Saint Nicholas (Renz, ed.)
The Play of the Three Maries at the Tomb (Zytowski)

The Play of the Three Shepherds (Zytowski)
Rachel (Gundry, ed.)
La Rappresentazione di Anima e di Corpo (Cavalieri)
The Shepherds (Gundry, ed.)
The Shepherds (Koch)
The Shephardes Playe (La Montaine)
Sponsus (Smoldon, ed.)
The Star (Gundry, ed.)
Thomas of Canterbury (Zytowski)
Visitatio Sepulchri (Smoldon, ed.)

APPENDIX H

LISTING BY SUBJECT

Advent/Christmas

Amahl and the Night Visitors (Menotti)
Baboushka (Swann)
Behold Your King (Patente)
Bethlehem (full-length version) (Boughton)
Bethlehem (abridged version) (Boughton)
The Birth of Our Lord (Bingham)
Candle Tree (Swann)
Cherry Tree Carol (Berger)
A Christmas Carol (Musgrave)
A Christmas Carol (Sandow)
A Christmas Carol (Tosh)
The Christmas Rose (Bridge)
The Christmas Story (Schütz)
The Christmas Troubadour (Mainville)
The Christymas Playe (Boren)
A Conversation Between Mary and the Angel Gabriel (Bingham)
Della's Gift (Welcher)
El Niño (Adams)
Erode the Greate (La Montaine)
L'enfance du Christ (Berlioz)
Father of the Child (Barab)
La Fiesta de la Posada (Brubeck)
The Finding of the King (Broome)
The First Nowell (Vaughan Williams)
A Gift of Song (Caldwell)
The Gift of the Magi (Brown)
The Gift of the Magi (Conte)
The Gift of the Magi (Ekstrom)
The Gift of the Magi (Gillis)
The Gift of the Magi (Magney)
Good King Wenceslas (Shephard)
Good Tidings from the Holy Beast (Locklair)
The Greenfield Christmas Tree (Moore)
Herod, Do Your Worst (Kelly)
In the Fullness of Time (Caldwell)
The Lessons of Advent (La Montaine)
The Little Thieves of Bethlehem (Stuart)

The Long Christmas Dinner (Hindemith)
Martin Avdeich: A Christmas Miracle (Downard)
The Miracle of the Nativity (Pendleton)
A Mystery for Christmas (McKinney)
The Mystery of the Nativity (Martin)
The Nativity (Gossec)
The Nativity (Webber)
Nativity According to St. Luke (Thompson)
The Nativity: A Mystery Play (Ekmon & Fyffe)
A Nativity in Threes (Barnard)
Nativity Play (Tcherepnin)
The Night of the Star (Caldwell)
Novellis, Novellis (La Montaine)
Officium Pastorum (Smoldon, ed.)
One Christmas Long Ago (Mayer)
Only A Miracle (Barab)
An Opera for Christmas (Neumann)
The Other Wise Man (Van Grove)
The Play of Balaam and His Ass (Zytowski)
The Play of Herod (Greenberg)
The Play of the Three Shepherds (Zytowski)
Please Get Out of the Way While We Rehearse (Welsh)
The Promise (Bass)
Rachel (Gundry, ed.)
St. Nicholas (Shephard)
Scrooge (Bricusse)
The Shepherd's Play (Shephard)
The Shephardes Playe (La Montaine)
The Shepherds (Koch)
The Shepherds (Gundry, ed.)
Simeon (Bingham)
Song of Simeon (Arnold)
The Star (Gundry, ed.)
A Swiss Nativity (Burkhard)
The Visitation (Bush)
The Wise Women (Susa)
Wondrous Love (Hunkins)
Yehu (Zádor)

Passion/Easter

Behold Your King (Patente)
Beloved Son (Brubeck)
Calvary (Pasatieri)
Christ, the Man from Galilee (Rizzo)

Comoedia de Christi Resurrectione (Orff)
The Easter Story (Schütz)
Good Friday (Miles)
The Greek Passion (Martinu)
Judas Iscariot (Welsh)
The Lament of Mary (Smoldon, ed.)
The Last Supper (Birtwistle)
The Last Supper (Malipiero)
Maastricht Easter Play (Hollman Morrison, ed.)
Magdalene (Bingham)
Marie-Magdeleine (Massenet)
Meditations on the Seven Last Words (Sateren)
The Nazarene (Gillis)
On the Road to Emmaus (Bingham)
An Opera for Easter (Neumann)
The Passion According to Pilate (Welsh)
Passion and Resurrection (Harvey)
The Passion of Our Lord Jesus Christ According to St. Luke (Owen)
Pilate (Hovhaness)
The Pilgrim (Proulx)
The Play of the Three Maries at the Tomb (Zytowski)
St. John Passion (Bach)
St. Luke Passion (Penderecki)
St. Matthew Passion (Bach)
Saturday, 29 A.D. (Schweizer)
See the Promised Dawn Arise (Cooman & Gay)
The Seven Last Words of Christ (Dubois)
The Stranger (Smoldon, ed.)
Thieves (Cooman)
Visitatio Sepulchri (Smoldon, ed.)

Parables

The Egg (Menotti)
L'enfant Prodigue (Debussy)
The Father's Love (Bass)
The Judas Tree (Dickinson)
The Prodigal Son (Britten)
Sponsus (Smoldon, ed.)

Miracles

Amahl and the Night Visitors (Menotti)
By the Pool of Siloam (Bingham)

Caedmon (Shephard)
Jericho Road (Aria)
Lazarus (Daniels)
Lazarus and His Beloved (Holdridge)
The Legend of St. Christopher (d'Indy)
The Legend of St. Christopher (Parker)
The Martyrdom of St. Magnus (Davies)
The Miracle of Nemirov (Silverman, F.)
The Play of Saint Nicholas (Renz, ed.)
The Promise of Peace (Raigorodsky)
The Raising of Lazarus (Bingham)
Tobias and the Angel (Bliss)
Tobias and the Angel (Castelnuovo-Tedesco)

Missions

God's Word in their Hearts (Butler)

Pentecost

Day of Pentecost (Sateren)

APPENDIX I

LISTING BY TYPE OR STYLE OF WORK

The works in this Appendix have been categorized according to either the composer's own designation or my own observations based upon the most obvious musical and dramatic elements of each individual score. Certain works lend themselves to alternative styles of presentation, which, of course, is a matter of personal taste and is to be placed in the hands of the stage director or conductor. For example, a work intended to be performed after the manner of a medieval music drama may work equally well when performed in a realistic or *verismo* style.

After the Manner of A Medieval Music Drama

The Burning Fiery Furnace (Britten)
Cherry Tree Carol (Berger)
The Christymas Playe (Boren)
A Conversation Between Mary and the Angel Gabriel (Bingham)
Curlew River (Britten)
Dance of Death (Distler)
Erode the Greate (La Montaine)
Everyman (Scott)
The Fall of Lucifer (Burgon)
The Flood (Stravinsky)
The First Nowell (Vaughan Williams)
The Glory Coach (Barnard)
Good Tidings from the Holy Beast (Locklair)
In the Fullness of Time (Caldwell)
Laud to the Nativity (Respighi)
The Lessons of Advent (La Montaine)
The Lord's A Wonder (Franceschina)
The Maastricht Easter Play (Hollman & Morrison, ed.)
Maria Egiziaca (Respighi)
Martin's Lie (Menotti)
The Miracle of the Nativity (Pendleton)
A Mystery for Christmas (McKinney)
Naboth's Vineyard (Goehr)
The Nativity (Webber)
Nativity According to St. Luke (Thompson)
The Nativity: A Mystery Play (Ekmon and Fyffe)
A Nativity in Threes (Barnard)

Nativity Play (Tcherepnin)
Noah (Salzman & Sahl)
Novellis, Novellis (La Montaine)
Noye's Fludde (Britten)
Officium Pastorum (Smoldon, ed.)
Passion and Resurrection (Harvey)
The Passion of Our Lord Jesus Christ According to St. Mark (Owen)
Peregrinus (Smoldon, ed.)
Perelandra (Swann)
The Pilgrim (Proulx)
Planctus Mariae (Smoldon, ed.)
The Play of Balaam and His Ass (Zytowski)
The Play of Daniel (Greenberg, ed.)
The Play of Herod (Greenberg, ed.)
The Play of Saint Nicholas (Renz, ed.)
The Play of the Three Maries at the Tomb (Zytowski)
The Play of the Three Shepherds (Zytowski)
The Prodigal Son (Britten)
Rachel (Gundry, ed.)
The Shephardes Playe (La Montaine)
The Shepherds (Koch)
The Shepherds (Gundry, ed.)
Song of Simeon (Arnold)
Sponsus (Smoldon, ed.)
The Star (Gundry, ed.)
Tales of A Magic Monastery (Bingham)
Thomas of Canterbury (Zytowski)
The Vision of Christ (Beversdorf)
The Visitation (Bush)
Visitatio Sepulchri (Smoldon, ed.)
What Men Live By (Martinu)

May Be Included in a Service of Worship

In nearly all instances, these works are intended to replace the sermon, dramatize the Scripture reading, or in some manner supplement and/or support the worship service.

The Awakening (Bingham)
Baboushka (Swann)
The Birth of Our Lord (Bingham)
By the Pool of Siloam (Bingham)
A Conversation Between Mary and the Angel Gabriel (Bingham)
Dance of Death (Distler)
Day of Pentecost (Sateren)
The Fall of Lucifer (Burgon)

The Last Supper (Malipiero)
Magdalene (Bingham)
Meditations on the Seven Last Words (Sateren)
Officium Pastorum (Smoldon, ed.)
On the Road to Emmaus (Bingham)
An Opera for Christmas (Neumann)
An Opera for Easter (Neumann)
An Opera for Everyman (Neumann)
Our Faith (Sateren)
Peregrinus (Smoldon, ed.)
Piece Together (Bingham)
Planctus Mariae (Smoldon, ed.)
The Play of the Three Maries at the Tomb (Zytowski)
The Play of the Three Shepherds (Zytowski)
The Raising of Lazarus (Bingham)
Ruth (Bingham)
Ruth and Naomi (Kondorossy)
The Sacrifice of Isaac (Bingham)
Saturday, 29 A.D. (Schweizer)
See the Promised Dawn Arise (Cooman & Gay)
The Shepherds (Gundry, ed.)
The Shepherds' Play (Shephard)
Simeon (Bingham)
Sponsus (Smoldon, ed.)
The Star (Gundry, ed.)
Thieves (Cooman)
Visitatio Sepulchri (Smoldon, ed.)
The Woman at Jacob's Well (Bingham)

Choral Drama (Passion, Cantata, Oratorio, Choric Drama, etc.)

These works designated by the composer as choral forms, are predominantly choral music or are dominated by the chorus rather than the soloists.

The Apocalypse (Gallico)
Athalia (Handel)
Behold Your King (Patente)
Beloved Son (Brubeck)
Belshazzar (Handel)
Bethlehem (full-length version) (Boughton)
Bethlehem (Abridged version) (Boughton)
Birds of A Feather (Berger)
Cherry Tree Carol (Berger)
The Christmas Story (Schütz)
Dance of Death (Distler)

Day of Pentecost (Sateren)
The Death of the Bishop of Brindisi (Menotti)
Deborah (Handel)
The Easter Story (Schütz)
Elijah (Mendelssohn)
Esther (Handel)
The Father's Love (Bass)
La Fiesta de la Posada (Brubeck)
The Gift of the Magi (Conte)
Here Comes Our King (Sateren)
Jeanne d'Arc au Bûcher (Honegger)
Jephtha (Handel)
Joseph (Handel)
Joshua (Handel)
Judas Iscariot (Welsh)
Judas Maccabaeus (Handel)
Juditha Triumphans (Vivaldi)
Judith (Chadwick)
The King's Contest (Mechem)
Laud to the Nativity (Respighi)
The Legend of St. Christopher (Parker)
The Lessons of Advent (La Montaine)
The Light in the Wilderness (Brubeck)
Marie-Magdeleine (Massenet)
Meditations on the Seven Last Words (Sateren)
Murder in the Cathedral (Pizzetti)
The Mystery of the Nativity (Martin)
The Nativity (Gossec)
Our Faith (Sateren)
Paradise Lost (Penderecki)
The Passion According to Pilate (Welsh)
The Passion of Our Lord Jesus Christ According to St. Mark (Owen)
Passion with Tropes (Freund)
The Pilgrim's Progress (Bantock)
The Promise of Peace (Raigorodsky)
La Rappresentazione di Anima e di Corpo (Cavalieri)
The Redeemer (Cundick)
The Redeemer (Cundick)
A Representation of the Book of Job (Blodgett)
St. John Passion (Bach)
St. Luke Passion (Penderecki)
St. Matthew Passion (Bach)
Saint Paul (Mendelssohn)
Samson (Handel)
Saul (Handel)
Saul, King of Israel (Gabriel)

The Seven Last Words of Christ (Dubois)
The Shorter Pilgrim's Progress (Kelly)
Solomon (Handel)
Song of Songs (Castelnuovo-Tedesco)
The Temptation of St. Anthony (Gray)
Tobias and the Angel (Castelnuovo-Tedesco)
The Walk (Goemanne)
Yiphtah and His Daughter (Berger)

Contemporary Chamber Opera

Abraham and Isaac (Boren)
Aceldama (Sleeper)
Amahl and the Night Visitors (Menotti)
And David Wept (Laderman)
The Binding of Isaac (Peterson)
Calvary (Pasatieri)
Candle Tree (Swann)
A Christmas Carol (Musgrave)
The Christmas Rose (Bridge)
The Christmas Troubadour (Mainville)
Daniel in the Lion's Den (Pinkham)
David (Goldman)
Dunstan and the Devil (Williamson)
The Egg (Menotti)
Emma (Boren)
Esther (Meyerowitz)
Eve's Odds (Trinkley)
Faith and the Sewing Circle (Welsh)
Father of the Child (Barab)
A Fisherman Called Peter (Owen)
A Gift of Song (Caldwell)
The Gift of the Magi (Brown)
Good Friday (Miles)
Jericho Road (Aria)
Job (Dallapiccola)
Jonah and the Whale (Argento)
The Judas Tree (Dickinson)
Judith (Smith)
Lazarus (Daniels)
Lazarus and His Beloved (Holdridge)
The Lion, the Witch and the Wardrobe (McCabe)
The Little Thieves of Bethlehem (Stuart)
Luther (Tikka)
Martin Avdeich: A Christmas Miracle (Downard)

The Martyrdom of St. Magnus (Davies)
The Martyrs' Mirror (Parker)
The Masque of Angels (Argento)
The Miracle of Nemirov (Silverman, F.)
Moses, Prince of Egypt (De Lisa)
The Night of the Star (Caldwell)
One Christmas Long Ago (Mayer)
Only A Miracle (Barab)
The Other Wise Man (Van Grove)
Perelandra (Swann)
Pilate (Hovhaness)
Please Get Out of the Way While We Rehearse (Welsh)
The Promise (Bass)
The Rape of Lucretia (Britten)
The Red Sea (Williamson)
Ruth (Berkeley)
Ruth (Hagemann)
Ruth (Van Grove)
Samson at Gaza (Alexander)
Samuel (Brantley)
Saul (Reutter)
Savitri (Holst)
See the Promised Dawn Arise (Cooman & Gay)
The Shepherds of the Delectable Mountains (Vaughan Williams)
Singer's Glen (Parker)
Thieves (Cooman)
Tobias and the Angel (Bliss)
The Village Singer (Paulus)
The Visitors (Swann)
Who is My Neighbor (Wells)
The Wise Women (Susa)
The Wrestler (Adler)

Grand/Full-scale Opera

Belshazzar's Feast (Root)
Cain (Denev)
Cecilia (Refice)
The Children's Crusade (Pierne)
David (Milhaud)
The Dialogues of the Carmelites (Poulenc)
El Niño (Adams)
Francesco: A Musical Biography (Kreutz)
Galileo Galilei (Laderman)
Der Golem (d'Albert)

The Golem (Sitsky)
The Greek Passion (Martinu)
Hérodiade (Massenet)
Holofernes (Reznicek)
I Am the Way (Hines)
Jeremiah (Fink)
Joseph (Méhul)
Judith (Fink)
The Last Supper (Birtwistle)
The Legend of St. Christopher (d'Indy)
Móses (Durkó)
Moses and Aaron (Schoenberg)
Nabucco (Verdi)
Palestrina (Pfitzner)
The Pilgrim's Progress (Vaughan Williams)
Salome (Strauss)
Samson and Delilah (Saint-Saëns)
Saul (Castelnuovo-Tedesco)
Saul and David (Nielsen)
Saul, King of Israel (Sargon)
The Temptation of St. Antoine (Soler)
X (The Life and Times of Malcolm X) (Davis)

Humorous/Entertainment

Birds of A Feather (Berger)
Caedmon (Shephard)
A Christmas Carol (Sandow)
A Christmas Carol (Tosh)
Comoedia de Christi Resurrectione (Orff)
David and Goliath (Salomon)
Della's Gift (Welcher)
Eve's Odds (Trinkley)
The Finding of the King (Broome)
The Gift of the Magi (Magney)
Good King Wenceslas (Shephard)
The Greenfield Christmas Tree (Moore)
Herod, Do Your Worst (Kelly)
Jonah (Beeson)
The Long Christmas Dinner (Hindemith)
The Masque of Angels (Argento)
A Nativity in Threes (Barnard)
Noah (Salzman & Sahl)
Noah and the Stowaway (Kalmanoff)
The Perfect Choir (Moore)

The Rites of Man (Neumann)
St. Nicholas (Shephard)
The Village Singer (Paulus)

Multi-media

The Children's Crusade (Lebowsky)
El Niño (Adams)
Jephthah's Daughter (Harrison)
The Walk (Goemanne)

In the Style of Musical Theatre

Christ, the Man from Galilee (Rizzo)
The Door (Peninger)
Exodus and Easter (Silver)
The Gift of the Magi (Ekstrom)
God and Abraham (Kingsley)
Hannah (Silver)
Mass (Bernstein)
Ruth (Ain)
Scrooge (Bricusse)
Two By Two (Rodgers)
Up from Paradise (Silverman, S.)

APPENDIX J

WORKS INCLUDING CHILDREN'S VOICES

These works all include some combination of children's voices in addition to adult voices. The annotations in the main section of this book will further define their use. One asterisk (*) indicates that children's solo voices are used; two asterisks (**) indicate that children's voices are optional.

*	Amahl and the Night Visitors (Menotti)
**	The Apocalypse (Gallico)
**	*Baboushka* (Swann)
**	Bel and the Dragon (Gardner)
	Bontzye Schweig (Swann)
	Caedmon (Shephard)
*	Candle Tree (Swann)
*	The Children's Crusade (Lebowsky)
	The Children's Crusade (Pierne)
	A Christmas Carol (Musgrave)
	A Christmas Carol (Sandow)
	A Christmas Carol (Tosh)
	Comoedia de Christi Resurrectione (Orff)
	David (Burroughs)
	David (Goldman)
	The Death of the Bishop of Brindisi (Menotti)
*	Elijah (Mendelssohn)
	Erode the Greate (La Montaine)
	La Fiesta de la Posada (Brubeck)
	The Finding of the King (Broome)
	A Gift of Song (Caldwell)
	The Glory Coach (Barnard)
	God's Word in their Heart (Butler)
*	Good King Wenceslas (Shephard)
*	The Greenfield Christmas Tree (Moore)
	Hannah (Silver)
*	In the Fullness of Time (Caldwell)
	Jeanne d'Arc au Bûcher (Honegger)
	Jericho Road (Aria)
	Jonah (Mathias)
**	A Journey With Jonah (Wyton)
	The Legend of St. Christopher (d'Indy)
*	The Legend of St. Christopher (H. Parker)

**	The Lessons of Advent (La Montaine)
	The Lion, the Witch and the Wardrobe (McCabe)
	Martin's Lie (Menotti)
	Mass (Bernstein)
*	Nativity According to St. Luke (Thompson)
*	The Night of the Star (Caldwell)
	Noah (Salzman & Sahl)
	Noye's Fludde (Britten)
	An Opera for Christmas (Neumann)
**	An Opera for Easter (Neumann)
	Paradise Lost (Penderecki)
	Pepito's Golden Flower (Caldwell)
**	Pilgrim's Progress (Kelly)
	The Play of St. Nicholas (Renz, ed.)
	Ruth and Naomi (Kondorossky)
*	Sacrifice of Isaac (Bingham)
	St. Luke Passion (Penderecki)
**	St. Nicholas (Shephard)
	Samuel (Butler)
	Samuel (Brantley)
	Samuel: The Boy Who Talked With God (Young)
	Scrooge (Bricusse)
**	The Shephardes Playe (La Montaine)
	Singer's Glen (Parker)
	A Swiss Nativity (Burkhard)
	The Tower of Babel (Rubinstein)
	The Visitors (Swann)
	The Walk (Goemanne)
	The Wrestler (Adler)

TITLE INDEX

A

Abraham and Isaac (Boren)	79
Aceldama (Sleeper)	14, 300
Amahl and the Night Visitors (Menotti)	219
And David Wept (Laderman)	190
The Apocalypse (Gallico)	141
Asmedai (Tal)	363
L'Assassinio nella Cattedrale (Pizzetti)	259
Athalia (Handel)	155
The Awakening (Bingham)	62

B

Baboushka (Swann)	310
Behold the Sun (Goehr)	363
Behold Your King (Patente)	249
Bel and the Dragon (Gardner)	142
Beloved Son (Brubeck)	96
Belshazzar (Handel)	156
Belshazzar's Feast (Root)	271
Bethlehem (full-length version) (Boughton)	83
Bethlehem (abridged) (Boughton)	84
Billy Budd (Britten)	363
Birds of A Feather (Berger)	54
The Birth of Our Lord (Bingham)	63
Bontzye Schweig (Swann)	311
The Bridegroom (Smoldon, ed.)	358
The Burning Fiery Furnace (Britten)	88
By the Pool of Siloam (Bingham)	64

C

Caedmon (Shephard)	14, 290
Cain (Denev)	14, 126
Cain and Abel (Fleisher)	14, 363
Calvary (Pasatieri)	248
Candle Tree (Swann)	312
Cecilia (Refice)	263
La Cena (Malipiero)	202
Cherry Tree Carol (Berger)	55
The Children's Crusade (Lebowsky)	198
The Children's Crusade (Pierne)	256
Christ, the Man from Galilee (Rizzo)	268
A Christmas Carol (Averill)	365

A Christmas Carol (Cohen)	365
A Christmas Carol (Gray)	366
A Christmas Carol (Hagemann)	366
A Christmas Carol (Hart)	366
A Christmas Carol (Herrmann)	366
A Christmas Carol (Musgrave)	233, 366
A Christmas Carol (Sandow)	276, 366
A Christmas Carol (Shapcott)	366
A Christmas Carol (Tosh)	320, 366
A Christmas Carol (Treharne)	366
A Christmas Carol (Wadely)	366
The Christmas Rose (Bridge)	87
The Christmas Story (Schütz)	286
The Christmas Troubadour (Mainville)	201
Christus (Rubinstein)	363
The Christymas Playe (Boren)	80
Il combattimento di Tancredi e Clorinda (Monteverdi)	228
The Combat of Tancredi and Clorinda (Monteverdi)	228
A Comedy During Christ's Resurrection (Orff)	240
Comoedia de Christi Resurrectione (Orff)	240
A Conversation Between Mary and the Angel Gabriel (Bingham)	65
Curlew River (Britten)	89

D

Dance of Death (Distler)	129
Daniel in the Lion's Den (Pinkham)	258
David (Burroughs)	101
David (Goldman)	147
David (Milhaud)	227
David and Goliath (Salomon)	274
David et Jonathas (Charpentier)	14, 364
Day of Pentecost (Sateren)	280
The Death of the Bishop of Brindisi (Menotti)	220
Debora e Jaele (Pizzetti)	364
Deborah (Handel)	158
Della's Gift (Welcher)	332
Les Dialogues des Carmélites (Poulenc)	260
The Dialogues of the Carmelites (Poulenc)	260
The Door (Peninger)	254
Dunstan and the Devil (Williamson)	339

E

The Easter Story (Schütz)	285
The Egg (Menotti)	221
Elijah (Mendelssohn)	216

Emma (Boren)	81
L'enfance du Christ (Berlioz)	58
L'enfant prodigue (Auber)	364
L'enfant prodigue (Debussy)	124
Erode the Greate (La Montaine)	192
Esther (Handel)	159
Esther (Meyerowitz)	224
Esther (Sosin)	304
Eve's Odds (Trinkley)	14, 321
Everyman (Scott)	288
Exodus and Easter (Silver)	294

F

Faith and the Sewing Circle (Welsh)	334
The Fall of Lucifer (Burgon)	99
Father of the Child (Barab)	47
The Father's Love (Bass)	51
La Fiesta de la Posada (Brubeck)	97
The Finding of the King (Broome)	94
The First Murder (Scarlatti)	283
The First Nowell (Vaughan Williams)	325
A Fisherman Called Peter (Owen)	242
The Flood (Stravinsky)	306
Francesco: A Musical Biography (Kreutz)	14, 188

G

Galileo Galilei (Laderman)	191
A Gift of Song (Caldwell)	104
The Gift of the Magi (Brown)	95
The Gift of the Magi (Conte)	14, 116
The Gift of the Magi (Ekstrom)	134
The Gift of the Magi (Gillis)	143
The Gift of the Magi (Magney)	200
The Glory Coach (Barnard)	49
God and Abraham (Kingsley)	185
God's Word in Their Heart (Butler)	103
Der Golem (d'Albert)	38
The Golem (Sitsky)	299
Good Friday (Miles)	225
Good King Wenceslas (Shephard)	14, 291
Good Tidings from the Holy Beast (Locklair)	199
The Greek Passion (Martinu)	204
The Greenfield Christmas Tree (Moore)	229
Griechische Passion (Martinu)	204

H

Hannah (Silver)	295
Here Comes Our King (Sateren)	281
Herod, Do Your Worst (Kelly)	181
Hérodiade (Massenet)	206
Historia, der...Geburt....Jesu Christi (Schütz)	286
Historia der...Auferstehungs....Jesu Christi (Schütz)	285
Holofernes (Reznicek)	267

I

I Am the Way (Hines)	172
In the Fullness of Time (Caldwell)	106

J

Jeanne d'Arc au Bûcher (Honegger)	175
Jephthah's Daughter (Harrison)	168
Jephtha (Handel)	160
Jepthe (Monteclair)	364
Jeremiah (Fink)	135
Jericho Road (Aria)	42
Le jeu de la Nativité (Tcherepnin)	316
Joan of Arc at the Stake (Honegger)	175
Job (Dallapiccola)	120
Job (Finney)	364
Johannes Passion (Bach)	44
Jonah (Beeson)	52
Jonah (Mathias)	209
Jonah and the Whale (Argento)	40
Joseph (Handel)	161
Joseph (Méhul)	215
Joshua (Handel)	162
The Journey With Jonah (Wyton)	341
Judas Iscariot (Welsh)	335
Judas Maccabaeus (Handel)	163
The Judas Tree (Dickinson)	128
The Judgment of Saint Francis (Flagello)	364
The Judgment of Sheba (Goldsworthy)	148
Judith (Chadwick)	115
Judith (Goossens)	150
Judith (Honegger)	177
Judith (Smith)	302
Judith and Holofernes (Fink)	136
Juditha Triumphans (Vivaldi)	330
La Juive (Halevy)	364

K

The King's Contest (Mechem)	214

L

The Lament of Mary (Smoldon, ed.)	352
The Last Supper (Birtwistle)	14, 76
The Last Supper (Malipiero)	202
Laud to the Nativity (Respighi)	264
Lauda per la Natività del Signore (Respighi)	264
Lazarus (Daniels)	121
Lazarus and His Beloved (Holdridge)	173
The Legend of St. Christopher (d'Indy)	179
The Legend of St. Christopher (Parker)	246
La légende de Saint Christophe (d'Indy)	179
The Lessons of Advent (La Montaine)	195
The Light in the Wilderness (Brubeck)	98
The Lion, the Witch and the Wardrobe (McCabe)	211
The Little Thieves of Bethlehem (Stuart)	14, 307
I Lombardi (Verdi)	364
The Long Christmas Dinner (Hindemith)	171
The Lord's A Wonder (Franceschina)	137
Luther (Tikka)	14, 319

M

The Maastricht Easter Play (Hollman, ed.)	350
Magdalene (Bingham)	65
Maria Egiziaca (Respighi)	265
Marie-Magdeleine (Massenet)	207
Martin Avdeich: A Christmas Miracle (Downard)	130
Martin's Lie (Menotti)	222
The Martyrdom of St. Magnus (Davies)	122
The Martyrs' Mirror (Parker)	243
The Masque of Angels (Argento)	41
Mass (Bernstein)	59
Matthaeus Passion (Bach)	45
Meditations on the Seven Last Words (Sateren)	281
The Miracle of Nemirov (Silverman, F.)	297
The Miracle of the Nativity (Pendleton)	253
Mr. Scrooge (Kalmanoff)	366
Mosè in Egitto (Rossini)	364
Moses (Rubinstein)	364
Moses and Aaron (Schoenberg)	284
Moses, Prince of Egypt (De Lisa)	125
Mózes (Durkó)	132
Murder in the Cathedral (Pizzetti)	259

A Mystery For Christmas (McKinney) 213
The Mystery of the Nativity (Martin) 203

N

Naboth's Vineyard (Goehr) 145
Nabucco (Verdi) 328
La Nativité (Gossec) 151
The Nativity (Gossec) 151
The Nativity (Webber) 331
The Nativity: A Mystery Play (Ekmon & Fyffe) 134
Nativity According to St. Luke (Thompson) 317
A Nativity in Threes (Barnard) 50
Nativity Play (Tcherepnin) 316
The Nazarene (Gillis) 144
The Night of the Star (Caldwell) 108
El Niño (Adams) 14, 35
Noah (Salzman & Sahl) 275
Noah and the Stowaway (Kalmanoff) 180
Novellis, Novellis (La Montaine) 195
Noye's Fludde (Britten) 90

O

The Obligation of the First Commandment (Mozart) 232
Officium Pastorum (Smoldon, ed.) 351
One Christmas Long Ago (Mayer) 210
On Christmas Night (Vaughan Williams) 366
On the Road to Emmaus (Bingham) 67
Only A Miracle (Barab) 48
An Opera for Christmas (Neumann) 235
An Opera for Easter (Neumann) 236
An Opera for Everyman (Neumann) 237
The Other Wise Man (Van Grove) 323
Our Faith (Sateren) 282
The Outcast (Ain) 37
Out of the Depths (Yahres) 365

P

Palestrina (Hans Pfitzner) 255
Paradise Lost (Penderecki) 250
Parsifal (Wagner) 365
Passio et mors domini nostri Jesu Christi secundum Lucam (Penderecki) 252
The Passion According to Pilate (Welsh) 336
The Passion and Death of Our Lord Jesus Christ According to St. Luke (Penderecki) 252
Passion and Resurrection (Harvey) 170
The Passion of Our Lord Jesus Christ According to St. Mark (Owen) 241

Passion with Tropes (Freund)	139
Pepito's Golden Flower (Caldwell)	109
Peregrinus (Smoldon, ed.)	351
Perelandra (Swann)	313
The Perfect Choir (F. Moore)	231
Piece Together (Bingham)	68
Pilate (Hovhaness)	178
The Pilgrim (Proulx)	261
The Pilgrim's Progress (Bantock)	46
Pilgrim's Progress (Kelly)	183
The Pilgrim's Progress (Vaughan Williams)	326
Planctus Mariae (Smoldon, ed.)	352
The Play of Balaam and His Ass (Zytowski)	345
The Play of Daniel (Greenberg, ed.)	353
The Play of Herod (Greenberg, ed.)	354
The Play of Saint Nicholas (Renz, ed.)	355
The Play of the Three Maries at the Tomb (Zytowski)	346
The Play of the Three Shepherds (Zytowski)	347
Please Get Out of the Way While We Rehearse (Welsh)	338
Il primo Omicidio (Scarlatti)	283
The Prodigal Son (Britten)	92
The Promise (Bass)	365
The Promise of Peace (Raigorodsky)	263
La Prophète (Meyerbeer)	365

R

Rachel (Gundry, ed.)	357
The Raising of Lazarus (Bingham)	69
The Rape of Lucretia (Britten)	93
La Rappresentazione di Anima e di Corpo (Cavalieri)	113
The Redeemer (Cundick)	119
The Red Sea (Williamson)	340
A Representation of the Book of Job (Blodgett)	78
The Representation of the Soul and Body (Cavalieri)	113
The Rites of Man (Neumann)	238
Ruth (Berkeley)	57
Ruth (Bingham)	70
Ruth (Hagemann)	14, 154
Ruth (Van Grove)	324
Ruth and Naomi (Kondorossy)	187

S

La sacra rappresentazione di Abram e d'Isaac (Pizzetti)	365
The Sacrifice of Isaac (Bingham)	71
St. John Passion (Bach)	44

St. Luke Passion (Penderecki)	252
St. Matthew Passion (Bach)	45
St. Nicholas (Shephard)	14, 292
Saint Paul (Mendelssohn)	218
Salome (Strauss)	305
Samson (Handel)	165
Samson and Dalila (Delilah) (Saint-Saëns)	273
Samson at Gaza (Alexander)	39
Samuel (Brantley)	84
Samuel (Butler)	103
Samuel: The Boy Who Talked with God (Young)	343
Saturday, 29 A.D. (Schweizer)	14, 287
Saul (Castelnuovo-Tedesco)	111
Saul (Handel)	166
Saul (Reutter)	266
Saul and David (Nielsen)	239
Saul at Endor (Tal)	365
Saul, King of Israel (Gabriel)	140
Saul, King of Israel (Sargon)	278
Savitri (Holst)	174
Die Schuldigkeit des ersten Gebotes (Mozart)	232
Scrooge (Bricusse)	86, 366
See the Promised Dawn Arise (Cooman & Gay)	14, 118
Les sept paroles du Christ (Dubois)	131
The Seven Last Words of Christ (Dubois)	131
Sharing the Prophets (Gottlieb)	152
The Shephardes Playe (La Montaine)	197
The Shepherds' Play (Shephard)	14, 293
The Shepherds (Gundry, ed.)	357
The Shepherds (Koch)	185
The Shepherds at the Manger (Smoldon, ed.)	351
The Shepherds of the Delectable Mountains (Vaughan Williams)	328
The Shorter Pilgrim's Progress (Kelly)	184
Simeon (Bingham)	72
Singer's Glen (Parker)	245
Sodom (Addison)	365
Solomon (Handel)	167
Song of Simeon (Arnold)	43
Song of Songs (Castelnuovo-Tedesco)	112
Sponsus (Smolden, ed.)	358
The Star (Gundry, ed.)	359
The Stranger (Smoldon, ed.)	351
Suor Angelica (Puccini)	365
A Swiss Nativity (Burkhard)	100

T

Tales of a Magic Monastery (Bingham)	73
The Temptation of St. Anthony (Gray)	153
The Temptation of St. Antoine (Soler)	303
La tentation de Ste. Antoine (Soler)	303
Thieves (Cooman)	14, 117
Thomas of Canterbury (Zytowski)	348
Der Thurm zu Babel (Rubinstein)	272
Tobias and the Angel (Bliss)	77
Tobias and the Angel (Castelnuovo-Tedesco)	112
The Tower of Babel (Rubinstein)	272
To the Ends of the Earth (Franceschina)	138
The Triumph of Judith (Vivaldi)	330
Two by Two (Rodgers)	269

U

Up From Paradise (Silverman, S.)	297

V

Das verlorne Paradies (Rubinstein)	365
The Village Singer (Paulus)	249
The Vision of Christ (Beversdorf)	61
The Visitation (Bush)	102
Visitatio Sepulchri (Smoldon, ed.)	360
The Visitors (Swann)	315
The Visit to the Tomb (Smoldon, ed.)	360

W

The Walk (Goemanne)	146
What Men Live By (Martinu)	205
Who is My Neighbor (Wells)	333
The Wise Women (Susa)	14, 308
The Woman at Jacob's Well (Bingham)	75
Wondrous Love (Hunkins)	178
The Wrestler (Adler)	36

X

X (The Life and Times of Malcolm X) (Davis)	123

Y

Yehu (Zádor)	344
Yiphtah and His Daughter (Berger)	56

Z

Die Zeller Weinacht (Burkhard)	100